Economic Growth in Latin America and the Impact of the Global Financial Crisis

Mauricio Garita
Universidad del Valle de Guatemala, Guatemala

Celso Fernando Cerezo Bregni
Universidad del Valle de Guatemala, Guatemala

A volume in the Advances in Finance, Accounting, and Economics (AFAE) Book Series

IGI Global
DISSEMINATOR OF KNOWLEDGE

Published in the United States of America by
IGI Global
Business Science Reference (an imprint of IGI Global)
701 E. Chocolate Avenue
Hershey PA, USA 17033
Tel: 717-533-8845
Fax: 717-533-8661
E-mail: cust@igi-global.com
Web site: http://www.igi-global.com

Library of Congress Cataloging-in-Publication Data

Names: Garita, Mauricio, editor. | Cerezo Bregni, Celso Fernando, 1976- editor.
Title: Economic growth in Latin America and the impact of the global financial crisis / Mauricio Garita and Celso Fernando Cerezo Bregni, editors.
Description: Hershey, PA : Business Science Reference, [2017]
Identifiers: LCCN 2017033732| ISBN 9781522549819 (hardcover) | ISBN 9781522549826 (ebook)
Subjects: LCSH: Latin America--Economic conditions--1945- | Global Financial Crisis, 2008-2009.
Classification: LCC HC125 .E37356 2017 | DDC 330.98/0041--dc23 LC record available at https://lccn.loc.gov/2017033732

This book is published in the IGI Global book series Advances in Finance, Accounting, and Economics (AFAE) (ISSN: 2327-5677; eISSN: 2327-5685)

British Cataloguing in Publication Data
A Cataloguing in Publication record for this book is available from the British Library.

For electronic access to this publication, please contact: eresources@igi-global.com.

Advances in Finance, Accounting, and Economics (AFAE) Book Series

ISSN:2327-5677
EISSN:2327-5685

Editor-in-Chief: Ahmed Driouchi, Al Akhawayn University, Morocco

MISSION

In our changing economic and business environment, it is important to consider the financial changes occurring internationally as well as within individual organizations and business environments. Understanding these changes as well as the factors that influence them is crucial in preparing for our financial future and ensuring economic sustainability and growth.

The **Advances in Finance, Accounting, and Economics (AFAE)** book series aims to publish comprehensive and informative titles in all areas of economics and economic theory, finance, and accounting to assist in advancing the available knowledge and providing for further research development in these dynamic fields.

COVERAGE

- International Economics
- Bankruptcy
- Accounting information systems
- Evidence-Based Studies
- Corporate finance
- Economics of Agriculture and Biotechnology
- Accounting Standards
- Investments and Derivatives
- Managerial Accounting
- Applied economics

IGI Global is currently accepting manuscripts for publication within this series. To submit a proposal for a volume in this series, please contact our Acquisition Editors at Acquisitions@igi-global.com or visit: http://www.igi-global.com/publish/.

The Advances in Finance, Accounting, and Economics (AFAE) Book Series (ISSN 2327-5677) is published by IGI Global, 701 E. Chocolate Avenue, Hershey, PA 17033-1240, USA, www.igi-global.com. This series is composed of titles available for purchase individually; each title is edited to be contextually exclusive from any other title within the series. For pricing and ordering information please visit http://www.igi-global.com/book-series/advances-finance-accounting-economics/73685. Postmaster: Send all address changes to above address.

Titles in this Series

For a list of additional titles in this series, please visit:
https://www.igi-global.com/book-series/advances-finance-accounting-economics/73685

Financial Entrepreneurship for Economic Growth in Emergig Nations
Atsede Woldie (University of South Wales, UK) and Brychan Thomas (University of South Wales, UK)
Business Science Reference • ©2018 • 304pp • H/C (ISBN: 9781522527008) • US $225.00

Technological Integration as a Catalyst for Industrial Development and Economic Growth
Bryan Christiansen (PryMarke, LLC, USA) and Ülkü Yüksel (The University of Sydney Business School, Australia)
Business Science Reference • ©2017 • 272pp • H/C (ISBN: 9781522523192) • US $185.00

Handbook of Research on Economic, Financial, and Industrial Impacts on Infrastructure ...
Ramesh Chandra Das (Katwa College, India)
Business Science Reference • ©2017 • 466pp • H/C (ISBN: 9781522523611) • US $230.00

Handbook of Research on Policies and Practices for Sustainable Economic Growth and ...
George M. Korres (University of Aegean, Greece) Elias Kourliouros (University of Aegean, Greece) and Maria P. Michailidis (University of Nicosia, Cyprus)
Business Science Reference • ©2017 • 440pp • H/C (ISBN: 9781522524588) • US $255.00

NFC Payment Systems and the New Era of Transaction Processing
Vibha Kaw Raina (Birla Institute of Technology, India)
Business Science Reference • ©2017 • 193pp • H/C (ISBN: 9781522523062) • US $155.00

Social, Health, and Environmental Infrastructures for Economic Growth
Ramesh Chandra Das (Katwa College, India)
Business Science Reference • ©2017 • 355pp • H/C (ISBN: 9781522523642) • US $200.00

Method of Systems Potential (MSP) Applications in Economics Emerging Research and ...
Grigorii Pushnoi (Independent Researcher, Russia)
Business Science Reference • ©2017 • 162pp • H/C (ISBN: 9781522521709) • US $135.00

For an enitre list of titles in this series, please visit:
https://www.igi-global.com/book-series/advances-finance-accounting-economics/73685

IGI Global
DISSEMINATOR OF KNOWLEDGE

701 East Chocolate Avenue, Hershey, PA 17033, USA
Tel: 717-533-8845 x100 • Fax: 717-533-8661
E-Mail: cust@igi-global.com • www.igi-global.com

Table of Contents

Detailed Table of Contents

The study of the IPOs are for a period of 10 years; hence, each company that came out with an IPO between 2004 and 2013 has been studied in terms of the paid up capital raised initially and then broken down into six sectors according to the type of industry they belong. The research is based on the assumption that the subprime crisis had a global effect and hence many developed countries suffered in terms of fall in exports, rise in debt defaults and reduced earrings of the corporate. However, the effect on India was minimal but the worldwide panic was there. The researchers have studied the impact of the subprime crisis on the IPOs issued during pre- and post-subprime crisis. The researchers have used statistical test to study the impact of subprime crisis on the Indian stock market. This compilation is a culmination of comprehensive in-depth study as well as practical experience.

order to understand the impact an economic crisis can have on taxes. Therefore, the study presents a research based on a historical approach with the purpose of understanding the different concepts concerning the elites and the evolution of the economic circumstances around it. Also, the discussion concerning inequality and development that evidence that not much has changed.

The information security is importance as a strategic process to improve and maintain the continuity of the company. There have been developed various methodologies and risk management, safety guidelines information, however, does not go beyond operational and strategic part of business. Although some methodologies are based on international standards to implement controls to mitigate risks, but not the financial factors that could be impacted by these risks are analyzed. In some companies the legal aspect as a financial category, economic losses is not analyzed as a risk or information theft materializes. There are several methodologies based on guidelines and recommendations and provide general guidance on the management of information security; therefore, for purposes of this scientific research it will be taken into account some relevant points of those standards, which will undoubtedly help establish an appropriate risk methodology and subsequently to the definition of financial criteria for decision-making.

The objective of this chapter is the analysis of the primary education in Guatemala and if the amount of investment during the period 2002–2015 is significant for the number of children promoted by school year, and if these investments were impacted by the economic crisis of 2008. The results of the investigation demonstrate that the variables with significance where the number of teachers and the budget per year, without relation to economic growth and no impact by the economic crisis on 2008 and with no significant relation with the rate of drop out, which was an important result, especially in primary school. The data analyzed also show that the budget per year for the Ministry of Education doesn't suffer an impact after the economic crisis in 2008, where the author expected to find some problem after the crisis, but that the number of teachers hired in 2009 almost doubles the amount of teachers who were hired in 2008.

The present chapter analyzes the importance of telecommunications and its economic effects by identifying the relation between the amount of telephone lines, both fixed and mobile, and the economy of Latin America as a region since year 1975 to 2015. The relation is demonstrated using a linear regression model. The case of Guatemala is analyzed in more in detail, where telecommunications have developed at an important pace since the privatization of the former public telco operator along crucial regulatory reforms.

The present chapter analyzes fiscal privileges in Guatemala from a taxation point of view, identifying the cost that they incur through the tax expenditure methodology. The chapter also discusses the historical situation of Guatemala concerning taxes and its consequence for the social situation and its relation. Therefore, the conclusion of this chapter is that fiscal privileges are politics aimed at minorities that cost more to the society than the benefits they have in Guatemala, as a consequence there is a sacrifice in taxation by benefiting certain sectors.

Due to the fact that the active weighted average interest rate that the banks of the national financial system have applied to the loan portfolio has been stable in recent years, it was considered important to calculate the impact of this measure on the performance of the balance of the loan portfolio by economic activity in Guatemala from 2008 to 2016; it was considered this time frame since the consulted web portals shows more information as of 2008. With the above information, it will be possible to observe the important variations and what events could propitiate it, the percentage of growth and which economic sectors have most financed their operations. The increase in the loan portfolio, in addition to being considered a strategic objective of any financial institution to increase its market share and income, is also a sign of confidence among corporate users, family members, and other entities involved in maintaining the national economic stability.

Foreword

Independently of the Kondratieff's long-term (40-50 years) economic cycle, the existence of high country risks has traditionally and primarily defined the Latin America and the Caribbean countries as they were negatively demarcated by their economic, social and political instability mainly caused by their external debt. In the past, these factors adversely affected both economic growth and welfare to generate business-related disturbances worldwide. Although many economic policy recipes focused on guaranteeing a minimum level of sustainable economic growth focused on creating a wealthy middle class, these attempts failed in many Latin American and the Caribbean countries, which adversely affected the entire continent resulted from the domino effect created.

However, the birth of the digital economy and the Economy 4.0 due to the Fourth Industrial Revolution impulse by the intensive use of the ICTs (Information and Communication Technologies), are positively transforming Latin America and the Caribbean regions and countries to create irreversible socio-economic transformations. In fact, Mexico and Brazil have been recently defined as EAGLE (Emerging and Growth-Leading Economies) countries, while Colombia, Peru, and Argentina are EAGLEs Nest (from Spanish, Nido de las Águilas). These nations have the role to impulse the Latin American and the Caribbean's economic growth, and they are increasing their geopolitical and socioeconomic importance due to their outstanding macroeconomic results and their potential to impulse Latin America and the Caribbean by following a similar model used in Europe to achieve sustainable welfare and growth. So, it is essential to develop the Industry 4.0 taking into account a triple environmental, social and economic impact in the digitalization process to achieve increasing rates of sustainable development. This strategy will impulse Latin America and the Caribbean through five Latin American EAGLEs countries (Argentina, Brazil, Colombia, Mexico, and Peru) by using growth axes and poles, as happens in the European Union.

Complementary to the creation of economic growth axes and poles, the growing geopolitical role of the People's Republic of China, Russia, India, and the European Union is forcing Latin America and the Caribbean to sign commercial agreements with some Asian and European countries, as an attractive alternative to the USA. One example is the case of the TPP (Trans-Pacific Partnership) Agreement signed on February 6, 2016, as an expansion of the Trans-Pacific Strategic Economic Partnership Agreement, where of the nine country members, three are Latin Americans: Chile, Peru, and Mexico. Also, other examples are the numerous agreements signed between the European Union and the Latin American countries, and even within some Latin American nations focused on regional economic growth.

The signing of these treaties and the US withdrawal from some key worldwide agreements, close with the First Global Financial Crisis (2008-2012) born in the USA, formed by the Great Global Recession (2008-2009) and the Sovereign Debt Crisis (2010-2012), is weakening the leadership of the United States on the planet. As a result, the People's Republic of China will hold a geopolitical and economic leadership in the next ten or fifteen years, where Latin America and Asia have a stronger role to play.

This book provides a valuable window to analyze the impact of both the Great Global Recession and the Sovereign Debt Crisis on the Latin American countries. A crisis that began on September 15, 2008, with the bankruptcy of Lehman Brothers, the fourth-largest investment bank in the United States, behind Goldman Sachs, Morgan Stanley, and Merrill Lynch, as the first worldwide crisis born in the USA. This valuable book examines the impact of both types of crisis in Latin America and Europe from different perspectives to enrich a global vision formed by various socioeconomic and business scenarios observed.

The countries of Latin America and the Caribbean are facing now a big challenge and have a unique opportunity for changing paradigms to benefit their populations. Moreover, this book contributes to illuminate the path focused on achieving higher welfare and economic growth. And, in this sense, this book is a good step in that direction.

José Manuel Saiz-Alvarez
Tecnologico de Monterrey, Mexico

José Manuel Saiz-Alvarez *is a Ph.D. in Honors, Economics and Business Administration, Autonomous University of Madrid (Spain), Ph.D. with Honors, Political Science and Sociology, Pontifical University of Salamanca (Spain). Research Professor, EGADE Business School, Tecnológico de Monterrey (Mexico). Visiting Professor, The Catholic University of Santiago de Guayaquil (Ecuador). He was Director of the BA Doctoral Program, Nebrija University (Spain) and Director of the Master in Microcredits and Social Inclusion, Pontifical University of Salamanca (Spain, and Guatemala). Member of GEM Jalisco and Academic Leader at Tecnológico de Monterrey. Diploma of recognition, House of Representatives of the Capitol of Puerto Rico. Diploma of Honor, Valahia University of Targoviste (Romania). Honorary Professor, Autonomous University of Madrid (Spain). International Advisor, Institute of Social Innovation BOSTAN (Turkey) and the Catholic University of Santiago de Guayaquil (Ecuador). Accredited in Spain by the National Agency for the Evaluation of Quality and Accreditation. More than 200 publications in editorials and indexed journals of international prestige. Scientific committees' member of indexed journals in Europe, America, and Asia. Who is in the World from 2011.*

Preface

Discussing a global financial crisis, such as the one that took place during the period 2008-2012, can be a challenging project. The reason for this challenge is that the perspectives on the effect that the crisis had, the way the capacity was handled and the process in which the crisis was resolved, if it has been indeed resolved, lead to a discussion that deepens more and more.

The financial crisis of 2009 began as a crisis based on two factors: income and loans. Concerning income, the first important aspect is that unemployment was an important factor when the crisis began. Unemployment was, in 2009, near to 10% in Nevada, 12% in Michigan and 9.9% in Rhode Island. Later, as the crisis developed, the unemployment in 2010 for Michigan grew 2%, Rhode Island 2% and Nevada in 3%. One of the most failed concepts concerning the crisis, is that unemployment began when the impact was felt and not before. The impact was before the crisis and deepened when the crisis began to grow.

The second factor of the financial crisis is the easiness for getting a loan. The banks diminished their regulations and began to give loans to everyone that ask for it, because there was an excess of cash in the financial system. Although one can think that this only happened in the United States, in Spain it was the same procedure. The case of Spain, as in the United States, began in 2002 when the loans were given not only for assets but also for personal expenditures. Considering assets, the idea was to finance house ownership that eventually will lead to better prices in the market because of construction costs. The result was very different, since this created a housing bubble, such as the one in the United States that resulted in the financial crisis. To consider that the crisis began in 2008 would be erroneous because crisis is developed through time.

These two factors will be imperative when understanding the book and the process in which it was written. The book is written for an audience that wants to know more about the financial crisis and its effect in Latin America. The book can be divided into three blocks, being the first one the discussion concerning the effect of the financial crisis, the capacity of handling the crisis through a welfare state in the European union and finally the role of the elites in the financial crisis process.

The second block centers in Latin America, where the studies conclude that the crisis had important effects on the social, economic, and political arena. The third and final block centers on the capacity of Central America, in specifically Guatemala, in handling the crisis and the effect that this had on the country. The reason why Guatemala was chosen is as a case for understanding the effects of the crisis given the economic and social circumstances.

The book can be read as a whole or through chapters. It is written with an interconnection between chapters that lead the reader to a conclusion of the effect concerning the financial crisis but it can also be read individually. When reading the book individually, the advice is to chose the block and read it thoroughly.

The book is composed of nine chapters, written by the editors and authors from Central America, India, United States, Spain, and Canada. The authors have experience in the banking industry, economic institutions, government, credit agencies, academia and social sector. This is an important asset concerning the book because it is written by authors that know the financial crisis at first-hand and that they have participated in its resolution. These attributes give the book more stability and a contextual framework that will not be found in any book.

The first chapter, titled "A Study to Analyze the Impact of the Sub-Prime Crisis on IPOs," is written from the methodological perspective as a way to understand the financial crisis and how this crisis bounds with the international crisis that it created. The study centers at the heart of the crisis, the Sub-Prime, that where the main focus on the development of the financial crisis and one of the aspect that was studied the most. The chapter also offers a comparative perspective with other countries, such as India, that as a BRIC country, it has an important input in the world economy. The result of the paper is a very interesting argument about the understanding of the crisis.

The second chapter, "The Transmission of the Great Recession (2008-2009) and the Sovereign Debt Crisis (2010-2012) to Latin America," is a demonstration of how the financial crisis evolved from a crisis centered on loans and personal consumption to a crisis that advanced into a government crisis, a sovereign debt crisis, that is still affecting the World, in specifically countries in the European Union. The authors focus, after the theoretical discussion, in Latin America. An economic region that has not been studied to depth because of the difficulty of analyzing Latin America as a block. As a result, the the authors share an important insight into understanding how the crisis has its effect in Latin America and how it can be understood from this perspective.

The third chapter, written by the one of the editors in collaboration, discusses the effect that the crisis had in the European Union. The European Union, which was created to foment economic development, had an interesting effect in the global financial crisis, due that the governments participation solved, in some cases, and accelerated the crisis. In this paper, both authors conclude that the Welfare State will be into the discussion given the crisis with the main focus being on the possibility of maintaining a welfare state- The chapter concludes in the importance of preparing as a country for possible outcomes.

The fourth chapter, written by editor Mauricio Garita-Gutiérrez, is a chapter focused on a historical approach in Central America. The reason for centering the study in Central America is basically the importance of analyzing a smaller block than Latin America. This leads to how the economic and financial process are based on history and not just on a governmental decision. In this paper, the author analyzes the creation of fiscal privileges in Central America and how they advanced into the current situation that the countries have. It is important to analyze the history of fiscal privileges given that that the governments are extremely important for the process of resolving an economic crisis. Given that fiscal privileges remove the government capacity of solving the crisis, a historical approach serves as a perfect example for a better understanding of the government roles.

Chapter 5 was written by an expert in information security, and therefore, the chapter explains in great depth the different approaches to information security and why it is important. The author also takes into account a methodology, which he explains broadly, in which he demonstrates what is the effect of the crisis in information issues. As a result, the chapter explains not only, why there is an effect in information but also how it can be solved.

The sixth chapter was written by an academic with experience in the public education sector. Since the crisis can affect the roles of the states as demonstrated in the European Union Effect and the fiscal privileges, the author centers in a most important effect: education. Education in Guatemala is fundamental for development given that the country has a high illiteracy rating, poor math and writing skills, according to the Pisa measurement and the lack of investment by the governments. The author analyzes all the aspects to lead the reader to the conclusion that one must invest in education if one wants future growth.

Chapter 7, written by the editor Celso Cerezo, centers on telecommunication. Celso has had experiencing handling diverse projects in the last ten years. This is why the paper transforms into a hands-on experience that can be important to the development of a country. With great detail, Celso explains the process in Latin America, its effects and the capacity that the industry has on growing.

Chapter 8 is the third contribution of the editor, Mauricio Garita, analyzing in more depth the situation concerning fiscal privileges and its effect in Guatemala. The author centers in the capacity of affecting economy, behooving part of a private sector and disturbing development. The conclusion offered by the chapter is that fiscal privileges cost more than the results they have.

Finally, the book closes with a credit analysis, focusing on the personal consumption data, to understand how credit has changed and how this can be the next follow-up to the economic crisis. The author explains greatly what is the process for debt to grow and hos this impacts the financial system.

The book as a whole is incomplete without the reader reflecting on the issues at hand. With all the effects that the economy has had, with the impacts that the societies have felt, there is only one valid conclusion. That one should be better prepared for the next financial crisis.

Mauricio Garita-Gutiérrez
Universidad del Valle de Guatemala, Guatemala
July 17, 2017

Acknowledgment

To God that gave me the opportunity to follow this path and to publish this book. To my wife, Sonia, and my son, Míkel, for the support and comprehension on this book. To everyone who reads each and every one of the chapters, we hope that it will guide you to your calling. - Mauricio Garita

To my wife, Zully, for her love and support. To my daughters, Anika and Katina, for inspiring me every day. - Celso Cerezo

Chapter 1
A Study to Analyze the Impact of the Sub-Prime Crisis on IPOs

Rakshita Dubey
Credit Suisse, India

Arti Chandani
Symbiosis International University, India

Mita Mehta
Symbiosis International University, India

ABSTRACT

The study of the IPOs are for a period of 10 years; hence, each company that came out with an IPO between 2004 and 2013 has been studied in terms of the paid up capital raised initially and then broken down into six sectors according to the type of industry they belong. The research is based on the assumption that the subprime crisis had a global effect and hence many developed countries suffered in terms of fall in exports, rise in debt defaults and reduced earrings of the corporate. However, the effect on India was minimal but the worldwide panic was there. The researchers have studied the impact of the subprime crisis on the IPOs issued during pre- and post-subprime crisis. The researchers have used statistical test to study the impact of subprime crisis on the Indian stock market. This compilation is a culmination of comprehensive in-depth study as well as practical experience.

DOI: 10.4018/978-1-5225-4981-9.ch001

INTRODUCTION

An IPO is like a negotiated transaction- the seller chooses when to come public, and it is unlikely that it's a time favourable to you. - By Warren Buffett

Initial Public Offer or offering shares to the public for the first time is a process where in a company issues shares/ stock / small shareholding of its company to the public or people at large in order to raise capital or money for their long term capital requirements by passing on the right to decision making of the company, to the public.

From the "publican" during the Roman republic to the modern day issues of Alibaba, the basic nature of IPO has not changed. All that is different is the methodology. The basic planning is crucial to the whole process as this is where the company decides the amount which it requires, sources of capital, method of allotment, price at which shares need to be issued and also the time of issue keeping in mind the economy.

The study has been conducted to find out the reason for the number of successful IPO's before 2008 in order to find out the exact nature of event due to which the companies after 2008 reduced their exposure to capital markets. Moreover the reasons could range from interest rates, capital market restrictions, FII's, global economy slowdown to even war and natural calamity. The Sectoral analysis would further throw light on the major companies that went for an IPO and what are the reasons for their subsequent under or over subscription. The study even though has been conducted in isolation for India but the factors may be external as well for the change in company's ideology for IPO's.

The year 2006 saw the surge in IPO's in India with successful IPOs' like ONGC, NTPC, TCS, Jet Airways, Cairn India etc. The total volume raised grew at the rate of 20-45% as compared to the past. The major reason for such an overwhelming response from the public was boom in stock market prices and investor confidence in the market as well as in the company. The period of 2004 to 2008 may be termed as golden years of IPO as a major chunk of shares were easily subscribed by the public and some over even oversubscribed to the extent of 95%. However IPO scams like that of Yes Bank actually caught the attention of investors later on who now got aware of the intricacies of IPO's.

The year 2008 onwards saw a huge decline in IPO's in the markets all over the world. The recession struck continents namely USA, Europe etc. had investors who became aware of the situations all over the world and starting pulling out funds from where they had invested thus leading to fall in stock markets all over the world. The companies also started to make provisions to cater to the losses if any due to this and hence most of them held up their requirements of the long term finances.

The research will aim to find out the trends in IPO's, volume of funds raised from primary market, valuation of the shares and book building mechanism used to raise capital. The study would also try to analyze the important IPO's of the respective period and the reason for the boom and oversubscription or vice versa as the case may be. Researchers would also analyze the international trends in IPO to be able to have awareness regarding the market situation abroad as well in order to get a holistic picture of the trend and hence get a conclusion regarding the various issues that took place while raising the money at the end of the research.

Objectives of the Research

The objective of the research can be broadly said to be the following:

1. To study the IPO's of different sectors during the period of 2004-2013
2. To study the impact of subprime crisis on the amount raised by IPOs
3. To analyze the impact of subprime crisis on the IPOs of different sectors of Indian stock market.

BACKGROUND

Singh et.al (2014), "Short Run Performance of IPO Market in India": The researchers analyzed the performance of IPOs in India. The researchers in their paper has clearly given that in the time period for measuring the performance was 30 days and the sample included 89 companies. There were the companies which issued IPOs during the time period of 2006-2009. The researcher has been able to analyze the pre listing information on which the IPO pricing is based. The researcher used the logistic regression model to test the hypotheses and concluded that many IPOs gave significant returns on the listing day price but did not give good returns in the short-run and this made the researchers to conclude that the market over reacts to the IPOs.

Chopra Rohini Inder (2009), "Price Performance of IPO's in Indian Capital Market": The researcher has analyzed the IPO's on the NSE for the period of 1999-2008 by considering their prices of issue into consideration. An analysis of the issue price has been undertaken for varied periods of time i.e. 1week, 1month, 3 months, 6 months, 9months and finally one year. Along with the price analysis, an analysis on the factors affecting the IPO was also carried out with a motive to recognize the basic reasons for the subscription by public to the various IPO's of the same period. It was found that most of issues were underpriced specially in the short run periods (day from listing until 6 months of the issue). Hence it can be inferred that the market capitalization of the various companies listed on NSE in the period 2003-2008 are an effect of underpricing and hence there is a possibility that the actual market capitalization in far more than what is stated.

Das Sajal (2014), "Underpricing of Initial Public Offerings: A study based on mega issues listed on National Stock Exchange"**:** The research paper is based on the top 20 mega issues that got listed on the NSE during the period of 2001 and 2010 in order to understand the pricing behavior of the same. There are 9 that belong to the boom period and remaining 11 belong to the recessionary period. It was found that there is not much of a relation between the IPO's that belong to the boom period and those belonging to the Recessionary period with respect to the pricing. Moreover it can also not be completely found that these mega issues are underpriced to the extent of 100% as compared to those in the previous periods. There are only 25% issues that can be called as underpriced, that too without any surety.

Katalina M. Bianco (2009), "The Subprime Lending Crisis: Causes and Effects of the Mortgage Meltdown": The researchers have discussed the report published by International Monetary fund (IMF) in the year 2008. The report took the official estimated of the global losses which banks and financial institutions have undergone. The researchers have discussed the roots of the subprime crisis namely housing bubble, low interest rates, and criticism of Greenspan, rise of subprime lending, declining risk premium etc. They also analyzed the impact of the subprime crisis on stock market and other industries. They have discussed in detail the reasons and the impact of the subprime crisis. All have understood the problem but the question as to how to resolve this, remains unanswered.

Different Sectors of Capital Market

The IPO's that have got listed on the National Stock Exchange during the period of 2004 till 2013 have been segregated into various sectors of the economy. With the help of this, the researcher will be able to analyze the economic condition of the economy as a whole along with the independent sectoral analysis to achieve the reasons for the subscription of shares by the public for the various issues. The Sectors are as follows:

1. **Computers, IT and Allied Services:** For the purpose of the research, this sector includes all the companies that either is in the manufacture of computer software, hardware or is providing IT solutions to its clients. They may be manufacturing the component or simply providing the logistical support to the clients with respect to the same. In the research there are 30 companies that fall under this category including Tech Mahindra, TCS, Data Matics Ltd. etc.

Mobile internet has also given an impetus to the sector. Dealership and OEM website have seen spurt in traffic from mobiles.

2. **Banking and Financial Services:** For the purpose of the research, this sector includes all types of banks i.e. scheduled banks, unscheduled banks etc. financial institutions, financial consultancy firms, intermediaries providing consultancy, long term funding options etc. This category includes any business formed to provide capital to other businesses, advisory services and even act as financial intermediaries. This category includes companies like ICICI Bank, IDFC Bank, Yeas Bank etc. with a total of 45 companies for analysis. The banks saw the spurt of women in the sector since 1950s.
3. **Manufacturing and Extraction, Processing of Minerals, Gems etc.:** The researcher has considered all the entities that are involved in the production of tangible goods, extraction of raw materials, refining of a raw material. It also includes businesses involved in refining, polishing and making jewellery out of the raw materials so extracted. The extraction could be of precious/ semi-precious metals, gems, stones, natural products etc. TATA Steel, Bharti Infratech, TBZ Jewellers, along with other companies forms a total of 109 companies for the analysis.
4. **Pharmaceuticals and Healthcare Products and Services:** This sector, for the purpose of research, includes all companies involved in the manufacture, packaging and/or sale of pharma products, directly or indirectly. All the companies selling healthcare products or are involved in both manufacture and sale of the same, are also considered for the purpose of analysis in this sector. 22 companies including Lotus eye care hospitals, Alpha Labs, Religare Enterprises Ltd. form a part of the study in this sector.
5. **Construction and Engineering:** Companies involved in the construction, development of all types of infrastructure projects, both short term and long term, and provide engineering services for the same or in addition to the same are included in this sector. The sector excludes any company that provides long term finance for these projects; incidentally they are analyzed under the "Banking and Financial Services" sector. PVK Power and Infrastructure, Paravanath developers along with 52 other companies have been able to successfully raise capital from the NSE during the period of study.
6. **Others:** It includes companies belonging to any other sector, apart from the above mentioned sectors. They may be Oil and Gas, FMCG, Retail, Power and Transmission, Petrochemicals, Aviation etc. There are 130 companies that have been characterized under this heading owing to their non-belongingness to the above listed 5 sectors.

Each of the sectors have been analyzed with reference to the amount of shares offered to the public, Issue price, total issue size, overall sector performance, and factors affecting the subscription by public based on the scenario of the Indian economy, over the period of 10 years i.e. 2004 to 2013. These sectors are further studied into pre and post subprime crisis to understand and analyze the impact.

Research Gap

The researchers, based on the existing literature have found that there has been extensive research on the reasons of the subprime crisis and the impact of the subprime crisis on various stock market, countries, industries and sector. However, not much research has been done to analyze the impact of the subprime crisis on the capital market. With this, the following gaps were identified:-

- Impact of subprime crisis on the IPOs has not been studied
- There has not been research to understand the impact of subprime on IPOs by comparing it with the pre subprime period

Research Question

The present study tries to answer the question whether was there any impact of subprime crisis on the IPOs issued in the Indian capital market

Hypothesis

- **H1:** There is no difference in the amount raised by the companies for pre and post subprime crisis time period
- **H2:** There is no difference in the amount raised by way IPO among the companies of different sector during pre-subprime crisis
- **H3:** There is no difference in the amount raised by way IPO among the companies of different sector during post-subprime crisis
- **H4:** There is no difference in the amount raised by IPOs among the companies of different sectors for pre and post subprime crisis

Analysis of IPO's for the Period of 2004-2008

Considering the fact that the years 2003-2004 have been called as the two golden years for stock markets and henceforth IPO's, the data vouches for the fact that they were truly in real sense most capital raising years for companies till then. However as the economy progressed the year 2007, saw the highest Capital raising by a company, listing on NSE. This can be clearly seen in the Table 1 where the total paid up capital is approximately Rs. 33, 68,356 lakhs for the year 2007. This was period where markets were at its peak, consumers were have enough purchasing power to buy whatever they wanted and overall economy was in its growing phase.

The major reasons for such a boom in 2004 onwards with respected to the IPO's is the growth of Indian Economy during the same time due to initiation of the 10th Five Year Plans (2002-2007), a GDP growth rate of 7.5% (projections) and the investor confidence in the Indian Companies during that time. The year 2004 and 2007 can be called as the most successful years for the IPO's.

The year 2008 has seen a decline in the total capital which was raised by issue of IPOs. The decrease in the amount of capital was close to 49% which is too big and this is the impact of the subprime crisis. This is the time when the subprime crisis started in US and it was expected to take the world and other economies into the wave. The subprime crisis took the globe through a roller coaster where people were not aware as to what was happening and how it will impact them. With the passage of time, things started becoming clear and the reasons and impact was known.

Analysis of IPO's in the Respective Sectors for the Period 2004-2008

The period of 2003-2008 saw a huge surge in the number of companies going for an IPO and thus raising crores of money through the National Stock Exchange. The sectoral net change in the total capital raised has been summarized in Table 2. It is clearly visible that for the year 2003, most amount of money was raised by companies of the Pharma sector i.e. approx. 25% of the total paid up capital. For the booming year 2007, the IT sector was at the peak of its operations and hence the companies of the same were expanding and hence raising money from the public to finance the same.

The year 2005 was a year where the researcher saw a number of IPO's from the Banking and Financial services sector, the major one being that of YES Bank.

Table 1. Total paid up capital raised during 2004-2008

Year	Total Paid Up Capital (Rs. In Lakh)
2004	₹ 2,897,401.98
2005	₹ 1,757,034.81
2006	₹ 2,330,893.65
2007	₹ 3,368,356.57
2008	₹ 1,696,714.97

Table 2. Sectoral description of total paid up capital raised through NSE

Year	2004	2005	2006	2007	2008
Computers, IT and Allied Services (Rs. In lakhs)	₹ 544,063.44	₹ 77,840.56	₹ 107,756.48	₹ 161,360.26	₹ 18,174.98
Banking and Finance (Rs. In lakhs)	₹ 349,427.59	₹ 1,090,903.35	₹ 371,890.00	₹ 680,094.92	₹ 49,134.42
Manufacturing and extraction, processing of minerals, gems etc. (Rs. In lakhs)	₹ 5,880.00	₹ 185,015.25	₹ 227,160.91	₹ 572,957.60	₹ 77,426.01
Pharmaceutical and Healthcare products and services (Rs. In lakhs)	₹ 78,774.95	₹ 9,288.00	₹ 22,585.68	₹ 30,268.39	₹ 11,822.00
Construction and Engineering (Rs. In lakhs)	₹ 0.00	₹ 76,810.55	₹ 385,141.38	₹ 1,485,225.37	₹ 157,631.95
Others (Rs. In lakhs)	₹ 1,919,256.00	₹ 317,177.11	₹ 1,216,359.21	₹ 438,450.01	₹ 1,382,525.61
Total Paid Up Capital (Rs. In lakhs)	₹ 2,897,401.98	₹ 1,757,034.81	₹ 2,330,893.65	₹ 3,368,356.57	₹ 1,696,714.97

IN 2006 there was an overall hike in capital raised by most of the sectors of the Indian economy. However in 2007, the construction and engineering sector saw the maximum surge in amount raised, almost triple the amount from the previous year. The economic slowdown of 2008 saw a reduced number of companies seeking help of stock exchanges for meeting their capital requirements. 2004 saw a great response among the investors nearly 100% growth in the number of IPO's with emphasis on the IT sector with others.

The Yes Bank, ICICI Bank, Syndicate Bank etc. came in need of money which led to such a rise in the amount raised by the sector from 2005 onwards. The year 2007 saw a majority of infrastructure companies borrowing money from the public in huge amount thus leading to a majority of IPO's in year 2007 during the period of study.

Analysis of IPO's for the Period of 2009-2013

The analysis of the 5 year period is crucial to understand the amount of money raised after a global slowdown with that of 2004-2008. The comparative study will help us in determining the reasons for such a response by public to the various capital issues owing to economic factors as well as personal factors. In the period of 2009-2013, 2010 is said to have had the most amount of money raised.

The Table 3 clearly shows that 2010 was a major year where the total capital issued to the public rose more than 100% as compared to the previous year. Thereafter the issue size has been very small as compared to the history. On the whole the 6 year period of 2003-2008 saw more number of IPO's than that in 2009-2013.

The major reason is the world economic slowdown owing to the US subprime crisis and it's after effects throughout the world economy. Also the various scams that happened in India like Coalgate, Telecom License etc. at the end of 2010 led to a serious loss of investor confidence in the country as a whole of both domestic investors and FII's.

Analysis of IPO's in the Respective Sectors for the period 2009-2013

The respective sectors of the Indian economy saw varied response from the public post the global economic slowdown owing to the sub-prime crisis. The period saw a decline in the number of IPO's naturally because of the lost investor faith and Global Economic slowdown.

The year 2010 saw maximum IPO's during the period of 5 years, considered for the research. Moreover, the companies belonging to the manufacturing sector have raised capital from the public owing to the expansionary plans of the specific corporate, looking at the proposed sectoral growth, after the global economic slowdown.

The major reason is the reduced market demand due to economic slowdown, increased selling of stocks on the stock exchanges all over the globe, more focus on the manufacturing sector owing to the reduced services provided abroad and hence reduced forex earnings of the country. The remaining sectors couldn't perform very well due to the overall turmoil of the economy hence this period definitely saw reduced IPO's than the previous period.

Table 3. Total paid up capital raised during 2009-2013

Year	Total Paid Up Capital (Rs. In Lakhs)
2009	₹ 1,932,638.71
2010	₹ 5,200,378.75
2011	₹ 1,045,693.35
2012	₹ 656,167.64
2013	₹ 837,543.76

Table 4. Sectoral description of total paid up capital raised through NSE

Year	2009	2010	2011	2012	2013
Computers, IT and Allied Services	₹ 2,384.34	₹ 67,946.35	₹ 25,250.00	₹ 0.00	₹ 0.00
Banking and Finance	₹ 0.00	₹ 510,747.05	₹ 470,013.20	₹ 120,328.29	₹ 27,038.85
Manufacturing and extraction, minerals, gems etc.	₹ 27,337.50	₹ 3,034,863.14	₹ 465,845.01	₹ 435,580.00	₹ 9,441.60
Pharmaceutical and Healthcare products and services	₹ 6,150.00	₹ 73,602.50	₹ 34,980.00	₹ 0.00	₹ 0.00
Construction and Engineering	₹ 106,023.23	₹ 708,507.20	₹ 3,690.02	₹ 5,500.00	₹ 0.00
Others	₹ 1,790,743.64	₹ 804,712.51	₹ 45,915.13	₹ 94,759.35	₹ 801,063.31
Total	₹ 1,932,638.71	₹ 5,200,378.75	₹ 1,045,693.35	₹ 656,167.64	₹ 837,543.76

Comparative Analysis of IPO's for Period 2003-2008 and 2009-2013

After studying each of the sectors and the period independently, the researcher can now join the dots to get a holistic picture of the analysis. To do so, the researcher has broken the study again into years and the sectors for the entire period of 2004 to 2013. The majority of the money that got raised in Period 1 i.e. 2004-2008 was in the year 2007 and in Period 2 i.e. 2009-2013 was in the year 2010.

The remaining years have had average amount of capital rising as compared to these two years. More importantly it's clearly visible that in Period 1, approximately 55.75% of the money got raised out of the total amount of Rs. 2 crore lacs belonging to the entire 10 year period. Comparing it to the overall sum it if found that only 45% was raised in 2009-2013 out of which 23.79% in the year 2010. The Period 1 can be called a Golden Period in comparison to the other years as the amount raised was more on an overall basis in the relevant years.

The years 2004 and 2013 saw maximum IPO's from the "others" sector which includes companies belonging to Oil and Gas sector, Entertainment and media etc. as given in the figure 1. Rest other sectors were very slow and may be hesitant to raise capital during these years. The banking Sector was at its full swing in the year 2010 where the logical explanation could be the need of banks to expand operations after the global economic slowdown and hence a reversal of the banks business technique. Year 2007 saw an increased demand from the Construction and Infrastructure business due to the boom in the market, growth in demand for goods and a positive spending spree among the consumers. This led to a rise in the demand for housing projects and hence subsequently a rise in housing projects.

Analysis of the IPO's Raised by the Companies Through NSE

In 2004, 21 companies raised Rs.289 thousand lacs of rupees through the NSE where in majority of the money was from other sector companies and thence computer, IT and software companies. The growth rate of Services Sector was 9.1% complemented by a GDP Growth rate of 8.5%, first time such a high rate of growth after 1975-76 for Indian Economy. The sharp rise in IT Sector called for an extensive demand for money from the companies operating in the same leading to more number of IPO's by companies like TCS, Datamatics Technologies etc. The capital goods Sector was growing by this time along with the consumer durables, thus paving way for Golden period for the IPO's.

PVR Ltd, ICICI Bank, Yeas Bank, Shoppers Stop, IDFC Bank etc are few of the companies that went public and received a heart whelming response from the public in the year 2005.The relaxation of norms by the RBI led to an easy more progressive business outlook of banks thereby a more active banking sector along with the other companies.

Year 2006 saw a slow and steady growth in the demand for money from all the sectors of the economy. Approximately Rs. 23, 00,000 lacs was raised by all the companies in this year which accounts for 19.31% of the total amount raised in Period 1. Companies like Parasvnath Developers, Cairn India, J.K Cement, Reliance Petrochemicals etc were some of the renowned names among the list of 68 companies. The major reasons being real growth rate of the country being 9% followed by growth in the construction, finance and manufacturing business segments of the country, leading to more growth and hence increasing demand for money by the respective companies.

The growth in the Construction and Banking Sector continued in the year 2007 which can also be called as a Golden Goose in the entire 6 years of the Period 1 wherein a total of ₹ 33, 00, 00 lacs approx amount of money was raised i.e. 27.64% of the total period 1 capital raising. Majorly this year saw an increased spending from the consumers on all kinds of goods and services leading to increased pressure on companies to sell and earn profits, hence requiring more funding to provide for the growing needs. It was in this year that the Sub Prime Crisis started in the US and its effects could gradually be felt across borders. Also the end of the 10th Five year Plan marked a great end to a growing Economy trend.

Due to the fear of Economic Slowdown, there was a drastic reduction in IPO's in the year 2008 and 2009 leading to a period of slow growth. By this time the after effects of the Sub Prime crisis could be felt all across the globe, even in India but in a small way i.e. only through the Stock Market Downturn and hence subsequent fall in the value of the Market Capitalization of the respective companies. A total 53 companies raised money in these 2 years that too with a lot of caution. The rising fuel and oil prices, withdrawal of money of FII's from the Global Capital Markets and high Inflation in the economy caused a very pale response to the IPO's during this time.

The maximum capital was raised in the year 2010 out of all years in our period of study, corresponding to 23% of the total money. All the sectors were in need of capital to the tune of Rs. 53,00,000 lacs approximately this year owing to the gradual increase in investor confidence in the country, growth in demand from the consumers for goods and hence a pressure on the company to meet those demands. Companies like Talwalkars, Jaypee Infratech, Standard Charted, NTPC, SKS Microfinance, REC Ltd. and Coal India were the major capital raisers of this period in a total of approximately 70 companies that raised finances in this period. Most importantly India's biggest ever IPO came in this period of Coal India Ltd. that got oversubscribed to the extent of 55 times.

The subsequent years to 2010 again saw a slowdown in the economy leading to only 51 IPO's in a span of 3 years of the study period i.e. 2011-2013. Rs 24,00,000 lacs of mount was raised by companies like TATA Steel, Bharti Infratel, Muthoot Finance, Just Dial, SRS Ltd, TBZ Jewellers etc. The reduction in GDP to 5.5% in this span of time, spread of the news of various scams in the country namely coal scam, telecom license, Satyam etc. led to a huge shift in investor confidence from the Indian economy to other growing economies of the world like Thailand, Singapore etc.

A thorough analysis of the various IPO's and the time period, the entire study could be summed up as per the above Table 5. It can be very well seen that there were double the IPO's in the Period I as compared to the other period due to various factors as mentioned above. Similarly the amount of money raised from the public was more in Period I and Period II saw a slow and weak growth with the only exception being the year 2010 that saw the highest amount of money raised in comparison to any of the years in the period of study. This was primarily because of the Coal India Limited IPO.

Table 5. Total Amount of capital raised during the period of study

Period of Study	Total Paid up Capital Raised (Amount in Rs. Lakhs)	Number of IPO's
Period I (2004 to 2008)	12050401.97	273
Period II (2009 to 2013)	9672422.21	141
Total	21722824.18	414

Table 6. Number of IPO's sector wise during 2004-2013

Period of Time		Computers, IT and Allied Services	Banking and Finance	Manufacturing and extraction, processing of minerals, gems etc.	Pharmaceutical and Healthcare products and services	Construction and Engineering	Others
Period I	2004	4	3	1	4	0	9
	2005	8	9	5	1	2	22
	2006	5	9	31	3	16	22
	2007	16	8	28	3	16	25
	2008	2	1	1	2	5	12
Total		35	30	66	13	39	90
Period II	2009	1	0	3	1	3	13
	2010	4	5	22	5	15	18
	2011	2	9	14	4	1	8
	2012	0	2	2	0	1	4
	2013	0	1	1	0	0	2
Total		7	17	42	10	20	45
Grand Total		42	47	108	23	59	135

Hypothesis Testing

The researchers have used z-test to test the hypothesis and to ascertain whether is there any difference in the IPOs issued pre and post subprime crisis. There are 258 companies which have issued the IPOs during the period of 2004-2008, while the number of companies was 141 during the period of 2009-2013. The z-test was applied by the researchers and the result is given in the Table 7. The p value is greater than 0.05 therefore the researchers accept the null hypothesis. Thus there is no significant difference in the amount raised by the companies for pre and post subprime crisis.

The researchers have taken 7 different sectors to categorize the IPOs issued by different companies for pre subprime crisis i.e. 2004-2008. The F value is 4.24 which are greater than F crit and the p value is less than 0.05, as given in Table 8, which implied that there is a difference for within the different sectors for pre subprime crisis. Hence the researchers reject the null hypothesis. Thus there is a difference in the amount raised by way of IPO among the companies of different sectors during pre-subprime crisis.

The researchers have used single factor ANOVA to identify the difference in the amount of capital raised by the companies in different sector for the period of 2009-2013, which is post subprime crisis period. The result of the single factor ANOVA is presented in Table 9 and it shows that the F value of 0.662776 is less than the F

Table 7. Result of z-test

	Variable 1	Variable 2
Mean	46706.9844	68598.7391
Known Variance	15946150063	32188540516
Observations	258	141
Hypothesized Mean Difference	0	
z	-1.285319132	
P(Z<=z) one-tail	0.099340394	
z Critical one-tail	1.644853627	
P(Z<=z) two-tail	0.198680787	
z Critical two-tail	1.959963985	

Table 8. Single factor ANOVA for the period of 2004-2008

Source of Variation	SS	df	MS	F	P-value	F crit
Between Groups	2.95E+11	6	4.92E+10	4.204065	0.000429	2.125591
Within Groups	3.93E+12	336	1.17E+10			
Total	4.23E+12	342				

Table 9. Single factor ANOVA for the period of 2009-2013

Source of Variation	SS	df	MS	F	P-value	F crit
Between Groups	1.07969E+11	5	2.16E+10	0.662776	0.65231	2.281305
Within Groups	4.39842E+12	135	3.26E+10			
Total	4.50639E+12	140				

crit and the p value of 0.65231 is greater than 0.05, therefore the null hypotheses is accepted. There is no difference in the amount raised by way IPO among the companies of different sector during post-subprime crisis.

The researchers have further used two way ANOVA to find the difference with the 7 sectors of the companies for pre and post subprime crisis and for the time period of 2004-2008 and 2009-2013. There is no difference in the amount raised by IPOs during the pre and post subprime crisis as the F value of 0.337845469 is less than F crit 4.042652129 and the p value of 0.56379595 is greater than 0.05. The Table 10 shows the results of the two-way ANOVA.

Table 10. Two factor ANOVA for the time period 2004-2013

Source of Variation	SS	df	MS	F	P-value	F crit
Sample	94246462435	1	94246462435	0.337845469	0.563795095	4.042652129
Columns	4.75262E+12	5	9.50524E+11	3.407344912	0.010282348	2.408514119
Interaction	1.48122E+12	5	2.96243E+11	1.061944226	0.393112444	2.408514119
Within	1.33902E+13	48	2.78963E+11			
Total	1.97183E+13	59				

However there is a difference among the companies belonging to different sectors during pre and post subprime crisis as the F value of 3.407344912 is greater than F crit 2.408514119 and p value of 0.010282348 is less than 0.05.

Therefore the researchers conclude that there is no difference in the amount raised by IPOs during the pre and post subprime crisis however there is difference among the companies for the amount raised for pre and post subprime crisis.

SOLUTIONS AND RECOMMENDATIONS

The Indian capital market has not been affected much by the subprime crisis and this is considered to be a good sign. There was impact of this housing bubble on the various sectors which saw a downfall in terms of recruitment; bonus etc. to their employees as well as the demand was sluggish for this period. The Indian banking sector which is very much controlled and rigid came to the rescue of the crisis. Had the banks followed a policy of liberal sanctioning of the loan, India would have not been spared.

The number of IPOs which were issued post subprime crisis was less but the impact was not much, at least statistically. The Indian markets need to be much more insulated from these impacts and for this India need to strong policies and less dependence on the FII. The FII influence the market a lot as of now. The IPOs norms should also be sticker so that a company which issues the IPOs is there to do a long term business and the investors are going to provide money to get a decent return. The corporate governance norms should also be made mandatory instead of voluntary, which will pave way for building the confidence of the investors and thus the IPOs would be more successful and investor would be happy to invest in the market.

FUTURE RESEARCH DIRECTIONS

The present study focuses on the impact of the subprime crisis on the IPOs where the time period was 10 years. The IPOs are a powerful and effective way for raising the equity capital for any firm. In the recent past, India has seen the IPOs being issued from Café Coffee Day, Interglobe Aviation to name a few. Some of the microfinance companies have also issued the IPOs.

The subprime crisis had a wide spread impact across the economies. A similar study can be conducted in countries which were affected more. This will also increase the body of knowledge, as far as; subprime crisis is concerned and will give the new directions.

The world has seen a new crisis, Eurozone crisis. Researches can be conducted to see the impact Euro crisis on the various stock markets in terms of IPOs.

CONCLUSION

The research was conducted looking at two perspectives. Firstly to understand the amount of money raised during the two periods namely Period I (2003-2008) and Period II (2009-2013) by studying each year independently. It was found that Period I saw the most number of IPO's in terms of the paid up capital raised as well as number. There were about 279 IPO's in this period that raised approximately Rs. 1.21 crore lacs amount of money from the public. Considering the huge number, the researcher found that the major reason for such a boom in the IPO market is because of the successfully running 10th five year plan; Steady GDP Growth Rate of 7.5-8.5%, Global Economic cycles etc.

The Period II can be characterized as a slow growth period followed by a US Sub Prime Crisis who's after effects were felt all over the world later on till 2012. India was not affected that majorly unlike countries like U.K., Germany and other European Countries. The year 2010 saw India's biggest IPO ever in the form of Coal India Limited, a state owned Enterprise, whose shares were oversubscribed by 15 times. Not to forget the Reliance Power IPO in 2008 which was 50 times oversubscribed but failed badly later on due to the fall in markets later on due to the overpricing of the issue. The major reason for a slow capital raising period was the US Sub Prime Crisis, Loss of investor Confidence in the markets due to a sharp 2000 points fall in Sensex in the year 2008, knowledge of scams among the public of Satyam, Coal scam, Telecom License etc.

The manufacturing sector has been the most demanding in terms of money thus out of the 5 independent sectors; it is the one that has had most number of IPO's during the period of the study. The "others" sector that includes all other companies which are not in manufacturing, IT solutions, infrastructure etc. has raised most amount of capital. The sectoral analysis has helped the researcher to find out the reasons for the same. The major ones being independent policies issued by the Government of India for specific sectors, incentives to them and the successful five year plans that give boost to the country as a whole thus leading to an overall GDP Growth.

The research found that the year 2005 saw a number of IPO's from the Banking Sector due to the hyped issues of ICICI Bank, Yes Bank and Oriental Bank of Commerce. Similarly the year 2007 saw maximum IPO's from the Construction and Infrastructure development Sector due to the massive demand from the consumers and thus rising pressure of the companies like Parasvnath Developers to fulfil the demand of the same. In 2010 there was arising pressure of consumer goods and hence there was a boom in the manufacturing sector that led to most of the IPO's.

REFERENCES

Arti, C., & Mita, M. (2013). Women Leadership in Axis Bank: A Comparison of woman and man leader using CAMEL Model. *International Journal of Research in Commerce, IT & Management.*, *3*(2), 83–89.

Bianco, K. M. (2008). *The subprime lending crisis: Causes and effects of the mortgage meltdown.* CCH, Wolters Kluwer Law & Business.

Chopra, R. I. (2009). *Price performance of IPOs in Indian Stock Market.* Patiala, India: Thapar University.

List of IPOs During 2003-2013 Through NSE. (n.d.). Retrieved from http://www.nseindia.com/products/content/equities/ipos/ipos.htm

Mishra, P. K. (2012). Global Financial Crisis and Indian Capital Market- An Econometric Analysis. *International Journal of Applied Business and Economics Research.*, *10*(1), 11–29.

Samson, R., Mehta, M., & Chandani, A. (2014). Impact of Online Digital Communication on Customer Buying Decision. *Procedia Economics and Finance.*, *11*, 872–880. doi:10.1016/S2212-5671(14)00251-2

Sejal, D. (2014). Underpricing of Initial Public Offerings: A study based on mega issues listed on National Stock Exchange. *International Journal of Business and Management*, *1*(2), 75–85.

Singh, A. K., & Murthy, K. V. B. (2014). Short run performance of IPO Market in India. *International Journal of Financial Management.*, *4*(1), 11–22.

KEY TERMS AND DEFINITIONS

BFSI: Banking and Financial Services Industry (BFSI) which is the backbone of the Indian economy, includes different types of banks, insurance, mutual funds, etc.

Book-Building Process: It is a process through which the demand for the shares at different prices is determined and a final price is arrived for issuance of share. This is also known as price discovery mechanism.

IPO: It is the process of raising equity capital from the public for the very first time. Therefore, it is named as Initial Public offering. This is the way in which a company becomes public limited company.

IT: Information technology sector which is one of major driver of the Indian economy. This sector deals with the information technology companies which are majorly engaged in providing the services.

NSE: National Stock Exchange, established in 1992, is the leading stock exchange of India. It was the first exchange to offer fully-automated screen based trading platform to the length and breadth of the country.

Paid-Up Capital: The amount of capital which has been subscribed by the equity shareholder is known as paid up capital. The IPOs increases the paid up capital of the company.

Price Performance: The price performance of a share can be calculated by comparing its issue price and the price at which it is being traded. The time period for comparison could be as small as 1 day and it can be as long as 50 years.

Subprime Crisis: The subprime crisis originated from the United States during December, 2007 to mid-2009. A bubble was created in terms of housing industry which burst during this time, giving shocks and tremors to various companies and economies.

Underpricing: If the share is being traded in the market at a price which is lesser than its fair value, it is termed as underpriced.

Chapter 2
The Transmission of the Great Recession (2008-2009) and the Sovereign Debt Crisis (2010-2012) to Latin America:
An Econometric Study of the Two Crises Impact on the Region

Roberto J. Santillán-Salgado
Tecnológico de Monterrey, Mexico

Edgardo A. Ayala-Gaytán
Instituto Tecnológico de Estudios Superiores de Monterrey, Mexico

ABSTRACT

In this work we discuss econometric evidence on four major issues that relate to the six largest Latin American economies (Argentina, Brazil, Chile, Colombia, Mexico, and Peru) during the two consecutive international financial crises between 2008 and 2012. Our first concern has to do with the mechanism of transmission of the international financial crisis and its secondary effects on the real and financial sectors of our sample countries. The second aspect that we explore refers to the actual magnitude of both, real and financial effects of the crisis. Our third objective has to do with an evaluation of the role played by individual countries' external macroeconomic vulnerability. And, finally, we propose a contra-factual analysis of the growth performance of our sample of Latin American economies, with the growth performance they would have experienced in a hypothetical scenario of no external turmoil.

DOI: 10.4018/978-1-5225-4981-9.ch002

INTRODUCTION

The 2008-2009 Global Financial Crisis revealed the serious limitations of the financial regulatory framework in place in the United States at the time. And just a few months after probably the most critical episode of the crisis, the bankruptcy filing of Lehman Brothers on September 15, 2008, the government of Greece unchained a new ripple effect with the announcement that its fiscal deficit and public debt levels had been misreported throughout several years. The new Sovereign Debt Crisis (2010-2012) exposed the weaknesses of the Eurozone supervisory system, and Greece came very close to defaulting its sovereign bonds. The Greek sovereign bonds problem arose the attention of investors and rating agencies, and shortly thereafter, Ireland, Portugal and Spain were targeted by speculators, as their macroeconomic fundamentals were also deemed to be in poor shape (Santillán-Salgado et al. 2015).

The sequential outburst of these "twin crises" proved not only that financial regulation and supervisory bodies were inappropriate to monitor the participants in the global financial market, and limited in their ability to counterbalance the surge of serious threats to the international financial system. Governmental entities in charge of enforcing transparency and due diligence in the case of the United States, and compliance with the public finances targets of sovereign countries, in the case of the members of the European Union, were unable to anticipate the onslaught of savage speculation and bank failures that would follow the events described, forcing their governments to bail out numerous financial entities and non-financial corporations that were considered "too-big to fail". An overwhelming and unexpected default of thousands of complex securitized bond issues and the limited cross-national coordination of the authorities to stop the extreme turbulence observed in the global financial market during that period staged an extraordinarily dangerous financial risk situation[1].

The Global Financial Crisis affected Latin American countries less than most other geographical regions in virtue of the important modernization efforts and structural reforms implemented by the regional governments during the previous decade (although there is a wide dispersion in the timing of the Latin American structural reforms that initiated back in the 1970's in Chile), and also because the international price of many of the commodities they export, including oil, metals, minerals and agricultural products, reached historically high levels well into the period of intense financial volatility, and until the last weeks of the Summer of 2008: and even when there was a generalized collapse of commodities prices during the next six months, there was a significant recovery towards January of 2009.

Almost two decades earlier, at the beginning of the 1990s, the most pressing macroeconomic problems affecting Latin American countries were: how to stabilize inflation, how to achieve fiscal discipline, and how to liberalize trade and liberalize the financial industry (Gonzalez and Kruger 2003). At that time, Latin America was considered a region affected by chronic inflationary problems and by general macroeconomic instability.

However, by the end of the 1990s, the macroeconomy of the region was totally different, and inflationary pressures were no longer an issue in most regional countries. The region governments' preventive policies included the accumulation of foreign reserves as a buffer to sudden capital outflows, and fiscal policy was conducted with more responsibility than in the previous decades[2].

The public finances had been significantly improved, including the massive reduction of the public sector ownership of all sorts of productive assets, through many successful privatization experiences. Domestic financial systems were strengthened by an expanded and improved quality capital base, by a systematic upgrading of regulatory and supervisory frameworks, and by better risk management practices.

In terms of trade liberalization, different regional initiatives were well advanced by the end of the 1990s like, for example, the creation of the Mercosur, in 1991, or the accession of Mexico to the North American Free Trade Agreement in 1994. Also, financial reforms were already in an advanced stage in most of the larger economies of the region (Chile, Colombia, Mexico, Peru).

The relative macroeconomic stability observed in Latin America during the 2008-2009 financial crisis and the 2010-2012 sovereign debt crisis may be attributed to the compound effect of that series of structural reforms during the previous decades. While the reforms effects on economic growth were not very impressive during the first years of the new century, they were significant steps towards the development of a Latin American economic model. According to ECLAC[3] Latin American countries economic activity, measured by GDP at constant prices and in dollars, observed an average annual growth for the 2001-2014 period of 1.62%. While not totally unsatisfactory, that average is certainly low, considering the significant lag of the region's income per capita with respect to more developed geographical areas. According to Lipsky (2011), the Latin American macroeconomic stability that was present at the outburst of the Great Recession, helped preserve the significant progress in social and human welfare indicators achieved during recent decades. Structural reforms were in many cases fully operational and prevented output losses and, in that sense, "helped to ensure that pre-crisis improvements in living standards and reductions in income inequality...(were)... preserved". In stark contrast with previous crisis episodes, this time such gains were not reversed by the consequences of the Great Recession.

However, there was one exception to that favorable scenario. Mexico's economy maintains a very close commercial relationship with that of the U.S. and, due to the significant interweaving of both economies, in addition to the disproportionate size of the latter economy with respect to the former, when there is an economic slowdown in the U.S. (as was the case during the Great recession, due to the liquidity constrains imposed by the financial crisis), the effect is more than proportional on Mexico's economy[4]. Mexico experienced an annual real GDP contraction of -4.7% (-7% annualized during the first quarter) in 2009, only comparable to the crippling economic effect that resulted from the peso devaluation back in December 1994 (as can be observed in Figure 1, below). However, the important structural reforms that took place in that country during the years that followed that episode helped buffer the otherwise catastrophic effects that the financial crisis of 2008-2009 would have had.

In this work we discuss econometric evidence on four major issues that relate to the six largest Latin American economies[5] (Argentina, Brazil, Chile, Colombia, Mexico and Peru) during the two consecutive crises that took place between 2008 and 2012. Our first concern has to do with the *mechanism of transmission* of the international financial crisis and its secondary effects to the real and financial sectors of our sample countries. Following Blanchard et al. (2010), and Izquierdo, Romero and Talvi (2008), the contraction of the volume and relative value of the exports of goods and services plays a prominent role in an international financial crisis. Hence, the degree of openness of an economy to foreign trade, the relative importance of goods and services exports (plus migrant workers remittances), as well as the terms of trade, should capture the negative impact of external demand

Figure 1. Mexico's Real GDP and its Quarterly Growth Rate (1994Q1-2015Q1)

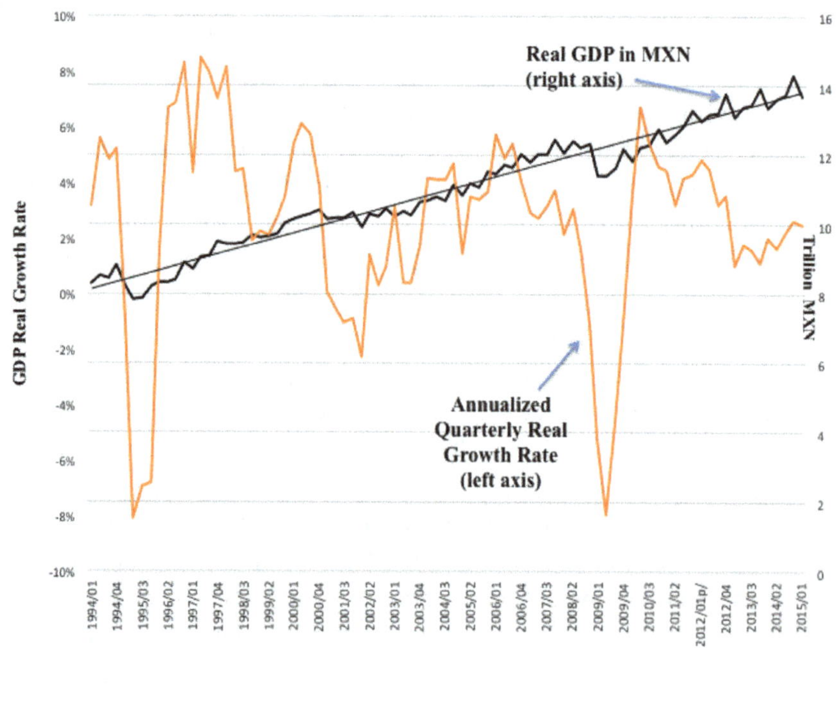

collapse and commodities prices drop when a crisis begins. Also, under financial openness, uncertainty in the world financial markets might cause a sudden stop of capital inflows and extreme volatility in the exchange rate, an increase in the sovereign spreads of interest rates, and a crash of the stock market. In such an environment, confidence and credit flows drop, leading to a consumption and investment crunch (Calvo 1998; Calvo & Reinhart 2000).

The second aspect that we explore refers to the actual magnitude of both, *real and financial effects of the crisis* over our sample of Latin American countries' economies. Our third objective has to do with an evaluation of the role played by individual countries' external macroeconomic vulnerability, a subject brought up by Blanchard, Farukee and Das (2010) and Llauvar, Salman y Chivakul (2010), when analyzing the context of the recent financial crisis and its impact on emerging countries. And, finally, we propose a contra-factual analysis of the growth performance of our sample of Latin American economies, with the growth performance they would have experienced in a hypothetical scenario of no external sector turmoil.

The following two sections present a brief review of the relevant literature on the subject. The fourth section presents our empirical model of transmission mechanisms and vulnerability, as well as our estimation results, and we conclude the chapter with some reflections on the Great Recession and its impact in Latin America.

The Transmission Mechanisms of International Financial Crises

In order to improve our understanding of the different channels through which the Great Recession was transmitted to Latin American countries, it is necessary to develop a comprehensive analysis of the external factors influencing both the real sector and the financial sector of emerging markets economies, as well as their interaction, during typical financial crises episodes. The review of the works of Calvo (1998), Calvo & Reinhart (2000), Izquierdo et al. (2008), and Blanchard et al. (2010) provides a comprehensive and detailed analysis of the influence of the most likely channels through which the Great Recession effects were transmitted to Latin America, and contributed to the conceptualization of the empirical model we implement later on in this work.

Both, Blanchard et al. (2010), and Izquierdo et al. (2008) suggest that the contraction of the volume and relative value of exports of goods and services during an international financial crisis plays a prominent role in its transmission (contagion) to other countries. Accordingly, the more open the external sector is, the greater the influence of international financial crises have on domestic economic activity. The effects on the terms of trade also determine the magnitude of the negative impact of the external demand collapse, and the consequent commodities prices drop at the beginning of the crisis.

The first one helps understand the impact of the financial crisis of 2008-2009 on emerging markets by exploring the role of the collapse in trade associated with a slowdown of the international economy, as well as the sharp decline in capital inflows "in the transmission of the crisis from the advanced economies". They center their attention on the last quarter of 2008 and the first quarter of 2009, when the annualized economic growth of a sample of seventeen advanced economies (where the EU is considered as one country) averaged -7.2% and -8.3%, and in a sample of twenty nine emerging countries, -1.9% and -3.2%, respectively. These growth rates were approximately 10% points below their 2007 values. While all the countries in their sample (advanced and emerging) had negative unexpected growth, the averages hide the fact that in as many as seven of the twenty nine emerging countries included in their sample, growth was at least 20% lower than the April 2008 forecast of the International Monetary Fund (IMF), but at the same time, in five countries (China and India included) the shortfall was less than 5%.

Blanchard et al.'s (2010) immediate goal is to answer the question of whether the different macroeconomic performance across emerging markets during the financial crisis can be satisfactorily explained. But a more ambitious goal they pursue is to better understand the role of trade and of financial channels in the transmission of shocks "in the transmission of the crisis from the advanced economies". To that end, they develop a simple open economy model, which allows for imperfect capital mobility and potentially contractionary effects of currency depreciation due to foreign debt exposure, with the aim to explain diverse types of responses across emerging markets.

The evidence they report suggests that emerging market countries were affected primarily by external shocks, mainly through a sharp decrease in their exports and, in the case of commodity producers, a sharp drop in their terms of trade, at the time that there was a sharp decrease in capital inflows, which helped compensate the trade deficits to some extent. The most significant explanatory global variable of negative changes in economic growth is the short-term external debt, suggesting the financial channel played a central role in the transmission of the crisis. Trade variables are also important.

However, they report there is little econometric evidence in support of the argument that a high volume of international reserves limited the decline in output in the crisis. As part of their efforts to explain of the differences observed across emerging countries, they argue that emerging countries were also differently exposed to the effects of the crisis in various ways: some of them had a large foreign-currency debt; some others had a large current account deficit, but they also reacted in many different ways. Most countries relied on fiscal and monetary expansionary actions, while some others relied on their international currency reserves to protect the exchange rate, and still others, instead, just let it adjust.

According to Calvo et al. (1993), the degree of financial openness will determine the importance of the negative influence of capital flows on economic growth during financial crises. The markets' response results in an increase of the sovereign spreads, and a collapse of emerging stock markets. As a consequence, investors' lost confidence generates significant capital outflows (flight to quality), reducing the country's foreign currency reserves, the exchange rate volatility attains extreme levels, and credit flows drop, creating the conditions for a consumption and investment crunch (also see: Calvo 1998; and, Calvo & Reinhart 2000).

The profound structural reforms implemented in several Latin American countries during the second half of the 1980s and the first years of the 1990s combined with the relative abundance of liquidity in the international market to augment the inflows of capital towards the region. These inflows resulted in the appreciation of the exchange rate of most regional currencies, booming stock and real estate markets, the accumulation of international reserves, a strong recovery of secondary market prices for foreign loans, and generalized economic growth (Calvo et al. 1993).

As noticed by Izquierdo et al. (2008), based on the study of Calvo et al. (1993), during the first years of the 1990s capital was flowing indiscriminately to the whole Latin American region, i.e., investors were not paying attention to the wide differences in macroeconomic policies (depth of economic reforms) and fundamental conditions of each country. However, the favorable influence of the structural reforms implemented in the late 1980s and the first years of the 1990s alone were not enough to explain the large volume and widespread distribution of foreign capital flows towards the region. Calvo et al. (1993) mention that "Capital flows to Latin America, which averaged about $8 billion a year in the second half of the 1980s, surged to $24 billion in 1990 and $40 billion in 1991."[6]. A major component of those flows was, indeed, related to macroeconomic reforms like, for example, in the case of Mexico (45% of the total), where capital inflow was associated to the important privatizations that were taking place in those two years, including airlines, mining, etc.

But reforms alone are not enough to explain why capital flowed to countries where no reforms had been undertaken and, by contrast was not flowing to countries where reforms "were introduced well before 1990". So Calvo et al. (1993) argue that there must be other not-yet-accounted-for, and common-to-the-region conditions propitiating them. They suggest that falling interest rates, slow economic activity, and increasing current account imbalances in the United States, motivated investors' interest in Latin America; there were clear opportunities they could take advantage of due to the region's renewed investment activity and its countries increasing solvency. These autonomous shocks seem validated by the evolution of the U.S. balance of payments' capital account, which recorded an increase in outflows and a reduction of inflows during 1990 and 1991, "after eight consecutive years of net inflows".

The same authors discuss that international capital flows affect emerging economies in at least four ways. First, by increasing the availability of capital in the domestic economy, they increase consumption and investment. Second, increased inflows of capital are usually associated with marked appreciation of the recipient country's real exchange rate so, the larger transfers received need to be absorbed to avoid inflationary pressures. If, for example, the capital inflows are directed towards real estate or other non-traded goods, these assets' relative prices will rise. Third, capital inflows are expected to get a response from domestic policymakers; for example, central banks interested in minimizing the effects of real exchange rate appreciation on the current account balance and on inflation, are likely to intervene in the market absorbing part of the foreign currency inflows in order to avoid their full monetization (and accompanying inflationary consequences). Those measures, however, are expected to raise domestic interest rates *vis à vis* foreign interest rates, with the consequent effects on the cost of domestic credit for both, the private and the public sectors. Fourth, capital inflows provide signals to world financial markets. They can be interpreted as reflecting increasingly attractive future investment opportunities in the receiving country.

To empirically contrast the validity of their arguments, Calvo et al. (1993) perform an econometric analysis on the role played by external factors over the accumulation of reserves and over the real exchange rate appreciation of ten Latin American countries during the period that goes from January 1988 to December 1991. Due to the lack of monthly information on international capital flows, they examine the joint behavior of international reserves and the real exchange rate, as an indirect estimate of its evolution. The analysis begins with principal components to describe the comovement among reserves data series, real exchange rate data series, and their dynamic interaction. Then, using Granger causality tests, they find that the accumulation of reserves precedes the real exchange rate appreciation, a clear indication that the initially identified external factors which influence investors' and lenders' decision to put their money in Latin America had significant consequences on the countries' exchange rates, and that they represent a clear example of external factors influence on the macroeconomy of emerging markets, in the sense of Díaz-Alejandro (1984).

Fifteen years later, Izquierdo et al. (2008) published a follow-up of Calvo et al.'s (1993) work, extending the period of the sample and analyzing the direct impact of external factors on the behavior of output performance, rather than attempting to account for the role of external factors on the behavior of capital inflows. Their econometric approach consists in the use of a Vector Error Correction Model (VECM) to model the relation between LAC7's[7] GDP and external factors, and they find that those factors account for a significant share of the observed variance in the GDP growth rate. Instead of estimating a VAR for each individual country, they estimate an index that captures output behavior of the typical Latin American country.

In addition to the external variables already discussed by Calvo et al. (1993), they extend the menu of explanatory variables in their econometric estimation. In first instance, they include the significant development of a large international emerging bond market since the early 1990s; in particular, they study the emerging market bond spreads or EMBI[8] spreads, which allow them to directly observe variations in the market price of risky assets, a relevant improvement with respect to the time when most external lending to Latin American countries took the form of commercial banks loans. They also include proxies for changes in external demand, terms of trade and international financial conditions (the average industrial production in the G-7 countries, an index of regional terms of trade, and the return on 10-year T-Bonds).

Another relevant contribution of Izquierdo et al.'s (2008) study is the confirmation that the terms of trade, which were reported not to play a major role in Latin America in the early 1990s (Calvo et al. 1993), first recorded a dramatic collapse as a consequence of the 1997 South East Asia financial crisis, and then surged after 2002, and continued their upward movement until the third quarter of 2006, providing the authors with a strong argument to include them "in their menu of external factors".

Izquierdo et al.'s (2008) results confirm that "external factors play a key role in explaining business fluctuations in Latin America, and that changes in the external environment can lead to large changes in economic performance". So they conclude that accounting for external factors is definitely important when the growth performance of Latin America is estimated. Their empirical model lets them develop a counterfactual exercise that highlights by how much the regional output dynamic could have been different from the observed outcome, in a similar vein to the analysis that we present in this work's empirical section.

Macroeconomic Vulnerability

Different authors have explored the dimensions of economic vulnerability to external shocks. The Great Recession and the 2008-2009 financial crisis were a privileged setting to evaluate which domestic economies characteristics can be said to increase vulnerability under external distress conditions. There are several examples of studies on vulnerability, some more sophisticated than others, coincident in general terms in recognizing that the trade and financial shocks play a major role in the macroeconomic performance of emerging countries, but differing in their methodological approach (e.g., Berkmen et al., 2009; or Lane and Milesi-Ferretti, 2010). In this section we will review in greater detail three of the most carefully crafted and representative studies in the recent literature, those of Blanchard et al. (2010), Llaunes et al. (2010) and Ihareta (2010).

Blanchard et al. (2010) develop a standard short-run static model that allows for imperfect capital mobility and potentially contractionary effects of a depreciation related to foreign currency debt exposure. They explore the nature of the relationship between financial variables, trade and economic growth, and estimate the magnitude and significance of their econometric adjustment. Although their analysis adopts an *ex-post* approach centered in a limited period that goes from Q4-2008 to Q1-2009 (one semester), it supplies valuable insights regarding what macroeconomic characteristics make an emerging country more vulnerable during a period of financial crisis.

The model's interpretation suggests how adverse financial and trade shocks are likely to decrease output; however, the role of policy response and the efficacy of its implementation, as well as its expected linkage to such variables as the initial foreign currency reserves of a country, and the fiscal flexibility with which it counts, renders the model significantly complex. Also, there are interactions between the initial conditions and the effects of the shocks on output; e.g., preexisting large foreign debt is likely to amplify the effects of the shocks. To empirically test the model, the authors propose a benchmark specification that allows them to analyze the performance heterogeneity of countries. That benchmark specification is "unexpected growth" defined as the "forecast error for output growth during the semester composed of 2008Q4 and 2009 Q1".

They first contrast unexpected growth with two trade variables, the export share of GDP (in percent) in 2007, and the "unexpected partner growth", defined as "the export-weighted average of actual growth in the country's trading partners, minus the corresponding forecast, scaled by the export share in GDP", and find that the fit with export share is relatively poor, but that with unexpected partner growth is definitely stronger. Next, they contrast unexpected growth with two financial variables, i.e., the ratio of short-term foreign debt to GDP, and the ratio of the current account deficit to GDP. Their working hypothesis with respect to this variable is that the larger the short-term debt to GDP ratio, and/or the initial current account deficit, the larger the likely adverse effects of a financial shock on economic growth. In this case, they find the relationship between unexpected growth and the initial current account deficit is much weaker than that for short-term debt. In the case of the latter, a cross-country regression yields an R^2 of 0.41, implying that an increase of 10% in the initial short-term debt to GDP ratio decreases unexpected growth by 3.3%.

As previously indicated, another variable of interest to measure macroeconomic vulnerability in Blanchard et al. (2010) is the balance of foreign currency reserves before the crisis, because reserves can play a useful role in limiting the effects of trade and financial shocks on output (and the exchange rate). They measure the role of reserves in their model as the ratio of reserves to short-term debt, and find that it is statistically and economically significant, when unexpected trade partner growth is controlled for. The coefficient indicates that a 50% increase in the ratio increases unexpected growth by 1.3%. However, to determine whether this effect comes from the denominator, or the numerator, or both, they run a regression where the log of the ratio of short-term to GDP and the log of the ratio of reserves to GDP are used separately, and find that the coefficient of the former variable is large and significant, while that on reserves "is incorrectly signed and insignificant". Interestingly enough, the authors mention that a possible explanation may be that "even when reserves were high, countries were reluctant to use them, for fear of using them too early, or that the use of reserves would be perceived as a signal of weakness, or that financial markets would consider the lower reserve levels inadequate".

Regarding whether countries with fixed exchange rates did better or worse in the crisis, Blanchard et al. (2010) model's results are ambiguous. They find that the outcome depends on such factors as the strength of the balance sheet effects of exchange rate depreciation (or devaluation), and the policies followed by governments to maintain the peg. They classify countries in two groups according to whether they had a fixed or a more flexible exchange rate regime in 2008, and found that countries with fixed exchange rates saw unexpected declines in real output by an average of 18.6% during the crisis semester, and those that had more flexible regimes only 11.3%. While this result apparently indicates that fixed rates are the potential source of an aggravated negative impact from crises, when running the regression in which the exchange rate regime is included as a regressor (in the form of a dummy variable), its coefficient is negative and insignificant.

The approach of Blanchard et al. (2010) is novel and reveals different dimensions of the vulnerability of emerging economies to the impact of international financial crises. Even while the model they use is much simplified, it showcases the great complexity of the subject. The short period of their analysis, which significantly limits the number of observations for model estimation imposes an additional constraint because, beyond the analysis of the macroeconomic variables deemed most relevant to explain the performance of the sample countries' GDP growth, it would be desirable to include some interactions between the variables, something that is not feasible with such a small sample. However, the main conclusions remain: a measure of vulnerability that is clearly the most significant in Blanchard et al.'s (2010) study, both from a statistical and economic perspectives, is short-term foreign debt. Trade, measured in terms of the trade-weighted growth in partner countries, also results economically significant in all the model's versions. However, its statistical significance is not always granted.

Next, we briefly discuss the work by Llaudes et al. (2010), who also study the most intense period of the 2008-2009 financial crisis and report that between Q3 of 2008 and Q1 of 2009 the global economy fell by 6% from its pre-crisis peak, and that real output in EMs fell by about 4%. However, they emphasize, these aggregate measures conceal considerable heterogeneity among individual EMs, and describe that those countries "in the worst affected quartile" -mainly located in emerging Europe- showed a negative real GDP growth of 11%, while those in the "least affected quartile" recorded a positive 1% GDP growth[9]. The authors explore the channels and factors that may explain the initial impact of the crisis differences using a sample of 50 emerging market economies, and measuring the impact of the crisis from different perspectives: actual decline of GDP, the stock market performance, the change in sovereign bonds spreads (a measure of perceived political risk in the international markets), and the slow-down of domestic credit.

The research approach makes use of a "unique measure of vulnerabilities" developed by IMF staff which, the authors claim, "allows a consistent comparison of vulnerabilities across EMs"[10]. Also, given that for most EMs in the sample this was an "externally driven" episode, the study centers on the external sector vulnerabilities of the sample countries, including: "current account deficits, reserve holdings, and external debt levels".

The general conclusions reported by Llaudes et al. (2010) are that: a) countries that before the crisis were more open to trade and financial transactions experienced a greater impact during the crisis; and b) that countries that had consistently worked to maintain macroeconomic equilibriums and reduce the external sector vulnerabilities, saw their efforts compensated with greater stability. Another interesting finding reported by these authors is the fact that countries holding larger (in relative terms) international currency reserves buffered the impact of the crisis. However, the reserves buffer effect had "diminishing returns", i.e., "at very high levels of reserves there is little discernable evidence of their moderating impact on output collapse". These authors findings about the buffer effect of international currency reserves contrasts with the contradictory results on the sign and significance of the estimated coefficient for the same variable reported by Blanchard et al. (2010). The differing results among the two works may be due to their different periods of analysis, i.e., in the Blanchard et al. (2010) analysis, the period runs from Q3 2008 to Q1 2009, while in Llaudes et al. (2010), the analysis includes one more quarter (Q3 2008).

One of the most interesting features of the Llaudes et al. (2010) study has to do with the emphasis it gives to the role of pre-crisis vulnerabilities in determining the magnitude of the Great Recession effects on EMs' economies. According to reported evidence based on the previously mentioned vulnerability index, EMs that had improved their fundamentals during the years preceding the crisis, entered that episode with less vulnerability and were, logically, less affected. This finding, according to the authors, highlights "the need for EMs...to protect themselves against future shocks".

To shed light on the variables and country characteristics that influenced the economic performance of their sample of EMs during the crisis, Llaudes et al. (2010) use regression analysis. They consider that, in most cases, for the EMs in the sample the 2008-2009 financial crisis was an "externally driven crisis", so they use the indicator-based external vulnerability index that is part of the internal semi-annual vulnerability exercise for emerging market economies (VEE) periodically estimated by the IMF staff.

The impact of the crisis on the real sector of the economy is measured as the percentage change seasonally adjusted quarterly GDP from peak to trough during the crisis; while the impact on the financial sector is measured as: a) the change in the monthly stock market index during the crisis; b) the collapse in real private sector credit growth from peak to trough, as well as the difference between pre and post crisis average monthly credit flows as a percentage of GDP; and, c) the rise in the average monthly EMBI sovereign spread, from trough to peak.

The basic specification used by the Llaudes et al.'s (2010) study expresses the real output contraction as a function of: a) pre-crisis vulnerabilities; b) trade connectedness with the rest of the world; and, c) international financial integration. The empirical evidence indicates that the least vulnerable EMs, on average, contracted 6% points less than the most vulnerable EMs. Also, the three previously mentioned factors that determine external vulnerability also resulted individually significant.

In some instances, EMs, with high current account deficits, thus more exposed to external factors, experienced sharper declines in domestic demand, which in turn resulted in a declining output. In other cases, countries with pre-crisis domestic demand booms fueled by external capital inflows, became vulnerable when the flows stopped in the middle of the crisis.

Trade linkages were another important determinant of output collapse. The statistical evidence reported by these authors indicates that EMs experienced an additional 1.5% reduction in real output for every 1% reduction in domestic demand. Also, pre-crisis reserve holdings were associated with positive but diminishing returns with respect to output collapse, and higher reserves had a positive return at low levels of reserve coverage but diminishing returns at high levels of coverage. Llaudes et al.'s (2010) econometric results show that, in line with Blanchard et al. (2010), reserves have no statistically significant effect at high levels, but become significant and "the magnitude of its impact increases" at low levels.

Regarding sovereign spreads, the country considered most vulnerable to external factors in Spring 2007 "experienced a greater widening in spreads than the country considered least vulnerable (by around 220 basis points)". In addition, countries with larger reserves experienced a smaller widening in spreads during the crisis period.

Two other factors that had an impact on sovereign spreads were: a) the accumulated inflation in the previous years; and, b) having an inflation-targeting regime. Lastly, and very much unexpected, "pre-crisis fiscal vulnerabilities do not show a significant impact on spreads". According to Llaunes et al. (2010), such evidence may reflect the forward looking nature of spreads that take into account the expected costs of the crisis on public finances, not the past fiscal balance situation.

Our brief review of the "vulnerability" literature ends with the work of Iraheta (2010), who proposes a methodology for the estimation of macroeconomic vulnerability indicators based on the normalized standard deviations with respect to their long-term trend. The indicators are used to compare the macroeconomic vulnerability of the sub region of Central America and the Dominican Republic (CADR) with the seven major economies of Latin America and the Caribbean (LAC7), prior to the international financial crisis. He also presents an assessment of the CADR, according to its macroeconomic conditions during the crisis, in order to identify the main weaknesses and macroeconomic challenges. In particular, he finds that during the crisis: (i) the fiscal imbalances were exacerbated due to the countercyclical stance adopted by all the governments of CADR in the face of the crisis, and ii) there was a need to improve the conditions of financing of the activities of the private non-financial corporations to recover the path of economic growth weakened by the crisis.

The macroeconomic vulnerability indicators used by Iraheta (2010) are based on the "Macroprudential Indicators of Stability of the Financial System" of Evans, et al. (2000), and a more recent document of Galician, et al. (2010), where they assess the financial crisis in Latin America from a set of " Market Sentiment Indicators and Vulnerability". Iraheta's (2010) definition of indicators of macroeconomic vulnerability is constrained by the availability of comparable statistical information for the LAC7 and CADR, but basically refer to:

1. **External Sector:** a1. Current Account; a2. Foreign Direct Investment; a3 International Investment Position; a4 Exchange Rate.
2. **Fiscal Sector:** b1. Net Domestic Assets of the General Government; b2. Net foreign assets of the General Government.
3. **Monetary Sector:** c1. Net foreign assets of the depository institutions; c2. Monetary supply; c3. Total domestic credit; c4. Total deposits.
4. **Real Sector:** d1. Production; d2. Rate of inflation; d3. Interest rates; d4. Exports.

The calculation of the regional macroeconomic vulnerability indicators is based on the association between vulnerability and volatility (Gallego, et al. 2010). The volatility is usually measured on the basis of their dispersion using standard deviations. To avoid possible bias in series with a trend, the dispersion of the series with respect to their trend is proposed as a measure of volatility. The interpretation of this measure is that a variable that shows high volatility represents a greater level of vulnerability than one that has lower volatility.

Iraheta's (2010) approach is more appropriate for an *ex post* assessment, and not to as a warning system of possible future crises events. However, its main contribution consists in developing a comprehensive conceptual model of the factors and variables that are deemed to influence the depth and breath of an international crisis contagion effects in a group of emerging economies.

The methodology is conducive to estimate what group of countries was better prepared to face the adverse effects of the global financial crisis in 2008. The analysis while the region CADR shares with the rest of Latin America a series of characteristics due to its common economic history, there are notable differences, most of them, highlighting an increased vulnerability in detriment of the CADR economies.

These remarkable works illustrate the relevance of performing an analysis of the factors that had greater influence in the transmission of the effects of the Great Recession to Latin America. The study of that experience serves the purpose of identifying and highlighting where the national structural weaknesses lie, as well as to propose a reflection on the response of governments and to evaluate the vulnerabilities of the region. In the following section we present our analysis of the Great Recession impact on Argentina, Brazil, Chile, Colombia, Mexico and Peru. We firmly believe that by learning from the past we can improve the odds of the region in the future.

Empirical Analysis of the Mechanisms of Transmission of the Great Recession Into Latin American Countries, and Their Macroeconomic Vulnerability

This section reports our econometric results on different models designed to represent the mechanisms of transmission of the Great Recession into the Argentina, Brazil, Chile, Colombia, Mexico and Peru. Our objective is to identify the main drivers of the recession and to estimate their impact on our sample countries' economies.

Calvo (1996), Calvo, Izquierdo & Mejía (1998) and Calvo & Reinhart (2000) stressed the importance of sudden stops of external capital inflows, leading to a consumption and investment abrupt crunch, and Reinhart and Rogoff (2008, 2009) extensively documented an inverse relationship between the current account deficit as a percentage of Gross Domestic Product (GDP), and the rate of growth of the economy that is consistent with the idea that external flows are a mechanism of transmission of financial crises. But more recent cross-section studies have advanced the idea that the impact of the Great Recession on representative emerging countries' economies was more significant for those countries with deficient fundamentals. For example, Salman, Chivakul & Llaudes (2010) run cross-section regressions to explain the variability in the total loss of economic activity between 2008Q3 and 2009Q1 for all emerging economies, and find that more vulnerable economies, i.e., those with lower international currency reserves in proportion to their current account deficit, short-term debt, or the basic money aggregate M2, suffered a greater loss in output. Blanchard et al. (2010) interpreted the link between current account deficit (as a percentage of GDP) and growth, as a measure of vulnerability of the economy because, in a sudden stop of external financial flows, those economies with larger current account deficits are forced to shrink their absorption of imports in a larger measure than those economies with a modest external imbalance.

In many studies long-term factors such as population growth, technological change and others are dismissed as irrelevant in the analysis of the impact and transmission mechanisms of financial crises. That approach is valid in cross-section studies that use information for only a few quarters, but in a panel estimation setting, where enough information from before and after to the event window (in this case, the recession period) is incorporated in the econometric models, long-term variables also must be included to estimate the way they affect output.

In that spirit we propose a simple *ad-hoc* model to explore the transmission of the Great Recession recession to Latin American countries in a panel data framework covering two alternative periods: 2000 to 2015 and 2003 to 2015. The two sample periods are included is with the intention to contrast the effect of the volatility period associated with the Argentinean financial crisis of 2001-2002, which was completely locally produced, over its Latin American neighbors.

To incorporate long-term factors that affect sustainable growth, we use the ratio of GDP to potential GDP as the relevant dependent variable. This choice has several advantages: first, that ratio reflects the gap of GDP to potential GDP, one of the most critical variables in the short-run macroeconomic analysis. Second, removing the "normal", long-run growth, is an easy way to incorporate the long-run fundamentals of an economy (e.g. population growth, human capital, technological change) without having to find proxies for each. And third, if the potential GDP measure captures well the long-run tendency, the only variability left to explain in the model is that originated by economic fluctuations, which are a function of the real, financial and vulnerability variables previously discussed.

The model can be represented as in equation (1), below, where y_{it} is the ratio of the actual seasonally adjusted GDP to potential GDP in country "i" during quarter "t", r_{it}, f_{it}, x_{it} are column vectors of real and financial mechanisms of transmission, as well as of vulnerability variables and, finally, ε_{it} represents the regression residuals. Equation (1) allows for fixed country effects $\left(\mu_i\right)$ and even though the model is presented as static, we introduced lags in the variables in our final estimations.

$$log\left(y_{it}\right) = \alpha + \mu_i + r_{it}'\beta + f_{it}'\gamma + x_{it}'\delta + \varepsilon_{it} \tag{1}$$

The gap of actual to potential GDP is the dependent variable in the model. There are several ways to estimate the potential GDP; some estimate a production function, or a Bayesian VAR system of the main drivers of long-run growth, but an easier to use option is to approximate potential GDP through the estimation of a secular tendency of GDP. In this work we opted for the latter alternative applying Hodrick and Prescott's filter with a lambda of 1,600 to the seasonally adjusted GDP series obtained after running the routine X-13. This method is easy to apply and provides reliable estimations of the long-run movement of the series.

Figure 2 presents the gap series for our sample of six Latin American countries and the United States during the Great Recession (2008Q2 to 2009Q2); the degree of synchronization across countries is highly significant. The peak and through of the Great Recession exactly coincides with that of the United States cycle in the cases of Argentina, Chile and Mexico, and there is just a one or two quarters discrepancy in the cases of Brazil, Colombia and Peru. For most of the Latin American sample countries, the drop in output was larger than in the case of United States, with the single exception of Colombia

The independent variables for the real mechanisms of transmission include the United States' GDP gap, built with the same methodology as the dependent variable, and the relative price of all commodities, fuel and non-fuel, as calculated by the International Monetary Fund.

Alternatively, we could use the World GDP gap, weighting each country's contribution according to its relative share in the total exports of the big-six Latin American countries, but that estimation requires a vast amount of data. Besides, a large proportion of the foreign trade of Latin American countries is made with the United States and the Great Recession originated in that country. Regarding the relative price of commodities, the first option was to use the terms of trade, but we could not assemble a sufficiently long series of exports and imports prices for all six countries in our sample.

The financial mechanisms variables should reflect the lending conditions of the emerging countries, which we identify as the interest rates and the financial inflows to the region. We opted for including the Emerging Markets Bond Index (EMBI) that is a major indicator of the spreads in emerging debt, as it measures the risk premium above the US Treasury securities returns that investors demand from each of the sample countries sovereign and corporate bonds. To measure the inflows we

Figure 2. GDP gap of the six big Latin American Countries and the United States during the Great Recession (2008-2009)

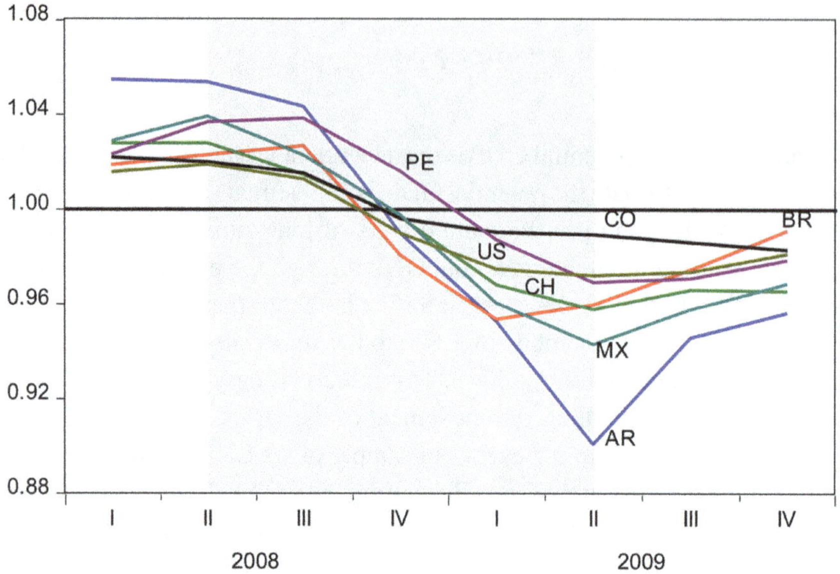

had the alternative of to use the net foreign capital inflows, as a proportion of GDP or, inversely, the current account balance to the GDP. We chose the last one because it plays a dual role, as a required financial flow and as a variable that reflect how vulnerable is the economy.

Finally, variables that measure the coverage (protection) represented by the international currency reserves of each country against some metrics were included in the vulnerability transmission mechanism vector. Specifically, we test the proportion of Reserves to short term debt plus the current account deficit, the proportion of Reserves to GDP and M2 to Reserves.

Equation (1) represents a static model with no lags but, in some estimations, some variables were lagged, in part to avoid a simultaneity bias, and because they have a forward effect on the GDP gap.

Additionally, as we remove the trend by dividing over present and potential GDP, many of the variables in the form of ratios to GDP, might be stationary. Thus testing for cointegration and making an error correction model is not an issue. In Table 1, we present some panel unit root test, and confirm most of them reject a common or country-specific unit root for the GDP gap and for the Current Account Balance ratio to GDP, although the evidence is ambiguous for the EMBI spreads. Based on this evidence, the model is run in the levels of the variables; no further differencing or detrending was deemed necessary.

Table 1. Panel Unit Roots Test for the 2000Q1 to 2015Q2 Sample Period

	GDP Gap	Latin America Current Acount (%GDP)	EMBI
Levin, Lin & Chu t*	-2.23887**	-1.58537*	3.04937
Im, Pesaran and Shin W-stat	-5.34084***	-1.75802**	1.56305
ADF - Fisher Chi-square	56.8509***	22.6875**	13.238
PP - Fisher Chi-square	47.2553***	47.7611***	59.4318***

Source: Authors' elaboration.

Table 2 presents six estimations differing in terms of the econometric method employed and the period of estimation. As mentioned before, two periods were studied: 2000Q1 to 2015Q2 and 2003Q1 to 2015Q2. The first period represents the whole sample, and the second has the advantage of removing the Argentinean financial crisis of 2001-2002, as well as the mild recession experienced in the United States between 2000 and 2003. This second period consists then of the expansion from 2003Q1 to 2008Q2, the Great Recession, and the posterior slow recovery. Columns 1 and 2 display the polled ordinary least squares assuming all fixed effects

Table 2. Different Models of the Mechanisms of Transmission of the Great Recession into Latin American countries

	Dependent Variable: GDP Gap (log)					
Variables	(1)	(2)	(3)	(4)	(5)	(6)
Constant	-0.000339	-0.004278	0.018669	0.01115	0.294862	0.103741
	(0.004645)	(0.00369)	(0.016086)	(0.014155)	(0.343548)	(0.077746)
US GDP Gap (log)	1.266855***	1.082753***	1.302466***	1.119042***	1.743362***	1.264519***
	(0.108836)	(0.079807)	(0.113968)	(0.083539)	(0.554696)	(0.143769)
Commodities Prices (log)	0.008842**	0.024511***	0.009255**	0.025337***	1.36E-02	0.030577***
	(0.003625)	(0.003495)	(0.003679)	(0.003588)	(0.010731)	(0.008008)
EMBI	-2.35E-06	1.11E-08	-3.05E-05	-1.34E-05	-0.000325	-0.000101
	(0.00000418)	(0.00000361)	(0.0000244)	(0.0000227)	(0.000371)	(0.0000777)
Current Account (% GDP)	-0.211606***	-0.093512***	-0.243658***	-0.128259***	-0.626678*	-0.226374***
	(0.03915)	(0.035393)	(0.042064)	(0.038951)	(0.322205)	(0.087264)
M2 to Reserves (ratio)	-0.000371	-0.001139*	-0.001919	-0.00391***	-0.041247	-1.92E-02
	(0.00069)	(0.000681)	(0.001424)	(0.00133)	(0.048262)	(0.012776)
Fix Effects	No	No	Yes	Yes	Yes	Yes
Instruments	No	No	No	No	Yes	Yes
Period	2000q1-2015q2	2003q1-2015q2	2000q1-2015q2	2003q1-2015q2	2000q1-2015q2	2003q1-2015q2
Observations	315	255	315	255	310	250
R2	0.433837	0.577854	0.440784	0.588993	-0.793594	0.397779
R2 adjusted	0.424676	0.569204	0.424283	0.573895	-0.847402	0.375196
F	47.35588	67.51575	26.71187	[illegible]	26.90623	37.10085

Source: Authors' estimations with data from the IMF and Bloomberg.

are $\mu_i = 0$, for the 2000Q1 to 2015Q2 and 2003Q1 and 2015Q2 samples. Columns (3) and (4) incorporate country fixed effects ($\mu_i \neq 0$), and Columns (5) and (6), the instrumental variable that takes into account the likely endogeneity of the Current Account Balance and the EMBI spreads, using their first two lags as instruments. All the estimations present the robust to heteroscedasticity and contemporaneous cross correlation of the country residuals. This is advisable because it is very likely that unobserved factors affect the entire region at the same time.

To prevent any possible contemporaneous correlation of Current Account and EMBI with the residual, we employ the first-lag of these variables in the first four estimations. As the last two sets of estimations instruments, these variables with their lags, the contemporaneous levels are the regressors. In all specifications, the vulnerability condition M2 to reserves was lagged by three periods.

In all six specifications, the signs of the coefficients are the expected ones. In the case of the real transmission mechanism our results suggest that the higher the US GDP gap or the price of commodities, the higher the GDP gap, because world demand is expanding and Latin America exports several commodities. Regarding the financial mechanism, we should expect that the lower the interest rates spreads, and the higher the amount of net inflows to the region (lower the Current Account Deficit), the higher the GDP gap. Finally, the higher the international currency reserves, and the lower the ratio of M2 to reserves, the less vulnerable the economy is, and the higher the GDP gap.

US GDP gap and the Current Account Balance are significant in all the specifications, and the absolute value of the estimated coefficients is larger for the whole sample, in comparison to the estimates obtained from the 2003Q1 to 2015Q2 subsample. The relative price of commodities is significant at least at 5% in all but one specification, EMBI is not significant in any specification, and M2 to reserves is significant in only two of the six. The goodness of the fit of the 2003Q1 to 2015Q2 estimations is higher than for the entire sample

Base on our estimations, we can calculate the output loss against a theoretical counter-factual scenario where the Great Recession never occurred (i.e., if the 2008Q2 gap had remained constant until 2009Q2). To this end we use the column's (6) results, and find a gap loss of -0.006 in 2008Q3, -0.046 in 20008Q4, -0.061 in 2009Q1 and -0.058 in 2009Q2, which are equivalent to a cumulative loss of -0.171.

However, as the GDP gap in all six countries was positive before the Great Recession (between 1.02 and 1.05), it is difficult to maintain that gap without adjusting back to the long run equilibrium even during normal years. Thus, the estimated lost output should be taken as a upper bound. Even though, the impact of the Great Recession on the big six Latin American countries looks very large, even larger than the drop in the GDP gap in USA (a cumulative loss of 0.124).

CONCLUSION

The complexity of the circumstances that conditioned such and extraordinary event as the Great Recession occurs very seldom. The extension and consequences associated are so vast that may still take many years to measure its true dimensions and, in some areas, simply never happen. This work inscribes in the literature that aims to understand and estimate the effects of the financial crisis, its associated economic recession and its follow-up across the Atlantic, over other geographical regions. Our interest centers in a sample of six Latin American countries that for the size of their economies, the availability of statistical information and relative macroeconomic stability were chosen as representative of how did the Great Recession impact Latin American emerging countries and, more specifically, their economic activity.

Our analysis contributes to complement and increase the precision of previous studies on the Great Recession impact on Latin America, and confirms the recessionary and turbulence effects were transmitted mainly through real and financial variables. However, the role of international reserves and the vulnerability of the countries remains inconclusive. Noticeably, we also find that the cumulative loss of economic growth of the average Latin American country in our sample was greater in relative terms, than the one experienced by the United States where the crises originated.

Among the limitations of our analysis include the fact that some of the variables probably need more refinement (we are thinking especially on the the vulnerability variables). For example, the statistics on short-term debt are only published once a year. Thus, the measures of coverage of reserves to current account deficit and short-term obligations could not be included in our estimations. Also, it was impossible to obtain a sufficiently long series of terms of trade, so we restricted its measurement just to the prices of internationally traded commodities prices.

Our econometric treatment of the effects of the Great Recession in Latin America could also be improved by incorporating the dynamic dimension of the process since, in more than one way, the model we present in this work is closer to a static view. One possibility is to test panel cointegration of GDP (not the gap), and use the Fully Modify Ordinary Least Squares (FMOLS) or the Dynamic Ordinary Least Squares (DOLS) techniques for the estimation. In addition, allowing for heterogeneity of the coefficients would be an interesting extension that can be performed under different econometric methods (e.g., FOMS, DOLS and the polled mean group autoregressive distributed lags, or PMGADL) that we plan to develop in the near future to refine the soundness and external validity of our findings. We present our current results with the hope that our readers will be understanding, and give us the benefit of considering it a first attempt of an exploratory nature that with some more work will in the future make additional contributions to the literature on the Great Recession and its effects on Latin America.

REFERENCES

Berkmen, P., Gelos, G., Rennhack, R., & Walsh, J. (2009). *The Global Financial Crisis: Explaining Cross-Country Differences in the Output Impact*. IMF Working Paper No.09/280. Washington, DC: International Monetary Fund.

Blanchard, O., Faruquee, H., & Das, M. (2010). *The Initial Impact of the Crisis on Emerging Market Countries. Brooking Papers on Economic Activity*. Washington, DC: Brookings Institution.

Calvo, G. (1998). Capital Flows and Capital Market-Crisis: The Simple Economics of Sudden Capital Stops. *Journal of Applied Econometrics, 1*(1), 35–54.

Calvo, G., & Reinhart, C. (2000). When Capital Inflows come to a Sudden Stop: Consequences and Policy Options. In P. Keenen & A. Swoboda (Eds.), *Key Issues in Reform of the International Monetary and Financial System*. Washington, DC: International Monetary Fund.

Calvo, G. A., Izquierdo, A., & Mejía, L. F. (2008). *Systemic sudden stops: the relevance of balance-sheet effects and financial integration (No. w14026)*. National Bureau of Economic Research. doi:10.3386/w14026

Diaz-Alejandro, C. F. (1984). *Good-bye Financial Repression, Hello Financial Crash*. Kellog Institute Working Papers Series No. 24.

Iraheta, B. J. M. (2010). Vulnerabilidad Macroeconómica en Centroamérica y República Dominicana ante la Crisis Financiera: Un Análisis Comparado con LAC7 (Documento de Trabajo No. 01–2010). San José, Costa Rica: Academic Press.

Izquierdo, A., Romero, R., & Talvi, E. (2008). *Booms and Busts in Latin America: The Role of External Factors*. Inter-American Development Bank: Centro de Estudio de Realidad Económica y Social.

Lane, P. R., & Milesi-Ferretti, G. M. (2010). *The Cross-Country Incidence of the Global Crisis*. IMF Working Paper No.10/171. Washington, DC: International Monetary Fund.

Lipsky, J. (2011). *Latin America in an Uneven Global Recovery: Managing Abundance*. Speech of the First Deputy Managing Director, III Forum économique International Amérique Latine et Caraïbes, International Monetary Fund, Paris, France.

Llaudes, R., Salman, F., Chivakul, M., & Dadayan, L. (2010). *The impact of the great recession on emerging markets* (IMF Working Paper No. 237). IMF Working Papers. Retrieved from http://www.rockinst.org/pdf/government_finance/2012-07-16-Recession_Local_ Property_Tax.pdf

Paulson, H. (2011). *On the Brink: Inside the Race to Stop the Collapse of the Global Financial System*. New York: Grand Central Publishing.

Reinhart, C. M., & Rogoff, K. (2009). *This time is different. In Eight Centuries of Financial Folly*. Princeton, NJ: Princeton University.

Rogoff, K., & Reinhart, C. (2008). Is the 2007 US sub-prime financial crisis so different? An international historical comparison. *The American Economic Review*, *98*(2), 339–344. doi:10.1257/aer.98.2.339

Salman, M. F., Chivakul, M., & Llaudes, M. R. (2010). The Impact of the Great Recession on Emerging Markets (No. 10-237). International Monetary Fund.

Santillán-Salgado, R. J., Fonseca-Ramírez, A., & Ortiz-Arango, F. (2015). La Crisis de la Deuda Soberana en la Eurozona (2009-2012). In La Gran Recesión (2007-2012): Lecciones y Oportunidades para México. EGADE-IMEF.

ENDNOTES

1 One of the literary narratives of the 2007-2009 Financial Crisis is the book authored by Henry Paulson, Secretary of the United States Treasury Department during that period. The book, was named "On the Brink: Inside the Race to Stop the Collapse of the Global Financial System". In his memories of the most turbulent months of the financial crisis, where he vividly recalls how close to a "meltdown" the United States' (and the world's) financial system was when Lehman Brothers declared bankruptcy, in September of 2008, the author makes honor to his chosen title.

2 For example, the decade of the 1980s is known in Latin America as a "lost decade" due to the depressed conditions that resulted from the External Debt Crisis that was detonated in 1982 by Mexico's default on its sovereign debt when its currency international reserves were exhausted after the price of oil slid down after it had reached a historically maximum quotation during the Summer months of 1981.

3 The Economic Commission for Latin America and the Caribbean (ECLAC), is a think tank focused on economic and social phenomena in the region, and sponsored by the United Nations.

4 Approximately 80% of Mexico's annual exports are made to the United States, so a desacceleration of that country's economy represents a drastic demand shock for the most dynamic sectors of the former country.

5 Venezuela's economy is large enough as to fit in this group, but the isolationist policy followed by its government has determined a very special macroeconomic evolution and, in particular, a very important contraction of its GDP, only explainable by domestic economic policies, thus introducing distortions that instead of adding clarity to the models, they produce confusing signals. For that reason, Venezuela was not included in this study.

6 Even some countries that had not engaged in structural reforms of their economy, received significant foreign capital inflows, including countries in Asia and the Middle East (Calvo et al. 1993).

7 LAC7 stands for the seven largest Latin American economies: Argentina, Brazil, Chile, Colombia, Mexico, Peru and Venezuela.

8 EMBI stands for "Emerging Markets Bond Index"; individual Latin American countries' EMBIs are compiled by JP Morgan.

9 The differences in reported economic growth between Llaudes et al (2010) and Blanchard et al. (2010) are due to a different sample of EMs and a different period of analysis. However, both studies are consistent when they identify the Q4 of 2008 and the Q1 of 2009 as the most profound period of the crisis.

10 A detailed description of the assessment of underlying vulnerabilities in Emerging Market countries methodology used by the IMF staff is presented in detail as Box 1, in Llaudes et al. (2010).

Chapter 3
Analysis on the European Union and the Concept of Welfare in the Context of the Economic Crisis the Cases of Spain, Portugal, Greece, and Italy

Luis Rodrigo Rodrigo Asturias Schaub
Universidad Rafael Landivar, Guatemala

ABSTRACT

The economic crisis of 2007 is still a matter of preoccupation for the countries around the World. The effect of the economic crisis is still in the agendas of many regions, including Europe. The present paper analyzes the effect of the economic crisis on one of the most important values of the European Union: wellbeing. The analysis leads us to the response of two main questions that elaborated the document: What is the current situation in Europe? What is the effect of the current situation in the wellbeing of Greece, Portugal, Spain, and Italy? The countries were chosen because of the similar situation they have concerning debt, inflation, unemployment and the search for immediate solutions. The empirical analysis based an inductive process and correlation and graphical analysis exemplify the situation of wellbeing in Europe.

DOI: 10.4018/978-1-5225-4981-9.ch003

INTRODUCTION

Europe is immersed in a debacle about its development and economic crisis. During the last ten years, the European system was based on the well-being policy that is reflected in the quality of life of its inhabitants and in its high indices of human development.

It is based on this was created a social treaty susceptible to maintain stability before an imminent union. The European Union (EU) raised this goal in the Maastricht Treaty, in which it established the main values and the recipe for them to be pre-eminent.

They set out to avoid a superpower, collaborate in security, maintain values and sustain the welfare offered over the years.

In 2007 the first challenge for the EU was presented, through the economic crisis that began in the United States as a financial crisis. This crisis, with more severe dimensions than in the thirties or the nineties, dismayed much of the world as it expanded through electronic banking and into the globalized market.

The case of Greece began to be news in the world media, when faced with a debt greater than 100% of its Gross Domestic Product (GDP). The EU resolution was to bail it out three times through loans, while the Greek people were struggling with political issues, lack of income, high unemployment and few ways to pay their debt in the long run. The case of Greece has not yet seen the solution and gives signs of difficulty in its recovery.

Spain becomes more evident in the stock market of Madrid, with the continuous falls that at the end of 2008 began to create concern. Unemployment began to grow and has remained within the highest ranks worldwide. The country has not recovered, has seen a significant drop in services offered and gives rise to massive movements that show discontent.

Italy and Portugal have similar problems. The Italian case has high debt rates, low inflation and low GDP growth, while Portugal exhibits the same picture, only with greater weaknesses.

It is common to analyze economic effects without noticing the social consequences. An analysis based on the Maastricht treaties is then drawn up to consider welfare in the most committed countries in Europe.

The Maastricht Treaty and the Welfare Concept

In its third article, this Treaty of the EU states the objective of "promoting peace, its values and the well-being of its peoples" (Royal Institute El Cano). By the subject that is treated is prudent to ignore the concepts of peace and values to focus on a concept of economic essence, that is the welfare.

Welfare is a broad word that the Royal Spanish Academy defines as "a set of things necessary to live well" or "Loose life supplied with all that leads well or spend well with tranquility." The official definition in the Castilian language does not include in itself, the concept of well-being so it should be categorized into more specific social welfare and economic welfare.

Economic well-being, according to the neoclassical welfare theory, assumed that at higher levels of income, greater well-being was obtained because the person could consume more and thus satisfy their needs (Fuentes and Rojas, 2001). Carl Menger (1997) stated in his book Principles of Political Economy that welfare is directly linked to the needs of man.

The measure of economic welfare is usually referred to GDP growth and the division of GDP between population, which would give us the GDP per head. Nordhaus and Tobin (1972) criticize this measure as it does not exemplify the nature of economic well-being and distorts the different welfare policies. In spite of this, the United Nations Development Program (UNDP, 2004) uses the GDP per capita in the Human Development Index to determine the well-being of a country, based on neoclassical economic theory. The reason for continuing with this measure is the transition from the term of economic welfare to social welfare that limits the purely economic approach.

Social welfare in economic terms is based on the idea of Keyes (1998) that integrated a psychosocial approach focused on social integration, social acceptance, social contribution, social updating and social coherence (Blanco and Diaz, 2005). Although Keyes mentioned a social welfare that is more focused on the psychological dimension, the economy has directed it towards referents Such as human development and poverty, in order to capture the essence of economic / social development.

The theory of human development focuses more specifically on social and political development as "the increase of the options that human beings can choose." The importance lies in the opportunities and in the conditions of being; Opportunities focus on nutrition and security while conditions are distributed in freedom, respect, instruction and values (UNDP, 2004). Their link with welfare would then fall into the quest to eradicate or erode the following elements: poverty, inequality, insecurity, malnutrition and disrespect.

The social and economic benefit in the Maastricht Treaty begins by establishing who can form the integration or who can accede to it. The criteria developed in the Treaty serve the purpose of maintaining a stable and sustainable economy based on basic principles: the rate of inflation can not exceed 1.5% of the three best performing Member States; The public deficit can not exceed 3% compared to GDP; Public debt should be less than 60% of GDP; A long-term interest rate of not more than 2% of the three Member States which show better results in price stability and a stable exchange rate (at Elcano Royal Institute).

Economic theory explains the impact that inflation can have on the economy, depending on whether it is anticipated or not anticipated (Fisher, 1986). In the case of anticipated inflation can be foreseen and decisions can be made with greater anticipation, while in the case of the unanticipated, it is difficult to conceptualize the costs and requires an intelligent work of the central bank. Riascos (1997) measured the impact of unanticipated inflation in Colombia in the years 1996-1997, concluding that in the long term annual consumption would decrease by 1.5%. The above example demonstrates the effect of inflation on consumption, since a rise in prices to a stable wage over time would mean consuming less at the same wage. If consumption is based on needs then the person would be being affected in their well-being. The Maastricht Treaty provided for the situation in its first paragraph.

The second and third paragraphs deal with the issue of debt. Public debt influences a country's poverty levels as it promotes a change in the country's budget planning and hence changes in economic and social policies. The payment will lead to a rise in taxes, whether direct or indirect or to companies as well as to individuals, the ultimate consequence being an effect on wages or profits and prices in general (World Bank, 2008). Existed by the International Monetary Fund and the World Bank, debt relief programs in low-income countries.

The foregoing explains the purpose of the EU to maintain the welfare and economic development of its members. The meaning of a treaty such as Maastricht is its economic character, it shows the importance of trade between nations and the development that this could represent the economy.

The Economic Crisis in Europe

The Maastricht Treaty strengthens the development of countries and reflects the well-being it generates. The current economic crisis begins in 2007 for Europe, with dimensions greater than the consequences of the Asian crisis of 1990 or the Great Depression of the thirties. GDP per capita during the crisis years fell sharply between 2007 and 2009. The region most affected by the economic crisis was Eastern Europe, according to Table 1, which clearly reflects the fall in the indicator during the crisis.

Table 1. Growth per capita GDP at PPP prices

GDP Growth per Capita at International PPP Prices	2007	2008	2009	2010	2011
Eastern Europe	10.90%	7.15%	-5.41%	4.81%	5.45%
Europe (General)	6.74%	3.28%	-4.05%	3.09%	3.31%
Western Europe	5.22%	1.81%	-3.74%	2.27%	2.44%

Source: Author's elaboration with IMF information

Apart from the fall in production per capita, which would mean a fall in the income of people, during the crisis a growth of the countries' external debt was observed. The causes of the increase were due to the use of countercyclical policies based on the Keynesian concept. The results of a countercyclical policy would facilitate the reduction of the interest rate, encourage the consumption of durable goods acquired through debt, reduce the financial costs of the companies, motivate new investments and reduce the debts of the citizen to offer a space for consumption (Muñoz, 2009).

The problem of Keynesian strategy is debt growth. It is advisable for a country not to encounter critical levels of indebtedness before the crisis so that this is almost impossible to overcome. Table 2 shows the growth of gross debt in the different regions of Europe from 2006 to 2011, showing that in Eastern Europe the gross debt was higher than allowed by Maastricht and that the average of Europe was approaching the critical point.

The increase in gross spending is evidence of the Eastern European decision on Keynesian bases to prevent a stronger fall than Table 1. The problem of debt growth obviously has to do with the ability to pay countries. The comparison between the income and expenditure of the countries of the European Union shows that there is an income deficit, which duplicates the provisions of the Maastricht agreements.

The current EU problem is therefore low per capita growth, a high level of gross debt and an income deficit that doubles the limits set by the Maastricht Treaty.

The lessons could be summarized in the spaces of: 1) The financial system; 2) Aggregate demand avoiding deflation; 3) International trade; 4) International finance and 5) The international character avoiding nationalism. The solutions proposed

Figure 1. Gross European debt (%GDP)

Source: Author's elaboration with IMF information. The red line identifies the maximum debt allowed by the Maastricht Treaty

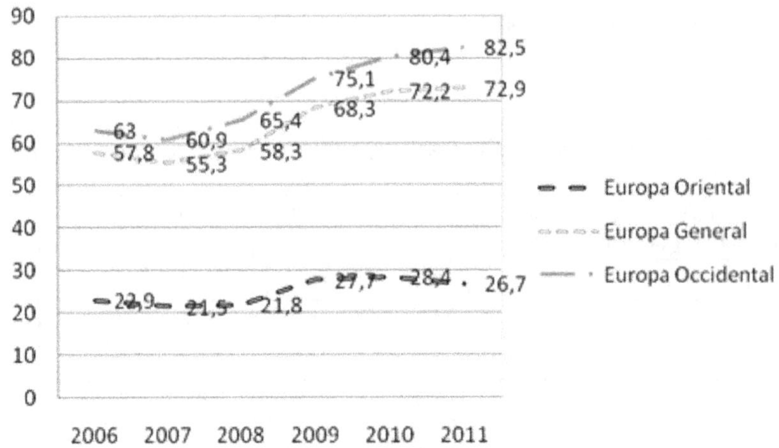

above were useful in the face of economic crises, especially during the 1990s, and continue the effects of globalization on international markets.

The problem of the EU with debt is general, but there are four countries with a critical situation, which affects their welfare. These are Portugal, Spain, Italy and Greece (PIGS).

Their economic situation serves as an example for the analysis of the effects of economic crises on human development and thus welfare.

Greece, Italy, Portugal, and Spain: Their Welfare Situation

Economic growth in Greece, Italy, Portugal and Spain was quite favorable during 2007, before the crisis. The years 2008-2011 marked a difference in the trend of their economies: GDP per capita declined significantly and only two countries show positive growth for 2011. Table 2 identifies their trend based on GDP growth over the years 2007-2011.

Per capita growth rates the ability of citizens in the countries cited to afford the goods and services they need. This includes spending on public systems such as education, health, welfare, safety and environmental protection. Based on the above definition, it can be concluded that the citizens of these countries find it difficult to afford their way of life.

A second point of analysis is the issue of debt, since inflation has remained relatively stable during the period under review. Table 3 summarizes the effect on these countries of the public debt for the year 2010 and the private debt for the year 2008.

The public debt as mentioned above compromises the nation's spending and priorities, a similar issue in the situation Of families and businesses. This table shows the financial situation of the country and the families that make up the risk analysis, exemplifying why these countries have a high risk for investment and the attraction of capital (Iranzo, 2008).

Table 2. GDP growth based on PPP per capita (International current prices)

GDP Growth Based on PPP per Capita (International Current Prices)	2007	2008	2009	2010	2011
Greece	7.11%	3.00%	-1.36%	-3.84%	-2.07%
Italy	3.80%	0.01%	-5.03%	1.76%	1.69%
Portugal	5.11%	2.03%	-1.67%	2.27%	-0.62%
Spain	4.90%	1.23%	-4.00%	0.39%	1.65%

Source: Author's elaboration with IMF information (2011)

Table 3. Comparison of public debt and private debt

Debt as% of GDP	Greece	Italy	Portugal	Spain
General Gross Public Debt (year 2011)	172.09%	116.5%	111.39%	69.46%
Private Debt (Families and companies year 2008)	103%	107%	198%	201%
Growth of private debt (year 2008)	40%	27%	44%	87%

Source: Elaboration of the author with information from the IMF, the Bank of Spain, World Fact Book and Alliance Bernstein

The above data show that in the growth and in the public debt the principles of the Maastricht Treaty can no longer be sustained for these countries, due to the excess of existing debt. It was previously identified that the Maastricht index on being violated would have an effect on the welfare of the Eurozone countries.

The likely consequence of a high rate of indebtedness in a company is bankruptcy. The debt of a company is identified when it can no longer achieve its operation, nor cover its labor, commercial, provisional or financial obligations. The effect of the fall in GDP growth, which implies a decline in consumption, investment and trade, leads to the breakdown of companies. Table 4 clearly shows the dynamics of employment and the crisis, as well as the correlation between unemployment and GDP growth.

The correlation in Greece and Spain shows that, given real GDP growth, unemployment will be reduced, clearly showing the behavior of an economy that, when growing, offers an improvement in consumption, investment, government spending and the trade balance. The case of Portugal is similar but with less force, while the case of Italy seems to show an independent relationship between GDP and unemployment.

Regarding the growth of the Human Development Index (HDI), the indicators of schooling and life expectancy are analyzed. In the case of life expectancy over

Table 4. Unemployment and Correlation Real GDP-Unemployment

Unemployment (in %)	2007	2008	2009	2010	2011	Correlation Real GDP-Unemployment
Greece	8.3	7.7	9.4	12.5	14.8	-0.751447685
Italy	6.2	6.8	7.8	8.5	8.6	0.009810044
Portugal	8.1	7.7	9.6	11	11.9	-0.348555067
Spain	8.3	11.3	18	20.1	19.4	-0.649653242

Source: Author's elaboration with IMF information.

the last five years, Greece, Italy and Spain show a significant decline, even more so when compared with 1995-2000 data. Chart 3 shows the behavior over the last 15 years in life expectancy. Despite the minimal change in the indicators, it is observed that the downward trend is clear, especially during the years 2005-2010.

The situation is similar when analyzing the average years of schooling. Greece during the period 1995-2000, showed a growth in the years of schooling of 14% and at present, during the period 2005-2010, shows a growth of 7%, a notable decline in the rate of growth in education.

The case of Portugal and Italy is similar, since Portugal decreases its growth from 11% to 2% in the period 2005-2011. The case of Italy is atypical since it has always been with negative growth of -2% during the periods 1995-2005. But during the last five years its growth has been of -11%. Figure 4 shows the change that exists in the educational theme of these countries.

The consequences can be observed in the Human Development Indicator, which presents the same trends as the previous indicators. The most worrying case is Italy, which is in negative growth. The one of Greece presents a decrease of 5% and the case of Portugal 3%. Within the group, the only country that is stable in terms of human development is Spain. Figure 5 clearly outlines what has been previously exemplified about the behavior of human development in those countries.

Figure 2. Percent change in life expectancy
Source: Elaboration of the author with information of the United Nations.

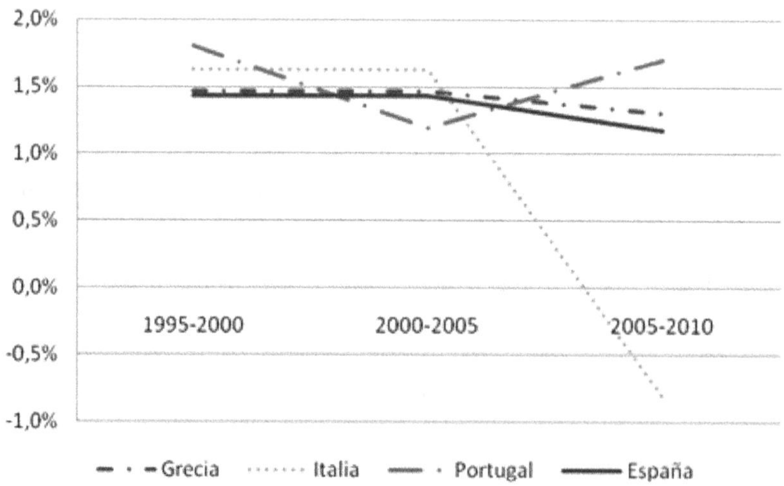

Figure 3. Percent change in life expectancy
Source: Elaboration by the author with information from the United Nations

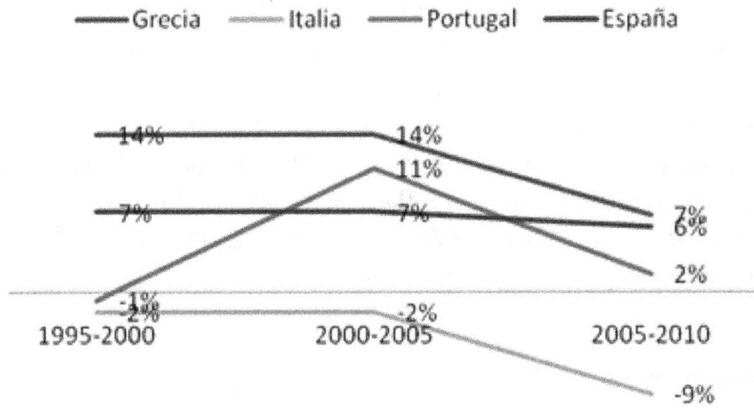

Figure 4. Percentage growth of the Human Development Indicator
Source: Elaboration by the author with information from the United Nations

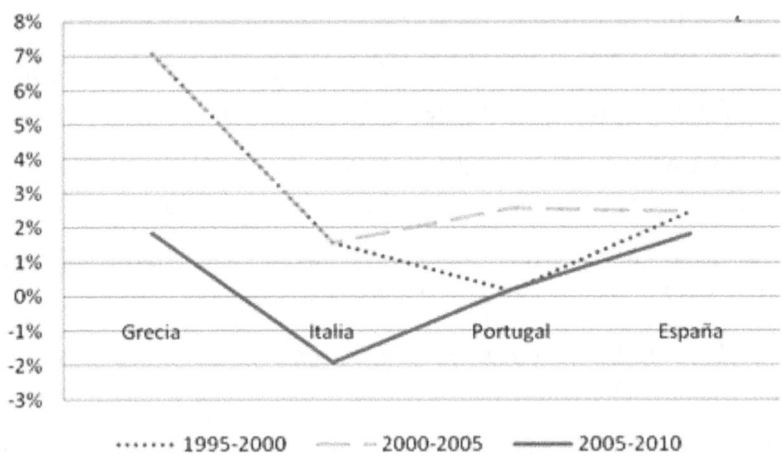

CONCLUSION

The essential principle of the Maastricht Treaty is to maintain well-being. Through the impetus of this principle, it elaborated certain economic rules that would regulate the impacts under a margin of prudence. In analyzing the situation in Europe, it is evident that the criteria of the Maastricht Treaties, with the exception of inflation, have not been followed, and that by not following such criteria, it can be inferred that welfare has been put at risk.

The analysis based on the HDI shows that the Maastricht Treaty does, from an empirical analysis, work to maintain well-being. The fact that the countries with the most worrisome situations in the EU have not focused on these parameters is demonstrated in the different indicators. Schooling fell, life expectancy was lower, and human development indicator as well.

The debt, which as a consequence presents an acceleration in unemployment, in turn is reflected in the indicators presented. The EU and the Maastricht Treaty demonstrate the foresight of a region that emphasizes its history, thus giving an example of how treaties should be drawn up, although they should be followed, evaluated and re-analyzed in times of crisis.

REFERENCES

Banco Mundial. (2008). *La deuda y el crecimiento, Material del curso de políticas de crecimiento*. Estados Unidos.

Blanco, A., & Díaz, D. (2005). El bienestar social: su concepción y medición. Psicotherma, 17(4).

Fisher, S. (1986). *The inflationary process: Shocks and Accommodation in the Israeli Economy: Maturing through crisis*. Harvard University Press.

Fondo Monetario Internacional. (2011). *Data mapper*. Obtenido de la siguiente dirección: http://www.imf.org/external/datamapper/index.php

Fuentes, N., & Rojas, M. (2001). Economic Theory and Subjective Well-Being: Mexico. In *Social Indicator Research*. Dialogos Bienestera.

Gobierno de Chile. (2011). *Guía práctica sobre la quiebra de una empresa. Dirección de trabajo*. Santiago de Chile.

Iranzo, S. (2008). *Introducción al riesgo país. Banco de España, documentos ocasionales No. 0802*. España.

Keyes, C. (1998). The Social Wellbeing. *Social Psychology Quarterly*, *61*(2).

Keynes, J. (2010). The General Theory of Employment and Interest and Money. Harcourt, Brace.

Maslow, A. (1943). *A Theory of Human Motivation*. Kindle Edition.

Menger, C. (1997). Principios de economía política (2nd ed.). Madrid: Unión Editorial, S.A.

Menger, C. (2003). *Economía y Bienestar Económico*. Barcelona: Ediciones Orbis.

Muñoz, R. (2009). *Política anticíclica*. Retrieved from http://ocw.usal.es/eduCommons/ciencias-sociales-1/hacienda-publica-i/contenidos/Comentarios/Comentario%201.pdf

Nordhaus, D., & Tobin, J. (1972). Is growth obsolete?. *Economic Research Journal, 38*.

Programa de las Naciones Unidas para el Desarrollo Humano. (2004). *Curso de Desarrollo Humano*. PNUD, República Dominicana.

Real Instituto Elcano. (2008). *Tratado de la Unión Europea*. España.

Riascos, A. (1997). Sobre el costo en bienestar de la inflación en Colombia. *Borradores de Economía, 82*, 1-25.

Chapter 4
Taxation and Elites in Central America:
A Historical Approach

Mauricio Garita
Universidad del Valle de Guatemala, Guatemala

ABSTRACT

The discussion of taxes in Central America has been based in economic and social crises. Because of these efforts, it is imperative to understand the history in order to understand the impact an economic crisis can have on taxes. Therefore, the study presents a research based on a historical approach with the purpose of understanding the different concepts concerning the elites and the evolution of the economic circumstances around it. Also, the discussion concerning inequality and development that evidence that not much has changed.

INTRODUCTION

Discussing taxes in Central America is a complex task, mainly because Central America has been dominated by different types of elites since its conception. Vilfredo Pareto (1935 [1848]) defined that elites could be divided into two concepts from a classical perspective that resembled the animal kingdom. The first concept was labeled as a lion, whereby the elites gained power by force. The second concept was the fox, symbolizing the fact that individuals gained access to the elitist arena by persuasion and skill. He also stated that for an elite to be created, there had to be restrictions in social mobility, knowledge, wealth and political inclusion. The last of these restrictions, political inclusion, stated the argument proposed by Weber (2012 [1922]) that elites, in search for a *status quo*, focus on power and domination.

DOI: 10.4018/978-1-5225-4981-9.ch004

According to Hirschman (1991), the consequences of power and domination in the political arena will lead to three reactive scenarios: perversity, futility and risk. Considering the perversity scenario, elites will deliberately act against any social, political and economic progress. In a futile scenario, the elite will advocate for small or inexistent social changes, and if there would be a social change, the elites would try to transform it into an unattainable aspect. Finally, in the third scenario, the elites will weigh the risk of social change and aim to reduce it with the purpose of maintaining the *status quo*, or gaining more advantages for society in general. In modern elite theory, the futile scenario is usually not considered because the elites use social change to gain advantages and improve their condition (Highley, 2001). Considering the history of Central America, the Spanish elite became an important factor in taxation since their colonization.

The First Elites: Spanish Colonization

To the Spaniards during the colonization period, specifically in the sixteen century, one of the most important interests was Indian labor. This led to the term *encomienda*[1], a Spanish system that gave control over a group of Indian labor and lands, with the purpose of maintaining the feudal system (Yeager, 1995). The *encomienda* was a payment to the *Peninsulares* or *ladinos*, in which they received as payment a group of *indios*[2] with the purpose of having workforce. The "owner" of the ones that were *encomended* had to evangelize them and also could charge tax.

The encomiendas led to a complicated discussion between the new elite that was being created because they "owned" labor and land, and the Spanish Crown was against this system because it would lead to a loss of power. The Spanish Crown tried to take control of the situation but the distance, the empowerment of the new Spanish elite, led by Pedro de Alvarado, Pedro Arias Dávila[3] and Contreras, utilized *encomiendas* as a way to benefit friends, family and allies (Helps, 1868). The *encomiendas* system changed the taxation dynamics in Central America, specifically for the Indian population because they were charged if they could not provide items that the Spanish needed. This forced the Indians to travel to other locations for work, thus creating another form of slavery: an economic slavery (MacLeod, 2007).

The Spanish elite and the new tax implementation (*encomiendas*) on Indians founded on the *encomiendas* concept blended in the conception of *castas,* a Spanish term for hierarchy. The *castas* were divided into four categories by race: Peninsultar[4], Criollo[5], Indio[6] and Negro[7]. Being part of an upper *casta,* such as the Peninsulares, led to a control of taxes and tribute payments which burdened the lower classes (Jestes, 2013). This social and economic blend helped the Spaniards in the development of two economic production lines: agricultural products and mining, which were very important concerning Central America.

One of the most important taxes, the royal fifth, affected commodities, including slavery and mining products with a 20% tax since 1520, but was reduced to 10% in 1736 to increase exportation and mining (Alban, Rivera, & Ayala, 1999). Although the *encomiendas* and taxes on Indians didn´t change, the reduction of the royal fifth demonstrated a change in the politics of Spain. Before the tax reduction, in 1717, the *Peninsulares* began to establish monopolies, specifically in tobacco production and trade, and began controlling the economy in Central America with the purpose of maintaining the *status quo*. The new strategy by the *Peninsulares* created discomfort in the New World and the foundation for the Bourbon Reforms.

Bourbon Reforms: The Power to the Comerciantes

In 1750, Guatemala had control of Central America through different mechanisms. The *ordenanzas* of the Ayuntamiento de Guatemala controlled food, minerals and other trade in Central America. The *comerciantes*, elites that helped establish the Spanish regime, controlled the commerce from Guatemala to Central America because they were the only ones that could fund producers, mainly because they had wealth but also because they had power given by the support of the *cabildo*. The *cabildo* created and owned the *Junta de Comercio*, which controlled taxes. This structure gave total control to the *comerciantes* because they controlled taxes, power and economy. Although it is important to state that the *comerciantes* were divided into two types*: the comerciantes de carrera (merchants by profession)* that were Spanish Peninsulares and *criollos* that handled the credit system of the New World charging high interest rates; and the *tratantes* that were low status *comerciantes* that depended on the *comerciantes de carrera* (Sena, 2007).

The *comerciantes* wanted liberalization from Spain, a common desire of the economic elite of the New World. One of the most important disagreements in the New World was the way monopolies were handled. The first fiscal reform in Guatemala was led by the *comerciantes* in 1758 motivated by a monopoly in Aguardiente, a monopoly that they wanted to seize. The problem was that the monopoly was going to be offered to a provider other than the Ayuntamiento - an institution controlled by the *comerciantes*. The fiscal reform was not needed as nine months later the monopoly was given to the Ayuntamiento (Wortman, 1975). Although this was taken as an act of disrespect against the Crown, the Spanish regime suggested changes in the tax regime of Central America.

In 1763, Francisco de Valdes[8] was assigned to control taxes and interrupted the control of the *comerciantes*. The Crown also changed the tax rates for commodities from 3% to 4%, and the tax for Indians that was previously 1% was doubled to 2%. This message sent by the Crown was clear: they would not accept a revolution from the New World. These changes gave birth to the Bourbon Reforms led by Felipe V and Carlos III, the purpose of which was to modernize the New World. One of the pillars of modernization was the tax structure as a result of the military agenda of Spain (Zeyfer, 2006). The necessity for a better army to fight the English and the Portuguese led to higher demands on fiscal revenues. This caused the creation of border controls, improvements in local governments (what are these?), the creation of vice royalties, the enforcement of monopolies and improved tax systems to counter smuggling. These reforms also provided more benefits to the Peninsulares, declaring them noble as soon as they stepped into the New World and with access to the wealth that the others could not obtain (Lynch & Humphreys, 1965). The Bourbon Reform in Central America had a positive effect for Spain because it controlled the production and created a better economic situation (Cuello, 1988). The reforms in Europe were very distant, though the Spanish introduced repressive policies, the inquisition and domestic reforms that affected Europe and Latin America. [9]

American colonies that were also gestating its separation from the Spanish Crown, and a better timing could not be possible.

Independence From Spain and the Central American Federation

The Bourbon Reform had a profound impact in Europe and in Central America. In Europe, the French Revolution, as well as the Napoleonic Wars that left Spain destroyed and without the capacity of managing its Central American colonies. This was seen as an opportunity for independence in South and Central America. In the South, independence was achieved in a short time but in Central America, it became violent. Jose Bustamante y Guerra was assigned to eradicate any ideas of liberation and thus Central America underwent a reign of terror (Grub, 2004). He wasn´t able to stop the liberalization movement and the discussions continued. The first movement was conceived in El Salvador by *Primer Grito de Independencia de Centro América* which was supported by the *criollos* because of the fiscal measures in place, the payment of taxes and the *alcabala* tax[10]. The *Primer Grito* led to the destitution of the Colonial Intendent of San Salvador, the dissolution of the Government Board and the negotiation of no retaliation against those who participated in the movement. The negotiation led the Spanish Crown in maintain control until the *Revolución de Riego*. The *Revolución de Riego* critiqued the lack of ability of the government, the inadequate acts of the treasury and the justice system and the obstacles to commerce, agriculture and other economic actives (Jaca, 1988).

The Cadiz Constitution gave economic liberty, strengthened indigenous rights and eliminated specific taxes. These benefits and the help of the *criollos* - that did not agree that only the *Peninsulares* could participate politically and access power - facilitated the Independence of Central America on the 15th of September of 1821, led by Gabino Gainza (*Peninsular)* and thirteen heroes of independence (*criollos).* This was a clear union between *Peninsulares* and *criollos* to gain separation from the Spanish Crown and avoid the rules and taxes imposed by it (Villalobos, 2013). Although the independence from the Spanish Crown was a reality, there was still a sentiment that it should be supported by a secondary act: the annexation of Mexico.

The annexation of Mexico was intended to confirm independence but it was not a planned process. Agustin de Iturbide[11] urged Gabino Gainza to consider an annexation to demonstrate the union of the *Estados Unidos de América*, and on the 29th of December 1821, the annexation was confirmed. From there on, Central America was a part of Mexico. The *notables*, a powerful elite, supported the idea of the annexation because it would give the military force needed to repel the Spanish Army. (Tovar, 2008). The annexation was not permanent because of the turmoil that the presence of Iturbide caused in the Mexican population. Personalities such as Iturbide were seen as part of the Spanish Crown and a remembrance of Spanish colonization. By 1823, Iturbide didn´t have the political strength to support the annexation and the independence of Central America was discussed again. The process of Central American independence was guided by Vicente Filísola, an Italian who was militarily trained in Spain and who fought with Iturbide for the Independence of Mexico (Fundación Enrique Bolaños, 2001)

By the 30th of June 1823, Central America was considered as independent but with a remembrance from the Spanish Crown. The constitution that was taken as part of Central America was the Spanish Constitution obviating the laws that were not appropriate for the independence. This act gave birth to the *República Federal de Centro América*, an act that created another separation of classes, this time not by *castas* but by their participation in the annexation of Mexico. Central America was divided between the *liberals* (freedom fighters) and the *serviles* (partial slavery) and in this division there were four groups:

- The *notables,* who were colonial functionaries, members of the municipal council, merchants and religious congregations.
- Those who supported annexing the Mexican Empire
- The *conservadores*, who protected their socioeconomic position that was inherited at the time of the Spanish Colonization.
- Those who rejected the annexation to other country and preferred a central rather than a federal government (Acosta, 2014).

Despite the differences created between *serviles* and liberals, the Constitution of the Republic of Central America, published 22nd of November 1824, had an interesting regulation concerning taxes. Article 69 established that only congress could decree extraordinary taxes and Article 178 determines that the legislative power regulates public expenditure, and decrees taxes to fulfill the Republic's necessities but that this has to be approved by congress (Constituyente, 1824).

Independence from Spain was a fact that Central America accepted, but the union of Central America was not a reality for the other countries. A second step towards independence was evidenced in the *Batalla de la Trinidad*[12] in Honduras. The purpose of this battle was to topple the current government, but it was impeded by Francisco Morazán. Morazán was born in a *criollo* family and during his political career he worked at the municipality, then took the position of general secretary during the period of Dionisio Herrera as *Primer Jefe*[13] of Honduras and President of the Representative Council (Santana, 2012). With his win in the *Batalla de la Trinidad,* he became *Primer Jefe* of Honduras. A series of events, including the discussion of high tax burden and abandonment by the state, led to the Civil War of Central America that culminated in an attack led by Morazán on the State of Guatemala, the state that governed Central America, and the control of the Central American Federation. He won the popular vote in 1930 and became President of the Federation. Morazán would become one of the leaders concerning social equity in Central America.

Even though Morazán was from an aristocratic family, his vision was very distant from the liberals protecting the *status quo*. He began fighting the oligarchy settled in Guatemala, the *notables* and *conservadores*, with a different view on what Central America should be. He declared free commerce, closed Catholic convents and transformed them into schools, and fought the invasions of the British in Nicaragua and Costa Rica (Cruz, 2009). During the presidency of Francisco Morazán, Mariano Galvez was proclaimed as *Jefe de Estado* of Guatemala. Mariano Galvez followed the vision of Morazán and expropriated ecclesiastical goods, abolished tithing, universalized primary education and encouraged grains and cochineal cultivation. During his government, the public revenues centered around the *alcabala*[14] tax, tobacco, hard liquor and *chicha*[15]

The Fall of the Central American Federation

The fiscal problems presented by the low *alcabala* tax, the cholera outbreak and the discomfort generated by the *notables* were the motivation needed for a new player in the political arena. The reign of Rafael Carrera began with an uprising sustained by the arguments of the Catholic Church, the *impuesto de capitación* (flat tax) and the agricultural policies. The *impuesto de capitación* was one of the most discomforting facts by the *notables* because it rejected the possibility of not paying revenues because of a social status (Instituto Centroamericano de Estudios Fiscales, 2009). Rafael Carrera, a *mestizo*[16] who came from a family with scarce resources, led the rebellion against Morazán's politics and social view in 1837. Carrera found support in the church and the *criollos* and with this support, the cholera outbreak and the fail of the Central American Federation, Morazán's presidency ended in 1838. This was also the end of the Federation that tried to unite again, following the example of the United States of America, during 1840 and 1852. These efforts only caused Central America to be separated into different sides and presented the opportunity for outside countries to enter into the Central American political agenda (Hernández, 2014).

Rafael Carrera assumed the role of Governor of Guatemala in 1844, a role that lasted until 1865 because of his permanence in power as a dictator. The support from the *criollos* introduced a new elite named the *Clan Aycinena* formed by *comerciantes* that were descendants of Juan Fermin Aycinena. Juan Fermin Aycinena, a *Peninsular*, was part of all the crucial steps that maintained the elite´s status quo in Central America. He participated in the Bourbon Reforms, he guided the modification caused by the Court of Cadiz, he managed to gain control of the intendancies by forming the *Clan Aycinena* and participated actively in the independence of Central America (Belaubre, 2009). His participation led him to be called as the most powerful man in the history of Central America.

The *Clan Aycinena* returned with the presidency of Rafael Carrera after Francisco Morazán expelled them because of their influence in the Central American political arena. Morazán also affected the Clan by expelling the Catholic congregations and turning the convents into public schools.

The *Clan Aycinena* included very powerful criollos and the evolution of the Clan demonstrates how they managed power. The *Clan Aycinena's* support of a *mestizo* for presidency was seen by the population as controversial. The strongest connection between *Clan Aycinena* and Rafael Carrera was religion, which led to a Holy War in Central America. He behooved the aristocracy and the Catholic Church by converting Guatemala into a concentration camp as the author Luis Cardoza y Aragon (1985) states in his book:

But this king of the Indians was no more than a bird of prey incubated and sustained for his service by the clergy, the English, and the aristocracy of the parish. The Indian, blinded by their misery and electrified by Carrera´s youth, talent and daring nature, followed him against their own benefit.

Rafael Carrera maintained the *alcabala tax* as the primordial source of public revenue followed by the income generated by the monopoly of alcoholic beverages. The fiscal problem during Rafael Carrera´s governing period was caused by the continuous expense in military operations with the purpose of maintaining his dictatorship. Rafael Carrera recognized this problem in 1863 when he stated that the effort of sustaining the army expedition to Honduras and El Salvador, the amortizations of the public debt and other commitments would demonstrate a deficit in the budget (Pompejano, 1997).

During the presidency of Rafael Carrera, the German government was given commercial benefits over other countries that traded in the region such as Sweden and Norway. German goods, which had the highest demand in Costa Rica, found a path to trade through the region and the Germans became an economic elite themselves. Thus began marriages between Germans and Spaniards, a European *metizaje* for maintaining control over the Indians (Schoonover, Germany in Central America, 1998).

The *new comerciantes* began a political work towards a tax change strategy that became successful in 1880, when the tax structure burdened the Indians with a change in obligations from in-kind trading to cash obligations. The *comerciantes* had the capability of administering power through politics, because they understood the importance of Congress and laws.

This also led to tax collection in wage labor. But before the tax reform, there was a discussion concerning the coffee industry. This led to a discussion concerning different tax structures for benefiting the industry. Tax relief to the industry, subsidies to improve production, road development for better transportation, and a legislation that cheapened work labor were set to encourage coffee expansion (Woodward, 1999). The same tax privileges were given to the sugar and cotton industry. These taxation decisions maintained the control of the *criollos*, but also gave space to the Germans and the United States of Americas citizens in the Central American elite.

With these reforms and the benefits obtained by the traditional and new elites, Rafael Carrera ended his reign with his death and was buried with the highest honors conceded by the Catholic Church. In his right hand rested a gift from Queen Victoria for the generosity of giving one fifth of the territory of Guatemala to Great Britain, a territory that would comprise the country of Belize (Kapuscinski, 2010).

Cotton, Coffee, Banana, and Taxes

The United States of America began its incursion in Central America during the 1820´s and 1830´s. During the American Civil War, Central America was an important discussion because both sides of the Civil War thought that the region should play an important role in their well-being and security. During the 1860´s, the North American elites saw an opportunity to introduce cotton into Central America, mostly because of the labor situation of the region, and because the Civil War led to freedom of slaves Therefore, when the Liberal Revolution of Guatemala took place in 1871 and the coffee expansion began, the cotton industry had already been in Central America for fifty years. During the Civil War (1861-1865), the Confederates handled the cotton trade in Central America. It is important to recall that the Confederates shared a similar vision with the elites of Central America, including for slavery. (Schoonover, 1991).

During this time, the imports from Central America grew considerably, as mentioned before, during the Liberal Revolution. The Liberal Revolution took place in 1871 under the leadership of Justo Rufino Barrios and Miguel García Granados who defeated Vicente Cerna, the successor of Rafael Carrera. The presidents of Guatemala after the Liberal Revolution, Justo Miguel García Granados, Justo Rufino Barrios and Lisandro Barillas focused on economic growth based on cotton, coffee and bananas. The focus of this economic growth was to export into the United States and it worked perfectly, as Figure 2 demonstrates (Revolution of 1871, n.d.).

After the presidency of Lizardo Barillas, José María Reina Barrios was appointed as President of Guatemala. The government of Reina Barrios was characterized by an important economic crisis in the coffee and silver markets. In an official communication by the government in 1897, the fall on prices of coffee and silver affected the region, specifically in Guatemala, and this led to a protectionist approach for this industry (La Ilustración Guatemalteca, 1897). Under these circumstances, Reina Barrios was heavily criticized by the media, specifically by the newspaper La República, saying that he was wasting money on railway construction and constructing buildings that weren´t necessary (La República, 1897). This discontent

Figure 1.
Source: Elaborated by the author with information from (Schoonover, 1991)

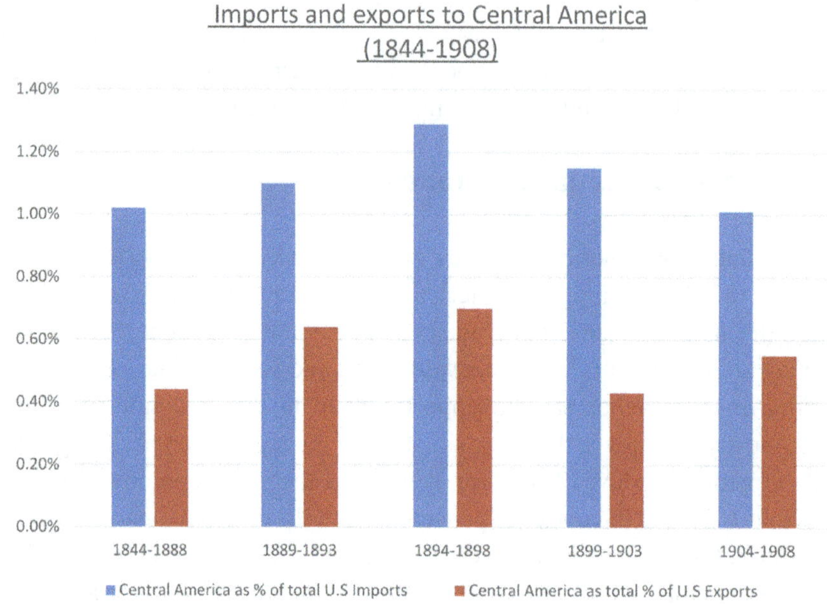

summed up with modification in taxes that benefited cotton and coffee and affected the presidency of Reina Barrios. He was assassinated by Edgar Zolliger, a British citizen and it is said that he was persuaded by Manuel Estrada Cabrera who wanted to be president.

After Reina Barrios' assassination, Manuel Estrada Cabrera rose to power in 1898 until he was overthrown in 1920. Manuel Estrada Cabrera added another commodity to the products of Guatemala that expanded into Central America: it was the bananas. With the implementation of the banana cultivation in the region came a company that affected Central America and the way politics were handled. This company was the United Fruit Company that came to be known as the UFCO. In the same way that Rafael Carrera gave all the power to the Spanish descendant's elite, Estrada Cabrera gave all the power to this company, and therefore another elite operated in Central America. There was the Spanish elite whose domination was smaller which each inclusion, the German elite that focused on the production of coffee, the North American Confederate elite that focused on cotton and now another North American elite that controlled the banana production.[17]

Tax exemptions that were given to coffee and cotton during the liberal revolution were now also granted to the UFCO[18]. Estrada Cabrera exempted the land that the UFCO was going to use for banana plantation of all the Guatemalan taxes. The taxation strategies changed from imposing the poor and discriminated to the exemption of taxes based on the industry. The participation of the UFCO and the Confederates in the cotton production made Central America an important region for the United States. Therefore, President Roosevelt and President Taft made Central America a priority for the United States and participated in the politics of all the countries in the region (Leonard, 1991).

The following years for Central America involved revolutions caused by the presence of the United States. The United States began taking more control over Central America as evidenced by their actions in Panama and Nicaragua, meanwhile countries such as Guatemala, Honduras, El Salvador and Costa Rica battled between supporting and rejecting the United States. During this time, cotton began to decrease in the region though coffee and bananas remained an important commodity. The Great War, World War II and the Cold War affected Central America because of the presence of the United States. This led to a political discussion that aggravated the countries until 1960, the year that the operation of *Bahia de Cochinos* failed and Central America began a revolution. First it was Guatemala, then Nicaragua, El Salvador and Honduras that began to fight between each other. Meanwhile, economic growth centered on agrarian production. The fight for land, labor and production ended in tax concessions for the companies who not only ruled the economic markets but also the political arena.

Controlling Power to Control Taxes: The Reality of Central America

After the Civil War of Guatemala, El Salvador and Nicaragua summed up with the brief trifling between Honduras and El Salvador[19], a united Central America was a euphemism. Central America became a mosaic of traditional elites and the new elites, which included a military elite in some countries.

Although there was also a common practice in Central America and should be discussed: the creation of chambers to represent the private sector. In every country of Central America, from Guatemala to Costa Rica, there are different chambers that represent the view of the elites and have the means to exercise control.

These organizations have become participants in the fiscal discussions and intermediators, a practice very distant from the one utilized by the Spaniards, since they had control of the taxation procedures. The Organization for Economic Co-operation and Development (2013) defined that challenges considering taxation in Central America were the small tax base, a large informal sector, weak governance and administrative capability, low levels of income *per capita*, domestic savings investments and possibly tax avoidance by the elites.

These sectors have united different elites, including transnational, local, traditional and industrial elites. Schneider (2012) established that elites develop cohesion and that cohesion is important because it gives the elites the ability to combine their social, economic and fiscal vision and include them into their state building agendas. This unification gave them the possibility to continue elaborating public policies and controlling taxes indirectly, as they had done so in the past since colonization. (Smith, 2014).

In a more specific detail, the mixture of controlling power, fighting tax reforms and obtaining tax privileges is the current challenge considering fiscal policy in the region. In Guatemala, as Barrientos and Figueroa (2015) demonstrate, there was an influence from CACIF to the Constitutional Court to challenge tax legislation. This challenge gives the private sector the possibility of not paying auxiliary assessments for the personal income tax. In the tax reform proposed in 2008-2012, CACIF was able to modify an article in the reform causing the tax burden to fall (Barrientos & Figueroa, 2015).

The capacity of the chamber to alter fiscal reforms should be analyzed under the view that when the Peace Accords were signed in 1996, the purpose was to equilibrate the economic elites so they would be less influential. This idea is even present in the elections were chosen candidates propose wealth distribution and increases in taxes but, in practice, the tax burden is not what it should be[20] (Steenbergen, 2012). For these reasons, it does not come as a surprise that Guatemala has the lowest tax burden in Latin America according to the United Nations Economic Commission for Latin America and the Caribbean. The average collection rate for Guatemala is 13%, meanwhile the average of Latin America is 23%. KPMG (2015), in its Global Tax Survey, rates Guatemala as the lowest in individual income with a 7% rate.

In El Salvador, the elites that dominated the coffee industry migrated to the financial sector with the purpose of increasing their wealth. (Instituto Centroamericano de Estudios Fiscales, 2015) This process was executed during the privatization of the national bank that led to an augmentation of the fiscal deficit to cover indebted businesses. Also, with the participation of the right-wing party that represents the private sector elite, the Alianza Republicana Nacionalista (ARENA), they managed avoid direct taxes and focus on the augmentation of indirect taxation. Barrientos et al. (2015) estate that the impediment to indirect taxes, the control of the financial sector, and the political power led by FUSADES and ARENA led to fiscal privileges for the banking industry and a control on tax policies.

In the case of Honduras, during the 1980´s to the 1990´s, there was a shift from agriculture to services which led the fiscal policy towards the benefit of this industry. The formula, similar to the one in El Salvador, was to grant fiscal privileges to the exportation industry to increase competitiveness. COHEP was able to exercise political influence over the governments to sustain the tax exemptions and fiscal privileges, even when the circumstances involved the presidency of Manuel Zelaya, as the private sector was capable of overthrowing the president (Pino, 2015).

In Nicaragua, during the period from 2008-2011, there was an important link between the political power and the elites to alter fiscal policy. This was evident when, in 2009, the fiscal reform was negotiated between COSEP and the government, excluding any other sectors. These reforms characterized by fiscal privileges and special tax treatment led to more control by the elites. As Medal (2015) stated, if the power of negotiation is not created for the participation of other economic agents, the fiscal policy of the country will continue to reflect the interests of the the economic and political elites, thus will continue to impact the fragility of Nicaraguan democracy.

Table 1. Central American Tax Burden (% of GDP)

Country	2011	2012	2013	2014	2015	2016
Guatemala	10.9%	10.8%	11.0%	10.8%	10.2%	10.4%
Costa Rica	13.0%	12.9%	13.2%	12.9%	13.2%	13.3%
Nicaragua	14.5%	15.1%	15.1%	15.4%	15.6%	
Honduras	14.8%	14.7%	15.0%	16.7%	17.9%	19.8%
El Salvador*	15.1%	15.5%	16.2%	15.9%	15.9%	15.8%

Source: Elaborated by the author with information from Icefi (2017). *El Salvador presents a gross tax burden because they have not deducted tax devolution for exportations or to income

Finally, in Costa Rica, the process was similar but with the domination of executive power. The economic elites not only influenced the fiscal policy decisions but they also controlled them with presidents who were part of the economic elite. The focus of the country has been aimed at exportation, similar to Honduras, and fiscal benefits have been granted for the growth of the industry. Considering the exportation sector, one of the most important exports is bananas that represented 12% of the GDP in 2014 with a value of USD 1.54 billion (OEC, 2014). Also, during every government from 1994, there have been specific private sector elites in important decision-making positions with the ability to alter the fiscal policy of the country (Rodriguez & Sancho, 2015).

CONCLUSION

In each one of the Central American countries, although they are apart, they demonstrate that the *comerciantes* are still in control of the political and economic power with the ability to make changes easily. This economic elite, though it may not be the same as it once was at the beginning of Spanish Central America, has used the same strategies for the last four hundred years. Therefore, the results in equality in the region had not changed with high levels of poverty, corruption, a lack of education and health, and with a compromised future. Instead of a more democratic society, we continue to have the illusion of power and with this illusion a change cannot be made.

This research demonstrates that the schemes used by the elites remain relatively the same but that they can be changed if there is more political participation in society. This political participation can be achieved with more knowledge and with the capacity of contributions from the state. The state, that has been used as a tool for creating wealth for the few, should be empowered to act in accordance with the social contract that the Central American countries have. If we continue this path, the path of control by elites, then the changes in Central America would be minimal and allowed, only if they do not alter the elites' *status quo*. Central American societies have to work towards a social contract that focuses on the well-being of every citizen so that every citizen is represented in the fiscal policy of Central America.

REFERENCES

Acosta, W. S. (2014). Del sueño unitario a la fragmentación: la República Federal de Centroamérica (1823-1838). In W. S. Acosta & M. S. Ulloa (Eds.), Centroamérica: casa común e integración regional (pp. 17-32). Universidad Nacional de Costa Rica.

Alban, J. V., Rivera, S. L., & Ayala, S. R. (1999). *Propriety and Permissiveness in Bourbon Mexico*. Rowman & Littlefield Publishers.

Belaubre, C. (2009). *Juan José Aycinena*. Guatemala: Asociación para el Fomento de los Estudios Históricos en Centroamérica .

Belaure, C. (n.d.). *Asociación para el Fomento de los Estudios Históricos en Centroamérica*. Retrieved from Red social de Juan Fermín Aycinena y su evoluación (1750-1808): http://www.afehc-historia-centroamericana.org/index.php?action=im_aff&id=1043

Bucheli, M. (2006). *Good dictator, bad dictator: United Fruit Company and Economic Nationalism in Central America in the Twentieth Century*. Chicago: University of Illinois.

Constituyente, A. N. (1824). *Constitución de la República Federal de Centroamérica*. Guatemala.

Cruz, F. P. (2009). *Morazán nuestro altivo héroe*. Havana: REvista Cubana de pensamiento e historia.

Cuello, J. (1988). The Economic Impact of the Bourbon Reforms and the Late Colonial Crisis of Empire at the Local Level: The Case of Saltillo, 17771817. *The Americas*, *44*(03), 301–323. doi:10.2307/1006909

D. A. D. C., S. J., & A, J. R. (2009). The consequences of radical reform: the French Revolution. *NBER Working Papers*.

D. K.-P. (2008). *New York Times*. Retrieved from Big Fruit: http://www.nytimes.com/2008/03/02/books/review/Kurtz-Phelan-t.html

F. R., & F. S. (2015). Costa Rica: favorecer a los exportadores, sacrificando la inversión social y el desarollo democrático. In I. C. Fiscales (Ed.), *Política fsical: expresión del poder de las élites centroamericanas* (pp. 313-390). FyG.

Fundación Enrique Bolaños. (2001). *Fundación Enrique Bolaños*. Retrieved from Vicente Filísola: http://www.enriquebolanos.org/data/docs/Biografia%20de%20Vicente%20Filisola%20v1.pdf

Grub, U. (2004). *Asociación para el Fomento de los Estudios Históricos en Centroamérica*. Bustamante y Guerra.

Guatemala Imprenta Nueva. (1830). Exposición que al comenzar la actual legislatura ordinaria, hizo al Congreso Federal de esta República. Author.

H. S. (2014). State Building and Taxation in Latin America. *Latin American Research Review*, 258–262.

Helps, A. (1868). *The Spanish conquest in America.* Harper & Brothers.

Hernández, M. S. (2014). *Centroamérica 1850-1950: los debates fundamentales sobre la unión política regional.* Universidad Nacional de Costa Rica.

Highley, J. (2001). *Elite Theory in Political Sociology.* Estados Unidos.

Hirshman, A. (1991). *Retórica de la instransigencia.* Academic Press.

ICEFI. (2017). *Perfiles macrofiscales 8.* ICEFI.

Instituto Centroamericano de Estudios Fiscales. (2009). *Historia de la tributación de Guatemala.* Superintendencia de Administración Tributaria.

Instituto Centroamericano de Estudios Fiscales. (2015). *Política fiscal: expresión del poder de las élites centroamericanas.* FyG editores.

J. L., & R. H. (1965). *The Origins of the Latin American Revolutions, 1808-1826.* Academic Press.

Jaca, B. B. (1988). *Causas del pronunciamiento de 1820 y de su éxito.* Madrid: Universidad Nacional de Educación a Distancia.

Jestes, R. (2013, June 15). *Native Heritage Project.* Retrieved from Las Castas – Spanish Racial Classifications: https://nativeheritageproject.com/2013/06/15/las-castas- spanish-racial-classifications/

Kapuscinski, R. (2010). *Cristo con un fusil al hombro.* Anagrama.

KPMG. (2015). Retrieved from 2015 Global Tax Rate Survey: https://assets.kpmg.com/content/dam/kpmg/pdf/2015/11/global-tax-rate-survey-2015-v2- web.pdf

La Ilustración Guatemalteca. (1897). Retrieved from La Ilustración Guatemalteca: https://archive.org/stream/ilustracionguate00guat#page/376/mode/2up

La República. (1897). Retrieved from https://archive.org/stream/ilustracionguate00guat#page/390/mode/2up

Leonard, T. (1991). *Central America and the United States: The Search for Stability.* Academic Press.

Lopez, M. (2013). Elite theory. *Sociopedia*, 1-12.

MacLeod, M. (2007). *Spanish Central America: A Socioeconomic History, 1520–1720.* LLILAS Special Publications.

Medal, J. L. (2015). Nicaragua: Política Fiscal para cargar a los contribuyentes las pérdidas privadas y los privilegios de las élites. In I. C. Fiscales (Ed.), *Política Fiscal: Expresión del poder de las élites centroamericanas* (pp. 273–319). FyG Editores.

OEC. (2014). *The observatory of economic complexity*. Retrieved from http://atlas.media.mit.edu/en/

Organisation for Economic Co-operation and Development. (2013). *Organisation for Economic Co-operation and Development*. Retrieved from What drives tax morale?: http://www.oecd.org/ctp/tax-global/TaxMorale_march13.pdf

Pareto, V. (1935). *The mind and society. A treaty on general sociology*. Dover: Nueva York.

Pino, H. N. (2015). Honduras: El abuso de las exoneraciones tributarias como dogma fiscal. In I. C. Fiscales (Ed.), *Política fiscal: expresión del poder de las élites centroamericanas* (pp. 211–273). FyG Editores.

Pompejano, D. (1997). *La crisis del antiguo régimen en Guatemala, 1839-1871*. Editorial Universitaria.

R. B., & W. F. (2015). Guatemala: Poder de veto a la legislación tributaria y captura fallida del negocio de la inversión pública. In I. C. Fiscales (Ed.), *Política Fiscal: epresión del poder de las élites centroamericanas* (pp. 25-128). FyG.

R. B., R. C., M. G., L. M., J. U., C. A., . . . Trejo, C. P. (2015). El Salvador: una política fiscal diseñada como base y garant{ia para un sistema económico rentista y expoliador. In I. C. Fiscales (Ed.), Política fiscal: expresión del poder de las élites centroamericans (pp. 129-208). FyG Editores.

Revolution of 1871. (n.d.). Retrieved from Revolution of 1871 - History - Guatemala - Central America: guatemala history, crop guatemala, guatemala people, guatemala money, coffee elite: http://www.countriesquest.com/central_ america/guatemala/history/revolution_of_1871.htm

Rock, D. (1992). *1516-1982: From Spanish Colonization to the Falklands War*. University of California Press.

Santana, A. (2012). *Vida, obra y pensamientos de Francisco Morazán*. Fundación Biblioteca Ayaucho.

Schneider, A. (2012). *State-Building and Tax Regimes in Central America*. Cambridge Press. doi:10.1017/CBO9781139094061

Schoonover, T. (1991). *The United States in Central America, 1860–1911: Episodes of Social Imperialism and Imperial Rivalry in the World System*. Duke University Press Books.

Schoonover, T. (1998). *Germany in Central America*. University of Alabama Press.

Sena. (2007). *La sociedad Colonial, Siglos XVI y XVII*. Banco de la República de Colombia.

SIECA. (n.d.). *Anexo A*. Retrieved from Anexo A: http://www.sieca.int/PortalData/Documentos/8F59A1A1-DC31-441F-AD66- 1B1739F37CB0.pdf

Smith, R. S. (1948). Sales taxes in New Spain, 15751770. *The Hispanic American Historical Review*, *28*(1), 2–37. doi:10.2307/2508188

Steenbergen, V. (2012). *Tax reform in Guatemala: analyzing the mechanisms of interest group influence*. Retrieved from London School of Economics: http://www.lse.ac.uk/IPA/images/Documents/PublicSphere/2013/6-tax-reform-guatemala- 2012.pdf

Tovar, G. S. (2008). *Centro de Estudios Politicos y Constitucionales*. Retrieved from La Federación Centroamericana: http://www.cepc.gob.es/Controls/Mav/getData.ashx?MAVqs=~ aWQ9MzI1MjImaWRlPTEwM zcmdXJsPTEzJm5hbWU9UlBJXzAwNV8xMT gucGRmJmZpbGU9UlBJXzAwNV8xMTgucG RmJnRhYmxhPUFydGljdWxvJmNvbn RlbnQ9YXBwbGljYXRpb24vcGRm

Villalobos, R. (2013). *Prensa Libre*. Retrieved from Criolla independencia: http://www.prensalibre.com/revista_d/Independencia_de_Guatemala-fiestas_patrias-verdadera_independencia-historia_de_la_independencia_0_991701023.html

Villatoro, D. (2015). *Plaza Pública*. Retrieved from https://www.plazapublica.com.gt/content/guatemala-es-el-pais-con-la-carga-tributaria-mas- baja-de-america-latina: https://www.plazapublica.com.gt/content/guatemala-es-el-pais-con-la- carga-tributaria-mas-baja-de-america-latina

Weber, M. (2012). *Sociologia del poder: Los Tipos De Dominacion*. Madrid: Alianza Editoria.

Woodward, R. L. (1999). *Central America: A Nation Divided*. Oxford Press.

Wortman, M. (1975). Bourbon Reforms in Central America: 1750-1786. The Americas, 222-238.

Yeager, T. (1995). Encomienda or Slavery? The Spanish Crowns choice of labour organization in Sixteen-Century Spanish America. *The Journal of Economic History*, *55*(04), 842–859. doi:10.1017/S0022050700042182

Zeyfer. (2006). *Historia de Honduras*. Retrieved from Reformas Borbónicas: http://www.historiadehonduras.hn/Historia/Colonial/reformasborbonicas.htm

ENDNOTES

1 The *encomienda* was a right given by the King of Spain by his will and was not an obligation. In Spanish, this translates as "á merced y voluntad del Rey" (a market and volunteers of the king).

2 In this work we use the Word "indian" and not "indigenous" because it was used in the original documents.

3 Better known as Pedrarias.

4 Born in Spain.

5 A person of Spanish descent born in Central America or the New World.

6 Descendent of the original habitants of the New World.

7 Black African descent.

8 Spanish general known for his leadership during the 80 years war.

9 The support to Carlos IV by Louis XIV led to the implementation of the same reforms in France which uplifted to the injustice of the Bourbons. France went against the alliance of Spain and England, resulting in the occupation of Bilbao and San Sebastian. As a consequence, Spain allied with France and England was left out, meaning Spain could not access Central America for ten years because of the continuing war. The alliance between Spain and France was not sufficient to cope with the revolution that was gestating in the citizens of France. As Acemoglu et al. (2009) stated, there were only two types of oligarchies that dominated in Europe: the landed nobility which sustained its wealth by agriculture and the urban-based oligarchy that controlled commerce and entry barriers. The French Revolution began as a threat and ended as a reality. Maybe it was a premonition to the Central American colonies that were also gestating its separation from the Spanish Crown, and a better timing could not be possible.

10 The alcabala tax was used in the fourteen century as a tax to fund war but for the Spanish Crown it was aimed to gain profit from sales. The tax affected the sale price and not the prime cost, which was seen as unfair (Smith, 1948).

11 Known as Agustín de México, was a succesfull general for the Mexican Army and was vital for Mexico independence.

12 November 11th, 1827.

13 The term "primer jefe" is used because it denotes a political figure as a president of a country but who was under the supervision of the President of Central America who was located in Guatemala.

14 The alcabala tax had a reduction of approximately 100% from 1826 to 1831.

15 Beverage made with sugar, *jocote* (fruit) and water.

16 His ancestry was a mix of Indian and *criollo.*

17 The banana industry was born in Costa Rica with the Central American Railroad. Martin Keith, a young entrepreneur working on the railroad in Costa Rica began growing bananas at the side of the railroad. This gave him the idea of a new business in which he could control the production of bananas and the transportation via the railroads (Daniel, 2008). With this vision and a president who wanted to stay in power, the United Fruit Company began its operations in the region. Given its growth due the demand of bananas in the United States and the easiness of commerce developed by the cotton and coffee industry, the growth of UFCO was extremely quick which gave them the capability of lobbying. In 1901, the UFCO managed to get a concession from Estrada Cabrera for transportation between Puerto Barrios in the Atlantic Coast of Guatemala and New Orleans. In 1904, they granted UFCO with the concession for 99 years, of the railroad efforts of which Reina Barrios was criticized and that became to be known as the International Railways of Central America (IRCA). In 1906, Estrada Cabrera granted UFCO with the exclusivity in banana production in Guatemala (Bucheli, 2006).

18 The UFCO went to control 40% of the Guatemalan Economy.

19 Also known as "La guerra del futbol". For more information about this event, we recommend Ryszard Kapuscinki´s book titled "La Guerra del Futbol".

20 When analyzing tax burden there is usually the rule that it should be sufficient to the plan of the country, the problema in Central America is often the lack of a development plan (exception can be found in Costa Rica).

Chapter 5
Information Security Management as a Business Strategy and Its Financial Impact

Israel E. Mendoza
Universidad del Valle de Guatemala, Guatemala & Superintendencia de Bancos, Guatemala

ABSTRACT

The information security is importance as a strategic process to improve and maintain the continuity of the company. There have been developed various methodologies and risk management, safety guidelines information, however, does not go beyond operational and strategic part of business. Although some methodologies are based on international standards to implement controls to mitigate risks, but not the financial factors that could be impacted by these risks are analyzed. In some companies the legal aspect as a financial category, economic losses is not analyzed as a risk or information theft materializes. There are several methodologies based on guidelines and recommendations and provide general guidance on the management of information security; therefore, for purposes of this scientific research it will be taken into account some relevant points of those standards, which will undoubtedly help establish an appropriate risk methodology and subsequently to the definition of financial criteria for decision-making.

DOI: 10.4018/978-1-5225-4981-9.ch005

INTRODUCTION

The information has taken important value for any business today, the reason is because certain information has value which is given by its content, however it must be protected against threats that exist at all times and that they may affect the business, its operations and therefore incur financial losses. Companies know that risks can not be eliminated but can be managed. However, when performing a risk analysis without finding the purpose or objective of its rationale, it is not relevant, due to it, a management methodology is presented, (ISO/IEC 27001:2013, 2013), where it analyzes its financial impact and the variations that could have an impact when making an investment or expense implementing controls that This methodology is based on a consulting firm (Datasec-MeycorKP, 2016) which emphasizes the alignment of risks with the implementation of controls to obtain the expected risk, at the same time, giving the results consistent. In order to understand the scope and purpose of risk management and to deepen the financial impact that could affect the company, a comparison has been made of the financial situation of the company with a history of its financial statements with a company that is listed on The Italian stock market (MCK:IM_Bloomberg, 2016), both with the same scope of labor market work, so that the comparative is coherent; The results obtained from the financial analysis can be studied and analyzed by experts in the field to make financial management decisions that could impact potential financial losses (Gerardo Guajardo Cantú, 2008).

LITERARY REVIEW

Risk Management

(ISACA, 2013), efines risk management as "a process to achieve an optimal balance between concrete opportunities for profit and minimize vulnerabilities and loss", "Risk management means that the risk is managed in such a way that Does not have a significant impact on the business process, and that acceptable levels of assurance and predictability are established on the desired results of any significant activity of the organization".

According to the National Institute of Cybersecurity of Spain. (UNISDR, 2009), defines risk as the combination of the probability of an event occurring and its negative consequences, consequently taking into account factors that influence that risk which are the vulnerability, which is a mistake or Deficiency in business processes that could present a threat to violate the security of a system causing business losses. However in terms of information security there is a technological risk that must be managed which, according to the definition given in Resolution JM-102-2011 of Guatemala (Junta Monetaria, 2011).

According to the National Institute of Cybersecurity of Spain (INCIBE, 2016) he threat is an event or a condition that can cause a substantial impact on economic damages or losses, for example, operational human error threats of natural or environmental origin such as floods, Earthquakes, etc., failures in computer systems and communications, etc., another factor that influences is the probability that an event occurs at any given time, the RAE (Real Academia Española, 2016) comments that probability is a process Random, ratio between the number of favorable cases and the number of possible cases; Therefore, this combination of probability and vulnerability can compromise the security of business information and therefore there may be an exposure to a threat.

Information assets can be categorized by groups and have no standard or standard to regulate their classification, however there are general criteria to better identify them, which helps to classify them according to their utility and purpose for which they exist. For example, information assets may be hardware assets (Cambridge Dictionary, 2016), which is any equipment or device that possesses electronic parts, Software asset, which comprises language code and / or applications developed by Systems programmers, Information asset which includes everything that has value in paper or electronic information such as financial statements, software licenses, patents, passwords of a computer system, etc., Assets of people or human resources and physical assets that can be furniture, filing cabinets, keys, data center of the Department of Informatics, etc.

The valuation of information assets is fundamental in the management of risks as it reflects the impact of the risk combined with the exposure to which it is exposed resulting in a level of risk. (ICONTEC, 2010) recommends the valuation of assets in terms of Confidentiality whose purpose is to protect information that is private or sensitive to unauthorized disclosure, in terms of Availability, which is when assets are accessed when required and in terms of Integrity, which is when it is required that there is validity and certainty of the information.

There are several ways to manage risk management, however. The Colombian Standard (NTC5254, 2004) defines the general stages of good risk management and management taking into account the definition and establishment of scope and limits involving both internal and external general factors That have an influence on the business processes, secondly a risk assessment must be carried out, a process in which the business risks that may affect and compromise the information security of the information assets are identified, in turn evaluating Both influence or impact on the business, however, it is necessary to carry out a risk treatment after the identification of the risks since at this stage the strategies that are performed to deal with the risks identified in the risk assessment stage are defined. The risk that exists after implementing controls at the stage of treatment of the potential risks that result from a possible threat is the residual risk and acceptable risk which management is responsible for responding to and accepting them, however, is not enough With obtaining this result since it is necessary to have information exchange with other areas of work of the business to identify if there are still important risks and to measure how effective the process and risk management has been, this stage is commonly known as Monitoring and Review Of the risks (ICONTEC, 2010).

Within the risk management framework, policies are high-level declarations of management's intention, expectations and direction. In order to achieve compliance it is necessary to plan the implementation of controls or countermeasures (indirect expenses for controls) And the organization must consider the costs and benefits of implementation. If the costs of specific controls or countermeasures exceed the mitigation benefits of a given risk, the organization may choose to accept the risk instead of incurring the mitigation cost, this is recommended by (ISO/IEC TR 13335-3:1998, 1998).

Factors that Impact Financially When Investing in Business Risk Management

When looking for a financial interpretation of investment in business risk management, it is necessary to have a clear definition of financial decisions to evaluate the business situation and according to (Scott Besley, 2009) focus on the Cash Flow that are the movement of input and output of cash resources of the company, the Balance Sheet which gives the business the financial situation in a certain date or period and the Income Statement which gives the utility or said in other words, "The profits of the business in a certain period". The financial analysis is based on financial reasons which seek to evaluate the profitability of the company or ability to obtain an additional profit or the gain obtained by a resource or by investments, the leverage whose objective is to use the debt for investments and to obtain profits, the Liquidity that is the company's ability to meet its obligations and commitments and also evaluates the performance of operational activities to measure the efficiency of the use of business resources (Polimeni, Fabozzi, & Adelberg, 2008). Every financial reason gives a result which is an indicator that measures financial health; some financial indicators published by (Cámara de Comercio de Medellín de Antioquia, 2016), are shown in the Appendix.

The Net Present Value that is also known as the net present value allows us to calculate the future flows and bring them to a present value. The purpose of this concept is to know if the business can produce gains or losses derived from an investment (William G. Sullivan, 2004).

METODOLOGY

The risk management analysis is based on a Datasec methodology (Datasec-MeycorKP, 2016), a company specialized in auditing and implementation of an ISMS. The steps to calculate the risks are as follows:

Stage 1: Initially defines the scope and limits of such analysis by identifying business processes. Scope is limited to business processes that are relevant and critical.

Example: Business processes are limited to internal operations following: "Purchasing process, customer service process, process financial transactions".

Stage 2: Information assets related to processes are identified, can be done by tabulating the assets in an excel sheet, grouping them by asset groups, indicating the name, a brief description of the asset as follows:

Stage 3: The impact is calculated.

A value of Confidentiality, Availability and Integrity is assigned in the column "Value" at its own discretion, for each asset, as follows:

Subsequently, the numeric average of Confidentiality, Availability and Integrity of the asset groups is extracted, for example, for the Physical Assets Group, the confidentiality is 2 for the Physical Asset "Wiring Rack Cabinet" and for the Physical Asset "Office Manager of technology support services "is 2, then the average of both assets will be of a value equal to 2:

Figure 1. Groups of assets and the value of its Impact

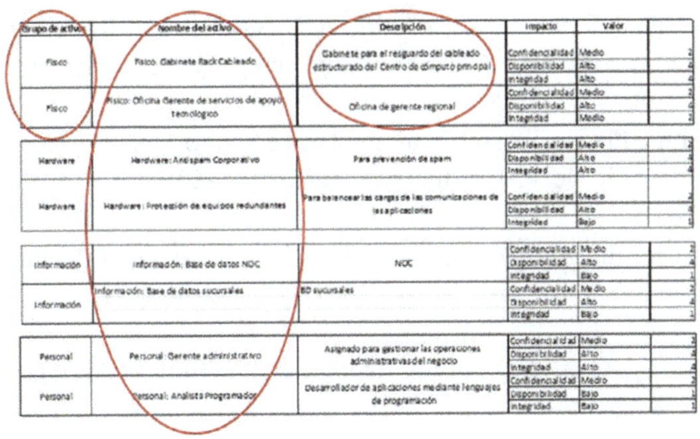

Grupo de activo	Nombre del activo	Descripción	Impacto	Valor	
Fisco	Fisico: Gabinete Rack Cableado	Gabinete para el resguardo del cableado estructurado del Centro de cómputo principal	Confidencialidad	Medio	2
			Disponibilidad	Alto	4
			Integridad	Alto	4
Fisco	Fisico: Oficina Gerente de servicios de apoyo tecnológico	Oficina de gerente regional	Confidencialidad	Medio	2
			Disponibilidad	Alto	4
			Integridad	Medio	2
Hardware	Hardware: Antispam Corporativo	Para prevención de spam	Confidencialidad	Medio	2
			Disponibilidad	Alto	4
			Integridad	Alto	4
Hardware	Hardware: Protección de equipos redundantes	Para balancear las cargas de las comunicaciones de las aplicaciones	Confidencialidad	Medio	2
			Disponibilidad	Alto	4
			Integridad	Bajo	1
Información	Información: Base de datos NOC	NOC	Confidencialidad	Medio	2
			Disponibilidad	Alto	4
			Integridad	Bajo	1
Información	Información: Base de datos sucursales	BD sucursales	Confidencialidad	Medio	2
			Disponibilidad	Alto	4
			Integridad	Bajo	1
Personal	Personal: Gerente administrativo	Asignado para gestionar las operaciones administrativas del negocio	Confidencialidad	Medio	2
			Disponibilidad	Alto	4
			Integridad	Alto	4
Personal	Personal: Analista Programador	Desarrollador de aplicaciones mediante lenguajes de programación	Confidencialidad	Medio	2
			Disponibilidad	Bajo	1
			Integridad	Bajo	1

Figure 2. Impact Criteria value

Grupo	Amenaza	Probabilidad	Vulnerabilidad	Exposición	Impacto	Riesgo	Nivel Riesgo
Información	Fuga de información.	Media	Alta	Alto	Alto	7	Mayor
Personal	Falta del Personal.	Alta	Media	Alto	Alto	7	Mayor
Personal	Desastre Natural	Media	Alta	Alto	Alto	7	Mayor
Físico	Falta del Personal.	Alta	Media	Alto	Medio-Alto	6	Importante
Físico	Acceso sin autorización.	Media	Alta	Alto	Medio-Alto	6	Importante
Información	Uso inadecuado de medios de almacenamiento de información	Media	Media	Medio	Alto	6	Importante
Información	Falta del Personal.	Alta	Media	Alto	Medio-Alto	6	Importante
Información	Modificación de información sin autorización	Alta	Media	Alto	Medio-Alto	6	Importante
Personal	Contaminación ambiental.	Media	Media	Medio	Alto	6	Importante
Personal	Comportamiento indebido y fuera de lugar de un funcionario.	Baja	Alta	Medio	Alto	6	Importante
Software	Copia no autorizada de información/software de la institución.	Alta	Media	Alto	Medio-Alto	6	Importante
Software	Ataque por código malicioso (Virus, Troyano, etc.).	Media	Alta	Alto	Medio-Alto	6	Importante
Software	Modificación sin autorización de servicios y/o sistemas	Media	Alta	Alto	Medio-Alto	6	Importante
Físico	Fuego (En instalaciones físicas)	Media	Alta	Alto	Medio	5	Significativo
Físico	Agua (inundación)	Alta	Media	Alto	Medio	5	Significativo
Físico	Falla del servicio eléctrico y aire acondicionado.	Media	Alta	Alto	Medio	5	Significativo
Físico	Desastre Natural	Media	Alta	Alto	Medio	5	Significativo
Hardware	Fuego (En la plataforma tecnológica)	Media	Alta	Alto	Medio	5	Significativo
Hardware	Cambios sin autorización en infraestructura de hardware	Media	Alta	Alto	Medio	5	Significativo
Hardware	Falla del servicio eléctrico y aire acondicionado.	Media	Alta	Alto	Medio	5	Significativo
Hardware	Desastre Natural	Media	Alta	Alto	Medio	5	Significativo
Hardware	Agua (inundación)	Alta	Media	Alto	Medio	5	Significativo
Hardware	Abuso de Funciones y Permisos.	Media	Alta	Alto	Medio	5	Significativo
Información	Acceso sin autorización a información interna de la institución.	Baja	Alta	Medio	Medio-Alto	5	Significativo
Información	Ataque por código malicioso (Virus, Troyano, etc.).	Media	Media	Medio	Medio-Alto	5	Significativo
Información	Comportamiento indebido y fuera de lugar de un funcionario.	Baja	Alta	Medio	Medio-Alto	5	Significativo
Información	Abuso de Funciones y Permisos	Media	Media	Medio	Medio-Alto	5	Significativo
Personal	Incumplimiento de leyes, contratos y reglamentación.	Baja	Media	Bajo	Alto	5	Significativo
Personal	Abuso de Funciones y Permisos.	Baja	Media	Bajo	Alto	5	Significativo
Personal	Dificultad para atender solicitudes de los colaboradores de la empresa.	Baja	Media	Bajo	Alto	5	Significativo
Software	Acceso sin autorización. (A sistemas y/o servicios que brinda TI)	Baja	Alta	Medio	Medio-Alto	5	Significativo
Software	Instalación de software no autorizado.	Baja	Alta	Medio	Medio-Alto	5	Significativo
Software	Impacto debido a mal funcionamiento del software.	Baja	Alta	Medio	Medio-Alto	5	Significativo
Físico	Falta de mantenimiento.	Baja	Alta	Medio	Medio	4	Poco Significativo
Hardware	Retiro no autorizado de hardware de las instalaciones	Baja	Alta	Medio	Medio	4	Poco Significativo
Hardware	Falta de mantenimiento.	Baja	Alta	Medio	Medio	4	Poco Significativo
Hardware	Acceso sin autorización.	Baja	Alta	Medio	Medio	4	Poco Significativo
Personal	Robo	Baja	Media	Bajo	Medio-Alto	4	Poco Significativo
Software	Robo (De software propiedad de la institución)	Baja	Media	Bajo	Medio	3	Menor

- The average of Confidentiality of Physical Assets is equal to (2 + 2) / 2 = 2.
- The same is done with Availability and Integrity for the group of Physical Assets:
- The average Physical Asset Availability is equal to (4 + 4) / 2 = 2.
- The average Physical Asset Integrity equals (4 + 2) / 2 = 3.

The impact for the group of physical assets is the average of the three previous results, that is,

Impact = (Average Confidentiality + Average Availability + Average Integrity) / 3

Figure 3. Average confidentiality of assets

Grupo	Amenaza	Riesgo	Nivel de Riesgo	Tratamiento del riesgo	Nueva Probabilidad	Nueva Vulnerabilidad	Nueva Exposición	Nuevo Impacto	Nuevo riesgo	Nuevo Nivel de Riesgo
Información	Fuga de información.	7	Mayor	Mitigar	Media	Alta	Alto	Medio-Alto	6	Importante
Personal	Falta del Personal	7	Mayor	Mitigar	Media	Media	Medio	Medio-Alto	5	Significativo
Información	Falta del Personal	6	Importante	Mitigar	Alta	Media	Alto	Medio	5	Significativo
Información	Modificación de información sin autorización	6	Importante	Mitigar	Media	Media	Medio	Medio-Alto	5	Significativo
Información	Uso inadecuado de medios de almacenamiento de información	6	Importante	Mitigar	Media	Media	Medio	Medio-Alto	5	Significativo
Software	Ataque por código malicioso (Virus, Troyano etc.).	6	Importante	Mitigar	Media	Alta	Alto	Medio	5	Significativo
Software	Modificación sin autorización de servicios y/o sistemas	6	Importante	Mitigar	Media	Alta	Alto	Medio	5	Significativo
Físico	Acceso sin autorización.	6	Importante	Mitigar	Media	Media	Medio	Medio	4	Poco Significativo
Físico	Falta del Personal.	6	Importante	Mitigar	Media	Media	Medio	Medio	4	Poco Significativo
Personal	Contaminación ambiental.	6	Importante	Mitigar	Media	Media	Medio	Medio	4	Poco Significativo
Software	Copia no autorizada de información/software de la institución	6	Importante	Mitigar	Media	Media	Medio	Medio	4	Poco Significativo
Hardware	Abuso de Funciones y Permisos.	5	Significativo	Mitigar	Baja	Alta	Medio	Medio	4	Poco Significativo
Hardware	Agua (Inundación)	5	Significativo	Mitigar	Media	Media	Medio	Medio	4	Poco Significativo
Hardware	Cambios sin autorización en infraestructura de hardware	5	Significativo	Mitigar	Baja	Alta	Medio	Medio	4	Poco Significativo
Hardware	Falla del servicio eléctrico y aire acondicionado.	5	Significativo	Mitigar	Baja	Alta	Medio	Medio	4	Poco Significativo
Hardware	Fuego (En la plataforma tecnológica)	5	Significativo	Mitigar	Baja	Alta	Medio	Medio	4	Poco Significativo
Información	Acceso sin autorización a información interna de la institución.	5	Significativo	Mitigar	Baja	Alta	Medio	Medio	4	Poco Significativo
Información	Ataque por código malicioso (Virus, Troyano etc.).	5	Significativo	Mitigar	Media	Media	Medio	Medio	4	Poco Significativo
Personal	Abuso de Funciones y Permisos.	5	Significativo	Mitigar	Baja	Media	Bajo	Medio-Alto	4	Poco Significativo
Personal	Dificultad para atender solicitudes de los colaboradores de la SIB.	5	Significativo	Mitigar	Baja	Media	Bajo	Medio-Alto	4	Poco Significativo
Software	Instalación de software no autorizado.	5	Significativo	Mitigar	Baja	Media	Bajo	Medio-Alto	4	Poco Significativo
Software	Acceso sin autorización. (A sistemas y/o servicios que brinda TI)	5	Significativo	Mitigar	Baja	Alta	Medio	Medio	4	Poco Significativo
Software	Impacto debido a mal funcionamiento del software.	5	Significativo	Mitigar	Baja	Media	Bajo	Medio-Alto	4	Poco Significativo
Hardware	Acceso sin autorización.	4	Poco Significat	Mitigar	Baja	Media	Bajo	Medio	3	Menor
Personal	Desastre Natural	7	Mayor	Aceptar	Media	Media	Medio	No aplica	0	NA
Personal	Comportamiento indebido y fuera de lugar de un funcionario.	6	Importante	Transferir	Media	Media	Medio	No aplica	0	NA
Físico	Agua (Inundación)	5	Significativo	Transferir	Media	Media	Medio	No aplica	0	NA
Físico	Desastre Natural	5	Significativo	Aceptar	Media	Media	Medio	No aplica	0	NA
Físico	Falla del servicio eléctrico y aire acondicionado.	5	Significativo	Transferir	Media	Media	Medio	No aplica	0	NA
Físico	Fuego (En instalaciones físicas)	5	Significativo	Transferir	Baja	Media	Bajo	No aplica	0	NA
Hardware	Desastre Natural	5	Significativo	Aceptar	Baja	Alta	Medio	No aplica	0	NA
Información	Abuso de Funciones y Permisos.	5	Significativo	Transferir	Media	Media	Medio	No aplica	0	NA
Información	Comportamiento indebido y fuera de lugar de un funcionario.	5	Significativo	Transferir	Media	Media	Medio	No aplica	0	NA
Personal	Incumplimiento de leyes, contratos y reglamentación.	5	Significativo	Transferir	Media	Media	Medio	No aplica	0	NA
Físico	Falta de mantenimiento.	4	Poco Significat	Transferir	Media	Media	Medio	No aplica	0	NA
Hardware	Falta de mantenimiento.	4	Poco Significat	Aceptar	Baja	Media	Bajo	No aplica	0	NA
Hardware	Retiro no autorizado de hardware de las instalaciones	4	Poco Significat	Aceptar	Baja	Media	Bajo	No aplica	0	NA
Personal	Robo	4	Poco Significat	Transferir	Baja	Media	Bajo	No aplica	0	NA
Software	Robo (De software propiedad de la institución)	3	Menor	Transferir	Media	Alta	Alto	No aplica	0	NA

where impact (of physical assets) = (2 + 2 + 3) / 3 = 2.3, approaching fall = 2. And so forth is the average Integrity and Availability for Physical assets. In the same way, this average is realized for the hardware, software, personnel and information assets.

Stage 4: Exposure calculation.

To calculate the exposure of the assets, the threats are identified and a value is assigned to the probability and vulnerability of these occurrences. An excel box is tabulated as follows:

Combining probability with vulnerability results in Exposure associated with each asset group. The values are taken according to Table 1.

Step 5: Risk value.

Figure 4. Threats by asset group, its impact, and risk exposure

POSICION DE LIQUIDEZ
ALGUNOS INDICADORES FINANCIEROS

INDICADOR	FORMULA	IDEAL
DIAS DE ROTACION CARTERA	CARTERA PROMEDIO/VENTAS NETAS A CREDITO*#DIAS	↓
DIAS DE ROTACION INVENTARIO	INVENTARIO PROMEDIO/COSTO VENTAS*#DIAS	↓
DIAS DE ROTACION PROVEEDORES	PROVEEDORES PROMEDIO/COMPRAS*#DIAS	↑
CICLO OPERATIVO	DIAS CARTERA+DIAS INVENTARIO - DIAS PROVEEDORES	↓
RAZON CORRIENTE	ACTIVOS CORRIENTES / PASIVOS CORRIENTES	↑
PRUEBA ACIDA	(ACTIVO CORRINTES - INVENTARIOS)/ PASIVO CORREINTE	↑
EFICIENCIA ACTIVO OPERATIVO	VENTAS NETAS/ACTIVO OPERATIVO PROMEDIO	↑

DESEMPEÑO OPERATIVO
ALGUNOS INDICADORES FINANCIEROS

INDICADOR	FORMULA	IDEAL
RENTABILIDAD PATRIMONIO	UAI/PATRIMONIO PROMEDIO*100	↑
RENTABILIDAD OPERATIVA	UAII/ACTIVOS OPERATIVOS PROMEDIO * 100	↑
MARGEN BRUTO	UTILIDAD BRUTA/VENTAS NETAS *100	↑
MARGEN OPERATIVO	UAII/VENTAS NETAS * 100	↑
MARGEN ANTES IMPUESTOS	UAI/VENTAS NETAS * 100	↑
MARGEN NETO	UTILIDAD NETA/VENTAS NETAS *100	↑
CARGA ADMINISTRATIVA	GASTOS DE ADMINISTRACIÓN/VENTAS NETAS * 100	↓
CARGA DE MERCADEO Y VENTAS	GASTOS DE MERCADEO Y VENTAS/VENTAS NETAS*100	↓
CARGA OPERATIVA	GASTOS OPERATIVOS/VENTAS NETAS * 100	↓

Source: (Cámara de Comercio de Medellín de Antioquia, 2016)

Table 1. Exposure values scale

Probability	Vulnerability	Exposition
high	high	Very high
high	Half	High
high	Low	Medium
Half	high	High
Half	Half	Medium
Half	Low	Low
Low	high	Medium
Low	Half	Low
Low	Low	Very low

Source: Software MeycorKP, (Datasec-MeycorKP, 2016).

The final risk value is obtained from the combination of Impact and Exposure. For example, for the threat defined in Figure 2, in the Physical Asset Group, the impact is "Medium-High" and the Exposure is "Medium", then the risk is = 5, meaning "Significant."

The risk values are based on the following table:

In this way, the risks are obtained for each Asset Group associated with each identified threat.

Stage 6: Treatment of risks and acceptance of residual risk.

Finally, a risk treatment is carried out, implementing controls that will have a cost, that cost will be reflected in the financial statements. Then, step 4 (Exposure Calculation) is performed again, which causes the probability or vulnerability to be reduced by the implementation of controls, thus remaining a residual risk. The criteria for accepting residual risks are: "The risk is accepted if the Exposure-Impact value is: Unimportant, Minor, Trivial, Negligible or Not applicable".

Interpretation of the Heat Map

Risks can be expressed in a heat map (see Figure 3), where the Exposure value is placed on the "X" axis and the Impact value is on the "Y" axis. However, more emphasis is placed on the risks that are in the border with red which have high Impact and Exposure, therefore, the threats associated with these assets or groups of

Table 2. Exposure-impact and value risk associated

<table>
<tr><th>Exposición</th><th>Impacto</th><th>Riesgo</th><th>Valor riesgo</th></tr>
<tr><td>No aplica</td><td>No aplica</td><td>No aplica</td><td>0</td></tr>
<tr><td>muy bajo</td><td>bajo</td><td>Insignificante</td><td>1</td></tr>
<tr><td>Bajo
muy bajo</td><td>bajo
medio</td><td>Trivial</td><td>2</td></tr>
<tr><td>medio
bajo
muy bajo</td><td>bajo
medio
medio-alto</td><td>Menor</td><td>3</td></tr>
<tr><td>alto
medio
bajo
muy bajo</td><td>bajo
medio
medio-alto
alto</td><td>Poco Significativo</td><td>4</td></tr>
<tr><td>muy alto
alto
medio
bajo</td><td>bajo
medio
medio-alto
alto</td><td>Significativo</td><td>5</td></tr>
<tr><td>muy alto
alto
medio</td><td>medio
medio-alto
alto</td><td>Importante</td><td>6</td></tr>
<tr><td>muy alto
alto</td><td>medio-alto
alto</td><td>Mayor</td><td>7</td></tr>
<tr><td>muy alto</td><td>alto</td><td>Catastrófico</td><td>8</td></tr>
</table>

Source: Software MeycorKP, (Datasec-MeycorKP, 2016).

assets could cause losses, so it is categorized as critical risks, High and important. Risks that are yellow border are risks that have a significant degree of Impact and Exposure, which can be treated and evaluated if it is feasible to implement controls for their treatment. The risks that are on the green border are insignificant, minor, trivial or insignificant risks from which top management can accept them. (See the Appendix).

FINANCIAL ANALYSIS

In this analysis the following premises are contemplated.

The financial statements (Income Statement, Balance Sheet, Cash Flow) of the business are analyzed in a period of 3 years, due to the fact that, when implementing controls, a period of execution must be considered, which is considered between 1 and 2 years depending on the amount of work involved in implementing the controls, as they can sometimes be projects to mitigate certain risks such as improvements in technological infrastructure that require several stages of implementation before the

Figure 5. Heat Map

RIESGO DE ENDEUDAMIENTO
ALGUNOS INDICADORES FINANCIEROS

INDICADOR	FORMULA	IDEAL
NIVEL ENDEUDAMIENTO	PASIVO TOTAL/ACTIVO TOTAL * 100	↓
CONCENTRACIÓN DEL PASIVO	PASIVO CORRIENTE/PASIVO TOTAL * 100	↓
SOLVENCIA FINANCIERA	ACTIVO TOTAL/PASIVO TOTAL	↑
ENDEUDAMIENTO FINANCIERO	DEUDA FINANCIERA TOTAL /VENTAS NETAS * 100%	↓
CARGA FINANCIERA	GASTOS FINANCIEROS/VENTAS NETAS * 100	↓
COBERTURA GASTOS FINANCIEROS	UAII/GASTOS FINANCIEROS	↑
APALANCAMIENTO FINANCIERO	DEUDA FINANCIERA TOTAL /PATRIMONIO	?
APALANCAMIENTO TOTAL	PASIVO TOTAL/PATRIMONIO	?

Source: (Cámara de Comercio de Medellín de Antioquia, 2016)

Table 3. Relevant premises

This business manages a unit margin between 30% and 40%.
Administrative expenses of 8%.
Debt to cover investment and development expenses is $ 875,250.00 for risk mitigation.
Inputs handle between 15 to 30 credit days.
Accounts receivable at 60 days.
It is estimated that in year 3 reinvestment for risk mitigation by $ 100,000.00
The company must maintain one month of inventory.
The tax rate is 25%.

production stage and testing of the project, However, monitoring of project execution is necessary. All these factors influence the estimated time to perform a financial analysis and its impact, of which 3 years is an acceptable value.

Interpretation of the Comparison of Financial Indicators

The values obtained from the liquidity ratios, profitability leverage and activity of the 3 years of the company to analyze, are averaged; The result is compared to the same financial ratios of a company listed on the stock exchange, a company with a similar market and capital is chosen so that the comparison is reasonable. The company that has been selected, ventures into the Italian Networks and Telecommunications technological market (MCK:IM_Bloomberg, 2016).

The comparative result of the financial ratios averaged over 3 years for the company to be analyzed with respect to the company (MCK:IM_Bloomberg, 2016) will be shown according to Figure 6. For the indicator called "Lighthouse", if the value is colored Green, this indicates that the company is in acceptable terms in an ideal range with respect to its competitor, the arrow with direction up or down will indicate that trend of the value is better; Likewise, if the "Lighthouse" is red, it indicates that the company needs improvement or that top management needs to make decisions to improve in certain aspects; For this, a more detailed study should be carried out, which excludes this research.

RESULTS AND DISCUSSION

The results of the Risk Analysis of the Business Information Security Management System are shown below in a matrix which reflects the high, medium and low risks. The Appendix of this document describes the details of the threats associated with the identified threats.

Residual risk is also shown after the implementation of the controls. At first glance the following heat map shows the risk reduction in which there is only one risk with Exposure = High and Impact = Medium-High, which gives an "Important" risk. But there was already a reduction of risks when investing and implementing controls to manage the risks identified initially.

- **Statement:** The financial statements of the company analyzed is shown below; In the first instance the income statement with a profit after tax of 18%, 17% and 17% for the three years respectively, also highlights the gross margin that the company must have to meet its sales targets of 40% 39%

Figure 6. Example of a comparative table of two companies with financial indicators

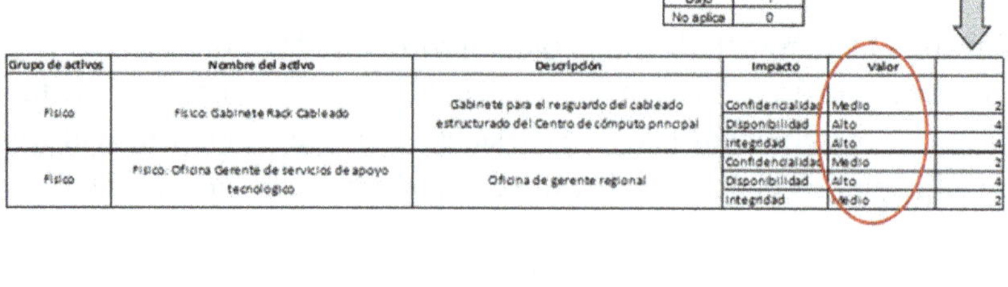

Figure 7. Risk Matrix

Source: Matrix Risk Analysis result using (Datasec-MeycorKP, 2016).

Average of confidentiality (two physical assets)

Grupo de activos	Nombre del activo	Descripción	Impacto	Valor	
Fisico	Fisico: Gabinete Rack Cableado	Gabinete para el resguardo del cableado estructurado del Centro de cómputo principal	Confidencialidad	Medio	2
			Disponibilidad	Alto	4
			Integridad	Alto	4
Fisico	Fisico: Oficina Gerente de servicios de apoyo tecnologico	Oficina de gerente regional	Confidencialidad	Medio	2
			Disponibilidad	Alto	4
			Integridad	Medio	2

Figure 8. Matrix of residual risk

Source: Result of Residual Risk using (Datasec-MeycorKP, 2016).

Amenazas	Descripción	Grupos de activos	Impacto	Impacto	Probabilidad	Vulnerabilidad	Exposición	Riesgo	Riesgo
Abuso de Funciones y Permisos.	Permisos sin autorización a falta de procedimiento s y politicas establecidas.	Físico	3	Medio-Alto	Alta	Baja	Medio	Significativo	5
		Hardware	3	Medio-Alto	Media	Alta	Alto	Importante	6
		Información	2	Medio	Baja	Media	Bajo	Menor	3
		Personal	3	Medio-Alto	Alta	Alta	Muy Alto	Mayor	7
		Software	2	Medio	Alta	Media	Alto	Significativo	5
		Terceras partes	3	Medio-Alto	Media	Media	Medio	Significativo	5
Acceso no autorizado a hardware	Acceso no autorizado a hardware a personal interno, subcontratistas, personas externas.	Físico	3	Medio-Alto	Media	Baja	Bajo	Poco Significativo	4
		Hardware	3	Medio-Alto	Baja	Alta	Medio	Significativo	5
		Información	2	Medio	Baja	Media	Bajo	Menor	3
		Personal	3	Medio-Alto	Baja	Baja	Muy Bajo	Menor	3
		Software	2	Medio	Media	Media	Medio	Poco Significativo	4
		Terceras partes	3	Medio-Alto	Alta	Media	Alto	Importante	6

and 39% for years 1 to 3 respectively; These aspects are important to have a consistent criterion of the profitability of the company.

On the balance sheet, the average liability / asset ratio over the three years was 26.12%, which is a good indicator of debt rationing, which gives a good margin of leverage for the company.

The cash flow during the three years was positive, as shown in Table 6, however during the first year is affected because it was the year in which debt is reflected, this confirms that when it is desired to mitigate risks associated with The Company will be affected cash flows.

This financial scheme aims to demonstrate that even with high capital, cash flows will always have a decrease since an investment or project to minimize the risks associated with information assets financially impact on extra expenses that the company disburses. However, it is an analysis in which it is necessary to have the financial indicators to evaluate until the margin limit of expenditure can be invested in adequate controls that to protect the information assets of the company.

Table 4. Statement of Income

INCOME STATEMENT			
	Año 2013	Año 2014	Año 2015
Income			
Revenue	**$ 38,203,709.83**	**$44,831,490.25**	**$ 49,591,818.34**
Cost	$ 22,922,171.45	$27,239,655.06	$ 30,153,186.49
Gross margin	**$ 15,281,538.38** **40%**	**$17,591,835.19** **39%**	**$ 19,438,631.85** **39%**
Expenses			
Operational expenses			
Expenses Sales	$ 1,146,111.29 3%	$ 1,344,944.71 3%	$ 1,487,754.55 3%
Administrative Expenses	$ 3,056,296.79	$ 3,586,519.22	$ 3,967,345.47
Interes paid	$ 28,445.63	$ 18,963.75	$ 9,481.88
Sales commissions	$ 1,910,185.49	$ 2,241,574.51	$ 2,479,590.92
Total expeditures	$ 6,141,039.23	$ 7,192,002.22	$ 7,944,172.84
Profit / Loss in Operation	$ 9,140,499.16 24%	$10,399,832.97 23%	$ 11,494,459.01 23%
ISR 25%	$ 2,285,124.79	$ 2,599,958.24	$ 2,873,614.75
Post-tax profits	$ 6,855,374.37 18%	$ 7,799,874.73 17%	$ 8,620,844.26 17%

The impact that can be observed derived from the investment that was made to mitigate the potential risks identified in the risk analysis causes that the cash flows are reduced, however by the profitability and solvency of the company, they do not have negative impact. Even so, it is necessary to take into account that all investment impacts on expenditure, therefore also impacts on net profit.

Profit after tax has yielded an acceptable profit, since investors can expect a profit percentage above 15%, which indicates that even with investment spending for risk mitigation, it will not represent financial losses.

The net present value, taking into account the initial investment expense $ 875,250.00 and the reinvestment of $ 100,000.00 in the third year whose destination was the implementation of controls to mitigate risks, gives an acceptable value, taking into account the cash flows originated for such investment. Since the NPV is> 0, then there is profit above the expected return.

Table 5. Balance Sheet

BALANCE SHEET	31/12/2013	31/12/2014	31/12/2015
Assets			
Current			
Cash and Banks	$ 2,744,774.13	$ 9,556,165.77	$ 17,633,361.47
Inventories	$ 1,910,180.95	$ 2,241,574.51	$ 2,479,590.92
Account receivable	$ 6,367,284.97	$ 7,471,915.04	$ 8,265,303.06
	$ 11,022,240.06	$ 19,269,655.32	$ 28,378,255.45
Noncurrent			
Machinery and equipment (controls)	$ 700,200.00	$ 525,150.00	$ 430,100.00
Total Assets	$ 11,722,440.06	$ 19,794,805.32	$ 28,808,355.45
Liabilities			
Circulating			
Loans Payable	$ 291,750.00	$ 145,875.00	$ -
Accounts payable	$ 1,802,565.87	$ 1,906,097.92	$ 2,171,022.25
Tax payable	$ 2,285,124.79	$ 2,599,958.24	$ 2,873,614.75
Total liabilities	$ 4,379,440.66	$ 4,651,931.17	$ 5,044,637.00
Capital			
Social capital	$ 50,000.00	$ 50,000.00	$ 50,000.00
Contributions	$ 437,625.00	$ 437,625.00	$ 437,625.00
Total Capital	$ 487,625.00	$ 487,625.00	$ 487,625.00
Acumulated utilities		$ 6,855,374.37	$ 14,655,249.10
Gains and Losses	$ 6,855,374.37	$ 7,799,874.73	$ 8,620,844.26
Heritage	$ 7,342,999.37	$ 8,287,499.73	$ 9,108,469.26
Total liabilities + Capital	$ 11,722,440.03	$ 19,794,805.26	$ 28,808,355.36

Table 6. Cash flow

Cashflow	2013	2014	2015
Income			
Sales	$ 33,856,096.77	$ 39,844,153.40	$ 44,217,128.30
Accounts Receivable Recovery		$ 6,771,219.35	$ 7,968,830.68
Total Income	$ 33,856,096.77	$ 46,615,372.75	$ 52,185,958.98
Expediture			
Cost	$ 24,430,139.61	$ 27,334,033.60	$ 30,163,883.57
Administrative Expenses	$ 3,250,185.29	$ 3,825,038.73	$ 4,244,844.32
Expenses Sales	$ 1,218,819.48	$ 1,434,389.52	$ 1,591,816.62
Sales Commissions	$ 2,031,365.81	$ 2,390,649.20	$ 2,653,027.70
Interest payment	$ 28,445.63	$ 18,963.75	$ 9,481.88
Loan payment	$ 145,875.00	$ 145,875.00	$ 145,875.00
Accounts payable payment		$ 1,802,565.87	$ 1,906,097.92
ISR payment previous year	$ -	$ 2,430,527.55	$ 2,772,011.18
Payment for reinvestments			$ 100,000.00
Total Expediture	$ 31,104,830.81	$ 39,382,043.23	$ 43,587,038.18
Balance of the year	$ 2,751,265.96	$ 7,233,329.52	$ 8,598,920.80
Initial capital or balance previous ye	$ 50,000.00	$ 2,801,265.96	$ 10,034,595.48
Final cash balance	$ 2,801,265.96	$ 10,034,595.48	$ 18,633,516.28

Table 7. Initial investment and annual cash flows

Initial investment (Risk mitigation)	Final cash balance		
	Year 1	Year 2	Year 3
$ -875,250.00	$ 2,801,265.96	$ 10,034,595.48	$ 18,633,516.28

Table 8. NOPAT (operating profit after taxes)

	Year 1	Year 2	Year 3
NOPAT	$ 6,855,374.37	$ 7,799,874.73	$ 8,620,844.26
NOPAT Margin	18%	17%	17%

Table 9. Net Present Value

NPV	$ 26,249,126.64

The result of the residual risk that is diminished in comparison with the original risks, is the product of a good managerial decision when dealing with the risks of the company taking into account its investment which is reflected in financial analysis.

CONCLUSION

Comparing the average financial indicators (Year 1, Year 2 and Year 3) of the company analyzed with the company MC Link SpA that enters the technological market of Networks and Telecommunications that is listed on the Italian stock Exchange (MCK:IM_Bloomberg, 2016) The following results were obtained:

In profitability, the company analyzed shows good results with a good profit margin obtained over cost of sales, therefore a satisfactory net operating margin compared to MC Link SpA; The company analyzed has a 39% operating margin on all of its production costs, which means that the overall execution cost is managed efficiently. The Return on Assets (ROA) is higher when compared to MC Link SpA. In conclusion, all the profitability indicators analyzed are greater than the Return of Equity (ROE). Your competitor, therefore the company can be attractive to investors in the first instance.

Figure 9. Financial Analysis

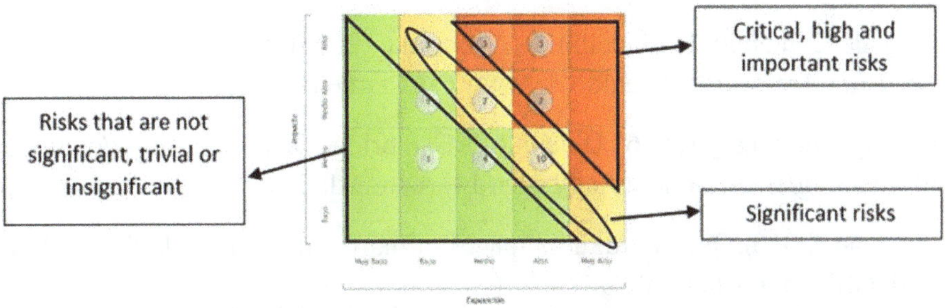

Source: Matrix Risk Analysis result using(Datasec-MeycorKP, 2016).

In the leverage indicators, one can conclude the following: When measuring the efficiency with which the company makes use of the resources, the following results were obtained: Financing with shareholders' equity (Assets/Equity) had a lower index in (MCK:IM_Bloomberg, 2016), the debt-to-equity ratio is acceptable, which means that the company's financing opportunities are not limited if required or for future projects that are viable. It should also be mentioned that debt on capital and on assets has adequate indexes since the company has indebtedness only for the implementation of the controls that mitigate the risks associated with its company.

The liquidity index is 4.09 on average for three years of the company analyzed, added to it is also an increase of Net Capital of $ 14,864,714.00, so it can be concluded that the company has the capacity to have cash to satisfy its current liabilities In the short term. It should be mentioned that MC Link SpA's capital is approximately $ 20 million, but its liquidity ratio is 0.56, which makes it an unreliable company in the face of any debt or liquidity contingency that arises in the face of any economic crisis.

In the activity analysis, inventory rotation has an index of about a quarter of the MC Link SpA indicator, however the accounts payable have a lower indicator (16.24), which would mean that the company had to pay in Less time to suppliers; This can be a disadvantage even for leverage and liquidity, at the same time, can be a good starting point and an opportunity for improvement to be taken into account by top management. The turnover of assets of the analyzed company is much lower, this indicator should also be improved, since there should be a more aggressive trend to increase this indicator, which would show a good increase in sales, innovation of new services and / or products, Employee training, process improvement, etc.

REFRENCES

Cámara de Comercio de Medellín de Antioquia. (2016). *Cámara de Comercio de Medellín de Antioquia*. Obtenido de www.camaramedellin.com.co

Cambridge Dictionary. (2016). Obtenido de Cambridge Dictionary: http://dictionary.cambridge.org/es/diccionario/ingles/hardware#translations

Damodaran. (2016). Obtenido de http://pages.stern.nyu.edu/~adamodar/New_Home_Page/datafile/totalbeta.html

Datasec-MeycorKP. (2016). Obtenido de Datasec.

Gerardo Guajardo Cantú, N. E. (2008). *Contabilidad financiera* (M. Hill, Ed.). México.

ICONTEC. (2010). *Compendio sistema de gestión de seguridad de la información (SGSI)*. Bogota, Colombia: Editorial Kimpress.

INCIBE. (2016). *Gestión de riesgos, una guía de aproximación para el empresario*. Obtenido de Instituto Nacional de Ciberseguridad: https://www.incibe.es/extfrontinteco/img/File/empresas/guias/Guia_gestion_riesgos/guiagestionriesgos.pdf

ISACA. (2013). *Manual de preparación al Examen CISM 2013*. Estados Unidos de América: ISACA. Recuperado el 20 de Septiembre de 2016, de http://www.isaca.org

ISO. IEC 27001:2013. (2013). Information technology - Security techniques - Information security management systems - Requeriments (2nd ed.). ISO.

ISO/IEC TR 13335-3:1998. (1998). *Information Technology. Guidelines for the Management of IT Security. Part 3: Techniques for the Management of IT Security*. ISO.

Junta Monetaria. (2011). Resolución JM-102-2011. Reglamento para la administración de riesgo tecnológico. Author.

MCK. IM Bloomberg. (2016). Obtenido de Bloomberg: http://www.bloomberg.com/quote/MCK:IM

MINFIN. (2016). Obtenido de Ministerio de Finanzas Públicas: http://www.minfin.gob.gt/index.php/comunicados-2014a/1839-22-fitch-ratings-asigna-calificacion-de-riesgo-crediticio

NASDAQ. (2016). *National Association of Securities Dealers Automated Quotation*. Obtenido de Mercado de Valores: http://www.nasdaq.com/

NTC5254. (2004). *Norma tecnica Colombiana, Gestión de Riesgos*. Bogotá, Colombia: ICONTEC.

Polimeni, R. S., Fabozzi, F. J., & Adelberg, A. H. (2008). Contabilidad de Costos (Conceptos y Aplicaciones para la Toma de Decisioens Gerenciales). McGraw-Hill.

Real Academia Española. (2016). *Diccionario de la lengua española* (E. D. Tricentenario, Ed.). Obtenido de RAE: www.rae.es

Scott Besley, E. F. (2009). Fundamentos de administración financiera. CENGAGE Learning.

UNISDR. (2009). *International Strategy for Disaster Reduction (UNISDR)*. Obtenido de UNISDR: http://www.unisdr.org/files/7817_UNISDRTerminologySpanish.pdf

William, G., & Sullivan, E. M. (2004). *Ingenieria Económica DeDegarmo* (D. Edición, Ed.). Pearson Prentice Hall.

10. Years US Treasury. (2016). Obtenido de Bloomberg: http://www.bloomberg.com/markets/rates-bonds/government-bonds/us

APPENDIX 1

Figure 10. Residual risk or remaining (Before reinvestment)

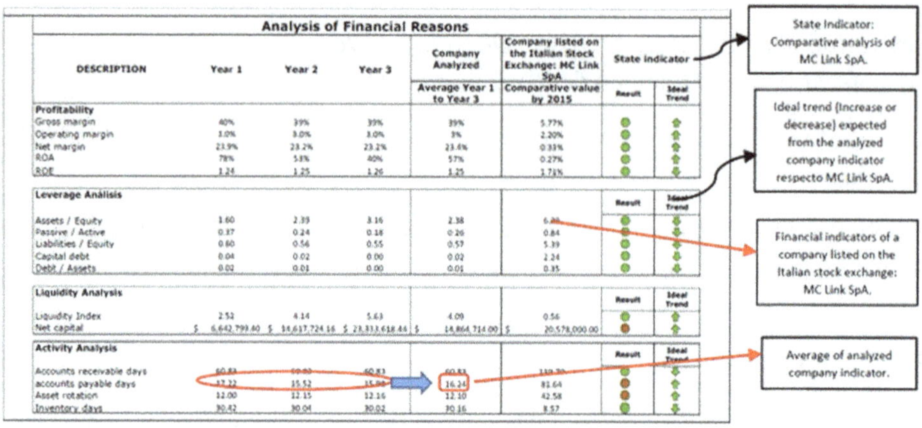

Analysis of Financial Reasons							
DESCRIPTION	Year 1	Year 2	Year 3	Company Analyzed	Company listed on the Italian Stock Exchange: MC Link SpA	State indicator	
				Average Year 1 to Year 3	Comparative value by 2015	Result	Ideal Trend
Profitability							
Gross margin	40%	39%	39%	39%	5.77%		
Operating margin	3.0%	3.0%	3.0%	3%	2.20%		
Net margin	23.9%	23.2%	23.2%	23.4%	0.33%		
ROA	78%	53%	40%	57%	0.27%		
ROE	1.24	1.25	1.26	1.25	1.71%		
Leverage Análisis						Result	Ideal Trend
Assets / Equity	1.60	2.39	3.16	2.38	[illegible]		
Passive / Active	0.37	0.24	0.18	0.26	0.84		
Liabilities / Equity	0.60	0.56	0.55	0.57	5.39		
Capital debt	0.04	0.02	0.00	0.02	2.24		
Debt / Assets	0.02	0.01	0.00	0.01	0.35		
Liquidity Analysis						Result	Ideal Trend
Liquidity Index	2.52	4.14	5.63	4.09	0.56		
Net capital	$ 6,642,799.40	$ 14,617,724.16	$ 23,333,618.44	$ 14,864,714.00	$ 20,578,000.00		
Activity Analysis						Result	Ideal Trend
Accounts receivable days	60.83	[illegible]	60.83	60.83	[illegible]		
accounts payable days	17.22	15.52	[illegible]	16.24	81.64		
Asset rotation	12.00	12.15	12.16	12.10	42.58		
Inventory days	30.42	30.04	30.02	30.16	8.57		

APPENDIX 2

Figure 11. Residual risk or remaining (After reinvestment)

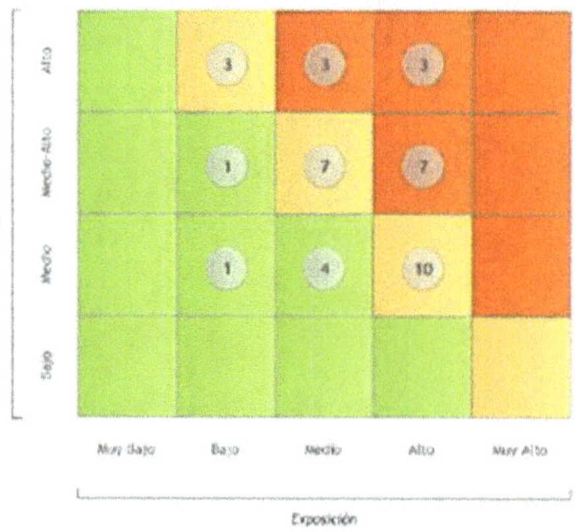

Source: Matrix Risk Analysis result using (Datasec-MeycorKP, 2016).

APPENDIX 3

Figure 12. Finance Ratios (Part 1)

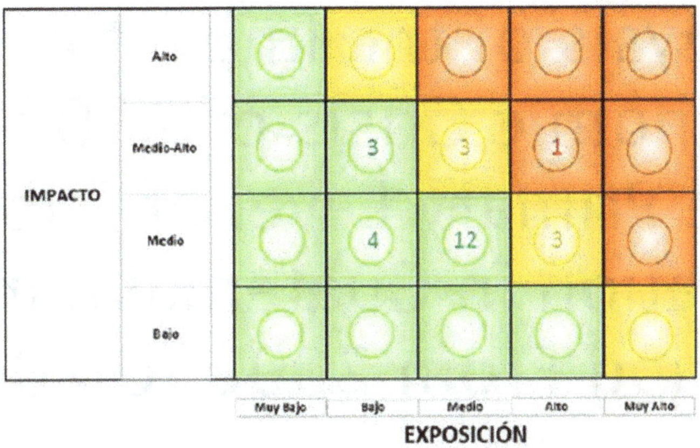

Source: Result of Residual Risk using (Datasec-MeycorKP, 2016).

APPENDIX 4

Figure 13. Finance Ratios (Part 2)

Analysis of Financial Reasons							
DESCRIPTION	Year 1	Year 2	Year 3	Company Analyzed	Company listed on the Italian Stock Exchange: MC Link SpA	State indicator	
				Average Year 1 to Year 3	Comparative value by 2015	Result	Ideal Trend
Profitability							
Gross margin	40%	39%	39%	39%	5.77%	● (green)	↑
Operating margin	3.0%	3.0%	3.0%	3%	2.20%	● (green)	↑
Net margin	23.9%	23.2%	23.2%	23.4%	0.33%	● (green)	↑
ROA	78%	53%	40%	57%	0.27%	● (green)	↑
ROE	1.24	1.25	1.26	1.25	1.71%	● (green)	↓
Leverage Análisis						Result	Ideal Trend
Assets / Equity	1.60	2.39	3.16	2.38	6.39	● (green)	↓
Passive / Active	0.37	0.24	0.18	0.26	0.84	● (green)	↓
Liabilities / Equity	0.60	0.56	0.55	0.57	5.39	● (green)	↓
Capital debt	0.04	0.02	0.00	0.02	2.24	● (green)	↓
Debt / Assets	0.02	0.01	0.00	0.01	0.35	● (green)	↓
Liquidity Analysis						Result	Ideal Trend
Liquidity Index	2.52	4.14	5.63	4.09	0.56	● (green)	↑
Net capital	$ 6,642,799.40	$ 14,617,724.16	$ 23,333,618.44	$ 14,864,714.00	$ 20,578,000.00	● (brown)	↑
Activity Analysis						Result	Ideal Trend
Accounts receivable days	60.83	60.83	60.83	60.83	139.70	● (green)	↓
accounts payable days	17.22	15.52	15.98	16.24	81.64	● (brown)	↑
Asset rotation	12.00	12.15	12.16	12.10	42.58	● (brown)	↑
Inventory days	30.42	30.04	30.02	30.16	8.57	● (green)	↓

Chapter 6
Analysis of the Impact of the Economic Crisis of 2008 on the Primary Level of Public Education in Guatemala, in the Period From 2002 to 2015

Sofía Jimena Roca
Universidad Del Valle de Guatemala, Guatemala

ABSTRACT

The objective of this chapter is the analysis of the primary education in Guatemala and if the amount of investment during the period 2002–2015 is significant for the number of children promoted by school year, and if these investments were impacted by the economic crisis of 2008. The results of the investigation demonstrate that the variables with significance where the number of teachers and the budget per year, without relation to economic growth and no impact by the economic crisis on 2008 and with no significant relation with the rate of drop out, which was an important result, especially in primary school. The data analyzed also show that the budget per year for the Ministry of Education doesn't suffer an impact after the economic crisis in 2008, where the author expected to find some problem after the crisis, but that the number of teachers hired in 2009 almost doubles the amount of teachers who were hired in 2008.

DOI: 10.4018/978-1-5225-4981-9.ch006

INTRODUCTION

The importance of primary education is due to "providing the foundations and building knowledge necessary to obtain later knowledge" (Arànega & Domènech, 2001). In Guatemala, primary education is mandatory and free of charge by law; the Ministry of Education (MINEDUC) is the responsable for it. The MINEDUC has a budget approved year by year by the Congress of the Republic, with which it must attend all the children and adolescents of school age.

The execution of this budget and investment in primary education and the results of such investment should be tangible in educational indicators, especially in the number of children finishing primary school; it is presumed that the greater growth of a country's economy increases the number of children ending the primary.

These indicators are analyzed through a linear regression to know if there is a relationship between investment and education, as well as an impact of the economic crisis on the year 2008.

LITERARY REVIEW

In Guatemala, free and mandatory primary education was instituted on January 2, of 1875 through the decree 130 that contained the Organic Law of Primary Public Instruction (González Orellana, 2007). This decree defined that: "Education shall not be limited to instruction, but will comprehend the development of all the faculties of the soul and the individual's physical activities "(González Orellana, 2007).

At present, the Constitution of the Republic (1985) indicates in Article 74 that "Habitants have the right and obligation to receive the initial, pre-primary, Primary and basic, within the age limits set by law. The education provided by The State is free. "So the primary education is 100% state responsibility by law. Then, what we understand by education? Education is a *process* 1 that have as target "modify *[to the human]* to complete it and optimize it, taking as reference an ideal model of person and society "(Luengo Navas, 2004). The importance of education focuses on the ability to change the humans and the direct impact on the formation of a society.

The entity in charge of designing, organizing and carrying out educational processes in Guatemala is the Ministry of Education (MINEDUC) and is based on the objectives defined in the National Curriculum Base (CNB). The CNB is the educational project of the Guatemala Government for the integral development of the human person, guatemalans and the plural nation (CNB). This is designed with for "Promoting a solid technical, scientific and humanistic formation as fundamental base for personal fulfillment, performance in productive work, the development of each person and national development" (Dirección de General de Gestión de Calidad Educativa).

The CNB indicates from the primary level that "It is expected that upon leaving the primary level, the students are able to communicate in two or more languages, use the thought logical, reflexive, critical and creative, in the construction of knowledge, technology and the arts and sciences of other cultures; contribute to the sustainable development of nature, societies and cultures of the country and the world; know about hygiene and individual and collective health, promote the improvement of the quality of life, act with security, freedom, accountability and honesty, to practice and promote values, democracy, culture of peace and respect for human rights. Also, that they respect, promote and value the art, culture and worldview of the Peoples. "(MINEDUC)

The CNB establishes its bases in competences, defined as "the capacity or disposition that has developed a person to face and solve problems of daily life and to generate new knowledge "(MINEDUC). Therefore, at the primary level, the childrens has to develop the competences of: mathematics, natural sciences and technology, social sciences, natural and social medium, artistic expression, physical education, citizen training and productivity and development.

But how are they evaluated? The evaluation in the CNB is defined through indicators of achievement that are the use of knowledge (MINEDUC); the evaluation will focus on observable evidence of student performance, demonstrating the development of skills. So "the evaluation made by a teacher about the performance of the group under their care may, in principle, be better than that through the application of evidence "(Martínez Rizo, 2004). Then, are the teachers the responsibles for assessing the development of competencies by students.

Teachers are a key player in the educational development of students. They are not only the ones who should evaluate their performance but the ones that have the tasks of guiding and facilitating the learning of competencies. In the profile of the graduate of the teaching profession, it is expected that: "(Teacher) Use methods to facilitate learning, grounded pedagogically, according to the needs, interests and expectations of the students and students "(González Orellana, 2007). The guide for the development of this learning is the CNB, which is divided by level, grade and areas of development.

MINEDUC is in charge of public education and executes it with budgets per year. Every year the Congress of the Republic approves a general budget of income of the State for the operation of the same the following year. From this budget of income is elaborated one of expenses in which are assigned amounts per institution and type of spending. The MINEDUC budget has increased by an average of 4.41% per year. The year in which the increase of the budget was greater was in 2009, in which the increase was of 18.85% in relation to 2008.

How to understand the increase of MINEDUC budget? One of the most important economic indicators, or the most important, because "it allows the measurement of the Economic evolution "(Banguat) is the Gross Domestic Product (GDP), which is responsible for measure the economic activity of a country. The Bank of Guatemala (BANGUAT) is the responsible for its calculation and performs it from three perspectives: production approach, the expense or income.

The current analysis uses the expenditure perspective of the GDP, as it reflects public expenditures carried out by the Government, in charge of public education. Under this approach GDP is defined as "final consumption expenditure plus gross fixed capital formation, plus the variation of stocks, plus exports, minus imports "(Banguat). This calculation makes an important division between the expenses of people and private institutions and expenditures by the general government. When analyzing the variation of the GDP is measured the economic growth of a country, so it can explain to us that a budget increase is linked to growth in a nation's economy.

It can be said, then, that education is important because of its transforming role of the human being and obligatory in Guatemala by law according to the Constitution of the Republic. That all children should be promoted if they have successfully competences described in the CNB; being the responsibility of teachers, in their role of facilitators, learning and improving them.

MINEDUC operates on a yearly basis and changes in the budget can be related to GDP as an indicator of economic growth country. The present work wants to determinate the influence of the variables described above with the number of children promoted; taking this indicator as a parameter of success in front of the school cycle and the time and money invested in the development of the same.

METHODOLOGY

The first step will be to calculate Pearson's correlation coefficient, defined by Seaber (1984) as a measure of similarity for quantitative variables. This coefficient is a numerical expression, between -1 and 1, indicating the ratio scale of two variables.

The coefficient (symbolized with the letter *r)* is calculated by dividing the sum of products of the deviations of each variant of X and Y, with respect to their means (sum that is denominated as covariance of X and Y), by the product of the standard deviations of both variables. This is expressed as follows, where N is the number of data.

$$r = \frac{N\sum_{i=1}^{N}(XY) - \left(\sum_{i=1}^{N}X\right)\left(\sum_{i=1}^{N}Y\right)}{\left[N\sum_{i=1}^{N}X^2 - \left(\sum_{i=1}^{N}X\right)^2\right]\left[N\sum_{i=1}^{N}Y^2 - \left(\sum_{i=1}^{N}Y\right)^2\right]}$$

The purpose of this analysis is to ensure that none of the variables to be used are in total dependence with any of the other variables analyzed. Based on the results obtained, the decision will be taken to maintain or not a variable in the model to be analyzed. The criterion to be used for the permanence of a variable will be the defined in Table 1.

Once the variables to be used have been delimited, the following methodology will be the Multiple regression analysis, whose objective is to construct a probabilistic model whose objective is to relates a dependent variable to more than one variable Independent (Devore, 2008).

The equation of the multiple regression model used is:

Y = b0 + b1x1 + b2x2 + ... + bnxn + e

where:

- Y is the variable to predict, the dependent variable.
- x1, x2, ... xn are the independent or explanatory variables of the variable Y.
- b0, b1, b2 ... bn are parameters that reflect the degree of influence of the variables independent of the dependent variable.
- e is the error that we make in the prediction of the parameters.

To perform the equation, we define the variables:

Table 1.

Value	Correlaction	Action
1 to 0.90	Positive high	Delete variable
0.89 to 0.35	Positive	Maintains variable
0.34 to 0	Low	Delete variable
0	Null	Delete variable
0 to -0.34	Low	Delete variable
-0.35 to -0.89	Negative	Maintains variable
-0.9 to -1	High Negative	Delete variable

1. Number of children promoted: total of children promoted of grade to the end of school year, according to the MINEDUC criteria.
2. Millions of quetzales executed: quantity of quetzales executed as part of programs for public primary education.
3. Number of teachers: number of teachers working at the primary level.
4. Rate of change in school drop-out: variation in the number of children drop out of school before September.
5. Rate of variation of GDP (calculated by destination of expenditure): change in the Gross Domestic Product obtained from the Banco de Guatemala database.

Then, the equation to analyze is:

Number of children promoted = b 0 + b 1 * Millions of quetzales executed + b 2 * Number Teachers + b 3 * variation rate dropout + b 4 * Rate of change of GDP + error

The multiple regression analysis will be performed through the eviews® software, where we will obtain the statistics of the model presented in Table 2.

In addition to the coefficient, a value called "t-statistic" is obtained for each variable. These statistical parameter will be used as a method of significance; the methods of significance accept or reject a null hypothesis, which allows to conclude about the variable analyzed. Statistic t is used as a method of significance in samples smaller tan 30 observations. The statistic t is calculated as follows where, x is the mean, mu is the value to be analyzed, S is the standard deviation and n is the size of the sample.

The first step in analyzing the significance of a variable is to define the hypotheses, which are defined as shown in Table 3.

Defined the hypotheses we continues to define the tcritical, for which we shall define the degrees of freedom, defined as n -1, where n is the number of observations.

Table 2.

Statistical	Interpretation
R squared *Statistic of the model*	It represents the percentage of variation of the variable Y that is explained by the model. It will be considered adequate if it is greater than 30%.
R squared adjusted *Statistic of the model*	It represents the percentage of Y that is explained by the model adjusted to the number of coefficients that it owns.
Coefficient *Statistical by variable*	It represents the degree of the influence of the independent variables on the dependent variable.

Table 3.

Hypothesis	Expression
Null hypothesis	Ho = b1 = 0
Alternative hypothesis	Ha = b1 ≠ 0

Once the degrees of freedom are obtained, the confidence interval must be determined. To apply the method: in this case, a 95% confidence interval apply a range of 99% because it is too accurate for the investigation or an interval of 90% since all the data will be obtained from official sources). The degrees of freedom and the confidence interval should refer to the *table t* (see Appendix 1) And find the corresponding interval.

If the t value is greater than the critical t value at the chosen significance level, the null hypothesis is rejected. Otherwise it can not be rejected (Gujarati & Porter). Variables that are rejected are removed from the model, one by one and the process is repeated for the obtaining statistics in Eviews®, and continues eliminating variables until the model has the adjusted R squared expected. The expected R squared adjusted is at least 0.4.

$$t = \frac{\bar{x} - \mu}{\frac{S}{\sqrt{n}}}$$

Once the model is defined, with an acceptable R squared and with the variables accepted within the significance test the model should be submitted to tests of multicolineality, heteroskedasticity and autocorrelation. These tests are performed to show if the model is adequate and complies with the assumptions that were assumed whe we wtart to develop and obtain the model. The assumptions that must being checked are shown in Table 4.

The multicollinearity test is analyzed through the inflation factor of the variance; calculated through the Eviews program. If this factor is less than 10 or equal to 1it means that there is no multicollinearity and the model is adequate to continue with its analysis. From not being appropriate factor it is necessary to eliminate variables of the model according to their t factor until that the factor is the right one.

The heteroskedasticity test is performed through White's analysis in Eviews. To the perform of this test the probability F must be greater than 0.05 so that there is no Heteroskedasticity and homocedasticity is present, which is correct, the variances of the different variables are equal.

Table 4.

Proof	Significance
Multicollinearity	Linear association between explanatory variables (x1, x2, x3, ... Xn)
Heterocedasticity	The disturbances ui that appear in the regression function are not homoscedastic; That is, they all have different variance.
Autocorrelation	Correlation between members of the series

When calculating the Linear Regression automatically Eviews calculates the Durbin coefficient Watson, which indicates whether or not autocorrelation exists. For this the table Durbin is consulted Watson (see Appendix 2). It looks for the amount of data analyzed and the amount of data variables, thus placing the upper and lower limits. Once the limits are determined, locate the Durbin Watson coefficient: if it is within the limits does not exist Autocorrelation, if it is located outside these if it exists. When there is autocorrelation it is necessary to correct it. If you need to do that calculate the Equation again through the Newey - West method and the coefficients found are suitable for use in the model.

ANALYSIS AND RESULTS

Derived from the analysis of the variables, the data were worked as two separate groups: clearly educational variables and economic variables. The first group focused on the teacher variables and dropout rate and in the second the variables of GDP and executed budget.

- Educational Variables (see Appendix 3)

Derived from the analysis of Pearson correlation coefficients the matrix of Coefficients was obteined (see Table 5).

From this, it is possible to define, based on the established criteria (see Table No. 1) that the two variables are maintained for the Multiple Regression analysis.

After decided the multiple regression model, the equation being obtained and adequate is:

Children promoted = 1358291 + 4.34 * teachers

Table 5.

	Promoted children	Primary level teachers	Drop rate
Promoted children	1		
Primary level teachers	0.703558375	1	
Drop rate	<0.534993976	<0.440884561	1

The final equation has an R ^ 2 of 0.49 and an adjusted R ^ 2 of 0.45. The elimination of variable abandonment rate was not expected since it was thought that the number of children who left school were significant against the number of children promoted annually.

The parameter 4.34 is the elasticity of the variable teachers with respect to promoted children, which means that an increase of one unit in the variable teachers modifies in 4.34 the number of children promoted. This shows that the greater number of teachers in the primary area, the greater the number of promoted children of the level will be obteined. If you want to increase the number of children promoted at the primary level, it is necessary to increase the number of teachers.

- Economic Variables (see Appendix 5)

Derived from the analysis of Pearson correlation coefficients the matrix of Coefficients was obteined (see Table 6).

From this, it is possible to define, based on the established criteria (see table No. 1) that the GDP variable has to be eliminated before continuing with Linear Regression.

After eliminate the variable, we performed the multiple regression model, as well as the (See Appendix No. 6), the equation being obtained and adequate:

Children promoted = 1399514 + 79.68 * budget

Table 6.

	Promoted children	Budget	GDP
Promoted children	1		
Budget	0.752052546	1	
GDP	:0.186931934	0.051159653	1

With an R ^ 2 of 0.56 and an adjusted R ^ 2 of 0.52. The elimination of the GDP variable was not expected since the economic growth of the country was thought to influence the number of children promoted. The 79.68 parameter is the elasticity of the variable teachers with respect to promoted children, which means that an increase of one unit in the budget variable (measured in millions of quetzales) modifies in 479.68 the number of children promoted. This shows that higher the budget executed in the primary area, the greater the number of children promoted of the level.

The results show that the number of children promoted depends on the quantity of teachers present at the level, as well as the amount of money executed in programs of primary education. It also demonstrates the null significant relationship of growth with the number of children promoted. The situation posed by the model does not allows us to conclude about the influence of the economic crisis on primary education as it presents us to the same as independent of the economic growth of the country; so same, there is no relation between the variables of budget and GDP leads us to see education as an independent activity of growth economic. No matter how much the country grows, the number of children promoted at the primary rate will continue to increase at an average annual rate of 1.97% if budget executed in primary level programs (representing an average of 40% of MINEDUC's total budget for 7 years).

CONCLUSION

The most significant finding within the investigation is to determine that the amount of children promoted at the primary level are unrelated to the economic growth of the country: the number of children promoted at the primary level of public education is maintained by over one million and a half since 2004, being in 2009 the year with more children promoted. The crisis has no effect on it.

It is possible to delimit that the number of teachers is significant for the number of children promoted, as well as the amount of money executed in primary education programs.

If it is desired to increase the number of children promoted from the primary it is necessary to increase the number of teachers available, as well as the amount of money executed in programs. It is not significant to increase the retention rate of children attending school (although a reduction in the abandonment rate must not be worked on), nor should it expected when the country is economically well children promoted at the primary level. Economic crises, such as the crisis of 2008, will affect the country but not primary education. If it continues receiving 40% of the budget of the and MINEDUC does not decline, stable growth in the promotion of primary school children in public education.

REFRENCES

Arànega, S., & Domènech, J. (2001). *Primary education: Challenges, dilemmas and proposals* (Vol. 160). Grao.

Banguat. (n.d.). Retrieved from System of National Accounts: Www.banguat.gob.gt/cuentasnac/TOMO_I.pdf

CNB. (n.d.). *The new curriculum.* Obtained from Http://cnbguatemala.org/index.php?title=El_nuevo_curr%C3%ADCornum

Devore, J. (2008). Probability and Statistics for Engineering and Sciences (7th Ed.). Cengage Learning.

General Management of Educational Quality Management. (n.d.). *National Curriculum Base.* Ministry of Education, Guatemala.

González Orellana, C. (2007). *History of education in Guatemala.* Editorial USAC.

Gujarati, D., & Porter, D. (n.d.). Econometrics (5th ed.). McGraw Hill.

Judicial Body. (n.d.). *Official statistics - Judicial Body.* Obtained from Http://www.oj.gob.gt/estadisticaj/files/population--total--by--municipal1.pdf

Luengo Navas, J. (2004). Education as an object of knowledge. He Concept of education. In M. d. Pozo Andrés, J. L. Álvarez Castillo, J. Luengo Navas, & E. Otero Urtza (Eds.), Theories and contemporary educational institutions. Madrid: Academic Press.

Martínez Rizo, F. (2004). Pass or fail? The meaning of the evaluation in basic education. *Mexican Journal of Educational Research, 9*(23), 817–839.

MINEDUC. (January 6, 2016). *Population exceeds 17.1 million.* Press Free.

Rosenthal, G. (2009). *The international economic crisis and its possible Consequences in Guatemala.* Academic Press.

Sánchez, M., & María, O. J. (1997). Education in multicultural society. *Papers, 53*, 139–148.

Spanish, R. A. (2001). *Dictionary of the Spanish Language* (22nd ed.). Retrieved from http://dle.rae.es/?id=UFbxsxz

APPENDIX 1

Figure 1.

Puntos de porcentaje de la distribución t

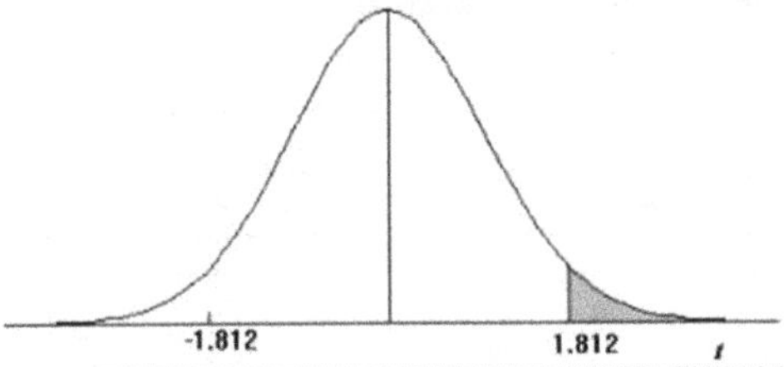

Ejemplo

Para ϕ = 10 grados de libertad:

P[t > 1.812] = 0.05
P[t < -1.812] = 0.05

r \ α	0,25	0,2	0,15	0,1	0,05	0,025	0,01	0,005	0,0005
1	1,000	1,376	1,963	3,078	6,314	12,706	31,821	63,656	636,578
2	0,816	1,061	1,386	1,886	2,920	4,303	6,965	9,925	31,600
3	0,765	0,978	1,250	1,638	2,353	3,182	4,541	5,841	12,924
4	0,741	0,941	1,190	1,533	2,132	2,776	3,747	4,604	8,610
5	0,727	0,920	1,156	1,476	2,015	2,571	3,365	4,032	6,869
6	0,718	0,906	1,134	1,440	1,943	2,447	3,143	3,707	5,959
7	0,711	0,896	1,119	1,415	1,895	2,365	2,998	3,499	5,408
8	0,706	0,889	1,108	1,397	1,860	2,306	2,896	3,355	5,041
9	0,703	0,883	1,100	1,383	1,833	2,262	2,821	3,250	4,781
10	0,700	0,879	1,093	1,372	1,812	2,228	2,764	3,169	4,587
11	0,697	0,876	1,088	1,363	1,796	2,201	2,718	3,106	4,437
12	0,695	0,873	1,083	1,356	1,782	2,179	2,681	3,055	4,318
13	0,694	0,870	1,079	1,350	1,771	2,160	2,650	3,012	4,221
14	0,692	0,868	1,076	1,345	1,761	2,145	2,624	2,977	4,140
15	0,691	0,866	1,074	1,341	1,753	2,131	2,602	2,947	4,073
16	0,690	0,865	1,071	1,337	1,746	2,120	2,583	2,921	4,015
17	0,689	0,863	1,069	1,333	1,740	2,110	2,567	2,898	3,965
18	0,688	0,862	1,067	1,330	1,734	2,101	2,552	2,878	3,922
19	0,688	0,861	1,066	1,328	1,729	2,093	2,539	2,861	3,883
20	0,687	0,860	1,064	1,325	1,725	2,086	2,528	2,845	3,850
21	0,686	0,859	1,063	1,323	1,721	2,080	2,518	2,831	3,819
22	0,686	0,858	1,061	1,321	1,717	2,074	2,508	2,819	3,792
23	0,685	0,858	1,060	1,319	1,714	2,069	2,500	2,807	3,768
24	0,685	0,857	1,059	1,318	1,711	2,064	2,492	2,797	3,745
25	0,684	0,856	1,058	1,316	1,708	2,060	2,485	2,787	3,725
26	0,684	0,856	1,058	1,315	1,706	2,056	2,479	2,779	3,707
27	0,684	0,855	1,057	1,314	1,703	2,052	2,473	2,771	3,689
28	0,683	0,855	1,056	1,313	1,701	2,048	2,467	2,763	3,674
29	0,683	0,854	1,055	1,311	1,699	2,045	2,462	2,756	3,660
30	0,683	0,854	1,055	1,310	1,697	2,042	2,457	2,750	3,646
40	0,681	0,851	1,050	1,303	1,684	2,021	2,423	2,704	3,551
60	0,679	0,848	1,045	1,296	1,671	2,000	2,390	2,660	3,460
120	0,677	0,845	1,041	1,289	1,658	1,980	2,358	2,617	3,373
∞	0,674	0,842	1,036	1,282	1,645	1,960	2,326	2,576	3,290

APPENDIX 2

Table 7.

Estadístico *d* de Durbin-Watson: puntos de significancia de d_L y d_U al nivel de significancia del 0.05

	$k'=1$		$k'=2$		$k'=3$		$k'=4$		$k'=5$		$k'=6$		$k'=7$		$k'=8$		$k'=9$		$k'=10$	
n	d_L	d_U	d_L	d_U	d_L	d_U	d_L	d_U	d_L	d_U	d_L	d_U	d_L	d_U	d_L	d_U	d_L	d_U	d_L	d_U
6	0.610	1.400	—	—	—	—	—	—	—	—	—	—	—	—	—	—	—	—	—	—
7	0.700	1.356	0.467	1.896	—	—	—	—	—	—	—	—	—	—	—	—	—	—	—	—
8	0.763	1.332	0.559	1.777	0.368	2.287	—	—	—	—	—	—	—	—	—	—	—	—	—	—
9	0.824	1.320	0.629	1.699	0.455	2.128	0.296	2.588	—	—	—	—	—	—	—	—	—	—	—	—
10	0.879	1.320	0.697	1.641	0.525	2.016	0.376	2.414	0.243	2.822	—	—	—	—	—	—	—	—	—	—
11	0.927	1.324	0.658	1.604	0.595	1.928	0.444	2.283	0.316	2.645	0.203	3.005	—	—	—	—	—	—	—	—
12	0.971	1.331	0.812	1.579	0.658	1.864	0.512	2.177	0.379	2.506	0.268	2.832	0.171	3.149	—	—	—	—	—	—
13	1.010	1.340	0.861	1.562	0.715	1.816	0.574	2.094	0.445	2.390	0.328	2.692	0.230	2.985	0.147	3.266	—	—	—	—
14	1.045	1.350	0.905	1.551	0.767	1.779	0.632	2.030	0.505	2.296	0.389	2.572	0.286	2.848	0.200	3.111	0.127	3.360	—	—
15	1.077	1.361	0.946	1.543	0.814	1.750	0.685	1.977	0.562	2.220	0.447	2.472	0.343	2.727	0.251	2.979	0.175	3.216	0.111	3.438
16	1.106	1.371	0.982	1.539	0.857	1.728	0.734	1.935	0.615	2.157	0.502	2.388	0.398	2.624	0.304	2.860	0.222	3.090	0.155	3.304
17	1.133	1.381	1.015	1.536	0.897	1.710	0.779	1.900	0.664	2.104	0.554	2.318	0.451	2.537	0.356	2.757	0.272	2.975	0.198	3.184
18	1.158	1.391	1.046	1.535	0.933	1.696	0.820	1.872	0.710	2.060	0.603	2.257	0.502	2.461	0.407	2.667	0.321	2.873	0.244	3.073
19	1.180	1.401	1.074	1.536	0.967	1.685	0.859	1.848	0.752	2.023	0.649	2.206	0.549	2.396	0.456	2.589	0.369	2.783	0.290	2.974
20	1.201	1.411	1.100	1.537	0.998	1.676	0.894	1.828	0.792	1.991	0.692	2.162	0.595	2.339	0.502	2.521	0.416	2.704	0.336	2.885
21	1.221	1.420	1.125	1.538	1.026	1.669	0.927	1.812	0.829	1.964	0.732	2.124	0.637	2.290	0.547	2.460	0.461	2.633	0.380	2.806
22	1.239	1.429	1.147	1.541	1.053	1.664	0.958	1.797	0.863	1.940	0.769	2.090	0.677	2.246	0.588	2.407	0.504	2.571	0.424	2.734
23	1.257	1.437	1.168	1.543	1.078	1.660	0.986	1.785	0.895	1.920	0.804	2.061	0.715	2.208	0.628	2.360	0.545	2.514	0.465	2.670
24	1.273	1.446	1.188	1.546	1.101	1.656	1.013	1.775	0.925	1.902	0.837	2.035	0.751	2.174	0.666	2.318	0.584	2.464	0.506	2.613
25	1.288	1.454	1.206	1.550	1.123	1.654	1.038	1.767	0.953	1.886	0.868	2.012	0.784	2.144	0.702	2.280	0.621	2.419	0.544	2.560
26	1.302	1.461	1.224	1.553	1.143	1.652	1.062	1.759	0.979	1.873	0.897	1.992	0.816	2.117	0.735	2.246	0.657	2.379	0.581	2.513
27	1.316	1.469	1.240	1.556	1.162	1.651	1.084	1.753	1.004	1.861	0.925	1.974	0.845	2.093	0.767	2.216	0.691	2.342	0.616	2.470
28	1.328	1.476	1.255	1.560	1.181	1.650	1.104	1.747	1.028	1.850	0.951	1.958	0.874	2.071	0.798	2.188	0.723	2.309	0.650	2.431
29	1.341	1.483	1.270	1.563	1.198	1.650	1.124	1.743	1.050	1.841	0.975	1.944	0.900	2.052	0.826	2.164	0.753	2.278	0.682	2.396
30	1.352	1.489	1.284	1.567	1.214	1.650	1.143	1.739	1.071	1.833	0.998	1.931	0.926	2.034	0.854	2.141	0.782	2.251	0.712	2.363
31	1.363	1.496	1.297	1.570	1.229	1.650	1.160	1.735	1.090	1.825	1.020	1.920	0.950	2.018	0.879	2.120	0.810	2.226	0.741	2.333
32	1.373	1.502	1.309	1.574	1.244	1.650	1.177	1.732	1.109	1.819	1.041	1.909	0.972	2.004	0.904	2.102	0.836	2.203	0.769	2.306
33	1.383	1.508	1.321	1.577	1.258	1.651	1.193	1.730	1.127	1.813	1.061	1.900	0.994	1.991	0.927	2.085	0.861	2.181	0.795	2.281
34	1.393	1.514	1.333	1.580	1.271	1.652	1.208	1.728	1.144	1.808	1.080	1.891	1.015	1.979	0.950	2.069	0.885	2.162	0.821	2.257
35	1.402	1.519	1.343	1.584	1.283	1.653	1.222	1.726	1.160	1.803	1.097	1.884	1.034	1.967	0.971	2.054	0.908	2.144	0.845	2.236
36	1.411	1.525	1.354	1.587	1.295	1.654	1.236	1.724	1.175	1.799	1.114	1.877	1.053	1.957	0.991	2.041	0.930	2.127	0.868	2.214

APPENDIX 3

Table 8.

Year	Promoted childrens	Primary level teachers	Drop rate
2002	1,370,101	55,151	0.082763239
2003	1,468,445	58,032	0.053685106
2004	1,546,901	61,547	0.074200722
2005	1,630,353	62,890	0.06560004
2006	1,660,665	64,606	0.060021697
2007	1,697,338	66,756	0.059309154
2008	1,787,844	70,982	0.061312082
2009	1,916,137	152,231	0.061377578
2010	1,874,837	84,759	0.062360429
2011	1,883,786	86,292	0.051865867
2012	1,827,018	90,858	0.054693329
2013	1,815,303	90,127	0.038929818
2014	1,784,535	90,116	0.039744353
2015	1,751,106	116,719	0.037107019

APPENDIX 4

Table 10.

Year	Promoted childrens	Budget	GDP
2002	1,370,101	2111.3	0.03866626
2003	1,468,445	2158.8	0.025307916
2004	1,546,901	2351.4	0.031520817
2005	1,630,353	2975	0.032601122
2006	1,660,665	3391.2	0.053797768
2007	1,697,338	3580.1	0.063040537
2008	1,787,844	3730.3	0.032810798
2009	1,916,137	4433.4	0.00526043
2010	1,874,837	4937.9	0.028694877
2011	1,883,786	5633	0.041620489
2012	1,827,018	5941.4	0.029698574
2013	1,815,303	5870.7	0.036975856
2014	1,784,535	6612.3	0.041741691
2015	1,751,106	7106.5	0.041487845

APPENDIX 5

Table 9.

Significance	Test	Result	Action
Multicollinearity	Variance inflation factor	1	Adequate
Heterocedasticity	White Test	0.5912	Adequate
Autocorrelation	Durbin - Watson	0.85	Not suitable, required calculation through Newey -

APPENDIX 6

Table 11.

Significance	Test	Result	Action
Multicollinearity	Variance inflation factor	1	Adequate
Heterocedasticity	White Test	0.7831	Adequate
Autocorrelation	Durbin - Watson	1.16	Adequate

Chapter 7
Telecommunications' Impact on Latin America's Economy:
A Close Up of Guatemala

Celso F. Cerezo
Universidad del Valle de Guatemala, Guatemala

ABSTRACT

The present chapter analyzes the importance of telecommunications and its economic effects by identifying the relation between the amount of telephone lines, both fixed and mobile, and the economy of Latin America as a region since year 1975 to 2015. The relation is demonstrated using a linear regression model. The case of Guatemala is analyzed in more in detail, where telecommunications have developed at an important pace since the privatization of the former public telco operator along crucial regulatory reforms.

INTRODUCTION

Since the invention of the telegraph in 1836 by Samuel Morse and the invention of the telephone, the world entered a new era. But it was until the 1970´s when most Latin American countries introduced fixed lines into their infrastructures. As Gutierrez (2002) stated almost two decades ago, "the transformation of telecommunications markets is occurring at a rapid pace around the world, with new technological developments, changing market structures, privatization of former public telecom operators (PTOs) in developing countries, convergence of services, and globalization of telephone operators along with the world economy". Nowadays this statement still holds true as markets are very dynamic and technology seems not to stop or even decelerate its development.

DOI: 10.4018/978-1-5225-4981-9.ch007

Even though the transition from state-owned telco operators into private and multinational operators had some difficulties in Latin America, the effect of PTO privatizations along the regulation reforms in each country, were crucial for the opening and development of the telecommunications markets in the region (Gutiérrez, 2002).

This advances in technology had its implications not only in the social area but also in the economies of the Latin American countries. This study analyses the relationship between teledensity and GDP per capita in Latin America, since the introduction of fixed copper lines in the region to year 2015. The study offers a close up into Guatemala where the industry is very busy and dynamic.

Brief History of the Telephone

The optic telegraph is considered to be the ancestor of the telephone (Huurdeman, 2003). On March 7th 1876, the U.S. Patent Office issued to Alexander Graham Bell, a young inventor, a patent named "improvements in telegraphy", which demonstrated the basic principles involved in a telephone. On the same day, Elisha Gray filed a caveat (preliminary patent document) for a similar instrument. This coincidence ignited one of the many debates around Bell´s questioned invention. Johann Phillipp Reis developed a version of the artifact in the early 1860´s, but his claim was defeated in court by Bell´s lawyers (Coe, 2006).

Also in 1871 Antonio Meucci, Italian engineer, also filed a caveat for his design of a "talking telegraph". For economical reasons, Meucci could not renew his caveat. Later he started a long legal battle. The United States House of Representatives passed a Resolution on June 11, 2002, honoring the work of Meucci.

By the end of 2014 the fixed and mobile telecommunications industry sector was very important generating around US$1.5 trillion of revenue. There are over seven billion mobile users and over 650 million fixed lines (Vodafone, 2014).

Table 1. Worldwide distribution of telephony at the end of the 19th *century*

Year	US	Europe	Rest of world	Total
1880	47.900	1.900	-	49.800
1885	147.700	58.000	11.800	217.500
1890	227.000	177.000	31.500	435.500
1900	1.355.000	800.000	100.000	2.255.000

Source: Coe, 1995.

Socio-Economic Benefits of Telecommunications in Latin America

The telecommunications industry generates significant economic and social benefits in Latin America. It affects the supply side of the economy, creates employment, increases productivity, and addresses intangible benefits to consumers. According to Deloitte, in 2011 the mobile phone industry contributed with US$27.7 billion to the nine countries of the region.[1] If we are to consider the wider economy the contribution is of US$84 billion. And if we are to consider as well the increase in productivity, as a spill-over effect in the wider economy, the total economic contribution boosts up to US$177 billion. In the same year, mobile operators hired 107 employees directly and 890,000 jobs were created indirectly (Deloitte, 2012).

Latin America: Previous Lessons From Privatization and Regulatory Reforms

Even though the 1980´s was not a promissory decade for telecommunications in Latin America (Jamison & Berg, 2000), the decades that followed the regulatory reforms as well as the privatization of PTO´s were much prosperous in terms of teledensity and economic growth. Gutierrez and Berg tracked these effects. Table 2 shows some results.

This table gives valuable information about the telecommunications industry in Latin America for the period 1986 to 1997. It seems clear how teledensity notably increased on both cellular and main lines. In cellular the ratio went from 0.01 to 1.14 lines per 100 inhabitants and in main lines from 6.2 to 11.4 inhabitants. This

Table 2. Economic and Demographic Indicators for Latin America

Indicators (Number of Countries in Parentheses)	1986-1990	1991-1995	1996-1997
GDP per capita (US$1995) (24)	2,493	2,662	2,858
Annual growh rate GDP per capita	1.25	1.65	3.46
Structural Policy Index (20)	0.425	0.581	NA
General Reform Index (17)	0.614	0.788	NA
Telecommunications Indicators			
Telecommunications Regulatory	0.29	0.43	0.75
Cellular subscribers per 100	0.01	0.31	1.14
Main lines per 100 inhabitants (24)	6.2	8.9	11.4

Source: Gutiérrez 2002.

is related to the increase of macroeconomic indicators. Annual growth rate GDP per capita increased from 1.25 (1986-1990) to 3.5 (1996-1997).

Data Analysis

The information used for this study was obtained from the World Bank. The 30 countries that conform the Latin America an the Caribbean region are: Antigua and Barbuda, Argentina, Belize, Bolivia, Brazil, Chile, Colombia, Costa Rica, Dominica, Dominican Republic, Ecuador, El Salvador, Grenada, Guatemala, Guyana, Haiti, Honduras, Jamaica, Mexico, Nicaragua, Panama, Paraguay, Peru, St. Kitts and Nevis, St. Vincent and the Grenadines, St. Lucia, Suriname, Trinidad and Tobago, Uruguay and Venezuela. They differ not only in land extension but also in cultural, political, economical and social factors.

The variables analyzed are gross domestic product per capita (GDP per capita) in 2010 prices as dependent variable and teledensity as independent or explanatory variable. For teledensity it was considered fixed or main lines and cellular or mobile lines per 100 inhabitants. A list of variables and it´s description:

Variable Description:

- GDPPC2010 Gross Domestic Product per capita in 2010 prices.
- CELL100P Cellular (mobile) lines per 100 inhabitants.
- FIXLIN100P Fixed (main) lines per 100 inhabitants.
- TOTLIN100P Total phones lines (cellular and fixed) per 100 inhabitants

When the information was plotted (teledensity vs GDPPC2010) a linear tendency was identified, so the model picked was a simple linear regression between the two variables with a confidence level of 95%. The simple regression model used is: $Y_i = a_0 + b_{0X}i + \in i$.

Catching Up: Economic and Demographic Analysis in Latin America From 1975 to 2015

One of the added values of this paper is to keep track on what happened after the decade of privatizations and forward. In this chapter we tracked and analyzed the GDP per capita and total teledensity (cellular and fixed phone lines) since 1975 (when main lines were introduced) to year 2015. Table 3 shows the GDP per capita (as prices of 2010) and total phones lines for the period. Information was retrieved form the World Bank database.

Previous data analyses have been made by other researches such as Ros (1999) and Gutiérrez (2002 and 2003). In this work the data analyses selected was a

Table 3. GDPPC (prices 2010) and TOTAL LINES PER 100 inhabitants for Latin America

YEAR	1975	1976	1977	1978	1979	1980	1981	1982	1983	1984	1985	1986	1987	1988
GDPPC2010	5813,085	6029,654	6178,932	6274,552	6538,345	6793,851	6666,243	6470,358	6159,930	6268,651	6360,714	6518,680	6611,467	6544,853
TOTLIN100p	2,824	2,976	3,233	3,530	3,767	4,015	4,162	4,407	4,536	4,808	5,065	5,218	5,419	5,663

YEAR	1989	1990	1991	1992	1993	1994	1995	1996	1997	1998	1999	2000	2001	2002
GDPPC2010	6509,714	6420,488	6537,080	6603,788	6741,641	6928,389	6927,134	7042,741	7285,116	7327,208	7220,703	7387,343	7353,906	7282,729
TOTLIN100p	5,868	6,248	6,671	7,297	7,910	8,871	9,801	11,146	13,273	15,839	20,677	26,668	31,918	35,185

YEAR	2003	2004	2005	2006	2007	2008	2009	2010	2011	2012	2013	2014	2015
GDPPC2010	7302,571	7660,305	7902,885	8223,520	8583,636	8815,745	8556,682	8943,098	9226,970	9377,880	9530,872	9513,683	9398,111
TOTLIN100p	39,849	48,729	60,506	71,505	84,350	97,571	105,548	114,315	122,880	127,544	132,969	131,900	128,082

Source: Elaborated by author with information from World Bank database.

linear regression, as it is intuitive to believe in a direct relationship between the variables. Figure 1 exhibits the results of the linear regression. The linear regression demonstrates the direct correlation between variables, teledensity and GDP per capita (2010 prices) as explained by an R Square value of 0.9549 (very close to 1). This is because telecommunications not only improve the efficiency of mostly all productive sectors, but also because of all the people it employs and goods consumed directly and indirectly.

A Close Up Into Guatemala

In this chapter we analyze the telecommunications development and impact in Guatemala. The former PTO GUATEL (now TELGUA) was founded in 1966. The first technology to be used was copper fixed lines, which were distributed in the main cities. Table 4 shows the teledensity for main lines since 1975 to 2015 as well as the development of the GDPPC (prices 2010). A linear regression analysis gave as a result an R square of 0.822 with 95% of confidence level.

The first cellular operator was COMCEL, which started operations in 1989. Since then, mobile phones subscribers have grown at a rapid pace. TELGUA, the former PTO introduced its mobile phone brand PCS Digital (now Claro) in 1997, followed by Bellsouth and Telefonica, both in year 2000. On 2015 the teledensity of mobile phones subscribers ended in 111.48 phones per 100 inhabitants. Table 5 shows the teledensity (cellular lines per 100 inhabitants) and its relation with GDP per capita (prices 2010). Same linear regression was applied and R squared resulted in 0.784.

Table 7 shows total density, which is the sum of mobile lines and fixed lines per 100 inhabitants. It is very interesting how total teledensity started in 0.768 in 1975 and increased to 122.055 at the end of 2015. A new linear regression was applied resulting on an R square of 0.747 with a confidence level of 95%, which is 0.207 less that R square for Latin America. See Figure 2.

Table 4. Linear regression – Teledensity vs GDP per capita in Latin America

TOTLINE vs GDPPCAP2010 Latam					
Period: 1975 - 2015					
Regression Statistics					
Multiple R	0.9772				
R Square	0.9549				
Adjusted R Square	0.9537				
Standard Error	232.7749				
Observations	41				
ANOVA					
	df	*SS*	*MS*	*F*	*Significance F*
Regression	1	43606299.1697	43606299.1697	804.7794	0.0000
Residual	38	2058998.1678	54184.1623		
Total	39	45665297.3375			
	Coefficients	*Standard Error*	*t Stat*	*P-value*	*Lower 95%*
Intercept	6471.3038	48.1156	134.4950	0.0000	6373.8990
2.82	22.9868	0.8103	28.3686	0.0000	21.3465
Upper 95%	*Lower 95%*	*Upper 95%*			
6568.7087	6373.8990	6568.70869			
24.6272	21.3465	24.62718			

Source: Elaborated by author with information from World Bank database. GDP per capita prices as of year2010.

Table 5. GDPPC (prices 2010) and MAIN LINES PER 100 inhabitants in Guatemala (1975-2015)

YEAR	1975	1976	1977	1978	1979	1980	1981	1982	1983	1984	1985	1986	1987	1988
GDPPC2010	2145,336	2246,045	2361,923	2419,715	2472,354	2502,862	2457,302	2312,234	2197,457	2154,713	2090,341	2044,079	2067,399	2098,448
FIXLIN100p	0,768	0,831	0,991	1,113	1,151	1,185	1,234	1,341	1,407	1,515	1,618	1,615	1,599	1,628

YEAR	1989	1990	1991	1992	1993	1994	1995	1996	1997	1998	1999	2000	2001	2002
GDPPC2010	2131,079	2146,595	2173,630	2225,921	2259,767	2296,931	2355,894	2371,312	2420,027	2484,760	2522,861	2554,782	2554,259	2591,329
FIXLIN100p	1,828	2,140	2,222	2,302	2,424	2,512	2,868	3,309	4,112	4,836	5,581	6,039	6,587	7,190

YEAR	2003	2004	2005	2006	2007	2008	2009	2010	2011	2012	2013	2014	2015
GDPPC2010	2594,926	2614,713	2638,290	2717,763	2825,138	2854,072	2806,980	2825,524	2880,415	2903,398	2947,972	3007,900	3069,044
FIXLIN100p	7,827	9,154	9,844	10,426	10,615	10,616	10,102	10,449	11,059	11,562	12,044	10,834	10,574

Source: Elaborated by author with information from World Bank database.

Table 6. GDPPC (prices 2010) and CELLULAR LINES PER 100 inhabitants in Guatemala (1990-2015)

YEAR	1990	1991	1992	1993	1994	1995	1996	1997	1998	1999	2000	2001	2002
GDPPC2010	2146,595	2173,630	2225,921	2259,767	2296,931	2355,894	2371,312	2420,027	2484,760	2522,861	2554,782	2554,259	2591,329
CELL100p	0,003	0,013	0,023	0,031	0,107	0,300	0,425	0,614	1,042	3,087	7,647	9,987	13,404

YEAR	2003	2004	2005	2006	2007	2008	2009	2010	2011	2012	2013	2014	2015
GDPPC2010	2594,926	2614,71	2638,29	2717,76	2825,14	2854,07	2806,98	2825,52	2880,41	2903,4	2947,97	3007,9	3069,04
CELL100p	16,868	25,617	35,5714	55,2408	89,3349	109,527	123,722	125,983	132,452	137,819	140,394	106,634	111,481

Source: Elaborated by author with information from World Bank database.

Table 7. GDPPC (prices 2010) and TOTAL LINES PER 100 in Guatemala (1975 – 2015)

YEAR	1975	1976	1977	1978	1979	1980	1981	1982	1983	1984	1985	1986	1987	1988
GDPPC2010	2145,336	2246,045	2361,923	2419,715	2472,354	2502,862	2457,302	2312,234	2197,457	2154,713	2090,341	2044,079	2067,399	2098,448
TOTLIN100p	0,768	0,831	0,991	1,113	1,151	1,185	1,234	1,341	1,407	1,515	1,618	1,615	1,599	1,628

YEAR	1989	1990	1991	1992	1993	1994	1995	1996	1997	1998	1999	2000	2001	2002
GDPPC2010	2131,079	2146,595	2173,630	2225,921	2259,767	2296,931	2355,894	2371,312	2420,027	2484,760	2522,861	2554,782	2554,259	2591,329
TOTLIN100p	1,828	2,143	2,236	2,325	2,456	2,619	3,169	3,734	4,727	5,878	8,669	13,687	16,574	20,594

YEAR	2003	2004	2005	2006	2007	2008	2009	2010	2011	2012	2013	2014	2015
GDPPC2010	2594,926	2614,713	2638,290	2717,763	2825,138	2854,072	2806,980	2825,524	2880,415	2903,398	2947,972	3007,900	3069,044
TOTLIN100p	24,695	34,771	45,416	65,667	99,950	120,143	133,824	136,433	143,510	149,381	152,438	117,468	122,056

Source: Elaborated by author with information from World Bank database.

Figure 1. Evolution of Teledensity in Guatemala (1975-2015)
Source: Elaborated by author with information from World Bank database.

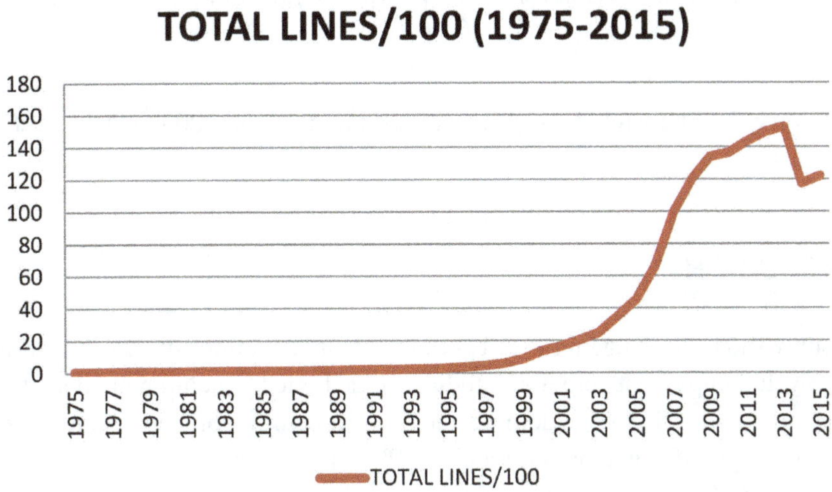

Table 8. Linear regression – Teledensity vs GDP per capita in Guatemala

TOTLINE100 vs GDPPC2010					
Period: 1975 - 2015					
Regression Statistics					
Multiple R	0,8645				
R Square	0,7473				
Adjusted R Square	0,7408				
Standard Error	147,6812				
Observations	41				
ANOVA					
	df	*SS*	*MS*	*F*	*Significance F*
Regression	1	2515626,3314	2515626,3314	115,3442	0,0000
Residual	39	850579,7590	21809,7374		
Total	40	3366206,0904			
	Coefficients	*Standard Error*	*t Stat*	*P-value*	*Lower 95%*
Intercept	2304,8326	27,8165	82,8584	0,0000	2248,5684
X	4,7081	0,4384	10,7398	0,0000	3,8214
Upper 95%	*Lower 95%*	*Upper 95%*			
2361,0969	2248,5684	2361,09686			
5,5948	3,8214	5,59476			

Source: Elaborated by author with information from World Bank database. GDP per capita prices as of year 2010.

It is very clear how teledensity accelerated rapidly from 2003 to 2013 as shown in Graph 1.

CONCLUSION

This study shows once again the effect of telecommunications on Latin America´s economy. It compliments previous studies on the topic by including and analyzing the past to decades. It´s been demonstrated the direct relation between teledensity (phone lines per 100 inhabitants) and GDPPC in 2010 prices in Latin America. The findings of other researches, about a strong correlation between teledensity and GDP, still hold true for nowadays.

Guatemala was analyzed in scope. The effect of teledensity over Guatemala´s GDP per capita was also demonstrated.

REFERENCES

Bastos, P. (1999). *The Political eEconomy of Latin American Telecommunications: Multinational Agreements and National Regulatory Systems*. Universidad do Rio de Janeiro.

Bortolotti, B., DSousa, J., Fantini, M., & Megginson, W. (2002). Privatization and the Sources of Performance Improvement in the Global Telecommunications Industry. *Telecommunications Policy*, *26*(5-6), 243–268. doi:10.1016/S0308-5961(02)00013-7

Coe, L. (1995). *The telephone and its several inventors*. McFarland & Company, Inc., Publishers.

Gensollen, M. & Laubie, A. (1995). *The role of telecommunications in economic development*. Academic Press.

GSMA. (2012). *Mobile telephony and taxation impact in Latin America*. GSMA.

Gutiérrez, L. (2002). *Regulatory Governance in the Latin American Telecommunications Sector*. Universidad del Rosario.

Gutiérrez, L. (2003). The Effect of Endogenous Regulation on Telecommunications Expansion and Efficiency in Latin America. *Journal of Regulatory Economics*, *23*(3), 257–286. doi:10.1023/A:1023412226826

Gutiérrez, L., & Berg, S. (2000). *Telecommunications Liberalization and Regulatory Governance: Lessons from Latin America*. University of Florida.

Heinz, W., & Zelner, B. A. (2001). The Institutional Environment for Telecommunications Investment. *Journal of Economics & Management Strategy*, *10*(1), 123–147. doi:10.1162/105864001300122575

Huurdeman, A. (2003). *The worldwide history of Telecommunications*. John Wiley & Sons, Inc. doi:10.1002/0471722243

International Telecommunications Union. (1993). *The Changing Role of Government in an Era of Deregulation. ITU Regulatory Colloquium No. 1*. ITU.

Jamison, M., & Berg, S. (2000). *Issues and Strategies in Latin American Telecommunications: The Global E-economy*. University of Florida.

Katz, R. (2009). The Economic and Social Impact of Telecommunications Output: A Theoretical Framework and Empirical Evidence for Spain. *Inter Economics*, *44*(1), 41–48. doi:10.1007/s10272-009-0276-0

Kridel, D., & Sappington, D. (n.d.). The Effects of Incentive Regulation in the Telecommunications Industry: A Survey. Journal of Regulatory Economics, 9, 269–306.

Megginson, W., & Netter, J. (2000). *From State to Market: A Survey of Empirical Studies on Privatization.* Academic Press.

Morgan, G., & Saunders, R. (1994). *Telecommunications and Economic Development.* Baltimore, MD: The John Hopkins University Press.

Oslin, G. P. (1992). *The Story of Telecommunications.* Mercer University Press.

Ros, A. (2003). *The Impact of Regulatory Process and Price Cap Regulation in Latin American Telecommunications Market.* Academic Press.

Vodafone Group Plc. (2014). *Annual Report 2014.* Retrieved from https://www.vodafone.com/content/annualreport/annual_report14/downloads/market_overview.pdf

World Bank. (2017). *Latin America and Guatemala Data.* Retrieved from World Bank: http://data.worldbank.org/

ENDNOTES

1 These countries are Ecuador, Argentina, Panama, Chile, Colombia, Uruguay, Mexico, and Peru.

Chapter 8
The Negotiation and Effects of Fiscal Privileges in Guatemala

Mauricio Garita
Universidad del Valle de Guatemala, Guatemala

ABSTRACT

The present chapter analyzes fiscal privileges in Guatemala from a taxation point of view, identifying the cost that they incur through the tax expenditure methodology. The chapter also discusses the historical situation of Guatemala concerning taxes and its consequence for the social situation and its relation. Therefore, the conclusion of this chapter is that fiscal privileges are politics aimed at minorities that cost more to the society than the benefits they have in Guatemala, as a consequence there is a sacrifice in taxation by benefiting certain sectors.

FISCAL PRIVILEGES: INTRODUCTION

In fiscal policy, privileges began as a practice to help certain industries prosper. Warrington (1993) described fiscal privileges as different tax treatment that could be applied to assets or savings. The difference in the treatment is focused on the results that the privilege and the beneficial consequences could have to the society. As the International Monetary Fund (2009) states, "Fiscal Policy is the use of Government expending and taxation to influence the economy"; therefore, this influence could lead to growth, poverty reduction, mitigation of an economic crisis and other factors. This highlights that the main importance of a fiscal privilege is its purpose and how it will improve the social contract that exists in a society.

DOI: 10.4018/978-1-5225-4981-9.ch008

Although the nature of the fiscal privilege aims to aid to society, in practice, it has been mostly used as a preservation of the elite. As Blaufarb (2012) states in his analysis of Provence, France, during the period of 1530 to 1830, nobles didn´t pay taxes from the outset and the use of fiscal privileges perpetuated this practice. In Granada, Spain, during the period of 1490 to 1495, the Spanish Crown offered, as an act for generosity and acceptance of the invasion, fiscal privileges such as the exemption of direct taxes Almería and Almueñécar (López, 1979). In Guatemala, this use of fiscal privilege has not been the exception. Since independence in 1821, an authoritarian state was created to benefit the economic privileges of the minorities (Commission for Historical Clarification, 1999).

In the long run, fiscal privileges have had a harmful effect on society by affecting the political efforts in a search for equality. When a group benefits from a fiscal privilege, it has consequences that could result in a distortion of the market prices, destruction of the possibility of competition, and interruption of a perfect market. On a political level, the consequences are seen on the income of the state; since the fiscal privileges reduce the income this negatively affects the state because it reduces the price of public goods. This is worse when the fiscal privileges are cumulative and have no positive effects for the well-being of citizens (Ihori, 2015).

This discussion led to the change of the term 'tax privileges' into the more positive term 'tax incentives'. It is also common to find the term 'tax benefits' in the same area. Although, there is an argument that tax privileges, tax incentives and tax benefits are the same, in the nature and political purpose, there is no significant difference. Tax incentives are often related to investments as a public policy to attract companies. The OECD (2014) refers to tax incentive as ineffective, inefficient, and often linked to abuse and corruption. Tax incentives are characterized by being poorly designed and often helping a particular minority.

Alexander Klem (2009) stated that the benefit of a tax incentive is hard to assess, difficult to quantify, and is often controversial in the long run. The Institute of Taxation and Economic Policy (2013) lists the pitfalls of tax incentives in four categories: 1) they are not crucial when a business decides their investment strategy, 2) it is impossible to design a tax benefit that would behoove the state, 3) it creates distortion in the market and disloyal competition, 4) is often paid by the citizen, and 5) the effect of small tax incentives is that they don't affect decision making but if the tax incentive is high, then it will affect the state.

An argument for tax incentives is often designed for business that need assistance to grow, such as in the case of entrepreneurs. The study elaborated by Harju & Konosen (2012) to examine if a tax incentive will positively affect entrepreneurs demonstrated that the policy is extremely costly and the results are minimal. Tax incentives do not motivate entrepreneurs in their decisions. The UNCTAD (1996) demonstrated that the consequences of the incentives between the United States and

Western Europe in the period of 1983-1995 where that the tax incentive cost USD 13,000 to USD 250,000 per job, and that this increased steadily.

Therefore, investment is not guided profoundly by taxes rather than by non-tax factors that include stable macroeconomic and fiscal policies, political stability, a strong institutional infrastructure, effective and transparent public administration, a skilled labor force, adequate mechanisms for conflict resolution, foreign exchange rules, language and culture, and market size and efficiency (Zolt & Easson, 2012).

Recently, in the European Union, the discussion concerning fiscal privileges and its implementation has been focused on the attraction of investment. Switzerland was at the center of the discussion when the Third Package of Fiscal Reforms was approved by the Senate in 2015. The Organization for Economic Co-operation and Development (OECD) as well as the European Union (EU) urged Switzerland to eliminate their fiscal privileges because they created a scheme of disloyal competence and distortion for the freedom of commerce. By this argument, the EU and the OECD managed to pressurize Switzerland into eliminating fiscal privileges by 2019 (Swiss Information, 2016). The World Trade Organization (WTO) followed the example set by the OECD and urged the United States to eliminate the fiscal privileges given to Boeing with the purpose of elaborating the airplanes produced in this country.

Therefore, fiscal privileges have been far from its collaborative subject and have become a tool of *status quo* for a minority which may be defined as the economic elite. Considering the implementation of fiscal privileges, this has varied depending on the law and the situation of the country in which they are being applied. The discussion concerning the potential benefits have been outweighed by the lack of results and, in the international context, the position in favor of tax privileges is becoming smaller.

The Birth of the Fiscal System of Guatemala: Privileges, Reforms and Taxes

Since Spanish Colonization, Guatemala´s fiscal system has been centered on benefiting the elite. Since the sixteenth century, the fiscal system taxed the indigenous population and exempted the Spaniards. The creation of a tax system based on *encomiendas*[1] maintained the *status quo,* taxing the indigenous population for every product they manufactured and needed by the Spanish Crown. This evolved in the period of the Bourbon Reforms, where the merchants, or *comerciantes,* were behooved by a tax privilege and were the only ones that could lend money (Zeyfer, 2006).

The merchants maintained the structure of tax privileges and, in 1880, they exempted the coffee industry of Guatemala with the purpose of encouraging coffee expansion. At the same time, the taxes to the indigenous population where changed and the obligations that they paid reduced given that their cash proceedings from their wage began to be taxed (Woodward, 1999). Eventually the tax privilege expanded to the sugar and cotton industry, benefiting the new investments made by German and North American citizens in Guatemala.

In 1898, the United Fruit Company (UFCO) took advantage of the tax privileges given to sugar and cotton, and demanded that they should be treated in the same way. This led to a horizontal operation by the UFCO by including cotton and coffee in their production and having the exclusive production of bananas in the country (Bucheli, 2006).

This practice continued and was instated by Jorge Ubico in 1944, who continued to give privileges to the UFCO and to the coffee industry. Only in the Presidency of Arévalo did the tax collection augment because of a change in the law that began to tax coffee production. The effect was substantial given that the Gross Domestic Product of Guatemala was integrated mostly by banana and coffee exportations (Smith, 2014). This motivated the creation of private sector chambers to defend future taxes and thus the Agricultural, Industrial, Financial and Commerce Chambers of Guatemala (CACIF[2]) was created in 1959.

The capacity of CACIF was demonstrated when President Ydigoras Fuentes tried to enact income tax in 1961. CACIF managed to veto the law by influencing the press and congress, thus the law proposal was withdrawn and new discussions began. The income tax was approved in 1963 with significant changes (SAT, 2014). One of the changes of the Decree 1559 was the second article which stated which organizations and persons were exempt from income tax. The law stated that the government, associations and social organizations, chambers, cooperatives, religious institutions, persons that were approved to be exempt by the Government, persons with an income less than Q1,800[3] and, those who worked in the agricultural industry that did not earn in excess of Q15,000[4] annually (Gobierno de la República de Guatemala, 1962). Although the exemptions effect of income tax managed to induce growth to the tax capacity of the state, even surpassing the barrier of 1% of the GDP in 1965, nothing has been accomplished since 1944. Even though the growth was considerably small, it was an improvement.

There was also a tax exemption given by President Ydigoras to the agricultural industry to protect them from the Central American Common Market, which meant that, with the benefits of the income law based on the income exemptions, the agricultural industry was almost completely tax exempt. In 1966, President Méndez Montengro tried to counter the exemptions given by Ydigoras by offering a fiscal reform. CACIF insisted that the reform should be discussed and proposed that certain taxes be modified. This led to the Decree 1627 during 1967 which exempted dividends and branch offices that were not in the country as demonstrated in the second article (Gobierno de la República de Guatemala, 1966). There were also

Figure 1. Ydigoras' Income Tax Effect
Source: Elaborated by the author with information from (Instituto Centroamericano de Estudios Fiscales, 2006)

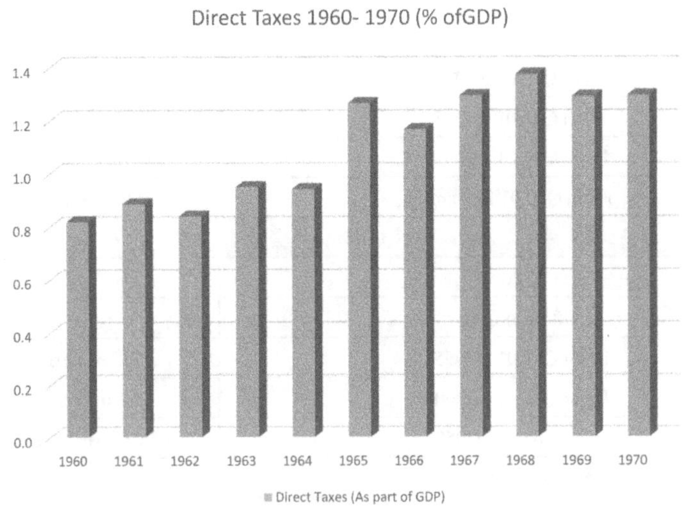

modifications in the decree to include products from petroleum and refineries but the agroindustry was not taxed.

In 1974, President Kjel Laugerud García tried to offer the traditional agro-industry with tax exemptions for banana production, but the private sector managed to delay the approval of the decree. Eventually the Decree 50-74[5] was approved in June 1974. Table 1 demonstrates the structure proposed for coffee and cotton based on the structure of FOB prices.

This had a negative impact on the private sector because it was based on the price of exportation, and in 1975, the price of coffee rose from USD 66 to USD300, applying a tax of 45% given the excess of price. In 1980, President Fernando Romeo Lucas García updated the FOB tax on coffee by adjusting the price of the market due to inflation and demand. Cotton was not included because the production was relatively small and the impact would have been non-existent.

Although something was added in the law that gave protection to the coffee sector, it was the addendum to the second article where they stated there was a limit in the tax that could not be over Q60 if the international prices in the international markets are between Q208.34 to Q250, over Q70 if prices are between Q250.01 and Q300, Q80 when the prices are between Q300.01 and Q350, and Q90 when they are over Q350.

Table 1. Decree 50-74 tax structure

Coffee	
FOB Prices	Tax
Unitl Q35	0%
From Q35.01 to Q40	5% over excess of Q35
From Q40.01 to Q45	15% over excess of Q40
From Q45.01 to Q50	30% over excess of Q45
From Q50.01 forward	45% over excess of Q50
Cotton	
FOB Prices	Tax
Q0.01 to Q50	Q0.75
From Q50.01 to Q55	17% over excess of Q50
From Q55.01 to Q60	15% over excess of Q55
From Q60.01 to Q50	30% over excess of Q60
From Q65.01 forward	45% over excess of Q65

Source: Elaborated by the author with information from (Gobierno de la República de guatemala, 1974)

Table 2. Coffee FOB tax price 1980

Coffee	
FOB Prices	Tax
-Unitl Q70	0%
From Q70.01 to Q75	25% over excess of Q70
From Q75.01 to Q80	30% over excess of Q75
From Q80.01 to Q85	35% over excess of Q80
From Q85.01 forward	45% over excess of Q85

Source: Elaborated by the author with information from (Gobierno de la República de Guatemala, 1980)

In 1982, the pseudo political stability that existed in Guatemala during the Civil War was broken by a *coup d'état* perpetrated by the polemic Efrain Rios Montt. During his government/dictatorship, Rios Montt created the Value-Added Law (Ley del Impuesto al Valor Agregado) as the Decree 97-84. The discussion concerning tax created a division in the private sector because it behooved certain industries and affected others. For this reason, the decree was briefly approved but it cost Ríos Montt his popularity (Cifuentes, 2007).

Decree 97-84 exempted economic activities such as universities, government, municipalities and business related to government, diplomatic missions, international organizations, individual and juridical persons that are under the temporary importation regime, associations, institutions that provide assistance, schools, the insurance related business and cooperatives under specific circumstances (Guatemala, 1987). Value-added tax didn´t have the expected effect and it became less effective when he endured a *coup d'état* by his Minister of Defense, Oscar Mejía Víctores.

One of the first difficulties that Mejía Víctores had to face was the opposition of the private sector, which managed to influence the president in reducing the value-added tax from 10% to 7%. The private sector continued to pressure the president in a day that came to be known as *Black Monday* because of the conflicting environment that was created between the two forces. *Black Monday* happened during a fiscal reform proposed by Mejía Víctores that included re-establishing the taxes for the importation of coffee, the selective tax on the beer consumption, the modification to value-added tax that included exemptions, paying of taxes by the domiciliary agencies located outside of Guatemala, and the taxes on petroleum (Reyes, 2017). The fiscal reform proposal was rejected and the Ministers of Finance, Commerce, Energy and the President of the Bank of Guatemala had to resign because of external pressures.

During the last decade, two of the most important taxes in the fiscal arena were created and implemented; value-added tax and income tax. The discussions of the elite began by reducing value-added tax and promoting exemptions, or privileges, for income tax. In 1986, Vinicio Cerezo, the first democratic president of the Civil War era, took the presidency and decided to implement a fiscal reform. The main purpose of the reform was to eliminate fiscal privileges and tax deductions related to income tax. Although the reform of President Cerezo was approved, it was quickly impugned by the Supreme Court and rejected. The decision of the Supreme Court happened during a level of pressure and conflict between the government and the private sector (Instituto Centroamericano de Estudios Fiscales, 2007). Although Cerezo did manage to approve a new constitution for Guatemala in 1985, it gave more participation to the private sector for government decisions.

An example of this is the Monetary Board, that is autonomous and that its obligations are to determine the monetary, exchange and credit policy of the country according to Article 133. The Monetary Board is integrated by the President of the Bank of Guatemala, the Minister of Finance, the Minister of Commerce, the Minister of industry, the Minister of Agriculture, a member of congress, a member of CACIF, a member of the private banks and a member of the state university (Gobierno de la República de Guatemala, 1985).

As Figure 2 demonstrates, the urgency for a fiscal reform was based on the lack of income and the growth of public expenditure. When Cerezo left office in 1990, Jorge Serrano Elías took office and intended to impose a fiscal reform given the circumstances considering the deficit and the public and private debt that the government was incurring. Serrano Elías managed to pass a fiscal reform based on taxing the middle and lower classes; therefore, the effects were not as expected. He left office after causing a *coup d'état* against himself to suspend the political power of congress that did not let him make decisions. As a consequence, he left for exile to Panama.

A reform was not discussed until the government of Álvaro Arzú in 1996. President Arzú signed the end of the Civil War on the 29th of December 1996 and began discussing the possibility of a fiscal reform with different stakeholders. The International Monetary Fund (IMF) had an agreement with Guatemala to reduce the tax burden to 8.5% of the GDP. The first tax approved during the government of President Arzú was a tax on estates, which was criticized by the private sector for being unfair. Decree 15-98 continued the fiscal privileges for different sectors by exempting them from the tax, including diplomatic missions, international organizations, universities, religious institutions, schools, professional committees and cooperatives, according to Article 12. It also gave a structure of exemptions for properties worth up to Q2,0000 and allowed landowners to calculate the estate's

Figure 2. Fiscal Deficit (1980-1990)
Source: Elaborated by the author with information from (Banco de Guatemala, 2016)

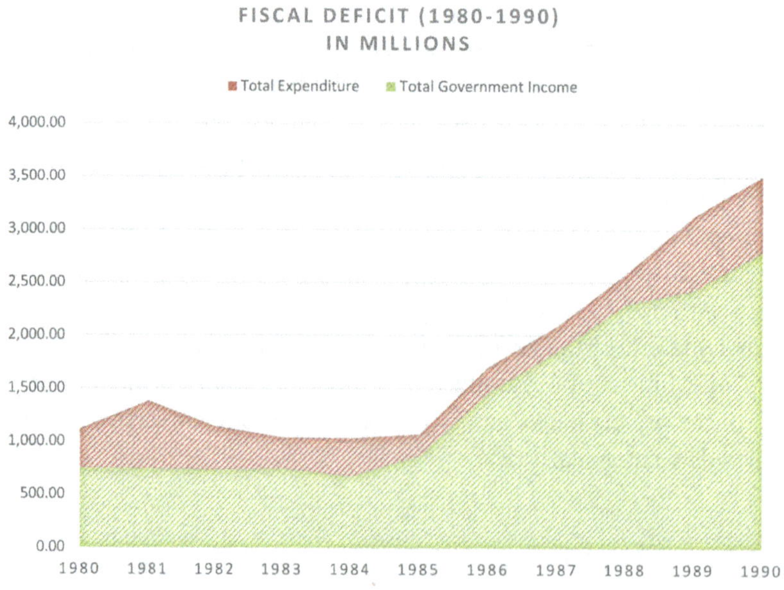

value (Gobierno de la República de Guatemala, 1998). This self-evaluation by the owner often resulted in under valuations so tax payments could be reduced.

President Arzú created the Superintendency of Tax Administration of Guatemala (SAT) with Decree 1-98. This change was important because it created an autonomous institution, not bound to the government, in order to collect taxes. One of the controversies of the SAT was the board of directors, that included a member of the private sector. The SAT was then assigned the collection of taxes and also the judicial capacity to create discussions concerning taxes.

In the last year of the government of President Arzú, a Fiscal Pact was approved. This fiscal pact aimed to develop a better infrastructure for fiscal policies, to strengthen transparency, and give stability to the country. The fiscal pact was finally signed by President Arzú's successor, President Alfonso Portillo, and the value-added tax was increased to 12%. This created a controversy in the country and the private sector rejected his policies. From 2004, regarding income, there has been small modifications which are reflected in Guatemala´s tax burden. The average of the tax burden of Guatemala from 1990-2013 is 13% of the GDP, therefore, in 2015, the United Nations Economic Commission for Latin American and the Caribbean (ECLAC) stated that Guatemala had the lowest tax burden in Latin America (Figure 3).

Tax Expense and Fiscal Privileges: Understanding the Effect

In the section above, the discussion concerning fiscal privileges was based on the inclusion of exemptions in the law by external pressures from the private sector. This has greatly affected the tax burden and therefore, the capacity of the government to

Figure 3. Comparison of tax burdens in Latin America
Source: Elaborated by the author with information from (ECLAC, 2015)

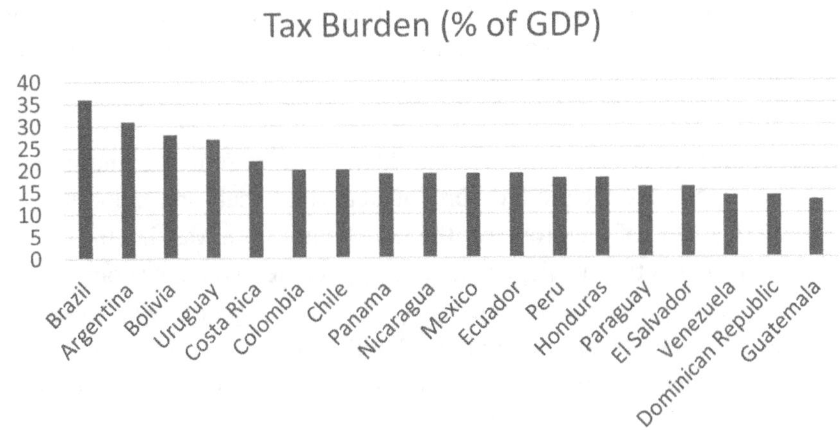

supply better services for the population. Surrey (1973) established the concept of *tax expense* as the difference between deductions, exemptions and other benefits that are not part of the tax structure. Tax expense includes elements of fiscal privileges that are exemptions, deductions, credits, reduced fees and deferments (SAT, 2015). Tax expenses have a negative outcome because they are regressive, generate unexpected stimulus, they are difficult to manage, distort the markets, and raise taxes in the long run.

In order to understand tax expense in Guatemala, it is important to recapture the fiscal privileges that existed and introduce an important decree that considerably affected the tax burden of Guatemala. The first decree is the law for the promotion of development of the export industry and confection (*maquila*) identified by the number 29-89. The law was inspired by Decree 65-89 that promoted free trade zones. With Decree 29-89, the free trade zones became obsolete because they were not necessary to engage in privileges.

Decree 29-89 is based on fiscal privileges to the export industry given that Article 12 states that the business or individuals that are dedicated to the exportation of goods or to the *maquila* industry can have the following benefits (privileges):

- Temporary suspension of the tariff rights and taxes to imports; this could include the value-added tax on different products or materials. Also, the law exempts any other activity that helps the production process, such as research. Applicable only one time.
- Total exemption of the income tax for products that are assembled in Guatemala and exported outside Central America. This exemption is stipulated for ten years.
- Temporary suspension of the taxes or tariffs from the import of products that are necessary for the production of the goods. This could include the value-added tax of the products. Applicable only one time.
- Total exemption of the tariff rights and value-added taxes regarding the import of machinery, parts, components, and accessories needed for the production process.

Article 13 also states that there is a possibility of reimbursement of the total of the income tax exemption on the products produced in Guatemala and exported outside Central America. One of the problems the law did not state was that the company could be renamed and the privilege would be applicable to the new company. This methodology has been used considerably by various companies with the purpose of benefiting themselves from exemptions. Another important fact was that the law was created to attract the textile industry but as time passed and the law continue to exist, different companies such as bakeries, mining, call centers and bottling plants became exempt (Gramajo & Ramirez, 2016).

The decree was complemented with a second decree that reformed certain aspects but maintained the privileges; this is Decree 19-2016, the emerging law for job creation. The reason for updating the previous decree was based on a demand by the World Trade Organization (WTO). The new decree added the possibility of exempting value-added tax from the acquisition of local products in Article 12 and expanded the reimbursement policy in Article 13.

According to Olmstead (2015), 47 mega-companies are registered in this law and 19 of those companies offer their services to the government of Guatemala. This is contrary to the spirit of the law, given that it was for exportation outside Central America.

This decree with the exemptions that the value-added tax and the income tax give amounts to 30,876 taxpayers that are exempt from taxes. The division is 272 banks, 1,683 cooperatives, 6,430 schools divided into 4,333 private and 118 universities and learning centers. Concerning religious institutions, there are 2,816 institutions that are exempt and 52 business chambers are also included in the total amount of institutions.

Figure 4 illustrates the impact of the tax expense during the period 2009-2015, which demonstrates that even though tax expense has diminished considerably, it is still 2.5% of the GDP. This reduction, in 2012, was because of the new structure of the income concern to individuals who had exemptions, such as the deduction of social security, and the regularization of the income tax payment. The amount exempted in 2012 on income tax was Q18,750 million or USD 2,500[6] million and, because of this modification, it diminished to Q2,894 million or USD 385 million.

Figure 4. Tax expense as a percentage of the GPD
Source: Elaborated by the author with information from (SAT, 2016)

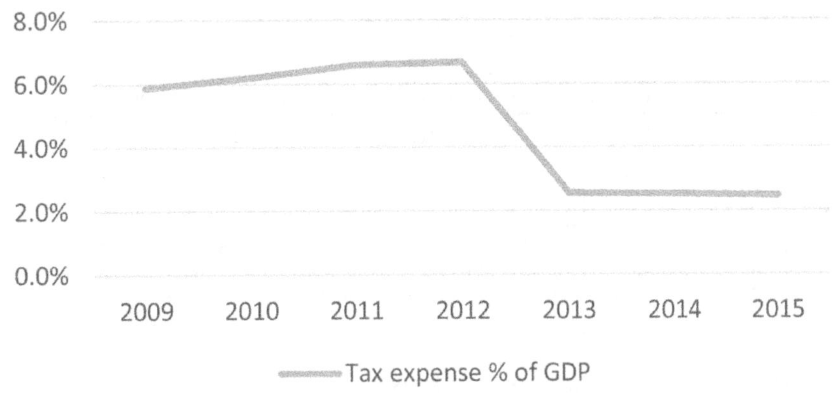

The problem is that, even though the income tax had an important reduction on the tax expenditure, the value-added tax remained constant during this period and it rose in 2015.

The total tax expense reached its highest point in 2012, when it amounted Q 26,330.70 million. From then on, it fell to Q 10,825.30 million in 2013 but surged in 2015 to Q12,062 million. Although there was a considerable reduction of the income tax expense given the new reforms implemented, value added-tax did not change and this was because companies settled in Decree 29-89 began to use the exemption of the value-added tax from 2011. Therefore, the exemption in 2011 was Q 237.30 million and in 2015 it almost doubled to Q406.17 million. Both Decree 29-89 and Decree 65-89 have grown considerably, demonstrating that the use of this fiscal privilege has become more attractive. Even though we do not have the data for 2016, given that there was a reform, it could be assumed that the amount will grow in the future.

An important reality of the tax expenditure is that, on average, only 12.2% are constitutional privileges meaning that the remaining 87.8% are exemptions by law that include Decrees 29-89 and 65-89, religious institutions, cooperatives, mining industries, banks and electric generation companies. The tax expenditure has considerably affected the amount of tax collected and has altered the capacity of financing the government.

This has impacted the goals for tax collection that the Tax Administration has declared year after year. This has had important consequences when analyzing the fiscal deficit of Guatemala given that the average difference in the income and expenditure projected in the budget in the years 2009-2015 has been Q 9,292 million and, as mentioned, the average tax expenditure in the same years were of Q 17,702.50 million, meaning that it could influence the differences between income and expenditure. Although, there are obligations not taken into account with the budget, fiscal privileges have an important impact in this process.

Table 3. Tax expense as percentage of the GPD

Most Relevant Tax Expenditure Per Tax as Percentage of Total Exempted								
Year	2009	2010	2011	2012	2013	2014	2014	
Income Tax	71.7%	71.7%	71.0%	71.2%	26.7%	25.6%	30.3%	
ISO	4.3%	3.9%	4.1%	3.5%	7.9%	7.6%	6.8%	
Value-Added Tax	22.2%	22.5%	22.9%	23.6%	61.1%	63.8%	60.2%	

Source: Elaborated by the author with information from (SAT, 2016)

Figure 5. Tax Expenditure Decree 29-89 and 65-89 (as % of total tax expenditure)
Source: Elaborated by the author with information from (SAT, 2016)

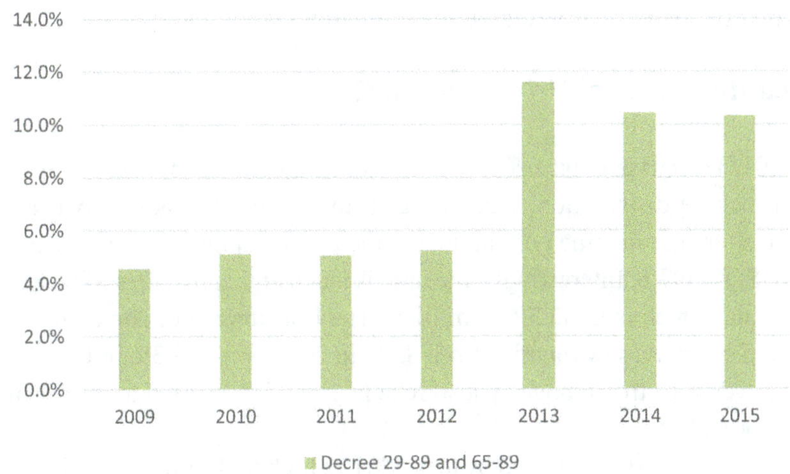

Figure 6. Tax Collection Comparison 2009-2015
Source: Elaborated by the author with information from (SAT, 2016)

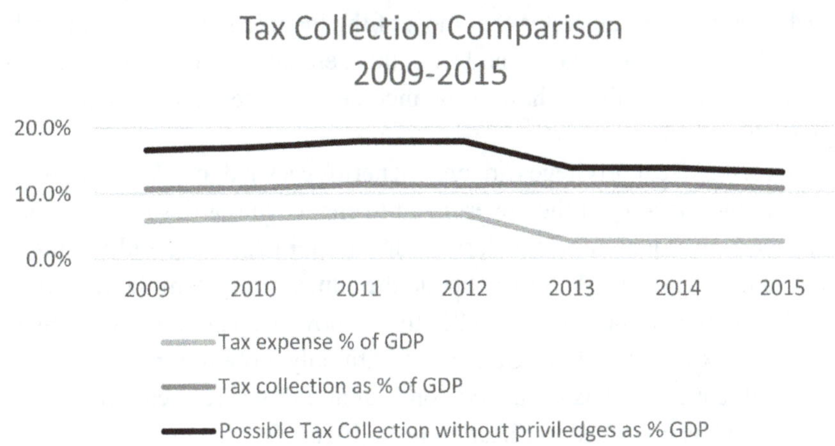

Therefore, fiscal privileges in Guatemala, from a taxation point of view, have been extremely harmful. The actual social and economic situation of Guatemala is not appropriate for a country to give tax exemptions.

The Reality of Fiscal Privileges in Guatemala

Oxfam (2015) discussed that fiscal privileges in Guatemala have had an important effect on income distribution. According to the study, the ratio between multi-millionaires' annual income per capita and the poorest quintile annual income per capita is USD 7,397.8. Interestingly, the ratio is much higher than the GDP per capita of Guatemala, which is USD 3,440 million. The last survey conducted to measure poverty in Guatemala saw this rise from 8.1% in 2006, with 59.3% of Guatemalans living in poverty. Extreme poverty also rose from 15.3% in 2006 to 23.4% in 2014 (Prensa Libre, 2015).

According to a study published by Icefi (2015), high multidimensional poverty in Guatemala exists in households with minors, less than 18 years of age. In 2006, the total multidimensional poverty rate was 53.8% and in 2014 it increased to 54.8%. In the same years, extreme poverty in the same households rose from 16.3% to 20.5%. Another important fact is that the income distribution is extremely inequitable in Guatemala. Table 4 demonstrates that most of the income in Guatemala is held by the highest 40% of the population, and from this percentage, 76% are in the highest 20%, which means that almost half of the income of Guatemala is concentrated in the highest 20%.

Therefore, the fiscal privileges are only benefiting a small part of the population and affecting the capacity of the government to engage in politics for better health, education, and development. Considering education, in 2014, 3.2 million boys and girls between the ages of 0-17 were outside the education system. Of the 50.1% of children that do not attend school, 75.8% live in poverty. The initial coverage rate in education is extremely low in Guatemala with only a 6% reported in 2014. The expenditure in education has remained constant and this is reflected in the results that Guatemala has produced in different tests (Figure 7).

Table 4. Income distribution in Guatemala

Years	2000	2006	2011	2014
Income by highest 40% of the population	78.1	78.3	76.4	74
Income by lowest 40% of the population	10.6	10.1	11.7	12.9

Source: Elaborated by the author with information from (World Bank, 2014)

Figure 7. Expenditure in education
Source: Elaborated by the author with information from (Instituto Centroamericano de Estudios Fiscales, 2016)

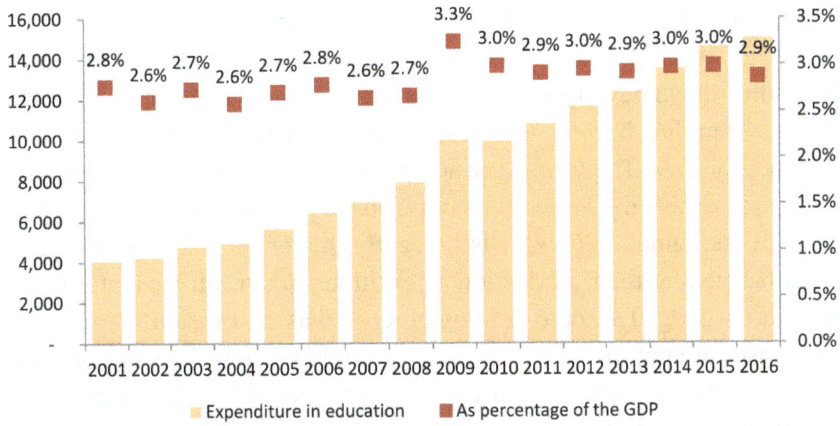

The situation is similar in the health sector. The vaccine programs only cover 59% of the population that depend on the government for health. Malnutrition in extreme poverty is reported to be 65.9% with a rate of 17.4% suffering from malnutrition. The indigenous population is the most vulnerable because they have a malnutrition rate of 61.2% and rural areas are the most vulnerable areas in Guatemala with a malnutrition rate of 53%. The investment in food and nutritional health was 1.3% in 2012 and it diminished in 2014 to 0.9% of the GDP (Instituto Centroamericano de Estudios Fiscales, 2014). Given this situation, discussing privileges in Guatemala seems illogical, since there is a necessity for investment in health and education.

One of the arguments for privileges in Guatemala is competitiveness and attraction of investment, but the World Economic Forum (2016) identified that the most problematic factors for doing business are crime and theft, corruption, and an inadequate supply of infrastructure. Taxes are in the position 13 of 16, which demonstrate that it is not a priority. Therefore, a sacrifice is being made by the population that needs the government not only to live but to survive. With the necessities of the population and the importance of advancing into a more inclusive society, fiscal privileges are obsolete and without function in these economies.

CONCLUSION

Since the colonization period, the negotiation of taxes has always been a privilege of the few, either by heritage, by nationality, by race or by economic activity. This discussion has led to a fiscal system in Guatemala that is not aimed at development and the eradication of poverty given that the situation has worsened in the last years. The fiscal system has become a tool for taking advantage of tax payers through different mechanisms. The former president and vice-president of Guatemala were involved in a tax evasion scheme in customs and are currently on trial because of this emblematic case, named *La Línea*. Also, recently, the company Aceros de Guatemala is on trial because of their fabrication of fictitious organizations that served as a façade for tax paying. This case is being processed as tax evasion.

These cases are not the only ones, and currently Guatemala is in a situation of prosecuting tax evaders and fortifying the system. This will lead to an improvement in the future, but would not be enough because they are important exemptions in the economy that also affect the tax burden. Therefore, it is extremely important that decrees such as 29-89 should be discussed and reformed again, not in the way they were reformed in 2016, which brought privileges to different sectors. It is demonstrated in the present investigation that fiscal privileges have not improved competitiveness and economic growth but have had an effect on poverty, education, and health. The argument of competitiveness has been refuted given that this is not a priority for investors, but the important factors that are a priority concern the government and published expenditure for infrastructure and the reduction of crime and theft.

As a conclusion, it is important to ask: Who are we privileging? Because, as it is demonstrated, the larger part of society is paying the exemptions.

REFERENCES

Banco de Guatemala. (2016). *Estadísticas Fiscales*. Retrieved from Banguat: http://www.banguat.gob.gt/inc/ver.asp?id=/pim/pim16&e=115131&e=115213

Blaufarb, R. (2012). *The Politics of Fiscal Privilege in Provence, 1530s–1830s*. Catholic University of America Press.

Bucheli, M. (2006). *Good dictator, bad dictator: United Fruit Company and Economic Nationalism in Central America in the Twentieth Century*. Chicago: University of Illinois.

Cifuentes, M. (2007). *Efectos por el incumplimiento de los compromisos del pacto fiscal*. Retrieved from Universidad de San Carlos: http://biblioteca.usac.edu.gt/tesis/03/03_3090.pdf

Commission for Historical Clarification. (1999). *Comisión para el esclarecimiento histórico*. Author.

ECLAC. (2015). *Panorama Fiscal de América Latina y el Caribe 2015: Dilemas y espacios de políticas*. United Natinos.

Gobierno de la República de Guatemala. (1962). *Decreto 1559*. Retrieved from http://old.congreso.gob.gt/archivos/decretos/1962/gtdcx15591962.pdf

Gobierno de la República de Guatemala. (1966). *Congreso de Guatemala*. Retrieved from http://old.congreso.gob.gt/archivos/decretos/1966/gtdcx16271966.pdf

Gobierno de la República de Guatemala. (1980). *Decreto 51-80*. Retrieved from Congreso de Guatemala: http://old.congreso.gob.gt/archivos/decretos/1980/gtdcx00511980.pdf

Gobierno de la República de Guatemala. (1985). *Constitución Política de la República de Guatemala*. Author.

Gobierno de la República de Guatemala. (1998). *Congeso de la República*. Retrieved from Decreto 15-98: https://www.rgp.org.gt/docs/legislacion_registral/Ley%20del%20Impuesto%20Unico%20sobre%20Inmuebles.pdf

Gobierno de la República de Guatemala. (1974). *Decreto 50-74*. Retrieved from Congress of Guatemala: http://old.congreso.gob.gt/archivos/decretos/1974/gtdcx00501974.pdf

Gramajo, J., & Ramirez, G. (2016). *Ley de Empleo favorece a maquilas y Call Centers*. Academic Press.

Guatemala, G. d. (1987). *Decreto 97-24*. Retrieved from Congreso de Guatemala: http://old.congreso.gob.gt/archivos/decretos/1984/gtdly97-84.pdf

Ihori, T. (2015). *Fiscal Privileges, Consolidation Attempts and Pigouvian Taxes*. Tokyo: Public Choice Meetings.

Institute of Taxation and Economic Policy. (2013). *Tax Incentives: Costly for States, Drag on the Nation*. Retrieved from ITEP: http://itep.org/itep_reports/2013/08/tax-incentives-costly-for-states-drag-on-the-nation.php#.WOOpezs1-M8

Instituto Centroamericano de Estudios Fiscales. (2006). Guatemala ingresos de gobierno Central. Guatemala: Author.

Instituto Centroamericano de Estudios Fiscales. (2007). *Historia de la tributación en Guatemala*. Author.

Instituto Centroamericano de Estudios Fiscales. (2014). *Contamos! Protegiendo la nueva cosecha*. ICEFI.

Instituto Centroamericano de Estudios Fiscales. (2016). *Contamos¡ ¿Dond están los ausentes?*. ICEFI.

International Monetary Fund. (2009). *What is fiscal policy?*. International Monetary Fund.

J. H. & T. K. (2012). The impact of tax incentives on the economic activity of entrepreneurs. *NBER Working Papers*, 1-48.

Klem, A. (2009). Causes, Benefits, and Risks of Business Tax Incentives. *IMF Working Papers*, 1-28.

López, J. E. (1979). *Privilegios fiscales y la repoblación del Reino de Granada (1495-1520)*. Universidad de Málaga.

Prensa Libre. (2015). *Pobreza sube a 59.3%: son 9.6 millones de guatemaltecos los afectados*. Author.

Reyes, J. (2017). *La Hora*. Retrieved from La historia no miente... 1975-1986: http://lahora.gt/hemeroteca-lh/la-historia-no-miente-19751986/

SAT. (2014). *Historia de la tributación de Guatemala*. SAT.

SAT. (2015). *Estimación del gasto tributario del gobierno central*. SAT.

SAT. (2016). *Gasto Tributario*. SAT.

Swiss Information. (2016). *Swiss Info*. Retrieved from http://www.swissinfo.ch/spa/economia/respiro-a-multinacionales_aprueban-nuevos-privilegios-fiscales-para-corporativos/42226892

UCTAD. (1996). *Incentives and Foreign Direct Investment*. New York: United Nations.

Warrington, P. (1993). *The distortionary impact of taxation on irish saving media: The principle of fiscal priviledges*. Student Economic Review.

Woodward, R. L. (1999). *Central America: A Nation Divided*. Oxford Press.

World Bank. (2014). *Guatemala Data*. Retrieved from World Bank: http://www.worldbank.org/en/country/guatemala

Z. E., & E. A. (2012). *Tax incentives*. Washington, DC: World Bank Institute.

Zeyfer. (2006). *Historia de Honduras*. Retrieved from Reformas Borbónicas: http://www.historiadehonduras.hn/Historia/Colonial/reformasborbonicas.htm

ENDNOTES

1 The *encomienda* was a right given by the King of Spain by his will and not an obligation. In Spanish this translates as "á merced y voluntad del Rey."

2 Comité Coordinador de Asociaciones Agrícolas, Comerciales, Industriales y Financieras.

3 Q1,800 in today's currency, assuming that in 1963 there was a Q1 to USD 1 currency, this would be equivalent to USD 14,781.

4 Q15,000 in today's currency, assuming that in 1963 there was a Q1 to USD 1 currency, this would be equivalent to USD 123,179.59.

5 It is said that this law was elaborated by the private sector and that it was approved for this reason.

6 Q7.5 to USD 1 exchange rate.

Chapter 9
The Variation in the Weighted Average Interest Rate and Its Influence on the Credit Portfolio of the Guatemalan Financial System

Mayra Irasema Gaitan
University of the Valley of Guatemala (UVG), Guatemala

ABSTRACT

Due to the fact that the active weighted average interest rate that the banks of the national financial system have applied to the loan portfolio has been stable in recent years, it was considered important to calculate the impact of this measure on the performance of the balance of the loan portfolio by economic activity in Guatemala from 2008 to 2016; it was considered this time frame since the consulted web portals shows more information as of 2008. With the above information, it will be possible to observe the important variations and what events could propitiate it, the percentage of growth and which economic sectors have most financed their operations. The increase in the loan portfolio, in addition to being considered a strategic objective of any financial institution to increase its market share and income, is also a sign of confidence among corporate users, family members, and other entities involved in maintaining the national economic stability.

DOI: 10.4018/978-1-5225-4981-9.ch009

INTRODUCTION

Due to the fact that the active weighted average interest rate that the banks of the national financial system have applied to the loan portfolio has been stable in recent years; it was considered important to calculate the impact of this measure on the performance of the balance of the loan portfolio by economic activity in Guatemala from 2008 to 2016; it was considered this time frame since the consulted web portals show more information as of 2008.

With the above information, it will be possible to observe the important variations and what events could propitiate it, the percentage of growth and which economic sectors have most financed their operations. The increase in the loan portfolio, in addition to being considered a strategic objective of any financial institution to increase its market share and income, is also a sign of confidence among corporate users, family members and other entities involved in maintaining the national economic stability. Financing of productive activities should then also lead to an increase in employment, which in turn also impacts on other national macroeconomic variables, of which a correlation was also made over the same period. For the present study, the information that the 18 banking entities report to the Superintendence of Banks was used in a periodic manner and such information is available on the website of the Supervisory and Inspection Body.

Considering the importance of the financing that the banking entities provide to the different economic sectors and how it influences the increase of the economic activity of the country, it is important to evaluate how the credit portfolio has behaved in the national financial system and the relation that the interest rate has in the increase or contraction of the same. For this purpose, several aspects must be interweaved in order to analyze these behaviors. One of them is the leading interest rate fixed by the Bank of Guatemala on a monthly basis, since it is a tool that uses central banking to fulfill its mission ("To promote the stability in the general price level") has a direct influence on the effect of the increase or decrease of credit. This leading interest rate is a parameter that central banking suggests, and is then observed in performing active and passive operations.

After the crisis of 2008 originated in the United States of America, the loan portfolio contracted, banks were more prudent in lending and precautionary measures were established to avoid contagion to the National Financial System. At the end, in Guatemala, there was no adverse effect on the financial system, given the current regulations and supervision that could be considered to be still conservative in some respects. After this crisis, interest rates were at their historical lows in some countries even in the negative, that is, that having the money in some investment or deposit was not remunerated, but the opposite, it lost value. The goal was to encourage people to circulate money to increase investment and boost the economy.

In this context, during the last 8 years the active interest rate has shown downward behavior which should encourage companies and individuals to contract debt at favorable rates, so the present document aims to show the relationship between the variables of interest leader rate, weighted average active rate and balance of the loan portfolio in the Guatemalan financial system.

LITERARY REVIEW

Economic Growth

The economic growth of a country refers to the increase of indicators such as:

- Growth in the production of goods and services,
- Increase energy consumption,
- Increased investment (public and private),
- Increased savings,
- Investment (public and private)

If these indicators increase, the theory tells us that the well-being of the population of a country should improve as well; in other words, there is a positive relationship between both indicators.

GROSS DOMESTIC PRODUCT - GDP

GDP refers in macroeconomic terms to the monetary value of goods and services produced in a country or region over a given period. In Guatemala, GDP has shown a positive behavior, growing above 3% since 2011, and according to expert estimates, at the end of 2016 will be around 3.6%.

FINANCE SYSTEM

In Guatemala, the national financial system is made up of banks, financial companies, brokerage houses, offshore entities, insurers and bondholders; and according to the publication of the SIB, the financial system consists of Table 1.

In Guatemala, the Superintendence of Banks is the supervisory and inspection body for these entities; and, as part of its supervision work, makes available to users information on supervised entities such as:

Table 1.

Chart 1	
Composition of the Supervised Financial System	
At September 30th, 2016	
Quantity	**Description**
18	Financial institutions
13	Financial Companies
14	Storage Companies
28	Insurance companies
3	Exchange houses
6	Entities outside the square - Off shore
10	Brokerage house
6	Credit card issuing companies
5	Other Institutions
10	Financial Groups

Source: Own elaboration with data published by the Superintendence of Banks.

- Balance sheet, income statement and its chart.
- Historically applied interest rates
- Statistics Bulletins
- Evolution of the loan portfolio
- Quarterly reports
- Monthly supplements and statistical bulletins.
- And others.

This information is useful for performing analyzes and projections; for the development of this document, we refer to the information published by the SIB through its web page (www.sib.gob.gt) related to the loan portfolio balances and the active interest rate during the time frame of 2008 to 2016. The objective is to correlate the variables and analyze them.

For purposes of reporting to the Superintendence of Banks, banking entities segment their loan portfolio as follows in accordance with the Regulations for Credit Risk Management:

- Senior Business consists of business debtors with total indebtedness (including direct and indirect indebtedness) greater than Q5.0 million or USD650.0 thousand.

- Minor business, corporate loans with total indebtedness (direct and indirect) equal to or less than Q5.0 million or USD650.0 thousand.
- Consumption, credits that are not higher than Q3.0 million or US $ 390.0 thousand granted to a single individual person.
- Microcredit credits are granted to a single individual or legal entity for an amount not greater than Q160.0 thousand or USD20.8 thousand.
- Mortgages for housing are credit assets granted to individuals (final owners) with mortgages on real estate to finance the acquisition, construction, remodeling, repair of housing, or release of mortgage lien.

TOP RATE

It is one of the instruments used by the Central Bank to meet the objective of maintaining stability in the general price level. One of the effects of the downward movement in the rate is the impulse to increase the loan portfolio and on the contrary the increase in the leading rate contracts the portfolio and should increase savings. During the analyzed period the following behavior of the rate has been observed (see Table 2).

As we can see in Figure 1 and Table 2, since 2008 the top interest rate has slowed down basically by international external factors, the fall in prices in some

Table 2.

Chart 2 Top interest rate From 2008 to 2016			
Year	**First Semester**	**Second Semester**	**Anual Average**
2008	6.62	7.13	6.92
2009	6.33	4.68	5.50
2010	4.50	4.50	4.50
2011	4.63	5.22	4.93
2012	5.50	5.00	5.25
2013	5.09	5.17	5.13
2014	4.86	4.41	4.63
2015	3.64	3.13	3.38
2016	3.00	3.00	3.00

Source: Own elaboration with data published on the website of the Bank of Guatemala.
*Data up to 09/15/2016

Figure 1.

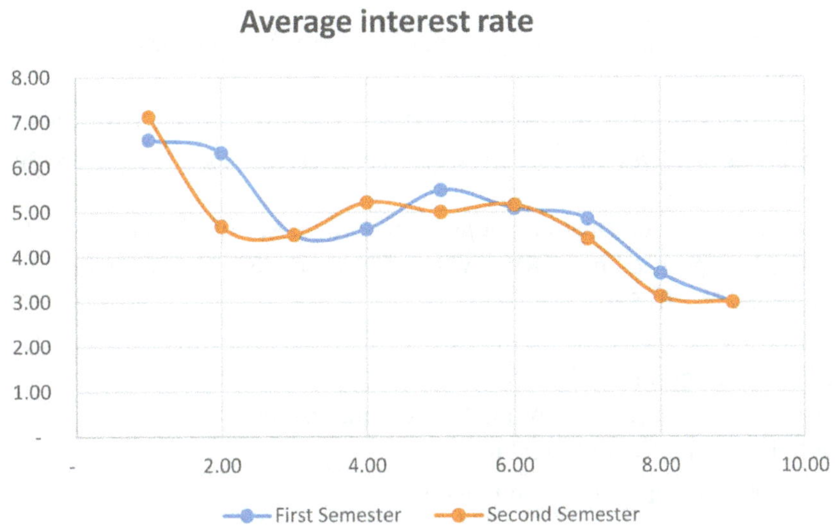

commodities and the impact of the subprime crisis. Guatemala is not exempt from the impact of the environment on its economy; that is why, when Central Bank sets the top interest rate, it is done based on observation, methodologies and models for its best determination.

The active interest rate is the price at which banks grant loans to debtors; and, *the passive interest rate*, is the percentage remuneration that the banks pay to the savers for the money that is deposited in any modality. It should be noted that each financial institution establishes the active and passive interest rate by which it will govern its operations with users. The difference between them, corresponds to the margin that the banks obtain for financial intermediation; this difference of rates is denominated "spread".

DEPOSITS

Banks raise funds with products such as savings, monetary and term deposits; and then set them through credits to applicants who require funding. This exercise is called "financial intermediation" and is also regulated by the SIB.

ANALYSIS OF RESULTS

Below we can see graphically the percentage growth that GDP has had since 2000 to date (see Table 3).

In the above chart, we see that the national GDP was growing at a steady pace, reaching its highest point in 2007 with 6.1% and its lowest peak in 2009 (subprime post-crisis) to 0.05%

According to the information obtained from the BANGUAT, the national GDP is composed of specific lines (18), of which 5 represent 63.3% of the total GDP (as of December 31st, 2015):

- Manufacturing Industries
- Agriculture, livestock, hunting, forestry and fishing;
- Wholesale and Retail Rental housing
- Transport, storage and communications.

Table 3.

Chart 3		
Annual amount of GDP (Figures in millions of Q)		
YERA	PIB Q	%
2001	146,977.85	-
2002	152,660.93	3.9%
2003	156,524.46	2.5%
2004	161,458.23	3.2%
2005	166,721.95	3.3%
2006	175,691.22	5.4%
2007	186,766.89	6.3%
2008	192,894.87	3.3%
2009	193,909.58	0.5%
2010	199,473.79	2.9%
2011	207,775.98	4.2%
2012	213,946.63	3.0%
2013	221,857.49	3.7%
2014	231,118.20	4.2%
2015	240,706.80	4.1%

Source: Own elaboration with information obtained from the website of the Bank of Guatemala.

Figure 2.

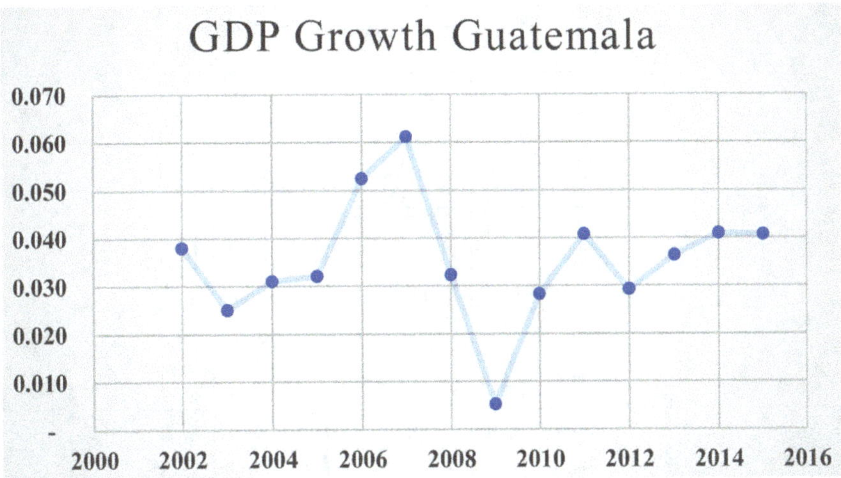

As it can be observed in the picture, the manufacturing sector shows growth in recent years, as it does agriculture. These sectors are composed of companies that can be considered as "Business Requesters".

The increase in GDP then indicates that the product of the sale of goods and services at the national level has increased and in recent years has remained above 0.03. Consequently, this should increase the demand for financing from domestic industries to finance their operations. This productive expansion must be financed by several channels, some of them can be: 1) Contribution of capital of the own shareholders; 2) with public offers; Or 3) Bank financing.

It is well known by all, that the cost of shareholder capital is an expensive way to get funds, public offerings of shares for being innovative instruments for some industries becomes less used; then, so using bank financing ends up being one of the options most frequented in our country.

CREDIT PORTFOLIO

The following Figures 4 and 5 then show the semi-annual balances of the consolidated loan portfolio and the weighted average interest rate applied to the five different classifications during the period from 2008 to July 2016 with the objective to see their relationship:

From 2008 to 2010 the portfolio grew moderately; however, the highest growth was reflected starting the year 2011, 2012, 2013, 2014 and 2015 compared to the previous year, basically in major business and minor business segments, which

Figure 3.

Cuadro 4
Cartera de créditos consolidada con saldos al cierre de cada semestre / crecimiento semestral y anual
del 30/06/2008 al 31/07/2016
Cifras en millones de quetzales

Criterio de Agrupación	30/06/2008	31/12/2008	30/06/2009	31/12/2009	30/06/2010	31/12/2010	30/06/2011	31/12/2011	30/06/2012	31/12/2012	30/06/2013	31/12/2013	30/06/2014	31/12/2014	30/06/2015	31/12/2015	30/06/2016	31/07/2016
Empresarial Mayor	38,846	40,311	40,372	41,387	40,400	43,201	44,850	49,185	51,544	59,906	61,771	67,649	69,327	73,623	79,254	86,444	85,006	84,948
Empresarial Menor	9,814	10,615	10,421	10,431	10,534	10,730	10,819	11,564	12,151	13,024	13,487	14,279	14,713	15,496	15,281	15,447	15,456	15,427
Consumo	16,817	17,408	17,671	17,988	18,738	20,179	21,848	24,178	26,322	28,709	30,811	32,958	35,223	37,336	40,462	43,733	46,487	46,659
Microcrédito	1,792	1,881	1,801	1,764	1,752	1,805	1,968	2,368	2,571	2,754	2,849	2,981	2,917	2,895	2,666	2,616	2,559	2,614
Hipo. p/ vivienda	5,487	5,919	6,183	6,319	6,317	6,329	6,422	6,608	6,934	7,188	7,356	7,638	7,717	7,801	7,884	8,046	8,226	8,235
Total	**72,755**	**76,135**	**76,448**	**77,889**	**77,740**	**82,243**	**85,907**	**93,903**	**99,521**	**111,581**	**116,274**	**125,505**	**129,897**	**137,150**	**145,547**	**156,287**	**157,734**	**157,882**

Crecimiento % s/ total	30/06/2008	31/12/2008	30/06/2009	31/12/2009	30/06/2010	31/12/2010	30/06/2011	31/12/2011	30/06/2012	31/12/2012	30/06/2013	31/12/2013	30/06/2014	31/12/2014	30/06/2015	31/12/2015	30/06/2016	31/07/2016
Semestral		**4.6%**	**0.4%**	**1.9%**	**-0.2%**	**5.8%**	**4.5%**	**9.3%**	**6.0%**	**12.1%**	**4.2%**	**7.9%**	**3.5%**	**5.6%**	**6.1%**	**7.4%**	**0.9%**	**0.1%**
Anual		**0%**		2.3%		5.6%		14.2%		18.8%		12.5%		9.3%		14.0%		1.0%

Cuadro 5
Tasa activa promedio ponderada aplicada a la cartera de créditos al cierre de cada semestre
del 30/06/2008 al 31/07/2016
Cifras en porcentajes

Criterio de Agrupación	30/06/2008	31/12/2008	30/06/2009	31/12/2009	30/06/2010	31/12/2010	30/06/2011	31/12/2011	30/06/2012	31/12/2012	30/06/2013	31/12/2013	30/06/2014	31/12/2014	30/06/2015	31/12/2015	30/06/2016	31/07/2016
Empresarial Mayor	8.17	8.9	8.96	8.78	8.45	7.83	7.33	6.98	6.94	6.79	6.68	6.67	6.62	6.53	6.43	6.39	6.43	6.42
Empresarial Menor	12.17	12.71	12.82	12.81	12.65	12.35	12.17	11.87	11.79	11.65	11.59	11.37	11.28	11.14	10.99	10.84	10.71	10.71
Consumo	21.19	22.74	23.86	25.96	26.06	26.31	25.8	25.66	25.45	25.77	26.03	26.2	26.23	25.96	24.23	23.97	22.71	22.58
Microcrédito	19.38	20.13	20.53	21.19	21.45	21.59	21.71	20.95	20.93	21.73	21.67	25.37	24.72	20.36	19.45	19.91	20.29	20.26
Hipotecario para vivienda	11.81	11.91	11.96	11.88	11.82	11.68	11.53	11.31	11.18	10.95	10.74	10.53	10.32	10.08	9.85	9.62	9.45	9.43

Figure 4.
Source: Own elaboration with information of the SIB website.

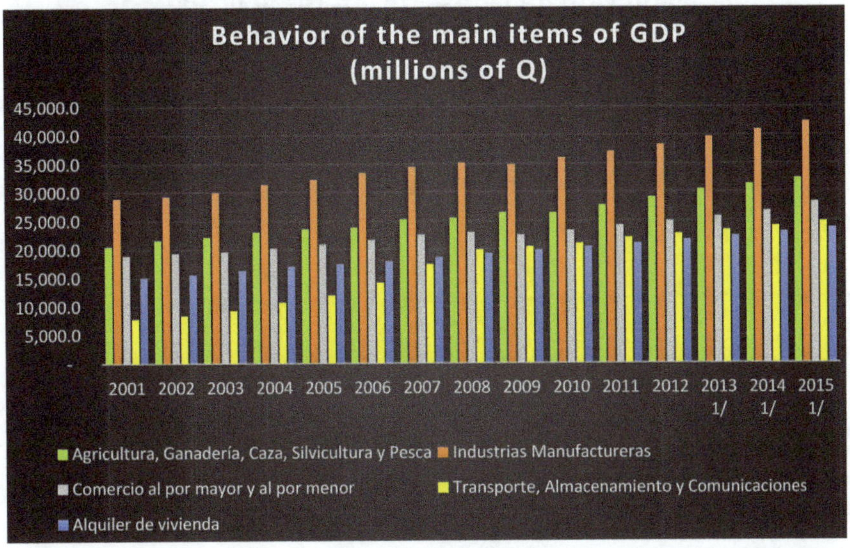

Figure 5.

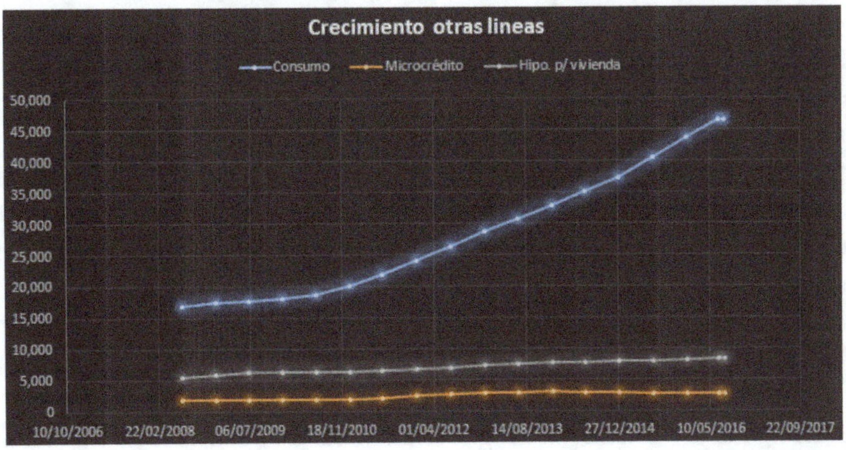

show a significant takeoff, however, for the last year we see a small contraction that could be influenced by the effects of the cancellation of important credits or by the migration of corporate loans to foreign banks.

The previous graph supports the assertion that the corporate loan portfolio has migrated and was not an effect of the increase in the interest rate applied, since far from increasing, it shows a decrease in the same period analyzed.

Figure 6.

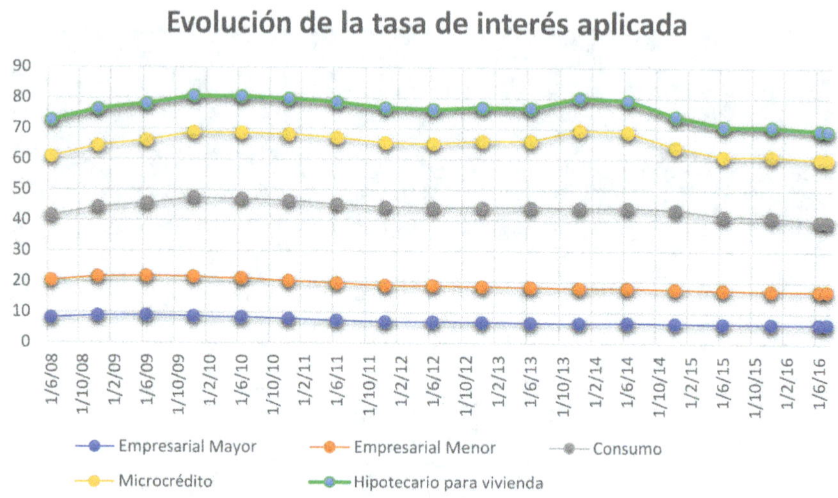

It is also interesting then to show the behavior of deposits (deposits of banks) in the course of recent years:

As we can see, the entities have made significant deposits in recent years and according to information provided by the SIB, to September 2016 such deposits reached Q202,708.0 million in both currencies, concentrating 73.5% of those deposits in the 4 main National Banks.

In addition, deposits are segmented into National Currency as follows:

It is important to note that, many of these banks, as the main collectors, are thus able to place and lend to the main industries (observed GDP graph). Finally, when correlating the variables leader rate, weighted average active rate applied by each segment of the loan portfolio, the following was obtained:

E Major: Business Major

Considering 1 or -1 when there is a high correlation and 0 when there is no correlation between the variables, the previous chart indicates that the leader rate and the rate applied to the senior business segment is correlated at 0.65.

E Minor: Smaller Business

In the case of the small business segment, there is a high correlation between the applied interest rate and the change in the leading rate.

Figure 7.
Source: Graph obtained from the tool of public use of the SIB in its web portal

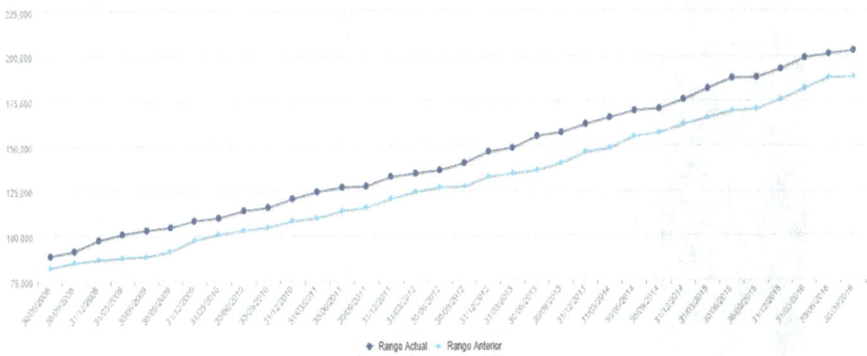

METHODOLOGY

The investigation is designed at the foreground showing the annual information of the weighted average interest rate in active operations and the balance of the total portfolio that is then broken down by segment to visualize the incidence of each one; In addition the leading interest rate factor of the same period is added to correlate the variables and to conclude how much the interest rate benefits in the increase of the credit. All information provided corresponds to the period from 2008 to 2016 that the 18 banking entities reported to the Superintendence of Banks. The means to analyze the information was through the correlation and analysis of variables with Excel.

CONCLUSION

1. The domestic Gross Domestic Product (GDP) has shown discrete growth in recent years, influenced to a large extent by growth in sectors of Manufacturing, Agriculture, among others, which represent a significant portion of GDP.
2. During the last 8 analyzed years, it is observed that the portfolio has had a dynamic behavior influenced by the movement of the interest rate applied to lending operations.
3. There is a variation in the active weighted average interest rate applied to the different portfolios (segments) which has influenced the portfolio change.

Figure 8.

BANCOS

CAPTACIONES CLASIFICADAS POR CANTIDAD DE CUENTAS Y MONTOS EN MONEDA NACIONAL

AL 30 DE SEPTIEMBRE DE 2016

(Cifras en miles de Quetzales)

INTERVALOS EN QUETZALES		MONETARIOS		DE AHORRO		A PLAZO		OTROS DEPÓSITOS 1/		OBLIGACIONES FINANCIERAS 2/		TOTAL	
DE MAS DE	HASTA	Cuentas	Valor	Cuentas	Valor	Cuentas	Valor	Cuentas	Valor	Cuentas	Valor	Cuentas	Valor
0	5,000	3,845,981	1,742,300	10,667,712	3,729,271	20,712	44,720	569,082	96,102	119	307	15,103,606	5,612,700
5,000	10,000	183,427	1,291,324	267,892	1,876,708	8,334	68,405	6,235	42,506	65	524	465,953	3,279,467
10,000	15,000	83,290	1,017,042	132,291	1,601,196	6,343	81,651	1,848	22,460	45	599	223,817	2,722,948
15,000	20,000	49,200	850,903	79,766	1,372,199	5,834	107,469	927	16,017	14	257	135,741	2,346,845
20,000	25,000	33,702	752,212	58,767	1,303,754	5,358	124,566	583	13,044	9	218	98,419	2,193,794
25,000	30,000	24,404	667,708	41,093	1,119,206	4,765	135,128	395	10,834	8	231	70,665	1,933,107
30,000	40,000	33,844	1,171,210	56,819	1,954,262	6,357	227,763	502	17,458	8	286	97,530	3,370,979
40,000	50,000	22,919	1,025,088	37,971	1,688,737	8,061	383,683	327	14,976	11	511	69,289	3,112,995
50,000	100,000	53,274	3,734,975	81,191	5,581,793	23,333	1,802,161	678	46,446	30	2,428	158,506	11,167,803
100,000	500,000	52,484	10,795,015	52,325	9,384,815	42,812	10,657,996	463	94,888	73	20,154	148,157	30,952,868
500,000	1,000,000	7,014	4,858,168	2,838	1,888,426	8,800	6,558,504	56	38,791	26	21,571	18,734	13,365,460
1,000,000	1,500,000	2,134	2,586,808	604	709,534	4,016	4,869,084	24	30,091	9	11,289	6,787	8,206,806
1,500,000	2,000,000	1,044	1,812,878	228	386,842	2,200	4,014,859	10	17,645	8	15,143	3,490	6,247,367
2,000,000	2,500,000	613	1,367,801	140	309,950	1,147	2,601,234	9	20,368	6	14,554	1,915	4,313,907
2,500,000	3,000,000	394	1,077,345	77	211,250	905	2,582,072	9	24,968	7	20,590	1,392	3,916,245
3,000,000	4,000,000	501	1,718,795	84	285,532	1,178	4,152,923	9	32,434	4	14,151	1,776	6,203,835
4,000,000	5,000,000	320	1,430,147	45	201,310	920	4,371,048	2	8,961	3	15,000	1,290	6,026,466
5,000,000	7,500,000	383	2,332,680	71	433,447	704	4,348,732	3	17,544	4	26,025	1,165	7,158,428
7,500,000	10,000,000	210	1,842,938	30	259,801	627	5,810,029	3	25,445	2	20,000	872	7,958,213
10,000,000	15,000,000	185	2,238,351	24	286,361	329	4,189,671	2	24,287	1	12,500	541	6,751,170
15,000,000	25,000,000	114	2,185,796	11	211,353	249	4,938,720	3	60,998	3	60,412	380	7,457,279
25,000,000		133	8,330,648	16	1,014,305	270	16,121,283	3	193,071	0		422	25,659,307
TOTAL		4,395,570	54,830,132	11,479,995	35,810,052	153,254	78,191,701	581,173	869,354	455	256,750	16,610,447	169,957,989

Figure 9.

CAPTACIONES CLASIFICADAS POR CANTIDAD DE CUENTAS Y MONTOS EN MONEDA EXTRANJERA
AL 30 DE SEPTIEMBRE DE 2016
(Cifras en miles de Quetzales)

INTERVALOS EN QUETZALES		MONETARIOS		DE AHORRO		A PLAZO		OTROS DEPÓSITOS 1/		OBLIGACIONES FINANCIERAS 2/		TOTAL	
DE MAS DE	HASTA	Cuentas	Valor	Cuentas	Valor	Cuentas	Valor	Cuentas	Valor	Cuentas	Valor	Cuentas	Valor
0	5,000	95,411	55,393	127,791	93,678	42	96	23,238	9,123	0	0	246,482	158,290
5,000	10,000	10,817	78,912	11,005	80,154	146	1,174	576	4,090	0	0	22,544	164,330
10,000	15,000	5,848	71,990	6,101	74,988	103	1,255	239	2,896	0	0	12,291	151,129
15,000	20,000	4,543	78,075	4,763	82,038	177	2,962	115	1,943	0	0	9,618	165,018
20,000	25,000	3,341	74,897	3,424	76,969	150	3,402	76	1,675	0	0	6,991	156,943
25,000	30,000	2,494	68,257	2,427	66,320	54	1,469	53	1,444	0	0	5,026	137,490
30,000	40,000	3,957	137,823	3,992	138,699	420	15,293	69	2,374	0	0	8,438	294,189
40,000	50,000	2,789	124,970	2,794	124,989	288	12,917	41	1,844	0	0	5,912	264,720
50,000	100,000	7,712	550,048	6,821	485,454	967	71,701	97	6,615	0	0	15,597	1,113,818
100,000	500,000	10,471	2,322,542	7,594	1,598,900	2616	661,271	92	18,810	0	0	20,773	4,601,523
500,000	1,000,000	2,166	1,524,405	1,028	702,464	1098	809,777	10	7,392	0	0	4,302	3,044,038
1,000,000	1,500,000	802	984,613	285	346,742	381	450,727	1	1,107	0	0	1,469	1,783,189
1,500,000	2,000,000	418	720,405	129	220,225	370	632,720	2	3,161	0	0	919	1,576,511
2,000,000	2,500,000	255	568,776	69	154,600	185	416,248	0	0	0	0	509	1,139,624
2,500,000	3,000,000	175	482,410	42	113,665	83	224,929	0	0	0	0	300	821,004
3,000,000	4,000,000	217	753,566	64	224,054	252	888,420	0	0	0	0	533	1,866,040
4,000,000	5,000,000	116	519,570	37	165,319	83	371,589	0	0	0	0	236	1,056,478
5,000,000	7,500,000	181	1,111,459	29	173,483	111	656,049	0	0	0	0	321	1,940,991
7,500,000	10,000,000	79	681,509	12	101,475	97	787,899	0	0	0	0	188	1,570,883
10,000,000	15,000,000	80	982,401	10	120,037	60	724,189	0	0	0	0	150	1,826,627
15,000,000	25,000,000	40	734,027	8	144,703	54	1,005,046	1	24,805	1	22,562	104	1,931,143
25,000,000		60	4,718,703	10	696,158	37	1,850,145	0	0	9	2,729,232	116	9,994,238
TOTAL		151,972	17,344,751	178,455	5,985,114	7,774	9,589,278	24,610	87,279	10	2,751,794	362,821	35,758,216

Figure 10.

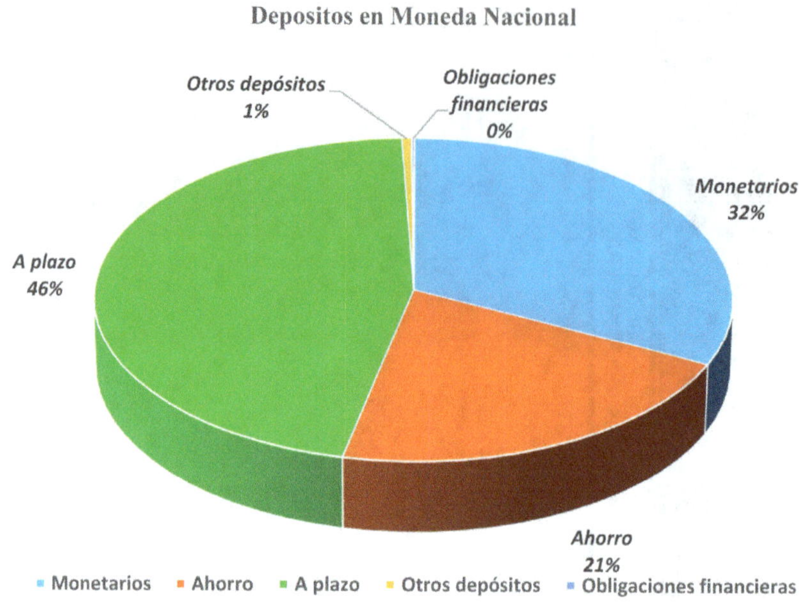

Figure 11.
Source: Own elaboration with information of the Statistical Bulletin referred to September 2016.

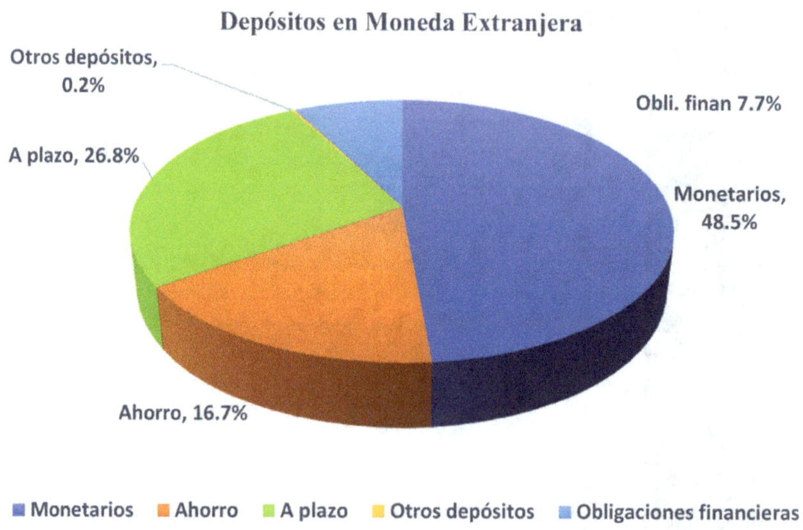

Table 4.

Description	*Top Rate*	*Growth E major*	*Senior Business Applied Rate*
Top Rate	**1.00**	**- 0.02**	**0.65**
Growth E Major	**- 0.02**	**1.00**	**- 0.38**
Senior Business Applied Rate	**0.65**	**- 0.38**	**1.00**

Table 5.

Description	*Top Rate*	*Growth E Minor*	**Small Business Applied Rate**
Top Rate	**1.00**	**0.39**	**0.71**
Growth E Major	**0.39**	**1.00**	**0.03**
Senior Business Applied Rate	**0.71**	**0.03**	**1.00**

Table 6.

Description	*Top Rate*	*Growth Consumption*	*Consumption Rate Applied*
Top Rate	**1.00**	**- 0.23**	**0.08**
Growth E Major	**- 0.23**	**1.00**	**0.58**
Senior Business Applied Rate	**- 0.08**	**0.58**	**1.00**

Table 7.

Description	*Top Rate*	*Microcredit Growth*	*Microcredit Applied Rate*
Top Rate	**1.00**	**0.27**	**0.08**
Growth E Major	**0.27**	**1.00**	**0.17**
Senior Business Applied Rate	**0.08**	**0.17**	**1.00**

Table 8.

Description	*Top Rate*	*Mortgage Growth For Housing*	*Mortgage for Housing Applied Rate*
Top Rate	**1.00**	**0.56**	**0.77**
Growth E Major	**0.56**	**1.00**	**0.27**
Senior Business Applied Rate	**0.77**	**0.27**	**1.00**

4. Until December 31st, 2015, the different portfolios (business, retail, consumption, microcredit and housing) have shown constant growth. However, in the six-month period of 2016, there is a slight contraction, possibly influenced by the fact that the economic sector has not grown at the expected rate.
5. The consumption portfolio has increased exponentially in recent years, despite the fact that the interest rate applied to this segment is high.
6. Deposits received by financial institutions in the different modalities have been growing in recent years; at the same time, it promotes the placement to industries or clients that require financing to grow in their operations.

REFERENCES

Balsells, E. (2006). *Competition and Regulation in the Banking Sector in Guatemala. Strengthening competition in the Central American Isthmus: National policies and institutions, regional coordination and participation in international negotiations*. CEPAL.

Banco de Guatemala. (2006). *Study of the National Economy*. Banco de Guatemala.

Banco de Guatemala. (2015). *Study of the National Economy*. Banco de Guatemala.

Díaz de León, A., & Greenham, L. (2001). Monetary policy and interest rates: recent experience for the case of Mexico. *Mexican Economy. New Age*, 213-258.

Related References

To continue our tradition of advancing academic research, we have compiled a list of recommended IGI Global readings. These references will provide additional information and guidance to further enrich your knowledge and assist you with your own research and future publications.

Adeyemo, O. (2013). The nationwide health information network: A biometric approach to prevent medical identity theft. In *User-driven healthcare: Concepts, methodologies, tools, and applications* (pp. 1636–1649). Hershey, PA: IGI Global. doi:10.4018/978-1-4666-2770-3.ch081

Adler, M., & Henman, P. (2009). Justice beyond the courts: The implications of computerisation for procedural justice in social security. In A. Martínez & P. Abat (Eds.), *E-justice: Using information communication technologies in the court system* (pp. 65–86). Hershey, PA: IGI Global. doi:10.4018/978-1-59904-998-4.ch005

Aflalo, E., & Gabay, E. (2013). An information system for coping with student dropout. In L. Tomei (Ed.), *Learning tools and teaching approaches through ICT advancements* (pp. 176–187). Hershey, PA: IGI Global. doi:10.4018/978-1-4666-2017-9.ch016

Ahmed, M. A., Janssen, M., & van den Hoven, J. (2012). Value sensitive transfer (VST) of systems among countries: Towards a framework. *International Journal of Electronic Government Research, 8*(1), 26–42. doi:10.4018/jegr.2012010102

Aikins, S. K. (2008). Issues and trends in internet-based citizen participation. In G. Garson & M. Khosrow-Pour (Eds.), *Handbook of research on public information technology* (pp. 31–40). Hershey, PA: IGI Global. doi:10.4018/978-1-59904-857-4.ch004

Aikins, S. K. (2009). A comparative study of municipal adoption of internet-based citizen participation. In C. Reddick (Ed.), *Handbook of research on strategies for local e-government adoption and implementation: Comparative studies* (pp. 206–230). Hershey, PA: IGI Global. doi:10.4018/978-1-60566-282-4.ch011

Aikins, S. K. (2012). Improving e-government project management: Best practices and critical success factors. In *Digital democracy: Concepts, methodologies, tools, and applications* (pp. 1314–1332). Hershey, PA: IGI Global. doi:10.4018/978-1-4666-1740-7.ch065

Akabawi, M. S. (2011). Ghabbour group ERP deployment: Learning from past technology failures. In E. Business Research and Case Center (Ed.), Cases on business and management in the MENA region: New trends and opportunities (pp. 177-203). Hershey, PA: IGI Global. doi:10.4018/978-1-60960-583-4.ch012

Akabawi, M. S. (2013). Ghabbour group ERP deployment: Learning from past technology failures. In *Industrial engineering: Concepts, methodologies, tools, and applications* (pp. 933–958). Hershey, PA: IGI Global. doi:10.4018/978-1-4666-1945-6.ch051

Akbulut, A. Y., & Motwani, J. (2008). Integration and information sharing in e-government. In G. Putnik & M. Cruz-Cunha (Eds.), *Encyclopedia of networked and virtual organizations* (pp. 729–734). Hershey, PA: IGI Global. doi:10.4018/978-1-59904-885-7.ch096

Akers, E. J. (2008). Technology diffusion in public administration. In G. Garson & M. Khosrow-Pour (Eds.), *Handbook of research on public information technology* (pp. 339–348). Hershey, PA: IGI Global. doi:10.4018/978-1-59904-857-4.ch033

Al-Shafi, S. (2008). Free wireless internet park services: An investigation of technology adoption in Qatar from a citizens perspective. *Journal of Cases on Information Technology, 10*(3), 21–34. doi:10.4018/jcit.2008070103

Al-Shafi, S., & Weerakkody, V. (2009). Implementing free wi-fi in public parks: An empirical study in Qatar. *International Journal of Electronic Government Research, 5*(3), 21–35. doi:10.4018/jegr.2009070102

Aladwani, A. M. (2002). Organizational actions, computer attitudes and end-user satisfaction in public organizations: An empirical study. In C. Snodgrass & E. Szewczak (Eds.), *Human factors in information systems* (pp. 153–168). Hershey, PA: IGI Global. doi:10.4018/978-1-931777-10-0.ch012

Related References

Aladwani, A. M. (2002). Organizational actions, computer attitudes, and end-user satisfaction in public organizations: An empirical study. *Journal of Organizational and End User Computing*, *14*(1), 42–49. doi:10.4018/joeuc.2002010104

Allen, B., Juillet, L., Paquet, G., & Roy, J. (2005). E-government and private-public partnerships: Relational challenges and strategic directions. In M. Khosrow-Pour (Ed.), *Practicing e-government: A global perspective* (pp. 364–382). Hershey, PA: IGI Global. doi:10.4018/978-1-59140-637-2.ch016

Alshawaf, A., & Knalil, O. E. (2008). IS success factors and IS organizational impact: Does ownership type matter in Kuwait? *International Journal of Enterprise Information Systems*, *4*(2), 13–33. doi:10.4018/jeis.2008040102

Ambali, A. R. (2009). Digital divide and its implication on Malaysian e-government: Policy initiatives. In H. Rahman (Ed.), *Social and political implications of data mining: Knowledge management in e-government* (pp. 267–287). Hershey, PA: IGI Global. doi:10.4018/978-1-60566-230-5.ch016

Amoretti, F. (2007). Digital international governance. In A. Anttiroiko & M. Malkia (Eds.), *Encyclopedia of digital government* (pp. 365–370). Hershey, PA: IGI Global. doi:10.4018/978-1-59140-789-8.ch056

Amoretti, F. (2008). Digital international governance. In A. Anttiroiko (Ed.), *Electronic government: Concepts, methodologies, tools, and applications* (pp. 688–696). Hershey, PA: IGI Global. doi:10.4018/978-1-59904-947-2.ch058

Amoretti, F. (2008). E-government at supranational level in the European Union. In A. Anttiroiko (Ed.), *Electronic government: Concepts, methodologies, tools, and applications* (pp. 1047–1055). Hershey, PA: IGI Global. doi:10.4018/978-1-59904-947-2.ch079

Amoretti, F. (2008). E-government regimes. In A. Anttiroiko (Ed.), *Electronic government: Concepts, methodologies, tools, and applications* (pp. 3846–3856). Hershey, PA: IGI Global. doi:10.4018/978-1-59904-947-2.ch280

Amoretti, F. (2009). Electronic constitution: A Braudelian perspective. In F. Amoretti (Ed.), *Electronic constitution: Social, cultural, and political implications* (pp. 1–19). Hershey, PA: IGI Global. doi:10.4018/978-1-60566-254-1.ch001

Amoretti, F., & Musella, F. (2009). Institutional isomorphism and new technologies. In M. Khosrow-Pour (Ed.), *Encyclopedia of information science and technology* (2nd ed.; pp. 2066–2071). Hershey, PA: IGI Global. doi:10.4018/978-1-60566-026-4.ch325

Andersen, K. V., & Henriksen, H. Z. (2007). E-government research: Capabilities, interaction, orientation, and values. In D. Norris (Ed.), *Current issues and trends in e-government research* (pp. 269–288). Hershey, PA: IGI Global. doi:10.4018/978-1-59904-283-1.ch013

Anderson, K. V., & Henriksen, H. Z. (2005). The first leg of e-government research: Domains and application areas 19982003. *International Journal of Electronic Government Research, 1*(4), 26–44. doi:10.4018/jegr.2005100102

Anttiroiko, A. (2009). Democratic e-governance. In M. Khosrow-Pour (Ed.), *Encyclopedia of information science and technology* (2nd ed.; pp. 990–995). Hershey, PA: IGI Global. doi:10.4018/978-1-60566-026-4.ch158

Baker, P. M., Bell, A., & Moon, N. W. (2009). Accessibility issues in municipal wireless networks. In C. Reddick (Ed.), *Handbook of research on strategies for local e-government adoption and implementation: Comparative studies* (pp. 569–588). Hershey, PA: IGI Global. doi:10.4018/978-1-60566-282-4.ch030

Becker, S. A., Keimer, R., & Muth, T. (2010). A case on university and community collaboration: The sci-tech entrepreneurial training services (ETS) program. In S. Becker & R. Niebuhr (Eds.), *Cases on technology innovation: Entrepreneurial successes and pitfalls* (pp. 68–90). Hershey, PA: IGI Global. doi:10.4018/978-1-61520-609-4.ch003

Becker, S. A., Keimer, R., & Muth, T. (2012). A case on university and community collaboration: The sci-tech entrepreneurial training services (ETS) program. In Regional development: Concepts, methodologies, tools, and applications (pp. 947-969). Hershey, PA: IGI Global. doi:10.4018/978-1-4666-0882-5.ch507

Bernardi, R. (2012). Information technology and resistance to public sector reforms: A case study in Kenya. In T. Papadopoulos & P. Kanellis (Eds.), *Public sector reform using information technologies: Transforming policy into practice* (pp. 59–78). Hershey, PA: IGI Global. doi:10.4018/978-1-60960-839-2.ch004

Bernardi, R. (2013). Information technology and resistance to public sector reforms: A case study in Kenya. In *User-driven healthcare: Concepts, methodologies, tools, and applications* (pp. 14–33). Hershey, PA: IGI Global. doi:10.4018/978-1-4666-2770-3.ch002

Bolívar, M. P., Pérez, M. D., & Hernández, A. M. (2012). Municipal e-government services in emerging economies: The Latin-American and Caribbean experiences. In Y. Chen & P. Chu (Eds.), *Electronic governance and cross-boundary collaboration: Innovations and advancing tools* (pp. 198–226). Hershey, PA: IGI Global. doi:10.4018/978-1-60960-753-1.ch011

Borycki, E. M., & Kushniruk, A. W. (2010). Use of clinical simulations to evaluate the impact of health information systems and ubiquitous computing devices upon health professional work. In S. Mohammed & J. Fiaidhi (Eds.), *Ubiquitous health and medical informatics: The ubiquity 2.0 trend and beyond* (pp. 552–573). Hershey, PA: IGI Global. doi:10.4018/978-1-61520-777-0.ch026

Borycki, E. M., & Kushniruk, A. W. (2011). Use of clinical simulations to evaluate the impact of health information systems and ubiquitous computing devices upon health professional work. In *Clinical technologies: Concepts, methodologies, tools and applications* (pp. 532–553). Hershey, PA: IGI Global. doi:10.4018/978-1-60960-561-2.ch220

Buchan, J. (2011). Developing a dynamic and responsive online learning environment: A case study of a large Australian university. In B. Czerkawski (Ed.), *Free and open source software for e-learning: Issues, successes and challenges* (pp. 92–109). Hershey, PA: IGI Global. doi:10.4018/978-1-61520-917-0.ch006

Buenger, A. W. (2008). Digital convergence and cybersecurity policy. In G. Garson & M. Khosrow-Pour (Eds.), *Handbook of research on public information technology* (pp. 395–405). Hershey, PA: IGI Global. doi:10.4018/978-1-59904-857-4.ch038

Burn, J. M., & Loch, K. D. (2002). The societal impact of world wide web - Key challenges for the 21st century. In A. Salehnia (Ed.), *Ethical issues of information systems* (pp. 88–106). Hershey, PA: IGI Global. doi:10.4018/978-1-931777-15-5.ch007

Burn, J. M., & Loch, K. D. (2003). The societal impact of the world wide web-Key challenges for the 21st century. In M. Khosrow-Pour (Ed.), *Advanced topics in information resources management* (Vol. 2, pp. 32–51). Hershey, PA: IGI Global. doi:10.4018/978-1-59140-062-2.ch002

Bwalya, K. J., Du Plessis, T., & Rensleigh, C. (2012). The "quicksilver initiatives" as a framework for e-government strategy design in developing economies. In K. Bwalya & S. Zulu (Eds.), *Handbook of research on e-government in emerging economies: Adoption, e-participation, and legal frameworks* (pp. 605–623). Hershey, PA: IGI Global. doi:10.4018/978-1-4666-0324-0.ch031

Cabotaje, C. E., & Alampay, E. A. (2013). Social media and citizen engagement: Two cases from the Philippines. In S. Saeed & C. Reddick (Eds.), *Human-centered system design for electronic governance* (pp. 225–238). Hershey, PA: IGI Global. doi:10.4018/978-1-4666-3640-8.ch013

Camillo, A., Di Pietro, L., Di Virgilio, F., & Franco, M. (2013). Work-groups conflict at PetroTech-Italy, S.R.L.: The influence of culture on conflict dynamics. In B. Christiansen, E. Turkina, & N. Williams (Eds.), *Cultural and technological influences on global business* (pp. 272–289). Hershey, PA: IGI Global. doi:10.4018/978-1-4666-3966-9.ch015

Capra, E., Francalanci, C., & Marinoni, C. (2008). Soft success factors for m-government. In A. Anttiroiko (Ed.), *Electronic government: Concepts, methodologies, tools, and applications* (pp. 1213–1233). Hershey, PA: IGI Global. doi:10.4018/978-1-59904-947-2.ch089

Cartelli, A. (2009). The implementation of practices with ICT as a new teaching-learning paradigm. In A. Cartelli & M. Palma (Eds.), *Encyclopedia of information communication technology* (pp. 413–417). Hershey, PA: IGI Global. doi:10.4018/978-1-59904-845-1.ch055

Charalabidis, Y., Lampathaki, F., & Askounis, D. (2010). Investigating the landscape in national interoperability frameworks. *International Journal of E-Services and Mobile Applications, 2*(4), 28–41. doi:10.4018/jesma.2010100103

Charalabidis, Y., Lampathaki, F., & Askounis, D. (2012). Investigating the landscape in national interoperability frameworks. In A. Scupola (Ed.), *Innovative mobile platform developments for electronic services design and delivery* (pp. 218–231). Hershey, PA: IGI Global. doi:10.4018/978-1-4666-1568-7.ch013

Chen, I. (2005). Distance education associations. In C. Howard, J. Boettcher, L. Justice, K. Schenk, P. Rogers, & G. Berg (Eds.), *Encyclopedia of distance learning* (pp. 599–612). Hershey, PA: IGI Global. doi:10.4018/978-1-59140-555-9.ch087

Chen, I. (2008). Distance education associations. In L. Tomei (Ed.), *Online and distance learning: Concepts, methodologies, tools, and applications* (pp. 562–579). Hershey, PA: IGI Global. doi:10.4018/978-1-59904-935-9.ch048

Chen, Y. (2008). Managing IT outsourcing for digital government. In A. Anttiroiko (Ed.), *Electronic government: Concepts, methodologies, tools, and applications* (pp. 3107–3114). Hershey, PA: IGI Global. doi:10.4018/978-1-59904-947-2.ch229

Chen, Y., & Dimitrova, D. V. (2006). Electronic government and online engagement: Citizen interaction with government via web portals. *International Journal of Electronic Government Research, 2*(1), 54–76. doi:10.4018/jegr.2006010104

Chen, Y., & Knepper, R. (2005). Digital government development strategies: Lessons for policy makers from a comparative perspective. In W. Huang, K. Siau, & K. Wei (Eds.), *Electronic government strategies and implementation* (pp. 394–420). Hershey, PA: IGI Global. doi:10.4018/978-1-59140-348-7.ch017

Chen, Y., & Knepper, R. (2008). Digital government development strategies: Lessons for policy makers from a comparative perspective. In H. Rahman (Ed.), *Developing successful ICT strategies: Competitive advantages in a global knowledge-driven society* (pp. 334–356). Hershey, PA: IGI Global. doi:10.4018/978-1-59904-654-9.ch017

Cherian, E. J., & Ryan, T. W. (2014). Incongruent needs: Why differences in the iron-triangle of priorities make health information technology adoption and use difficult. In C. El Morr (Ed.), *Research perspectives on the role of informatics in health policy and management* (pp. 209–221). Hershey, PA: IGI Global. doi:10.4018/978-1-4666-4321-5.ch012

Cho, H. J., & Hwang, S. (2010). Government 2.0 in Korea: Focusing on e-participation services. In C. Reddick (Ed.), *Politics, democracy and e-government: Participation and service delivery* (pp. 94–114). Hershey, PA: IGI Global. doi:10.4018/978-1-61520-933-0.ch006

Chorus, C., & Timmermans, H. (2010). Ubiquitous travel environments and travel control strategies: Prospects and challenges. In M. Wachowicz (Ed.), *Movement-aware applications for sustainable mobility: Technologies and approaches* (pp. 30–51). Hershey, PA: IGI Global. doi:10.4018/978-1-61520-769-5.ch003

Chuanshen, R. (2007). E-government construction and China's administrative litigation act. In A. Anttiroiko & M. Malkia (Eds.), *Encyclopedia of digital government* (pp. 507–510). Hershey, PA: IGI Global. doi:10.4018/978-1-59140-789-8.ch077

Ciaghi, A., & Villafiorita, A. (2012). Law modeling and BPR for public administration improvement. In K. Bwalya & S. Zulu (Eds.), *Handbook of research on e-government in emerging economies: Adoption, e-participation, and legal frameworks* (pp. 391–410). Hershey, PA: IGI Global. doi:10.4018/978-1-4666-0324-0.ch019

Ciaramitaro, B. L., & Skrocki, M. (2012). mHealth: Mobile healthcare. In B. Ciaramitaro (Ed.), Mobile technology consumption: Opportunities and challenges (pp. 99-109). Hershey, PA: IGI Global. doi:10.4018/978-1-61350-150-4.ch007

Comite, U. (2012). Innovative processes and managerial effectiveness of e-procurement in healthcare. In A. Manoharan & M. Holzer (Eds.), *Active citizen participation in e-government: A global perspective* (pp. 206–229). Hershey, PA: IGI Global. doi:10.4018/978-1-4666-0116-1.ch011

Cordella, A. (2013). E-government success: How to account for ICT, administrative rationalization, and institutional change. In J. Gil-Garcia (Ed.), *E-government success factors and measures: Theories, concepts, and methodologies* (pp. 40–51). Hershey, PA: IGI Global. doi:10.4018/978-1-4666-4058-0.ch003

Cropf, R. A. (2009). ICT and e-democracy. In M. Khosrow-Pour (Ed.), *Encyclopedia of information science and technology* (2nd ed.; pp. 1789–1793). Hershey, PA: IGI Global. doi:10.4018/978-1-60566-026-4.ch281

Cropf, R. A. (2009). The virtual public sphere. In M. Pagani (Ed.), *Encyclopedia of multimedia technology and networking* (2nd ed.; pp. 1525–1530). Hershey, PA: IGI Global. doi:10.4018/978-1-60566-014-1.ch206

D'Abundo, M. L. (2013). Electronic health record implementation in the United States healthcare industry: Making the process of change manageable. In V. Wang (Ed.), *Handbook of research on technologies for improving the 21st century workforce: Tools for lifelong learning* (pp. 272–286). Hershey, PA: IGI Global. doi:10.4018/978-1-4666-2181-7.ch018

Damurski, L. (2012). E-participation in urban planning: Online tools for citizen engagement in Poland and in Germany. *International Journal of E-Planning Research, 1*(3), 40–67. doi:10.4018/ijepr.2012070103

de Almeida, M. O. (2007). E-government strategy in Brazil: Increasing transparency and efficiency through e-government procurement. In M. Gascó-Hernandez (Ed.), *Latin America online: Cases, successes and pitfalls* (pp. 34–82). Hershey, PA: IGI Global. doi:10.4018/978-1-59140-974-8.ch002

de Juana Espinosa, S. (2008). Empirical study of the municipalitites' motivations for adopting online presence. In A. Anttiroiko (Ed.), *Electronic government: Concepts, methodologies, tools, and applications* (pp. 3593–3608). Hershey, PA: IGI Global. doi:10.4018/978-1-59904-947-2.ch262

de Souza Dias, D. (2002). Motivation for using information technology. In C. Snodgrass & E. Szewczak (Eds.), *Human factors in information systems* (pp. 55–60). Hershey, PA: IGI Global. doi:10.4018/978-1-931777-10-0.ch005

Demediuk, P. (2006). Government procurement ICT's impact on the sustainability of SMEs and regional communities. In S. Marshall, W. Taylor, & X. Yu (Eds.), *Encyclopedia of developing regional communities with information and communication technology* (pp. 321–324). Hershey, PA: IGI Global. doi:10.4018/978-1-59140-575-7.ch056

Devonshire, E., Forsyth, H., Reid, S., & Simpson, J. M. (2013). The challenges and opportunities of online postgraduate coursework programs in a traditional university context. In B. Tynan, J. Willems, & R. James (Eds.), *Outlooks and opportunities in blended and distance learning* (pp. 353–368). Hershey, PA: IGI Global. doi:10.4018/978-1-4666-4205-8.ch026

Di Cerbo, F., Scotto, M., Sillitti, A., Succi, G., & Vernazza, T. (2007). Toward a GNU/Linux distribution for corporate environments. In S. Sowe, I. Stamelos, & I. Samoladas (Eds.), *Emerging free and open source software practices* (pp. 215–236). Hershey, PA: IGI Global. doi:10.4018/978-1-59904-210-7.ch010

Diesner, J., & Carley, K. M. (2005). Revealing social structure from texts: Meta-matrix text analysis as a novel method for network text analysis. In V. Narayanan & D. Armstrong (Eds.), *Causal mapping for research in information technology* (pp. 81–108). Hershey, PA: IGI Global. doi:10.4018/978-1-59140-396-8.ch004

Dologite, D. G., Mockler, R. J., Bai, Q., & Viszhanyo, P. F. (2006). IS change agents in practice in a US-Chinese joint venture. In M. Hunter & F. Tan (Eds.), *Advanced topics in global information management* (Vol. 5, pp. 331–352). Hershey, PA: IGI Global. doi:10.4018/978-1-59140-923-6.ch015

Drnevich, P., Brush, T. H., & Luckock, G. T. (2011). Process and structural implications for IT-enabled outsourcing. *International Journal of Strategic Information Technology and Applications*, *2*(4), 30–43. doi:10.4018/jsita.2011100103

Dwivedi, A. N. (2009). Handbook of research on information technology management and clinical data administration in healthcare (Vols. 1–2). Hershey, PA: IGI Global. doi:10.4018/978-1-60566-356-2

Elbeltagi, I., McBride, N., & Hardaker, G. (2006). Evaluating the factors affecting DSS usage by senior managers in local authorities in Egypt. In M. Hunter & F. Tan (Eds.), *Advanced topics in global information management* (Vol. 5, pp. 283–307). Hershey, PA: IGI Global. doi:10.4018/978-1-59140-923-6.ch013

Eom, S., & Fountain, J. E. (2013). Enhancing information services through public-private partnerships: Information technology knowledge transfer underlying structures to develop shared services in the U.S. and Korea. In J. Gil-Garcia (Ed.), *E-government success around the world: Cases, empirical studies, and practical recommendations* (pp. 15–40). Hershey, PA: IGI Global. doi:10.4018/978-1-4666-4173-0.ch002

Esteves, T., Leuenberger, D., & Van Leuven, N. (2012). Reaching citizen 2.0: How government uses social media to send public messages during times of calm and times of crisis. In K. Kloby & M. D'Agostino (Eds.), *Citizen 2.0: Public and governmental interaction through web 2.0 technologies* (pp. 250–268). Hershey, PA: IGI Global. doi:10.4018/978-1-4666-0318-9.ch013

Estevez, E., Fillottrani, P., Janowski, T., & Ojo, A. (2012). Government information sharing: A framework for policy formulation. In Y. Chen & P. Chu (Eds.), *Electronic governance and cross-boundary collaboration: Innovations and advancing tools* (pp. 23–55). Hershey, PA: IGI Global. doi:10.4018/978-1-60960-753-1.ch002

Ezz, I. E. (2008). E-governement emerging trends: Organizational challenges. In A. Anttiroiko (Ed.), *Electronic government: Concepts, methodologies, tools, and applications* (pp. 3721–3737). Hershey, PA: IGI Global. doi:10.4018/978-1-59904-947-2.ch269

Fabri, M. (2009). The Italian style of e-justice in a comparative perspective. In A. Martínez & P. Abat (Eds.), *E-justice: Using information communication technologies in the court system* (pp. 1–19). Hershey, PA: IGI Global. doi:10.4018/978-1-59904-998-4.ch001

Fagbe, T., & Adekola, O. D. (2010). Workplace safety and personnel well-being: The impact of information technology. *International Journal of Green Computing, 1*(1), 28–33. doi:10.4018/jgc.2010010103

Fagbe, T., & Adekola, O. D. (2011). Workplace safety and personnel well-being: The impact of information technology. In *Global business: Concepts, methodologies, tools and applications* (pp. 1438–1444). Hershey, PA: IGI Global. doi:10.4018/978-1-60960-587-2.ch509

Farmer, L. (2008). Affective collaborative instruction with librarians. In S. Kelsey & K. St.Amant (Eds.), *Handbook of research on computer mediated communication* (pp. 15–24). Hershey, PA: IGI Global. doi:10.4018/978-1-59904-863-5.ch002

Favier, L., & Mekhantar, J. (2007). Use of OSS by local e-administration: The French situation. In K. St.Amant & B. Still (Eds.), *Handbook of research on open source software: Technological, economic, and social perspectives* (pp. 428–444). Hershey, PA: IGI Global. doi:10.4018/978-1-59140-999-1.ch033

Fernando, S. (2009). Issues of e-learning in third world countries. In M. Khosrow-Pour (Ed.), *Encyclopedia of information science and technology* (2nd ed.; pp. 2273–2277). Hershey, PA: IGI Global. doi:10.4018/978-1-60566-026-4.ch360

Filho, J. R., & dos Santos Junior, J. R. (2009). Local e-government in Brazil: Poor interaction and local politics as usual. In C. Reddick (Ed.), *Handbook of research on strategies for local e-government adoption and implementation: Comparative studies* (pp. 863–878). Hershey, PA: IGI Global. doi:10.4018/978-1-60566-282-4.ch045

Fletcher, P. D. (2004). Portals and policy: Implications of electronic access to U.S. federal government information services. In A. Pavlichev & G. Garson (Eds.), *Digital government: Principles and best practices* (pp. 52–62). Hershey, PA: IGI Global. doi:10.4018/978-1-59140-122-3.ch004

Fletcher, P. D. (2008). Portals and policy: Implications of electronic access to U.S. federal government information services. In A. Anttiroiko (Ed.), *Electronic government: Concepts, methodologies, tools, and applications* (pp. 3970–3979). Hershey, PA: IGI Global. doi:10.4018/978-1-59904-947-2.ch289

Forlano, L. (2004). The emergence of digital government: International perspectives. In A. Pavlichev & G. Garson (Eds.), *Digital government: Principles and best practices* (pp. 34–51). Hershey, PA: IGI Global. doi:10.4018/978-1-59140-122-3.ch003

Franzel, J. M., & Coursey, D. H. (2004). Government web portals: Management issues and the approaches of five states. In A. Pavlichev & G. Garson (Eds.), *Digital government: Principles and best practices* (pp. 63–77). Hershey, PA: IGI Global. doi:10.4018/978-1-59140-122-3.ch005

Gaivéo, J. M. (2013). Security of ICTs supporting healthcare activities. In M. Cruz-Cunha, I. Miranda, & P. Gonçalves (Eds.), *Handbook of research on ICTs for human-centered healthcare and social care services* (pp. 208–228). Hershey, PA: IGI Global. doi:10.4018/978-1-4666-3986-7.ch011

Garson, G. D. (1999). *Information technology and computer applications in public administration: Issues and trends*. Hershey, PA: IGI Global. doi:10.4018/978-1-87828-952-0

Garson, G. D. (2003). Toward an information technology research agenda for public administration. In G. Garson (Ed.), *Public information technology: Policy and management issues* (pp. 331–357). Hershey, PA: IGI Global. doi:10.4018/978-1-59140-060-8.ch014

Garson, G. D. (2004). The promise of digital government. In A. Pavlichev & G. Garson (Eds.), *Digital government: Principles and best practices* (pp. 2–15). Hershey, PA: IGI Global. doi:10.4018/978-1-59140-122-3.ch001

Garson, G. D. (2007). An information technology research agenda for public administration. In G. Garson (Ed.), *Modern public information technology systems: Issues and challenges* (pp. 365–392). Hershey, PA: IGI Global. doi:10.4018/978-1-59904-051-6.ch018

Gasco, M. (2007). Civil servants' resistance towards e-government development. In A. Anttiroiko & M. Malkia (Eds.), *Encyclopedia of digital government* (pp. 190–195). Hershey, PA: IGI Global. doi:10.4018/978-1-59140-789-8.ch028

Gasco, M. (2008). Civil servants' resistance towards e-government development. In A. Anttiroiko (Ed.), *Electronic government: Concepts, methodologies, tools, and applications* (pp. 2580–2588). Hershey, PA: IGI Global. doi:10.4018/978-1-59904-947-2.ch190

Ghere, R. K. (2010). Accountability and information technology enactment: Implications for social empowerment. In E. Ferro, Y. Dwivedi, J. Gil-Garcia, & M. Williams (Eds.), *Handbook of research on overcoming digital divides: Constructing an equitable and competitive information society* (pp. 515–532). Hershey, PA: IGI Global. doi:10.4018/978-1-60566-699-0.ch028

Gibson, I. W. (2012). Simulation modeling of healthcare delivery. In A. Kolker & P. Story (Eds.), *Management engineering for effective healthcare delivery: Principles and applications* (pp. 69–89). Hershey, PA: IGI Global. doi:10.4018/978-1-60960-872-9.ch003

Gil-Garcia, J. R. (2007). Exploring e-government benefits and success factors. In A. Anttiroiko & M. Malkia (Eds.), *Encyclopedia of digital government* (pp. 803–811). Hershey, PA: IGI Global. doi:10.4018/978-1-59140-789-8.ch122

Gil-Garcia, J. R., & González Miranda, F. (2010). E-government and opportunities for participation: The case of the Mexican state web portals. In C. Reddick (Ed.), *Politics, democracy and e-government: Participation and service delivery* (pp. 56–74). Hershey, PA: IGI Global. doi:10.4018/978-1-61520-933-0.ch004

Goldfinch, S. (2012). Public trust in government, trust in e-government, and use of e-government. In Z. Yan (Ed.), *Encyclopedia of cyber behavior* (pp. 987–995). Hershey, PA: IGI Global. doi:10.4018/978-1-4666-0315-8.ch081

Goodyear, M. (2012). Organizational change contributions to e-government project transitions. In S. Aikins (Ed.), *Managing e-government projects: Concepts, issues, and best practices* (pp. 1–21). Hershey, PA: IGI Global. doi:10.4018/978-1-4666-0086-7.ch001

Gordon, S., & Mulligan, P. (2003). Strategic models for the delivery of personal financial services: The role of infocracy. In S. Gordon (Ed.), *Computing information technology: The human side* (pp. 220–232). Hershey, PA: IGI Global. doi:10.4018/978-1-93177-752-0.ch014

Gordon, T. F. (2007). Legal knowledge systems. In A. Anttiroiko & M. Malkia (Eds.), *Encyclopedia of digital government* (pp. 1161–1166). Hershey, PA: IGI Global. doi:10.4018/978-1-59140-789-8.ch175

Graham, J. E., & Semich, G. W. (2008). Integrating technology to transform pedagogy: Revisiting the progress of the three phase TUI model for faculty development. In L. Tomei (Ed.), *Adapting information and communication technologies for effective education* (pp. 1–12). Hershey, PA: IGI Global. doi:10.4018/978-1-59904-922-9.ch001

Grandinetti, L., & Pisacane, O. (2012). Web services for healthcare management. In D. Prakash Vidyarthi (Ed.), *Technologies and protocols for the future of internet design: Reinventing the web* (pp. 60–94). Hershey, PA: IGI Global. doi:10.4018/978-1-4666-0203-8.ch004

Groenewegen, P., & Wagenaar, F. P. (2008). VO as an alternative to hierarchy in the Dutch police sector. In G. Putnik & M. Cruz-Cunha (Eds.), *Encyclopedia of networked and virtual organizations* (pp. 1851–1857). Hershey, PA: IGI Global. doi:10.4018/978-1-59904-885-7.ch245

Gronlund, A. (2001). Building an infrastructure to manage electronic services. In S. Dasgupta (Ed.), *Managing internet and intranet technologies in organizations: Challenges and opportunities* (pp. 71–103). Hershey, PA: IGI Global. doi:10.4018/978-1-878289-95-7.ch006

Gronlund, A. (2002). Introduction to electronic government: Design, applications and management. In Å. Grönlund (Ed.), *Electronic government: Design, applications and management* (pp. 1–21). Hershey, PA: IGI Global. doi:10.4018/978-1-930708-19-8.ch001

Gupta, A., Woosley, R., Crk, I., & Sarnikar, S. (2009). An information technology architecture for drug effectiveness reporting and post-marketing surveillance. In J. Tan (Ed.), *Medical informatics: Concepts, methodologies, tools, and applications* (pp. 631–646). Hershey, PA: IGI Global. doi:10.4018/978-1-60566-050-9.ch047

Hallin, A., & Lundevall, K. (2007). mCity: User focused development of mobile services within the city of Stockholm. In I. Kushchu (Ed.), Mobile government: An emerging direction in e-government (pp. 12-29). Hershey, PA: IGI Global. doi:10.4018/978-1-59140-884-0.ch002

Hallin, A., & Lundevall, K. (2009). mCity: User focused development of mobile services within the city of Stockholm. In S. Clarke (Ed.), Evolutionary concepts in end user productivity and performance: Applications for organizational progress (pp. 268-280). Hershey, PA: IGI Global. doi:10.4018/978-1-60566-136-0.ch017

Hallin, A., & Lundevall, K. (2009). mCity: User focused development of mobile services within the city of Stockholm. In D. Taniar (Ed.), Mobile computing: Concepts, methodologies, tools, and applications (pp. 3455-3467). Hershey, PA: IGI Global. doi:10.4018/978-1-60566-054-7.ch253

Hanson, A. (2005). Overcoming barriers in the planning of a virtual library. In M. Khosrow-Pour (Ed.), *Encyclopedia of information science and technology* (pp. 2255–2259). Hershey, PA: IGI Global. doi:10.4018/978-1-59140-553-5.ch397

Haque, A. (2008). Information technology and surveillance: Implications for public administration in a new word order. In T. Loendorf & G. Garson (Eds.), *Patriotic information systems* (pp. 177–185). Hershey, PA: IGI Global. doi:10.4018/978-1-59904-594-8.ch008

Hauck, R. V., Thatcher, S. M., & Weisband, S. P. (2012). Temporal aspects of information technology use: Increasing shift work effectiveness. In J. Wang (Ed.), *Advancing the service sector with evolving technologies: Techniques and principles* (pp. 87–104). Hershey, PA: IGI Global. doi:10.4018/978-1-4666-0044-7.ch006

Hawk, S., & Witt, T. (2006). Telecommunications courses in information systems programs. *International Journal of Information and Communication Technology Education, 2*(1), 79–92. doi:10.4018/jicte.2006010107

Helms, M. M., Moore, R., & Ahmadi, M. (2009). Information technology (IT) and the healthcare industry: A SWOT analysis. In J. Tan (Ed.), *Medical informatics: Concepts, methodologies, tools, and applications* (pp. 134–152). Hershey, PA: IGI Global. doi:10.4018/978-1-60566-050-9.ch012

Hendrickson, S. M., & Young, M. E. (2014). Electronic records management at a federally funded research and development center. In J. Krueger (Ed.), *Cases on electronic records and resource management implementation in diverse environments* (pp. 334–350). Hershey, PA: IGI Global. doi:10.4018/978-1-4666-4466-3.ch020

Henman, P. (2010). Social policy and information communication technologies. In J. Martin & L. Hawkins (Eds.), *Information communication technologies for human services education and delivery: Concepts and cases* (pp. 215–229). Hershey, PA: IGI Global. doi:10.4018/978-1-60566-735-5.ch014

Hismanoglu, M. (2011). Important issues in online education: E-pedagogy and marketing. In U. Demiray & S. Sever (Eds.), *Marketing online education programs: Frameworks for promotion and communication* (pp. 184–209). Hershey, PA: IGI Global. doi:10.4018/978-1-60960-074-7.ch012

Ho, K. K. (2008). The e-government development, IT strategies, and portals of the Hong Kong SAR government. In A. Anttiroiko (Ed.), *Electronic government: Concepts, methodologies, tools, and applications* (pp. 715–733). Hershey, PA: IGI Global. doi:10.4018/978-1-59904-947-2.ch060

Holden, S. H. (2003). The evolution of information technology management at the federal level: Implications for public administration. In G. Garson (Ed.), *Public information technology: Policy and management issues* (pp. 53–73). Hershey, PA: IGI Global. doi:10.4018/978-1-59140-060-8.ch003

Holden, S. H. (2007). The evolution of federal information technology management literature: Does IT finally matter? In G. Garson (Ed.), *Modern public information technology systems: Issues and challenges* (pp. 17–34). Hershey, PA: IGI Global. doi:10.4018/978-1-59904-051-6.ch002

Holland, J. W. (2009). Automation of American criminal justice. In M. Khosrow-Pour (Ed.), *Encyclopedia of information science and technology* (2nd ed.; pp. 300–302). Hershey, PA: IGI Global. doi:10.4018/978-1-60566-026-4.ch051

Holloway, K. (2013). Fair use, copyright, and academic integrity in an online academic environment. In *Digital rights management: Concepts, methodologies, tools, and applications* (pp. 917–928). Hershey, PA: IGI Global. doi:10.4018/978-1-4666-2136-7.ch044

Horiuchi, C. (2005). E-government databases. In L. Rivero, J. Doorn, & V. Ferraggine (Eds.), *Encyclopedia of database technologies and applications* (pp. 206–210). Hershey, PA: IGI Global. doi:10.4018/978-1-59140-560-3.ch035

Horiuchi, C. (2006). Creating IS quality in government settings. In E. Duggan & J. Reichgelt (Eds.), *Measuring information systems delivery quality* (pp. 311–327). Hershey, PA: IGI Global. doi:10.4018/978-1-59140-857-4.ch014

Hsiao, N., Chu, P., & Lee, C. (2012). Impact of e-governance on businesses: Model development and case study. In *Digital democracy: Concepts, methodologies, tools, and applications* (pp. 1407–1425). Hershey, PA: IGI Global. doi:10.4018/978-1-4666-1740-7.ch070

Huang, T., & Lee, C. (2010). Evaluating the impact of e-government on citizens: Cost-benefit analysis. In C. Reddick (Ed.), *Citizens and e-government: Evaluating policy and management* (pp. 37–52). Hershey, PA: IGI Global. doi:10.4018/978-1-61520-931-6.ch003

Hunter, M. G., Diochon, M., Pugsley, D., & Wright, B. (2002). Unique challenges for small business adoption of information technology: The case of the Nova Scotia ten. In S. Burgess (Ed.), *Managing information technology in small business: Challenges and solutions* (pp. 98–117). Hershey, PA: IGI Global. doi:10.4018/978-1-930708-35-8.ch006

Hurskainen, J. (2003). Integration of business systems and applications in merger and alliance: Case metso automation. In T. Reponen (Ed.), *Information technology enabled global customer service* (pp. 207–225). Hershey, PA: IGI Global. doi:10.4018/978-1-59140-048-6.ch012

Iazzolino, G., & Pietrantonio, R. (2011). The soveria.it project: A best practice of e-government in southern Italy. In D. Piaggesi, K. Sund, & W. Castelnovo (Eds.), *Global strategy and practice of e-governance: Examples from around the world* (pp. 34–56). Hershey, PA: IGI Global. doi:10.4018/978-1-60960-489-9.ch003

Imran, A., & Gregor, S. (2012). A process model for successful e-government adoption in the least developed countries: A case of Bangladesh. In F. Tan (Ed.), *International comparisons of information communication technologies: Advancing applications* (pp. 321–350). Hershey, PA: IGI Global. doi:10.4018/978-1-61350-480-2.ch014

Inoue, Y., & Bell, S. T. (2005). Electronic/digital government innovation, and publishing trends with IT. In M. Khosrow-Pour (Ed.), *Encyclopedia of information science and technology* (pp. 1018–1023). Hershey, PA: IGI Global. doi:10.4018/978-1-59140-553-5.ch180

Islam, M. M., & Ehsan, M. (2013). Understanding e-governance: A theoretical approach. In M. Islam & M. Ehsan (Eds.), *From government to e-governance: Public administration in the digital age* (pp. 38–49). Hershey, PA: IGI Global. doi:10.4018/978-1-4666-1909-8.ch003

Jaeger, B. (2009). E-government and e-democracy in the making. In M. Khosrow-Pour (Ed.), *Encyclopedia of information science and technology* (2nd ed.; pp. 1318–1322). Hershey, PA: IGI Global. doi:10.4018/978-1-60566-026-4.ch208

Jain, R. B. (2007). Revamping the administrative structure and processes in India for online diplomacy. In A. Anttiroiko & M. Malkia (Eds.), *Encyclopedia of digital government* (pp. 1418–1423). Hershey, PA: IGI Global. doi:10.4018/978-1-59140-789-8.ch217

Jain, R. B. (2008). Revamping the administrative structure and processes in India for online diplomacy. In A. Anttiroiko (Ed.), *Electronic government: Concepts, methodologies, tools, and applications* (pp. 3142–3149). Hershey, PA: IGI Global. doi:10.4018/978-1-59904-947-2.ch233

Jauhiainen, J. S., & Inkinen, T. (2009). E-governance and the information society in periphery. In C. Reddick (Ed.), *Handbook of research on strategies for local e-government adoption and implementation: Comparative studies* (pp. 497–514). Hershey, PA: IGI Global. doi:10.4018/978-1-60566-282-4.ch026

Jensen, M. J. (2009). Electronic democracy and citizen influence in government. In C. Reddick (Ed.), *Handbook of research on strategies for local e-government adoption and implementation: Comparative studies* (pp. 288–305). Hershey, PA: IGI Global. doi:10.4018/978-1-60566-282-4.ch015

Jiao, Y., Hurson, A. R., Potok, T. E., & Beckerman, B. G. (2009). Integrating mobile-based systems with healthcare databases. In J. Erickson (Ed.), *Database technologies: Concepts, methodologies, tools, and applications* (pp. 484–504). Hershey, PA: IGI Global. doi:10.4018/978-1-60566-058-5.ch031

Joia, L. A. (2002). A systematic model to integrate information technology into metabusinesses: A case study in the engineering realms. In F. Tan (Ed.), *Advanced topics in global information management* (Vol. 1, pp. 250–267). Hershey, PA: IGI Global. doi:10.4018/978-1-930708-43-3.ch016

Jones, T. H., & Song, I. (2000). Binary equivalents of ternary relationships in entity-relationship modeling: A logical decomposition approach. *Journal of Database Management, 11*(2), 12–19. doi:10.4018/jdm.2000040102

Juana-Espinosa, S. D. (2007). Empirical study of the municipalitites' motivations for adopting online presence. In L. Al-Hakim (Ed.), *Global e-government: Theory, applications and benchmarking* (pp. 261–279). Hershey, PA: IGI Global. doi:10.4018/978-1-59904-027-1.ch015

Jun, K., & Weare, C. (2012). Bridging from e-government practice to e-government research: Past trends and future directions. In K. Bwalya & S. Zulu (Eds.), *Handbook of research on e-government in emerging economies: Adoption, e-participation, and legal frameworks* (pp. 263–289). Hershey, PA: IGI Global. doi:10.4018/978-1-4666-0324-0.ch013

Junqueira, A., Diniz, E. H., & Fernandez, M. (2010). Electronic government implementation projects with multiple agencies: Analysis of the electronic invoice project under PMBOK framework. In J. Cordoba-Pachon & A. Ochoa-Arias (Eds.), *Systems thinking and e-participation: ICT in the governance of society* (pp. 135–153). Hershey, PA: IGI Global. doi:10.4018/978-1-60566-860-4.ch009

Juntunen, A. (2009). Joint service development with the local authorities. In C. Reddick (Ed.), *Handbook of research on strategies for local e-government adoption and implementation: Comparative studies* (pp. 902–920). Hershey, PA: IGI Global. doi:10.4018/978-1-60566-282-4.ch047

Kamel, S. (2001). *Using DSS for crisis management*. Hershey, PA: IGI Global. doi:10.4018/978-1-87828-961-2.ch020

Kamel, S. (2006). DSS for strategic decision making. In M. Khosrow-Pour (Ed.), *Cases on information technology and organizational politics & culture* (pp. 230–246). Hershey, PA: IGI Global. doi:10.4018/978-1-59904-411-8.ch015

Kamel, S. (2009). The software industry in Egypt as a potential contributor to economic growth. In M. Khosrow-Pour (Ed.), *Encyclopedia of information science and technology* (2nd ed.; pp. 3531–3537). Hershey, PA: IGI Global. doi:10.4018/978-1-60566-026-4.ch562

Kamel, S., & Hussein, M. (2008). Xceed: Pioneering the contact center industry in Egypt. *Journal of Cases on Information Technology*, *10*(1), 67–91. doi:10.4018/jcit.2008010105

Kamel, S., & Wahba, K. (2003). The use of a hybrid model in web-based education: "The Global campus project. In A. Aggarwal (Ed.), *Web-based education: Learning from experience* (pp. 331–346). Hershey, PA: IGI Global. doi:10.4018/978-1-59140-102-5.ch020

Kardaras, D. K., & Papathanassiou, E. A. (2008). An exploratory study of the e-government services in Greece. In G. Garson & M. Khosrow-Pour (Eds.), *Handbook of research on public information technology* (pp. 162–174). Hershey, PA: IGI Global. doi:10.4018/978-1-59904-857-4.ch016

Kassahun, A. E., Molla, A., & Sarkar, P. (2012). Government process reengineering: What we know and what we need to know. In *Digital democracy: Concepts, methodologies, tools, and applications* (pp. 1730–1752). Hershey, PA: IGI Global. doi:10.4018/978-1-4666-1740-7.ch086

Khan, B. (2005). Technological issues. In B. Khan (Ed.), *Managing e-learning strategies: Design, delivery, implementation and evaluation* (pp. 154–180). Hershey, PA: IGI Global. doi:10.4018/978-1-59140-634-1.ch004

Khasawneh, A., Bsoul, M., Obeidat, I., & Al Azzam, I. (2012). Technology fears: A study of e-commerce loyalty perception by Jordanian customers. In J. Wang (Ed.), *Advancing the service sector with evolving technologies: Techniques and principles* (pp. 158–165). Hershey, PA: IGI Global. doi:10.4018/978-1-4666-0044-7.ch010

Khatibi, V., & Montazer, G. A. (2012). E-research methodology. In A. Juan, T. Daradoumis, M. Roca, S. Grasman, & J. Faulin (Eds.), *Collaborative and distributed e-research: Innovations in technologies, strategies and applications* (pp. 62–81). Hershey, PA: IGI Global. doi:10.4018/978-1-4666-0125-3.ch003

Kidd, T. (2011). The dragon in the school's backyard: A review of literature on the uses of technology in urban schools. In L. Tomei (Ed.), *Online courses and ICT in education: Emerging practices and applications* (pp. 242–257). Hershey, PA: IGI Global. doi:10.4018/978-1-60960-150-8.ch019

Kidd, T. T. (2010). My experience tells the story: Exploring technology adoption from a qualitative perspective - A pilot study. In H. Song & T. Kidd (Eds.), *Handbook of research on human performance and instructional technology* (pp. 247–262). Hershey, PA: IGI Global. doi:10.4018/978-1-60566-782-9.ch015

Kieley, B., Lane, G., Paquet, G., & Roy, J. (2002). e-Government in Canada: Services online or public service renewal? In Å. Grönlund (Ed.), Electronic government: Design, applications and management (pp. 340-355). Hershey, PA: IGI Global. doi:10.4018/978-1-930708-19-8.ch016

Kim, P. (2012). "Stay out of the way! My kid is video blogging through a phone!": A lesson learned from math tutoring social media for children in underserved communities. In *Wireless technologies: Concepts, methodologies, tools and applications* (pp. 1415–1428). Hershey, PA: IGI Global. doi:10.4018/978-1-61350-101-6.ch517

Kirlidog, M. (2010). Financial aspects of national ICT strategies. In S. Kamel (Ed.), *E-strategies for technological diffusion and adoption: National ICT approaches for socioeconomic development* (pp. 277–292). Hershey, PA: IGI Global. doi:10.4018/978-1-60566-388-3.ch016

Kisielnicki, J. (2006). Transfer of information and knowledge in the project management. In E. Coakes & S. Clarke (Eds.), *Encyclopedia of communities of practice in information and knowledge management* (pp. 544–551). Hershey, PA: IGI Global. doi:10.4018/978-1-59140-556-6.ch091

Kittner, M., & Van Slyke, C. (2006). Reorganizing information technology services in an academic environment. In M. Khosrow-Pour (Ed.), *Cases on the human side of information technology* (pp. 49–66). Hershey, PA: IGI Global. doi:10.4018/978-1-59904-405-7.ch004

Knoell, H. D. (2008). Semi virtual workplaces in German financial service enterprises. In P. Zemliansky & K. St.Amant (Eds.), *Handbook of research on virtual workplaces and the new nature of business practices* (pp. 570–581). Hershey, PA: IGI Global. doi:10.4018/978-1-59904-893-2.ch041

Koh, S. L., & Maguire, S. (2009). Competing in the age of information technology in a developing economy: Experiences of an Indian bank. In S. Koh & S. Maguire (Eds.), *Information and communication technologies management in turbulent business environments* (pp. 326–350). Hershey, PA: IGI Global. doi:10.4018/978-1-60566-424-8.ch018

Kollmann, T., & Häsel, M. (2009). Competence of information technology professionals in internet-based ventures. In I. Lee (Ed.), *Electronic business: Concepts, methodologies, tools, and applications* (pp. 1905–1919). Hershey, PA: IGI Global. doi:10.4018/978-1-60566-056-1.ch118

Kollmann, T., & Häsel, M. (2009). Competence of information technology professionals in internet-based ventures. In A. Cater-Steel (Ed.), *Information technology governance and service management: Frameworks and adaptations* (pp. 239–253). Hershey, PA: IGI Global. doi:10.4018/978-1-60566-008-0.ch013

Kollmann, T., & Häsel, M. (2010). Competence of information technology professionals in internet-based ventures. In *Electronic services: Concepts, methodologies, tools and applications* (pp. 1551–1565). Hershey, PA: IGI Global. doi:10.4018/978-1-61520-967-5.ch094

Kraemer, K., & King, J. L. (2006). Information technology and administrative reform: Will e-government be different? *International Journal of Electronic Government Research, 2*(1), 1–20. doi:10.4018/jegr.2006010101

Kraemer, K., & King, J. L. (2008). Information technology and administrative reform: Will e-government be different? In D. Norris (Ed.), *E-government research: Policy and management* (pp. 1–20). Hershey, PA: IGI Global. doi:10.4018/978-1-59904-913-7.ch001

Lampathaki, F., Tsiakaliaris, C., Stasis, A., & Charalabidis, Y. (2011). National interoperability frameworks: The way forward. In Y. Charalabidis (Ed.), *Interoperability in digital public services and administration: Bridging e-government and e-business* (pp. 1–24). Hershey, PA: IGI Global. doi:10.4018/978-1-61520-887-6.ch001

Lan, Z., & Scott, C. R. (1996). The relative importance of computer-mediated information versus conventional non-computer-mediated information in public managerial decision making. *Information Resources Management Journal, 9*(1), 27–0. doi:10.4018/irmj.1996010103

Law, W. (2004). *Public sector data management in a developing economy.* Hershey, PA: IGI Global. doi:10.4018/978-1-59140-259-6.ch034

Law, W. K. (2005). Information resources development challenges in a cross-cultural environment. In M. Khosrow-Pour (Ed.), *Encyclopedia of information science and technology* (pp. 1476–1481). Hershey, PA: IGI Global. doi:10.4018/978-1-59140-553-5.ch259

Law, W. K. (2009). Cross-cultural challenges for information resources management. In M. Khosrow-Pour (Ed.), *Encyclopedia of information science and technology* (2nd ed.; pp. 840–846). Hershey, PA: IGI Global. doi:10.4018/978-1-60566-026-4.ch136

Law, W. K. (2011). Cross-cultural challenges for information resources management. In *Global business: Concepts, methodologies, tools and applications* (pp. 1924–1932). Hershey, PA: IGI Global. doi:10.4018/978-1-60960-587-2.ch704

Malkia, M., & Savolainen, R. (2004). eTransformation in government, politics and society: Conceptual framework and introduction. In M. Malkia, A. Anttiroiko, & R. Savolainen (Eds.), eTransformation in governance: New directions in government and politics (pp. 1-21). Hershey, PA: IGI Global. doi:10.4018/978-1-59140-130-8.ch001

Mandujano, S. (2011). Network manageability security. In D. Kar & M. Syed (Eds.), *Network security, administration and management: Advancing technology and practice* (pp. 158–181). Hershey, PA: IGI Global. doi:10.4018/978-1-60960-777-7.ch009

Marich, M. J., Schooley, B. L., & Horan, T. A. (2012). A normative enterprise architecture for guiding end-to-end emergency response decision support. In M. Jennex (Ed.), *Managing crises and disasters with emerging technologies: Advancements* (pp. 71–87). Hershey, PA: IGI Global. doi:10.4018/978-1-4666-0167-3.ch006

Markov, R., & Okujava, S. (2008). Costs, benefits, and risks of e-government portals. In G. Putnik & M. Cruz-Cunha (Eds.), *Encyclopedia of networked and virtual organizations* (pp. 354–363). Hershey, PA: IGI Global. doi:10.4018/978-1-59904-885-7.ch047

Martin, N., & Rice, J. (2013). Evaluating and designing electronic government for the future: Observations and insights from Australia. In V. Weerakkody (Ed.), *E-government services design, adoption, and evaluation* (pp. 238–258). Hershey, PA: IGI Global. doi:10.4018/978-1-4666-2458-0.ch014

i. Martinez, A. C. (2008). Accessing administration's information via internet in Spain. In F. Tan (Ed.), *Global information technologies: Concepts, methodologies, tools, and applications* (pp. 2558–2573). Hershey, PA: IGI Global. doi:10.4018/978-1-59904-939-7.ch186

Mbarika, V. W., Meso, P. N., & Musa, P. F. (2006). A disconnect in stakeholders' perceptions from emerging realities of teledensity growth in Africa's least developed countries. In M. Hunter & F. Tan (Eds.), *Advanced topics in global information management* (Vol. 5, pp. 263–282). Hershey, PA: IGI Global. doi:10.4018/978-1-59140-923-6.ch012

Mbarika, V. W., Meso, P. N., & Musa, P. F. (2008). A disconnect in stakeholders' perceptions from emerging realities of teledensity growth in Africa's least developed countries. In F. Tan (Ed.), *Global information technologies: Concepts, methodologies, tools, and applications* (pp. 2948–2962). Hershey, PA: IGI Global. doi:10.4018/978-1-59904-939-7.ch209

Means, T., Olson, E., & Spooner, J. (2013). Discovering ways that don't work on the road to success: Strengths and weaknesses revealed by an active learning studio classroom project. In A. Benson, J. Moore, & S. Williams van Rooij (Eds.), *Cases on educational technology planning, design, and implementation: A project management perspective* (pp. 94–113). Hershey, PA: IGI Global. doi:10.4018/978-1-4666-4237-9.ch006

Melitski, J., Holzer, M., Kim, S., Kim, C., & Rho, S. (2008). Digital government worldwide: An e-government assessment of municipal web sites. In G. Garson & M. Khosrow-Pour (Eds.), *Handbook of research on public information technology* (pp. 790–804). Hershey, PA: IGI Global. doi:10.4018/978-1-59904-857-4.ch069

Memmola, M., Palumbo, G., & Rossini, M. (2009). Web & RFID technology: New frontiers in costing and process management for rehabilitation medicine. In L. Al-Hakim & M. Memmola (Eds.), *Business web strategy: Design, alignment, and application* (pp. 145–169). Hershey, PA: IGI Global. doi:10.4018/978-1-60566-024-0.ch008

Meng, Z., Fahong, Z., & Lei, L. (2008). Information technology and environment. In Y. Kurihara, S. Takaya, H. Harui, & H. Kamae (Eds.), *Information technology and economic development* (pp. 201–212). Hershey, PA: IGI Global. doi:10.4018/978-1-59904-579-5.ch014

Mentzingen de Moraes, A. J., Ferneda, E., Costa, I., & Spinola, M. D. (2011). Practical approach for implementation of governance process in IT: Information technology areas. In N. Shi & G. Silvius (Eds.), *Enterprise IT governance, business value and performance measurement* (pp. 19–40). Hershey, PA: IGI Global. doi:10.4018/978-1-60566-346-3.ch002

Merwin, G. A. Jr, McDonald, J. S., & Odera, L. C. (2008). Economic development: Government's cutting edge in IT. In M. Raisinghani (Ed.), *Handbook of research on global information technology management in the digital economy* (pp. 1–37). Hershey, PA: IGI Global. doi:10.4018/978-1-59904-875-8.ch001

Meso, P., & Duncan, N. (2002). Can national information infrastructures enhance social development in the least developed countries? An empirical investigation. In M. Dadashzadeh (Ed.), *Information technology management in developing countries* (pp. 23–51). Hershey, PA: IGI Global. doi:10.4018/978-1-931777-03-2.ch002

Meso, P. N., & Duncan, N. B. (2002). Can national information infrastructures enhance social development in the least developed countries? In F. Tan (Ed.), *Advanced topics in global information management* (Vol. 1, pp. 207–226). Hershey, PA: IGI Global. doi:10.4018/978-1-930708-43-3.ch014

Middleton, M. (2008). Evaluation of e-government web sites. In G. Garson & M. Khosrow-Pour (Eds.), *Handbook of research on public information technology* (pp. 699–710). Hershey, PA: IGI Global. doi:10.4018/978-1-59904-857-4.ch063

Mingers, J. (2010). Pluralism, realism, and truth: The keys to knowledge in information systems research. In D. Paradice (Ed.), *Emerging systems approaches in information technologies: Concepts, theories, and applications* (pp. 86–98). Hershey, PA: IGI Global. doi:10.4018/978-1-60566-976-2.ch006

Mital, K. M. (2012). ICT, unique identity and inclusive growth: An Indian perspective. In A. Manoharan & M. Holzer (Eds.), *E-governance and civic engagement: Factors and determinants of e-democracy* (pp. 584–612). Hershey, PA: IGI Global. doi:10.4018/978-1-61350-083-5.ch029

Mizell, A. P. (2008). Helping close the digital divide for financially disadvantaged seniors. In F. Tan (Ed.), *Global information technologies: Concepts, methodologies, tools, and applications* (pp. 2396–2402). Hershey, PA: IGI Global. doi:10.4018/978-1-59904-939-7.ch173

Molinari, F., Wills, C., Koumpis, A., & Moumtzi, V. (2011). A citizen-centric platform to support networking in the area of e-democracy. In H. Rahman (Ed.), *Cases on adoption, diffusion and evaluation of global e-governance systems: Impact at the grass roots* (pp. 282–302). Hershey, PA: IGI Global. doi:10.4018/978-1-61692-814-8.ch014

Molinari, F., Wills, C., Koumpis, A., & Moumtzi, V. (2013). A citizen-centric platform to support networking in the area of e-democracy. In H. Rahman (Ed.), *Cases on progressions and challenges in ICT utilization for citizen-centric governance* (pp. 265–297). Hershey, PA: IGI Global. doi:10.4018/978-1-4666-2071-1.ch013

Monteverde, F. (2010). The process of e-government public policy inclusion in the governmental agenda: A framework for assessment and case study. In J. Cordoba-Pachon & A. Ochoa-Arias (Eds.), *Systems thinking and e-participation: ICT in the governance of society* (pp. 233–245). Hershey, PA: IGI Global. doi:10.4018/978-1-60566-860-4.ch015

Moodley, S. (2008). Deconstructing the South African government's ICT for development discourse. In A. Anttiroiko (Ed.), *Electronic government: Concepts, methodologies, tools, and applications* (pp. 622–631). Hershey, PA: IGI Global. doi:10.4018/978-1-59904-947-2.ch053

Moodley, S. (2008). Deconstructing the South African government's ICT for development discourse. In C. Van Slyke (Ed.), *Information communication technologies: Concepts, methodologies, tools, and applications* (pp. 816–825). Hershey, PA: IGI Global. doi:10.4018/978-1-59904-949-6.ch052

Mora, M., Cervantes-Perez, F., Gelman-Muravchik, O., Forgionne, G. A., & Mejia-Olvera, M. (2003). DMSS implementation research: A conceptual analysis of the contributions and limitations of the factor-based and stage-based streams. In G. Forgionne, J. Gupta, & M. Mora (Eds.), *Decision-making support systems: Achievements and challenges for the new decade* (pp. 331–356). Hershey, PA: IGI Global. doi:10.4018/978-1-59140-045-5.ch020

Mörtberg, C., & Elovaara, P. (2010). Attaching people and technology: Between e and government. In S. Booth, S. Goodman, & G. Kirkup (Eds.), *Gender issues in learning and working with information technology: Social constructs and cultural contexts* (pp. 83–98). Hershey, PA: IGI Global. doi:10.4018/978-1-61520-813-5.ch005

Murphy, J., Harper, E., Devine, E. C., Burke, L. J., & Hook, M. L. (2011). Case study: Lessons learned when embedding evidence-based knowledge in a nurse care planning and documentation system. In A. Cashin & R. Cook (Eds.), *Evidence-based practice in nursing informatics: Concepts and applications* (pp. 174–190). Hershey, PA: IGI Global. doi:10.4018/978-1-60960-034-1.ch014

Mutula, S. M. (2013). E-government's role in poverty alleviation: Case study of South Africa. In H. Rahman (Ed.), *Cases on progressions and challenges in ICT utilization for citizen-centric governance* (pp. 44–68). Hershey, PA: IGI Global. doi:10.4018/978-1-4666-2071-1.ch003

Nath, R., & Angeles, R. (2005). Relationships between supply characteristics and buyer-supplier coupling in e-procurement: An empirical analysis. *International Journal of E-Business Research, 1*(2), 40–55. doi:10.4018/jebr.2005040103

Nissen, M. E. (2006). Application cases in government. In M. Nissen (Ed.), *Harnessing knowledge dynamics: Principled organizational knowing & learning* (pp. 152–181). Hershey, PA: IGI Global. doi:10.4018/978-1-59140-773-7.ch008

Norris, D. F. (2003). Leading-edge information technologies and American local governments. In G. Garson (Ed.), *Public information technology: Policy and management issues* (pp. 139–169). Hershey, PA: IGI Global. doi:10.4018/978-1-59140-060-8.ch007

Norris, D. F. (2008). Information technology among U.S. local governments. In G. Garson & M. Khosrow-Pour (Eds.), *Handbook of research on public information technology* (pp. 132–144). Hershey, PA: IGI Global. doi:10.4018/978-1-59904-857-4.ch013

Northrop, A. (1999). The challenge of teaching information technology in public administration graduate programs. In G. Garson (Ed.), *Information technology and computer applications in public administration: Issues and trends* (pp. 1–22). Hershey, PA: IGI Global. doi:10.4018/978-1-87828-952-0.ch001

Northrop, A. (2003). Information technology and public administration: The view from the profession. In G. Garson (Ed.), *Public information technology: Policy and management issues* (pp. 1–19). Hershey, PA: IGI Global. doi:10.4018/978-1-59140-060-8.ch001

Northrop, A. (2007). Lip service? How PA journals and textbooks view information technology. In G. Garson (Ed.), *Modern public information technology systems: Issues and challenges* (pp. 1–16). Hershey, PA: IGI Global. doi:10.4018/978-1-59904-051-6.ch001

Null, E. (2013). Legal and political barriers to municipal networks in the United States. In A. Abdelaal (Ed.), *Social and economic effects of community wireless networks and infrastructures* (pp. 27–56). Hershey, PA: IGI Global. doi:10.4018/978-1-4666-2997-4.ch003

Okunoye, A., Frolick, M., & Crable, E. (2006). ERP implementation in higher education: An account of pre-implementation and implementation phases. *Journal of Cases on Information Technology*, *8*(2), 110–132. doi:10.4018/jcit.2006040106

Olasina, G. (2012). A review of egovernment services in Nigeria. In A. Tella & A. Issa (Eds.), *Library and information science in developing countries: Contemporary issues* (pp. 205–221). Hershey, PA: IGI Global. doi:10.4018/978-1-61350-335-5.ch015

Orgeron, C. P. (2008). A model for reengineering IT job classes in state government. In G. Garson & M. Khosrow-Pour (Eds.), *Handbook of research on public information technology* (pp. 735–746). Hershey, PA: IGI Global. doi:10.4018/978-1-59904-857-4.ch066

Owsinski, J. W., & Pielak, A. M. (2011). Local authority websites in rural areas: Measuring quality and functionality, and assessing the role. In Z. Andreopoulou, B. Manos, N. Polman, & D. Viaggi (Eds.), *Agricultural and environmental informatics, governance and management: Emerging research applications* (pp. 39–60). Hershey, PA: IGI Global. doi:10.4018/978-1-60960-621-3.ch003

Owsiński, J. W., Pielak, A. M., Sęp, K., & Stańczak, J. (2014). Local web-based networks in rural municipalities: Extension, density, and meaning. In Z. Andreopoulou, V. Samathrakis, S. Louca, & M. Vlachopoulou (Eds.), *E-innovation for sustainable development of rural resources during global economic crisis* (pp. 126–151). Hershey, PA: IGI Global. doi:10.4018/978-1-4666-4550-9.ch011

Pagani, M., & Pasinetti, C. (2008). Technical and functional quality in the development of t-government services. In A. Anttiroiko (Ed.), *Electronic government: Concepts, methodologies, tools, and applications* (pp. 2943–2965). Hershey, PA: IGI Global. doi:10.4018/978-1-59904-947-2.ch220

Pani, A. K., & Agrahari, A. (2005). On e-markets in emerging economy: An Indian experience. In M. Khosrow-Pour (Ed.), *Advanced topics in electronic commerce* (Vol. 1, pp. 287–299). Hershey, PA: IGI Global. doi:10.4018/978-1-59140-819-2.ch015

Papadopoulos, T., Angelopoulos, S., & Kitsios, F. (2011). A strategic approach to e-health interoperability using e-government frameworks. In A. Lazakidou, K. Siassiakos, & K. Ioannou (Eds.), *Wireless technologies for ambient assisted living and healthcare: Systems and applications* (pp. 213–229). Hershey, PA: IGI Global. doi:10.4018/978-1-61520-805-0.ch012

Papadopoulos, T., Angelopoulos, S., & Kitsios, F. (2013). A strategic approach to e-health interoperability using e-government frameworks. In *User-driven healthcare: Concepts, methodologies, tools, and applications* (pp. 791–807). Hershey, PA: IGI Global. doi:10.4018/978-1-4666-2770-3.ch039

Papaleo, G., Chiarella, D., Aiello, M., & Caviglione, L. (2012). Analysis, development and deployment of statistical anomaly detection techniques for real e-mail traffic. In T. Chou (Ed.), *Information assurance and security technologies for risk assessment and threat management: Advances* (pp. 47–71). Hershey, PA: IGI Global. doi:10.4018/978-1-61350-507-6.ch003

Papp, R. (2003). Information technology & FDA compliance in the pharmaceutical industry. In M. Khosrow-Pour (Ed.), *Annals of cases on information technology* (Vol. 5, pp. 262–273). Hershey, PA: IGI Global. doi:10.4018/978-1-59140-061-5.ch017

Parsons, T. W. (2007). Developing a knowledge management portal. In A. Tatnall (Ed.), *Encyclopedia of portal technologies and applications* (pp. 223–227). Hershey, PA: IGI Global. doi:10.4018/978-1-59140-989-2.ch039

Passaris, C. E. (2007). Immigration and digital government. In A. Anttiroiko & M. Malkia (Eds.), *Encyclopedia of digital government* (pp. 988–994). Hershey, PA: IGI Global. doi:10.4018/978-1-59140-789-8.ch148

Pavlichev, A. (2004). The e-government challenge for public administration. In A. Pavlichev & G. Garson (Eds.), *Digital government: Principles and best practices* (pp. 276–290). Hershey, PA: IGI Global. doi:10.4018/978-1-59140-122-3.ch018

Penrod, J. I., & Harbor, A. F. (2000). Designing and implementing a learning organization-oriented information technology planning and management process. In L. Petrides (Ed.), *Case studies on information technology in higher education: Implications for policy and practice* (pp. 7–19). Hershey, PA: IGI Global. doi:10.4018/978-1-878289-74-2.ch001

Planas-Silva, M. D., & Joseph, R. C. (2011). Perspectives on the adoption of electronic resources for use in clinical trials. In M. Guah (Ed.), *Healthcare delivery reform and new technologies: Organizational initiatives* (pp. 19–28). Hershey, PA: IGI Global. doi:10.4018/978-1-60960-183-6.ch002

Pomazalová, N., & Rejman, S. (2013). The rationale behind implementation of new electronic tools for electronic public procurement. In N. Pomazalová (Ed.), *Public sector transformation processes and internet public procurement: Decision support systems* (pp. 85–117). Hershey, PA: IGI Global. doi:10.4018/978-1-4666-2665-2.ch006

Postorino, M. N. (2012). City competitiveness and airport: Information science perspective. In M. Bulu (Ed.), *City competitiveness and improving urban subsystems: Technologies and applications* (pp. 61–83). Hershey, PA: IGI Global. doi:10.4018/978-1-61350-174-0.ch004

Poupa, C. (2002). Electronic government in Switzerland: Priorities for 2001-2005 - Electronic voting and federal portal. In Å. Grönlund (Ed.), *Electronic government: Design, applications and management* (pp. 356–369). Hershey, PA: IGI Global. doi:10.4018/978-1-930708-19-8.ch017

Powell, S. R. (2010). Interdisciplinarity in telecommunications and networking. In *Networking and telecommunications: Concepts, methodologies, tools and applications* (pp. 33–40). Hershey, PA: IGI Global. doi:10.4018/978-1-60566-986-1.ch004

Priya, P. S., & Mathiyalagan, N. (2011). A study of the implementation status of two e-governance projects in land revenue administration in India. In M. Shareef, V. Kumar, U. Kumar, & Y. Dwivedi (Eds.), *Stakeholder adoption of e-government services: Driving and resisting factors* (pp. 214–230). Hershey, PA: IGI Global. doi:10.4018/978-1-60960-601-5.ch011

Prysby, C., & Prysby, N. (2000). Electronic mail, employee privacy and the workplace. In L. Janczewski (Ed.), *Internet and intranet security management: Risks and solutions* (pp. 251–270). Hershey, PA: IGI Global. doi:10.4018/978-1-878289-71-1.ch009

Prysby, C. L., & Prysby, N. D. (2003). Electronic mail in the public workplace: Issues of privacy and public disclosure. In G. Garson (Ed.), *Public information technology: Policy and management issues* (pp. 271–298). Hershey, PA: IGI Global. doi:10.4018/978-1-59140-060-8.ch012

Prysby, C. L., & Prysby, N. D. (2007). You have mail, but who is reading it? Issues of e-mail in the public workplace. In G. Garson (Ed.), *Modern public information technology systems: Issues and challenges* (pp. 312–336). Hershey, PA: IGI Global. doi:10.4018/978-1-59904-051-6.ch016

Radl, A., & Chen, Y. (2005). Computer security in electronic government: A state-local education information system. *International Journal of Electronic Government Research*, *1*(1), 79–99. doi:10.4018/jegr.2005010105

Rahman, H. (2008). Information dynamics in developing countries. In C. Van Slyke (Ed.), *Information communication technologies: Concepts, methodologies, tools, and applications* (pp. 104–114). Hershey, PA: IGI Global. doi:10.4018/978-1-59904-949-6.ch008

Ramanathan, J. (2009). Adaptive IT architecture as a catalyst for network capability in government. In P. Saha (Ed.), *Advances in government enterprise architecture* (pp. 149–172). Hershey, PA: IGI Global. doi:10.4018/978-1-60566-068-4.ch007

Ramos, I., & Berry, D. M. (2006). Social construction of information technology supporting work. In M. Khosrow-Pour (Ed.), *Cases on information technology: Lessons learned* (Vol. 7, pp. 36–52). Hershey, PA: IGI Global. doi:10.4018/978-1-59140-673-0.ch003

Ray, D., Gulla, U., Gupta, M. P., & Dash, S. S. (2009). Interoperability and constituents of interoperable systems in public sector. In V. Weerakkody, M. Janssen, & Y. Dwivedi (Eds.), *Handbook of research on ICT-enabled transformational government: A global perspective* (pp. 175–195). Hershey, PA: IGI Global. doi:10.4018/978-1-60566-390-6.ch010

Reddick, C. G. (2007). E-government and creating a citizen-centric government: A study of federal government CIOs. In G. Garson (Ed.), *Modern public information technology systems: Issues and challenges* (pp. 143–165). Hershey, PA: IGI Global. doi:10.4018/978-1-59904-051-6.ch008

Reddick, C. G. (2010). Citizen-centric e-government. In C. Reddick (Ed.), *Homeland security preparedness and information systems: Strategies for managing public policy* (pp. 45–75). Hershey, PA: IGI Global. doi:10.4018/978-1-60566-834-5.ch002

Reddick, C. G. (2010). E-government and creating a citizen-centric government: A study of federal government CIOs. In C. Reddick (Ed.), *Homeland security preparedness and information systems: Strategies for managing public policy* (pp. 230–250). Hershey, PA: IGI Global. doi:10.4018/978-1-60566-834-5.ch012

Reddick, C. G. (2010). Perceived effectiveness of e-government and its usage in city governments: Survey evidence from information technology directors. In C. Reddick (Ed.), *Homeland security preparedness and information systems: Strategies for managing public policy* (pp. 213–229). Hershey, PA: IGI Global. doi:10.4018/978-1-60566-834-5.ch011

Reddick, C. G. (2012). Customer relationship management adoption in local governments in the United States. In S. Chhabra & M. Kumar (Eds.), *Strategic enterprise resource planning models for e-government: Applications and methodologies* (pp. 111–124). Hershey, PA: IGI Global. doi:10.4018/978-1-60960-863-7.ch008

Reeder, F. S., & Pandy, S. M. (2008). Identifying effective funding models for e-government. In A. Anttiroiko (Ed.), *Electronic government: Concepts, methodologies, tools, and applications* (pp. 1108–1138). Hershey, PA: IGI Global. doi:10.4018/978-1-59904-947-2.ch083

Riesco, D., Acosta, E., & Montejano, G. (2003). An extension to a UML activity graph from workflow. In L. Favre (Ed.), *UML and the unified process* (pp. 294–314). Hershey, PA: IGI Global. doi:10.4018/978-1-93177-744-5.ch015

Ritzhaupt, A. D., & Gill, T. G. (2008). A hybrid and novel approach to teaching computer programming in MIS curriculum. In S. Negash, M. Whitman, A. Woszczynski, K. Hoganson, & H. Mattord (Eds.), *Handbook of distance learning for real-time and asynchronous information technology education* (pp. 259–281). Hershey, PA: IGI Global. doi:10.4018/978-1-59904-964-9.ch014

Roche, E. M. (1993). International computing and the international regime. *Journal of Global Information Management, 1*(2), 33–44. doi:10.4018/jgim.1993040103

Rocheleau, B. (2007). Politics, accountability, and information management. In G. Garson (Ed.), *Modern public information technology systems: Issues and challenges* (pp. 35–71). Hershey, PA: IGI Global. doi:10.4018/978-1-59904-051-6.ch003

Rodrigues Filho, J. (2010). E-government in Brazil: Reinforcing dominant institutions or reducing citizenship? In C. Reddick (Ed.), *Politics, democracy and e-government: Participation and service delivery* (pp. 347–362). Hershey, PA: IGI Global. doi:10.4018/978-1-61520-933-0.ch021

Rodriguez, S. R., & Thorp, D. A. (2013). eLearning for industry: A case study of the project management process. In A. Benson, J. Moore, & S. Williams van Rooij (Eds.), Cases on educational technology planning, design, and implementation: A project management perspective (pp. 319-342). Hershey, PA: IGI Global. doi:10.4018/978-1-4666-4237-9.ch017

Roman, A. V. (2013). Delineating three dimensions of e-government success: Security, functionality, and transformation. In J. Gil-Garcia (Ed.), *E-government success factors and measures: Theories, concepts, and methodologies* (pp. 171–192). Hershey, PA: IGI Global. doi:10.4018/978-1-4666-4058-0.ch010

Ross, S. C., Tyran, C. K., & Auer, D. J. (2008). Up in smoke: Rebuilding after an IT disaster. In H. Nemati (Ed.), *Information security and ethics: Concepts, methodologies, tools, and applications* (pp. 3659–3675). Hershey, PA: IGI Global. doi:10.4018/978-1-59904-937-3.ch248

Ross, S. C., Tyran, C. K., Auer, D. J., Junell, J. M., & Williams, T. G. (2005). Up in smoke: Rebuilding after an IT disaster. *Journal of Cases on Information Technology*, *7*(2), 31–49. doi:10.4018/jcit.2005040103

Roy, J. (2008). Security, sovereignty, and continental interoperability: Canada's elusive balance. In T. Loendorf & G. Garson (Eds.), *Patriotic information systems* (pp. 153–176). Hershey, PA: IGI Global. doi:10.4018/978-1-59904-594-8.ch007

Rubeck, R. F., & Miller, G. A. (2009). vGOV: Remote video access to government services. In A. Scupola (Ed.), Cases on managing e-services (pp. 253-268). Hershey, PA: IGI Global. doi:10.4018/978-1-60566-064-6.ch017

Saekow, A., & Boonmee, C. (2011). The challenges of implementing e-government interoperability in Thailand: Case of official electronic correspondence letters exchange across government departments. In Y. Charalabidis (Ed.), *Interoperability in digital public services and administration: Bridging e-government and e-business* (pp. 40–61). Hershey, PA: IGI Global. doi:10.4018/978-1-61520-887-6.ch003

Saekow, A., & Boonmee, C. (2012). The challenges of implementing e-government interoperability in Thailand: Case of official electronic correspondence letters exchange across government departments. In *Digital democracy: Concepts, methodologies, tools, and applications* (pp. 1883–1905). Hershey, PA: IGI Global. doi:10.4018/978-1-4666-1740-7.ch094

Sagsan, M., & Medeni, T. (2012). Understanding "knowledge management (KM) paradigms" from social media perspective: An empirical study on discussion group for KM at professional networking site. In M. Cruz-Cunha, P. Gonçalves, N. Lopes, E. Miranda, & G. Putnik (Eds.), *Handbook of research on business social networking: Organizational, managerial, and technological dimensions* (pp. 738–755). Hershey, PA: IGI Global. doi:10.4018/978-1-61350-168-9.ch039

Sahi, G., & Madan, S. (2013). Information security threats in ERP enabled e-governance: Challenges and solutions. In *Enterprise resource planning: Concepts, methodologies, tools, and applications* (pp. 825–837). Hershey, PA: IGI Global. doi:10.4018/978-1-4666-4153-2.ch048

Sanford, C., & Bhattacherjee, A. (2008). IT implementation in a developing country municipality: A sociocognitive analysis. *International Journal of Technology and Human Interaction*, *4*(3), 68–93. doi:10.4018/jthi.2008070104

Schelin, S. H. (2003). E-government: An overview. In G. Garson (Ed.), *Public information technology: Policy and management issues* (pp. 120–138). Hershey, PA: IGI Global. doi:10.4018/978-1-59140-060-8.ch006

Schelin, S. H. (2004). Training for digital government. In A. Pavlichev & G. Garson (Eds.), *Digital government: Principles and best practices* (pp. 263–275). Hershey, PA: IGI Global. doi:10.4018/978-1-59140-122-3.ch017

Schelin, S. H. (2007). E-government: An overview. In G. Garson (Ed.), *Modern public information technology systems: Issues and challenges* (pp. 110–126). Hershey, PA: IGI Global. doi:10.4018/978-1-59904-051-6.ch006

Schelin, S. H., & Garson, G. (2004). Theoretical justification of critical success factors. In G. Garson & S. Schelin (Eds.), *IT solutions series: Humanizing information technology: Advice from experts* (pp. 4–15). Hershey, PA: IGI Global. doi:10.4018/978-1-59140-245-9.ch002

Scime, A. (2002). Information systems and computer science model curricula: A comparative look. In M. Dadashzadeh, A. Saber, & S. Saber (Eds.), *Information technology education in the new millennium* (pp. 146–158). Hershey, PA: IGI Global. doi:10.4018/978-1-931777-05-6.ch018

Scime, A. (2009). Computing curriculum analysis and development. In M. Khosrow-Pour (Ed.), *Encyclopedia of information science and technology* (2nd ed.; pp. 667–671). Hershey, PA: IGI Global. doi:10.4018/978-1-60566-026-4.ch108

Scime, A., & Wania, C. (2008). Computing curricula: A comparison of models. In C. Van Slyke (Ed.), *Information communication technologies: Concepts, methodologies, tools, and applications* (pp. 1270–1283). Hershey, PA: IGI Global. doi:10.4018/978-1-59904-949-6.ch088

Seidman, S. B. (2009). An international perspective on professional software engineering credentials. In H. Ellis, S. Demurjian, & J. Naveda (Eds.), *Software engineering: Effective teaching and learning approaches and practices* (pp. 351–361). Hershey, PA: IGI Global. doi:10.4018/978-1-60566-102-5.ch018

Seifert, J. W. (2007). E-government act of 2002 in the United States. In A. Anttiroiko & M. Malkia (Eds.), *Encyclopedia of digital government* (pp. 476–481). Hershey, PA: IGI Global. doi:10.4018/978-1-59140-789-8.ch072

Seifert, J. W., & Relyea, H. C. (2008). E-government act of 2002 in the United States. In A. Anttiroiko (Ed.), *Electronic government: Concepts, methodologies, tools, and applications* (pp. 154–161). Hershey, PA: IGI Global. doi:10.4018/978-1-59904-947-2.ch013

Seufert, S. (2002). E-learning business models: Framework and best practice examples. In M. Raisinghani (Ed.), *Cases on worldwide e-commerce: Theory in action* (pp. 70–94). Hershey, PA: IGI Global. doi:10.4018/978-1-930708-27-3.ch004

Shareef, M. A., & Archer, N. (2012). E-government service development. In M. Shareef, N. Archer, & S. Dutta (Eds.), *E-government service maturity and development: Cultural, organizational and technological perspectives* (pp. 1–14). Hershey, PA: IGI Global. doi:10.4018/978-1-60960-848-4.ch001

Shareef, M. A., & Archer, N. (2012). E-government initiatives: Review studies on different countries. In M. Shareef, N. Archer, & S. Dutta (Eds.), *E-government service maturity and development: Cultural, organizational and technological perspectives* (pp. 40–76). Hershey, PA: IGI Global. doi:10.4018/978-1-60960-848-4.ch003

Shareef, M. A., Kumar, U., & Kumar, V. (2011). E-government development: Performance evaluation parameters. In M. Shareef, V. Kumar, U. Kumar, & Y. Dwivedi (Eds.), *Stakeholder adoption of e-government services: Driving and resisting factors* (pp. 197–213). Hershey, PA: IGI Global. doi:10.4018/978-1-60960-601-5.ch010

Shareef, M. A., Kumar, U., Kumar, V., & Niktash, M. (2012). Electronic-government vision: Case studies for objectives, strategies, and initiatives. In M. Shareef, N. Archer, & S. Dutta (Eds.), *E-government service maturity and development: Cultural, organizational and technological perspectives* (pp. 15–39). Hershey, PA: IGI Global. doi:10.4018/978-1-60960-848-4.ch002

Shukla, P., Kumar, A., & Anu Kumar, P. B. (2013). Impact of national culture on business continuity management system implementation. *International Journal of Risk and Contingency Management, 2*(3), 23–36. doi:10.4018/ijrcm.2013070102

Shulman, S. W. (2007). The federal docket management system and the prospect for digital democracy in U S rulemaking. In G. Garson (Ed.), *Modern public information technology systems: Issues and challenges* (pp. 166–184). Hershey, PA: IGI Global. doi:10.4018/978-1-59904-051-6.ch009

Simonovic, S. (2007). Problems of offline government in e-Serbia. In A. Anttiroiko & M. Malkia (Eds.), *Encyclopedia of digital government* (pp. 1342–1351). Hershey, PA: IGI Global. doi:10.4018/978-1-59140-789-8.ch205

Simonovic, S. (2008). Problems of offline government in e-Serbia. In A. Anttiroiko (Ed.), *Electronic government: Concepts, methodologies, tools, and applications* (pp. 2929–2942). Hershey, PA: IGI Global. doi:10.4018/978-1-59904-947-2.ch219

Singh, A. M. (2005). Information systems and technology in South Africa. In M. Khosrow-Pour (Ed.), *Encyclopedia of information science and technology* (pp. 1497–1502). Hershey, PA: IGI Global. doi:10.4018/978-1-59140-553-5.ch263

Singh, S., & Naidoo, G. (2005). Towards an e-government solution: A South African perspective. In W. Huang, K. Siau, & K. Wei (Eds.), *Electronic government strategies and implementation* (pp. 325–353). Hershey, PA: IGI Global. doi:10.4018/978-1-59140-348-7.ch014

Snoke, R., & Underwood, A. (2002). Generic attributes of IS graduates: An analysis of Australian views. In F. Tan (Ed.), *Advanced topics in global information management* (Vol. 1, pp. 370–384). Hershey, PA: IGI Global. doi:10.4018/978-1-930708-43-3.ch023

Sommer, L. (2006). Revealing unseen organizations in higher education: A study framework and application example. In A. Metcalfe (Ed.), *Knowledge management and higher education: A critical analysis* (pp. 115–146). Hershey, PA: IGI Global. doi:10.4018/978-1-59140-509-2.ch007

Song, H., Kidd, T., & Owens, E. (2011). Examining technological disparities and instructional practices in English language arts classroom: Implications for school leadership and teacher training. In L. Tomei (Ed.), *Online courses and ICT in education: Emerging practices and applications* (pp. 258–274). Hershey, PA: IGI Global. doi:10.4018/978-1-60960-150-8.ch020

Speaker, P. J., & Kleist, V. F. (2003). Using information technology to meet electronic commerce and MIS education demands. In A. Aggarwal (Ed.), *Web-based education: Learning from experience* (pp. 280–291). Hershey, PA: IGI Global. doi:10.4018/978-1-59140-102-5.ch017

Spitler, V. K. (2007). Learning to use IT in the workplace: Mechanisms and masters. In M. Mahmood (Ed.), *Contemporary issues in end user computing* (pp. 292–323). Hershey, PA: IGI Global. doi:10.4018/978-1-59140-926-7.ch013

Stellefson, M. (2011). Considerations for marketing distance education courses in health education: Five important questions to examine before development. In U. Demiray & S. Sever (Eds.), *Marketing online education programs: Frameworks for promotion and communication* (pp. 222–234). Hershey, PA: IGI Global. doi:10.4018/978-1-60960-074-7.ch014

Straub, D. W., & Loch, K. D. (2006). Creating and developing a program of global research. *Journal of Global Information Management, 14*(2), 1–28. doi:10.4018/jgim.2006040101

Straub, D. W., Loch, K. D., & Hill, C. E. (2002). Transfer of information technology to the Arab world: A test of cultural influence modeling. In M. Dadashzadeh (Ed.), *Information technology management in developing countries* (pp. 92–134). Hershey, PA: IGI Global. doi:10.4018/978-1-931777-03-2.ch005

Straub, D. W., Loch, K. D., & Hill, C. E. (2003). Transfer of information technology to the Arab world: A test of cultural influence modeling. In F. Tan (Ed.), *Advanced topics in global information management* (Vol. 2, pp. 141–172). Hershey, PA: IGI Global. doi:10.4018/978-1-59140-064-6.ch009

Suki, N. M., Ramayah, T., Ming, M. K., & Suki, N. M. (2013). Factors enhancing employed job seekers intentions to use social networking sites as a job search tool. In A. Mesquita (Ed.), *User perception and influencing factors of technology in everyday life* (pp. 265–281). Hershey, PA: IGI Global. doi:10.4018/978-1-4666-1954-8.ch018

Suomi, R. (2006). Introducing electronic patient records to hospitals: Innovation adoption paths. In T. Spil & R. Schuring (Eds.), *E-health systems diffusion and use: The innovation, the user and the use IT model* (pp. 128–146). Hershey, PA: IGI Global. doi:10.4018/978-1-59140-423-1.ch008

Swim, J., & Barker, L. (2012). Pathways into a gendered occupation: Brazilian women in IT. *International Journal of Social and Organizational Dynamics in IT, 2*(4), 34–51. doi:10.4018/ijsodit.2012100103

Tarafdar, M., & Vaidya, S. D. (2006). Adoption and implementation of IT in developing nations: Experiences from two public sector enterprises in India. In M. Khosrow-Pour (Ed.), *Cases on information technology planning, design and implementation* (pp. 208–233). Hershey, PA: IGI Global. doi:10.4018/978-1-59904-408-8.ch013

Tarafdar, M., & Vaidya, S. D. (2008). Adoption and implementation of IT in developing nations: Experiences from two public sector enterprises in India. In G. Garson & M. Khosrow-Pour (Eds.), *Handbook of research on public information technology* (pp. 905–924). Hershey, PA: IGI Global. doi:10.4018/978-1-59904-857-4.ch076

Thesing, Z. (2007). Zarina thesing, pumpkin patch. In M. Hunter (Ed.), *Contemporary chief information officers: Management experiences* (pp. 83–94). Hershey, PA: IGI Global. doi:10.4018/978-1-59904-078-3.ch007

Thomas, J. C. (2004). Public involvement in public administration in the information age: Speculations on the effects of technology. In M. Malkia, A. Anttiroiko, & R. Savolainen (Eds.), *eTransformation in governance: New directions in government and politics* (pp. 67–84). Hershey, PA: IGI Global. doi:10.4018/978-1-59140-130-8.ch004

Treiblmaier, H., & Chong, S. (2013). Trust and perceived risk of personal information as antecedents of online information disclosure: Results from three countries. In F. Tan (Ed.), *Global diffusion and adoption of technologies for knowledge and information sharing* (pp. 341–361). Hershey, PA: IGI Global. doi:10.4018/978-1-4666-2142-8.ch015

van Grembergen, W., & de Haes, S. (2008). IT governance in practice: Six case studies. In W. van Grembergen & S. De Haes (Eds.), *Implementing information technology governance: Models, practices and cases* (pp. 125–237). Hershey, PA: IGI Global. doi:10.4018/978-1-59904-924-3.ch004

van Os, G., Homburg, V., & Bekkers, V. (2013). Contingencies and convergence in European social security: ICT coordination in the back office of the welfare state. In M. Cruz-Cunha, I. Miranda, & P. Gonçalves (Eds.), *Handbook of research on ICTs and management systems for improving efficiency in healthcare and social care* (pp. 268–287). Hershey, PA: IGI Global. doi:10.4018/978-1-4666-3990-4.ch013

Velloso, A. B., Gassenferth, W., & Machado, M. A. (2012). Evaluating IBMEC-RJ's intranet usability using fuzzy logic. In M. Cruz-Cunha, P. Gonçalves, N. Lopes, E. Miranda, & G. Putnik (Eds.), *Handbook of research on business social networking: Organizational, managerial, and technological dimensions* (pp. 185–205). Hershey, PA: IGI Global. doi:10.4018/978-1-61350-168-9.ch010

Villablanca, A. C., Baxi, H., & Anderson, K. (2009). Novel data interface for evaluating cardiovascular outcomes in women. In A. Dwivedi (Ed.), *Handbook of research on information technology management and clinical data administration in healthcare* (pp. 34–53). Hershey, PA: IGI Global. doi:10.4018/978-1-60566-356-2.ch003

Villablanca, A. C., Baxi, H., & Anderson, K. (2011). Novel data interface for evaluating cardiovascular outcomes in women. In *Clinical technologies: Concepts, methodologies, tools and applications* (pp. 2094–2113). Hershey, PA: IGI Global. doi:10.4018/978-1-60960-561-2.ch806

Virkar, S. (2011). Information and communication technologies in administrative reform for development: Exploring the case of property tax systems in Karnataka, India. In J. Steyn, J. Van Belle, & E. Mansilla (Eds.), *ICTs for global development and sustainability: Practice and applications* (pp. 127–149). Hershey, PA: IGI Global. doi:10.4018/978-1-61520-997-2.ch006

Virkar, S. (2013). Designing and implementing e-government projects: Actors, influences, and fields of play. In S. Saeed & C. Reddick (Eds.), *Human-centered system design for electronic governance* (pp. 88–110). Hershey, PA: IGI Global. doi:10.4018/978-1-4666-3640-8.ch007

Wallace, A. (2009). E-justice: An Australian perspective. In A. Martínez & P. Abat (Eds.), *E-justice: Using information communication technologies in the court system* (pp. 204–228). Hershey, PA: IGI Global. doi:10.4018/978-1-59904-998-4.ch014

Wang, G. (2012). E-democratic administration and bureaucratic responsiveness: A primary study of bureaucrats' perceptions of the civil service e-mail box in Taiwan. In K. Kloby & M. D'Agostino (Eds.), *Citizen 2.0: Public and governmental interaction through web 2.0 technologies* (pp. 146–173). Hershey, PA: IGI Global. doi:10.4018/978-1-4666-0318-9.ch009

Wangpipatwong, S., Chutimaskul, W., & Papasratorn, B. (2011). Quality enhancing the continued use of e-government web sites: Evidence from e-citizens of Thailand. In V. Weerakkody (Ed.), *Applied technology integration in governmental organizations: New e-government research* (pp. 20–36). Hershey, PA: IGI Global. doi:10.4018/978-1-60960-162-1.ch002

Wedemeijer, L. (2006). Long-term evolution of a conceptual schema at a life insurance company. In M. Khosrow-Pour (Ed.), *Cases on database technologies and applications* (pp. 202–226). Hershey, PA: IGI Global. doi:10.4018/978-1-59904-399-9.ch012

Whybrow, E. (2008). Digital access, ICT fluency, and the economically disadvantages: Approaches to minimize the digital divide. In F. Tan (Ed.), *Global information technologies: Concepts, methodologies, tools, and applications* (pp. 1409–1422). Hershey, PA: IGI Global. doi:10.4018/978-1-59904-939-7.ch102

Whybrow, E. (2008). Digital access, ICT fluency, and the economically disadvantages: Approaches to minimize the digital divide. In C. Van Slyke (Ed.), *Information communication technologies: Concepts, methodologies, tools, and applications* (pp. 764–777). Hershey, PA: IGI Global. doi:10.4018/978-1-59904-949-6.ch049

Wickramasinghe, N., & Geisler, E. (2010). Key considerations for the adoption and implementation of knowledge management in healthcare operations. In M. Saito, N. Wickramasinghe, M. Fuji, & E. Geisler (Eds.), *Redesigning innovative healthcare operation and the role of knowledge management* (pp. 125–142). Hershey, PA: IGI Global. doi:10.4018/978-1-60566-284-8.ch009

Wickramasinghe, N., & Geisler, E. (2012). Key considerations for the adoption and implementation of knowledge management in healthcare operations. In *Organizational learning and knowledge: Concepts, methodologies, tools and applications* (pp. 1316–1328). Hershey, PA: IGI Global. doi:10.4018/978-1-60960-783-8.ch405

Wickramasinghe, N., & Goldberg, S. (2007). A framework for delivering m-health excellence. In L. Al-Hakim (Ed.), *Web mobile-based applications for healthcare management* (pp. 36–61). Hershey, PA: IGI Global. doi:10.4018/978-1-59140-658-7.ch002

Wickramasinghe, N., & Goldberg, S. (2008). Critical success factors for delivering m-health excellence. In N. Wickramasinghe & E. Geisler (Eds.), *Encyclopedia of healthcare information systems* (pp. 339–351). Hershey, PA: IGI Global. doi:10.4018/978-1-59904-889-5.ch045

Wyld, D. (2009). Radio frequency identification (RFID) technology. In J. Symonds, J. Ayoade, & D. Parry (Eds.), *Auto-identification and ubiquitous computing applications* (pp. 279–293). Hershey, PA: IGI Global. doi:10.4018/978-1-60566-298-5.ch017

Yaghmaei, F. (2010). Understanding computerised information systems usage in community health. In J. Rodrigues (Ed.), *Health information systems: Concepts, methodologies, tools, and applications* (pp. 1388–1399). Hershey, PA: IGI Global. doi:10.4018/978-1-60566-988-5.ch088

Yee, G., El-Khatib, K., Korba, L., Patrick, A. S., Song, R., & Xu, Y. (2005). Privacy and trust in e-government. In W. Huang, K. Siau, & K. Wei (Eds.), *Electronic government strategies and implementation* (pp. 145–190). Hershey, PA: IGI Global. doi:10.4018/978-1-59140-348-7.ch007

Yeh, S., & Chu, P. (2010). Evaluation of e-government services: A citizen-centric approach to citizen e-complaint services. In C. Reddick (Ed.), *Citizens and e-government: Evaluating policy and management* (pp. 400–417). Hershey, PA: IGI Global. doi:10.4018/978-1-61520-931-6.ch022

Young-Jin, S., & Seang-tae, K. (2008). E-government concepts, measures, and best practices. In A. Anttiroiko (Ed.), *Electronic government: Concepts, methodologies, tools, and applications* (pp. 32–57). Hershey, PA: IGI Global. doi:10.4018/978-1-59904-947-2.ch004

Yun, H. J., & Opheim, C. (2012). New technology communication in American state governments: The impact on citizen participation. In K. Bwalya & S. Zulu (Eds.), *Handbook of research on e-government in emerging economies: Adoption, e-participation, and legal frameworks* (pp. 573–590). Hershey, PA: IGI Global. doi:10.4018/978-1-4666-0324-0.ch029

Zhang, N., Guo, X., Chen, G., & Chau, P. Y. (2011). User evaluation of e-government systems: A Chinese cultural perspective. In F. Tan (Ed.), *International enterprises and global information technologies: Advancing management practices* (pp. 63–84). Hershey, PA: IGI Global. doi:10.4018/978-1-60960-605-3.ch004

Zuo, Y., & Hu, W. (2011). Trust-based information risk management in a supply chain network. In J. Wang (Ed.), *Supply chain optimization, management and integration: Emerging applications* (pp. 181–196). Hershey, PA: IGI Global. doi:10.4018/978-1-60960-135-5.ch013

Compilation of References

10. Years US Treasury. (2016). Obtenido de Bloomberg: http://www.bloomberg.com/markets/rates-bonds/government-bonds/us

Acosta, W. S. (2014). Del sueño unitario a la fragmentación: la República Federal de Centroamérica (1823-1838). In W. S. Acosta & M. S. Ulloa (Eds.), Centroamérica: casa común e integración regional (pp. 17-32). Universidad Nacional de Costa Rica.

Adeyemo, O. (2013). The nationwide health information network: A biometric approach to prevent medical identity theft. In *User-driven healthcare: Concepts, methodologies, tools, and applications* (pp. 1636–1649). Hershey, PA: IGI Global. doi:10.4018/978-1-4666-2770-3.ch081

Adler, M., & Henman, P. (2009). Justice beyond the courts: The implications of computerisation for procedural justice in social security. In A. Martínez & P. Abat (Eds.), *E-justice: Using information communication technologies in the court system* (pp. 65–86). Hershey, PA: IGI Global. doi:10.4018/978-1-59904-998-4.ch005

Aflalo, E., & Gabay, E. (2013). An information system for coping with student dropout. In L. Tomei (Ed.), *Learning tools and teaching approaches through ICT advancements* (pp. 176–187). Hershey, PA: IGI Global. doi:10.4018/978-1-4666-2017-9.ch016

Ahmed, M. A., Janssen, M., & van den Hoven, J. (2012). Value sensitive transfer (VST) of systems among countries: Towards a framework. *International Journal of Electronic Government Research*, *8*(1), 26–42. doi:10.4018/jegr.2012010102

Aikins, S. K. (2008). Issues and trends in internet-based citizen participation. In G. Garson & M. Khosrow-Pour (Eds.), *Handbook of research on public information technology* (pp. 31–40). Hershey, PA: IGI Global. doi:10.4018/978-1-59904-857-4.ch004

Aikins, S. K. (2009). A comparative study of municipal adoption of internet-based citizen participation. In C. Reddick (Ed.), *Handbook of research on strategies for local e-government adoption and implementation: Comparative studies* (pp. 206–230). Hershey, PA: IGI Global. doi:10.4018/978-1-60566-282-4.ch011

Aikins, S. K. (2012). Improving e-government project management: Best practices and critical success factors. In *Digital democracy: Concepts, methodologies, tools, and applications* (pp. 1314–1332). Hershey, PA: IGI Global. doi:10.4018/978-1-4666-1740-7.ch065

Akabawi, M. S. (2011). Ghabbour group ERP deployment: Learning from past technology failures. In E. Business Research and Case Center (Ed.), Cases on business and management in the MENA region: New trends and opportunities (pp. 177-203). Hershey, PA: IGI Global. doi:10.4018/978-1-60960-583-4.ch012

Akabawi, M. S. (2013). Ghabbour group ERP deployment: Learning from past technology failures. In *Industrial engineering: Concepts, methodologies, tools, and applications* (pp. 933–958). Hershey, PA: IGI Global. doi:10.4018/978-1-4666-1945-6.ch051

Akbulut, A. Y., & Motwani, J. (2008). Integration and information sharing in e-government. In G. Putnik & M. Cruz-Cunha (Eds.), *Encyclopedia of networked and virtual organizations* (pp. 729–734). Hershey, PA: IGI Global. doi:10.4018/978-1-59904-885-7.ch096

Akers, E. J. (2008). Technology diffusion in public administration. In G. Garson & M. Khosrow-Pour (Eds.), *Handbook of research on public information technology* (pp. 339–348). Hershey, PA: IGI Global. doi:10.4018/978-1-59904-857-4.ch033

Aladwani, A. M. (2002). Organizational actions, computer attitudes and end-user satisfaction in public organizations: An empirical study. In C. Snodgrass & E. Szewczak (Eds.), *Human factors in information systems* (pp. 153–168). Hershey, PA: IGI Global. doi:10.4018/978-1-931777-10-0.ch012

Aladwani, A. M. (2002). Organizational actions, computer attitudes, and end-user satisfaction in public organizations: An empirical study. *Journal of Organizational and End User Computing*, *14*(1), 42–49. doi:10.4018/joeuc.2002010104

Alban, J. V., Rivera, S. L., & Ayala, S. R. (1999). *Propriety and Permissiveness in Bourbon Mexico*. Rowman & Littlefield Publishers.

Allen, B., Juillet, L., Paquet, G., & Roy, J. (2005). E-government and private-public partnerships: Relational challenges and strategic directions. In M. Khosrow-Pour (Ed.), *Practicing e-government: A global perspective* (pp. 364–382). Hershey, PA: IGI Global. doi:10.4018/978-1-59140-637-2.ch016

Al-Shafi, S. (2008). Free wireless internet park services: An investigation of technology adoption in Qatar from a citizens perspective. *Journal of Cases on Information Technology*, *10*(3), 21–34. doi:10.4018/jcit.2008070103

Al-Shafi, S., & Weerakkody, V. (2009). Implementing free wi-fi in public parks: An empirical study in Qatar. *International Journal of Electronic Government Research*, *5*(3), 21–35. doi:10.4018/jegr.2009070102

Alshawaf, A., & Knalil, O. E. (2008). IS success factors and IS organizational impact: Does ownership type matter in Kuwait? *International Journal of Enterprise Information Systems*, *4*(2), 13–33. doi:10.4018/jeis.2008040102

Ambali, A. R. (2009). Digital divide and its implication on Malaysian e-government: Policy initiatives. In H. Rahman (Ed.), *Social and political implications of data mining: Knowledge management in e-government* (pp. 267–287). Hershey, PA: IGI Global. doi:10.4018/978-1-60566-230-5.ch016

Amoretti, F. (2007). Digital international governance. In A. Anttiroiko & M. Malkia (Eds.), *Encyclopedia of digital government* (pp. 365–370). Hershey, PA: IGI Global. doi:10.4018/978-1-59140-789-8.ch056

Amoretti, F. (2008). Digital international governance. In A. Anttiroiko (Ed.), *Electronic government: Concepts, methodologies, tools, and applications* (pp. 688–696). Hershey, PA: IGI Global. doi:10.4018/978-1-59904-947-2.ch058

Amoretti, F. (2008). E-government at supranational level in the European Union. In A. Anttiroiko (Ed.), *Electronic government: Concepts, methodologies, tools, and applications* (pp. 1047–1055). Hershey, PA: IGI Global. doi:10.4018/978-1-59904-947-2.ch079

Amoretti, F. (2008). E-government regimes. In A. Anttiroiko (Ed.), *Electronic government: Concepts, methodologies, tools, and applications* (pp. 3846–3856). Hershey, PA: IGI Global. doi:10.4018/978-1-59904-947-2.ch280

Amoretti, F. (2009). Electronic constitution: A Braudelian perspective. In F. Amoretti (Ed.), *Electronic constitution: Social, cultural, and political implications* (pp. 1–19). Hershey, PA: IGI Global. doi:10.4018/978-1-60566-254-1.ch001

Amoretti, F., & Musella, F. (2009). Institutional isomorphism and new technologies. In M. Khosrow-Pour (Ed.), *Encyclopedia of information science and technology* (2nd ed.; pp. 2066–2071). Hershey, PA: IGI Global. doi:10.4018/978-1-60566-026-4.ch325

Andersen, K. V., & Henriksen, H. Z. (2007). E-government research: Capabilities, interaction, orientation, and values. In D. Norris (Ed.), *Current issues and trends in e-government research* (pp. 269–288). Hershey, PA: IGI Global. doi:10.4018/978-1-59904-283-1.ch013

Anderson, K. V., & Henriksen, H. Z. (2005). The first leg of e-government research: Domains and application areas 19982003. *International Journal of Electronic Government Research*, *1*(4), 26–44. doi:10.4018/jegr.2005100102

Anttiroiko, A. (2009). Democratic e-governance. In M. Khosrow-Pour (Ed.), *Encyclopedia of information science and technology* (2nd ed.; pp. 990–995). Hershey, PA: IGI Global. doi:10.4018/978-1-60566-026-4.ch158

Arànega, S., & Domènech, J. (2001). *Primary education: Challenges, dilemmas and proposals* (Vol. 160). Grao.

Arti, C., & Mita, M. (2013). Women Leadership in Axis Bank: A Comparison of woman and man leader using CAMEL Model. *International Journal of Research in Commerce, IT & Management.*, *3*(2), 83–89.

Baker, P. M., Bell, A., & Moon, N. W. (2009). Accessibility issues in municipal wireless networks. In C. Reddick (Ed.), *Handbook of research on strategies for local e-government adoption and implementation: Comparative studies* (pp. 569–588). Hershey, PA: IGI Global. doi:10.4018/978-1-60566-282-4.ch030

Balsells, E. (2006). *Competition and Regulation in the Banking Sector in Guatemala. Strengthening competition in the Central American Isthmus: National policies and institutions, regional coordination and participation in international negotiations*. CEPAL.

Banco de Guatemala. (2006). *Study of the National Economy*. Banco de Guatemala.

Banco de Guatemala. (2016). *Estadísticas Fiscales*. Retrieved from Banguat: http://www.banguat.gob.gt/inc/ver.asp?id=/pim/pim16&e=115131&e=115213

Banco Mundial. (2008). *La deuda y el crecimiento, Material del curso de políticas de crecimiento*. Estados Unidos.

Banguat. (n.d.). Retrieved from System of National Accounts: Www.banguat.gob.gt/cuentasnac/TOMO_I.pdf

Bastos, P. (1999). *The Political eEconomy of Latin American Telecommunications: Multinational Agreements and National Regulatory Systems*. Universidad do Rio de Janeiro.

Becker, S. A., Keimer, R., & Muth, T. (2012). A case on university and community collaboration: The sci-tech entrepreneurial training services (ETS) program. In Regional development: Concepts, methodologies, tools, and applications (pp. 947-969). Hershey, PA: IGI Global. doi:10.4018/978-1-4666-0882-5.ch507

Becker, S. A., Keimer, R., & Muth, T. (2010). A case on university and community collaboration: The sci-tech entrepreneurial training services (ETS) program. In S. Becker & R. Niebuhr (Eds.), *Cases on technology innovation: Entrepreneurial successes and pitfalls* (pp. 68–90). Hershey, PA: IGI Global. doi:10.4018/978-1-61520-609-4.ch003

Belaubre, C. (2009). *Juan José Aycinena*. Guatemala: Asociación para el Fomento de los Estudios Históricos en Centroamérica .

Belaure, C. (n.d.). *Asociación para el Fomento de los Estudios Históricos en Centroamérica*. Retrieved from Red social de Juan Fermín Aycinena y su evoluación (1750-1808): http://www.afehc-historia-centroamericana.org/index.php?action=im_aff&id=1043

Berkmen, P., Gelos, G., Rennhack, R., & Walsh, J. (2009). *The Global Financial Crisis: Explaining Cross-Country Differences in the Output Impact*. IMF Working Paper No.09/280. Washington, DC: International Monetary Fund.

Bernardi, R. (2012). Information technology and resistance to public sector reforms: A case study in Kenya. In T. Papadopoulos & P. Kanellis (Eds.), *Public sector reform using information technologies: Transforming policy into practice* (pp. 59–78). Hershey, PA: IGI Global. doi:10.4018/978-1-60960-839-2.ch004

Bernardi, R. (2013). Information technology and resistance to public sector reforms: A case study in Kenya. In *User-driven healthcare: Concepts, methodologies, tools, and applications* (pp. 14–33). Hershey, PA: IGI Global. doi:10.4018/978-1-4666-2770-3.ch002

Bianco, K. M. (2008). *The subprime lending crisis: Causes and effects of the mortgage meltdown*. CCH, Wolters Kluwer Law & Business.

Blanchard, O., Faruquee, H., & Das, M. (2010). *The Initial Impact of the Crisis on Emerging Market Countries. Brooking Papers on Economic Activity*. Washington, DC: Brookings Institution.

Blanco, A., & Díaz, D. (2005). El bienestar social: su concepción y medición. Psicotherma, 17(4).

Blaufarb, R. (2012). *The Politics of Fiscal Privilege in Provence, 1530s–1830s*. Catholic University of America Press.

Bolívar, M. P., Pérez, M. D., & Hernández, A. M. (2012). Municipal e-government services in emerging economies: The Latin-American and Caribbean experiences. In Y. Chen & P. Chu (Eds.), *Electronic governance and cross-boundary collaboration: Innovations and advancing tools* (pp. 198–226). Hershey, PA: IGI Global. doi:10.4018/978-1-60960-753-1.ch011

Bortolotti, B., DSousa, J., Fantini, M., & Megginson, W. (2002). Privatization and the Sources of Performance Improvement in the Global Telecommunications Industry. *Telecommunications Policy*, *26*(5-6), 243–268. doi:10.1016/S0308-5961(02)00013-7

Borycki, E. M., & Kushniruk, A. W. (2010). Use of clinical simulations to evaluate the impact of health information systems and ubiquitous computing devices upon health professional work. In S. Mohammed & J. Fiaidhi (Eds.), *Ubiquitous health and medical informatics: The ubiquity 2.0 trend and beyond* (pp. 552–573). Hershey, PA: IGI Global. doi:10.4018/978-1-61520-777-0.ch026

Borycki, E. M., & Kushniruk, A. W. (2011). Use of clinical simulations to evaluate the impact of health information systems and ubiquitous computing devices upon health professional work. In *Clinical technologies: Concepts, methodologies, tools and applications* (pp. 532–553). Hershey, PA: IGI Global. doi:10.4018/978-1-60960-561-2.ch220

Buchan, J. (2011). Developing a dynamic and responsive online learning environment: A case study of a large Australian university. In B. Czerkawski (Ed.), *Free and open source software for e-learning: Issues, successes and challenges* (pp. 92–109). Hershey, PA: IGI Global. doi:10.4018/978-1-61520-917-0.ch006

Bucheli, M. (2006). *Good dictator, bad dictator: United Fruit Company and Economic Nationalism in Central America in the Twentieth Century*. Chicago: University of Illinois.

Buenger, A. W. (2008). Digital convergence and cybersecurity policy. In G. Garson & M. Khosrow-Pour (Eds.), *Handbook of research on public information technology* (pp. 395–405). Hershey, PA: IGI Global. doi:10.4018/978-1-59904-857-4.ch038

Burn, J. M., & Loch, K. D. (2002). The societal impact of world wide web - Key challenges for the 21st century. In A. Salehnia (Ed.), *Ethical issues of information systems* (pp. 88–106). Hershey, PA: IGI Global. doi:10.4018/978-1-931777-15-5.ch007

Burn, J. M., & Loch, K. D. (2003). The societal impact of the world wide web-Key challenges for the 21st century. In M. Khosrow-Pour (Ed.), *Advanced topics in information resources management* (Vol. 2, pp. 32–51). Hershey, PA: IGI Global. doi:10.4018/978-1-59140-062-2.ch002

Bwalya, K. J., Du Plessis, T., & Rensleigh, C. (2012). The "quicksilver initiatives" as a framework for e-government strategy design in developing economies. In K. Bwalya & S. Zulu (Eds.), *Handbook of research on e-government in emerging economies: Adoption, e-participation, and legal frameworks* (pp. 605–623). Hershey, PA: IGI Global. doi:10.4018/978-1-4666-0324-0.ch031

Cabotaje, C. E., & Alampay, E. A. (2013). Social media and citizen engagement: Two cases from the Philippines. In S. Saeed & C. Reddick (Eds.), *Human-centered system design for electronic governance* (pp. 225–238). Hershey, PA: IGI Global. doi:10.4018/978-1-4666-3640-8.ch013

Calvo, G. (1998). Capital Flows and Capital Market-Crisis: The Simple Economics of Sudden Capital Stops. *Journal of Applied Econometrics*, *1*(1), 35–54.

Calvo, G. A., Izquierdo, A., & Mejía, L. F. (2008). *Systemic sudden stops: the relevance of balance-sheet effects and financial integration (No. w14026).* National Bureau of Economic Research. doi:10.3386/w14026

Calvo, G., & Reinhart, C. (2000). When Capital Inflows come to a Sudden Stop: Consequences and Policy Options. In P. Keenen & A. Swoboda (Eds.), *Key Issues in Reform of the International Monetary and Financial System.* Washington, DC: International Monetary Fund.

Cámara de Comercio de Medellín de Antioquia. (2016). *Cámara de Comercio de Medellín de Antioquia.* Obtenido de www.camaramedellin.com.co

Cambridge Dictionary. (2016). Obtenido de Cambridge Dictionary: http://dictionary.cambridge.org/es/diccionario/ingles/hardware#translations

Camillo, A., Di Pietro, L., Di Virgilio, F., & Franco, M. (2013). Work-groups conflict at PetroTech-Italy, S.R.L.: The influence of culture on conflict dynamics. In B. Christiansen, E. Turkina, & N. Williams (Eds.), *Cultural and technological influences on global business* (pp. 272–289). Hershey, PA: IGI Global. doi:10.4018/978-1-4666-3966-9.ch015

Capra, E., Francalanci, C., & Marinoni, C. (2008). Soft success factors for m-government. In A. Anttiroiko (Ed.), *Electronic government: Concepts, methodologies, tools, and applications* (pp. 1213–1233). Hershey, PA: IGI Global. doi:10.4018/978-1-59904-947-2.ch089

Cartelli, A. (2009). The implementation of practices with ICT as a new teaching-learning paradigm. In A. Cartelli & M. Palma (Eds.), *Encyclopedia of information communication technology* (pp. 413–417). Hershey, PA: IGI Global. doi:10.4018/978-1-59904-845-1.ch055

Charalabidis, Y., Lampathaki, F., & Askounis, D. (2010). Investigating the landscape in national interoperability frameworks. *International Journal of E-Services and Mobile Applications*, *2*(4), 28–41. doi:10.4018/jesma.2010100103

Charalabidis, Y., Lampathaki, F., & Askounis, D. (2012). Investigating the landscape in national interoperability frameworks. In A. Scupola (Ed.), *Innovative mobile platform developments for electronic services design and delivery* (pp. 218–231). Hershey, PA: IGI Global. doi:10.4018/978-1-4666-1568-7.ch013

Chen, I. (2005). Distance education associations. In C. Howard, J. Boettcher, L. Justice, K. Schenk, P. Rogers, & G. Berg (Eds.), *Encyclopedia of distance learning* (pp. 599–612). Hershey, PA: IGI Global. doi:10.4018/978-1-59140-555-9.ch087

Chen, I. (2008). Distance education associations. In L. Tomei (Ed.), *Online and distance learning: Concepts, methodologies, tools, and applications* (pp. 562–579). Hershey, PA: IGI Global. doi:10.4018/978-1-59904-935-9.ch048

Chen, Y. (2008). Managing IT outsourcing for digital government. In A. Anttiroiko (Ed.), *Electronic government: Concepts, methodologies, tools, and applications* (pp. 3107–3114). Hershey, PA: IGI Global. doi:10.4018/978-1-59904-947-2.ch229

Chen, Y., & Dimitrova, D. V. (2006). Electronic government and online engagement: Citizen interaction with government via web portals. *International Journal of Electronic Government Research*, *2*(1), 54–76. doi:10.4018/jegr.2006010104

Chen, Y., & Knepper, R. (2005). Digital government development strategies: Lessons for policy makers from a comparative perspective. In W. Huang, K. Siau, & K. Wei (Eds.), *Electronic government strategies and implementation* (pp. 394–420). Hershey, PA: IGI Global. doi:10.4018/978-1-59140-348-7.ch017

Chen, Y., & Knepper, R. (2008). Digital government development strategies: Lessons for policy makers from a comparative perspective. In H. Rahman (Ed.), *Developing successful ICT strategies: Competitive advantages in a global knowledge-driven society* (pp. 334–356). Hershey, PA: IGI Global. doi:10.4018/978-1-59904-654-9.ch017

Cherian, E. J., & Ryan, T. W. (2014). Incongruent needs: Why differences in the iron-triangle of priorities make health information technology adoption and use difficult. In C. El Morr (Ed.), *Research perspectives on the role of informatics in health policy and management* (pp. 209–221). Hershey, PA: IGI Global. doi:10.4018/978-1-4666-4321-5.ch012

Cho, H. J., & Hwang, S. (2010). Government 2.0 in Korea: Focusing on e-participation services. In C. Reddick (Ed.), *Politics, democracy and e-government: Participation and service delivery* (pp. 94–114). Hershey, PA: IGI Global. doi:10.4018/978-1-61520-933-0.ch006

Chopra, R. I. (2009). *Price performance of IPOs in Indian Stock Market*. Patiala, India: Thapar University.

Chorus, C., & Timmermans, H. (2010). Ubiquitous travel environments and travel control strategies: Prospects and challenges. In M. Wachowicz (Ed.), *Movement-aware applications for sustainable mobility: Technologies and approaches* (pp. 30–51). Hershey, PA: IGI Global. doi:10.4018/978-1-61520-769-5.ch003

Chuanshen, R. (2007). E-government construction and China's administrative litigation act. In A. Anttiroiko & M. Malkia (Eds.), *Encyclopedia of digital government* (pp. 507–510). Hershey, PA: IGI Global. doi:10.4018/978-1-59140-789-8.ch077

Ciaghi, A., & Villafiorita, A. (2012). Law modeling and BPR for public administration improvement. In K. Bwalya & S. Zulu (Eds.), *Handbook of research on e-government in emerging economies: Adoption, e-participation, and legal frameworks* (pp. 391–410). Hershey, PA: IGI Global. doi:10.4018/978-1-4666-0324-0.ch019

Ciaramitaro, B. L., & Skrocki, M. (2012). mHealth: Mobile healthcare. In B. Ciaramitaro (Ed.), Mobile technology consumption: Opportunities and challenges (pp. 99-109). Hershey, PA: IGI Global. doi:10.4018/978-1-61350-150-4.ch007

Cifuentes, M. (2007). *Efectos por el incumplimiento de los compromisos del pacto fiscal.* Retrieved from Universidad de San Carlos: http://biblioteca.usac.edu.gt/tesis/03/03_3090.pdf

CNB. (n.d.). *The new curriculum.* Obtained from Http://cnbguatemala.org/index.php?title=El_nuevo_curr%C3%ADCornum

Coe, L. (1995). *The telephone and its several inventors.* McFarland & Company, Inc., Publishers.

Comite, U. (2012). Innovative processes and managerial effectiveness of e-procurement in healthcare. In A. Manoharan & M. Holzer (Eds.), *Active citizen participation in e-government: A global perspective* (pp. 206–229). Hershey, PA: IGI Global. doi:10.4018/978-1-4666-0116-1.ch011

Commission for Historical Clarification. (1999). *Comisión para el esclarecimiento histórico.* Author.

Constituyente, A. N. (1824). *Constitución de la República Federal de Centroamérica.* Guatemala.

Cordella, A. (2013). E-government success: How to account for ICT, administrative rationalization, and institutional change. In J. Gil-Garcia (Ed.), *E-government success factors and measures: Theories, concepts, and methodologies* (pp. 40–51). Hershey, PA: IGI Global. doi:10.4018/978-1-4666-4058-0.ch003

Cropf, R. A. (2009). ICT and e-democracy. In M. Khosrow-Pour (Ed.), *Encyclopedia of information science and technology* (2nd ed.; pp. 1789–1793). Hershey, PA: IGI Global. doi:10.4018/978-1-60566-026-4.ch281

Cropf, R. A. (2009). The virtual public sphere. In M. Pagani (Ed.), *Encyclopedia of multimedia technology and networking* (2nd ed.; pp. 1525–1530). Hershey, PA: IGI Global. doi:10.4018/978-1-60566-014-1.ch206

Cruz, F. P. (2009). *Morazán nuestro altivo héroe.* Havana: REvista Cubana de pensamiento e historia.

Cuello, J. (1988). The Economic Impact of the Bourbon Reforms and the Late Colonial Crisis of Empire at the Local Level: The Case of Saltillo, 17771817. *The Americas*, *44*(03), 301–323. doi:10.2307/1006909

D. A. D. C., S. J., & A, J. R. (2009). The consequences of radical reform: the French Revolution. *NBER Working Papers.*

D. K.-P. (2008). *New York Times*. Retrieved from Big Fruit: http://www.nytimes.com/2008/03/02/books/review/Kurtz-Phelan-t.html

D'Abundo, M. L. (2013). Electronic health record implementation in the United States healthcare industry: Making the process of change manageable. In V. Wang (Ed.), *Handbook of research on technologies for improving the 21st century workforce: Tools for lifelong learning* (pp. 272–286). Hershey, PA: IGI Global. doi:10.4018/978-1-4666-2181-7.ch018

Damodaran. (2016). Obtenido de http://pages.stern.nyu.edu/~adamodar/New_Home_Page/datafile/totalbeta.html

Damurski, L. (2012). E-participation in urban planning: Online tools for citizen engagement in Poland and in Germany. *International Journal of E-Planning Research*, *1*(3), 40–67. doi:10.4018/ijepr.2012070103

Datasec-MeycorKP. (2016). Obtenido de Datasec.

de Almeida, M. O. (2007). E-government strategy in Brazil: Increasing transparency and efficiency through e-government procurement. In M. Gascó-Hernandez (Ed.), *Latin America online: Cases, successes and pitfalls* (pp. 34–82). Hershey, PA: IGI Global. doi:10.4018/978-1-59140-974-8.ch002

de Juana Espinosa, S. (2008). Empirical study of the municipalitites' motivations for adopting online presence. In A. Anttiroiko (Ed.), *Electronic government: Concepts, methodologies, tools, and applications* (pp. 3593–3608). Hershey, PA: IGI Global. doi:10.4018/978-1-59904-947-2.ch262

de Souza Dias, D. (2002). Motivation for using information technology. In C. Snodgrass & E. Szewczak (Eds.), *Human factors in information systems* (pp. 55–60). Hershey, PA: IGI Global. doi:10.4018/978-1-931777-10-0.ch005

Demediuk, P. (2006). Government procurement ICT's impact on the sustainability of SMEs and regional communities. In S. Marshall, W. Taylor, & X. Yu (Eds.), *Encyclopedia of developing regional communities with information and communication technology* (pp. 321–324). Hershey, PA: IGI Global. doi:10.4018/978-1-59140-575-7.ch056

Devonshire, E., Forsyth, H., Reid, S., & Simpson, J. M. (2013). The challenges and opportunities of online postgraduate coursework programs in a traditional university context. In B. Tynan, J. Willems, & R. James (Eds.), *Outlooks and opportunities in blended and distance learning* (pp. 353–368). Hershey, PA: IGI Global. doi:10.4018/978-1-4666-4205-8.ch026

Devore, J. (2008). Probability and Statistics for Engineering and Sciences (7th Ed.). Cengage Learning.

Di Cerbo, F., Scotto, M., Sillitti, A., Succi, G., & Vernazza, T. (2007). Toward a GNU/Linux distribution for corporate environments. In S. Sowe, I. Stamelos, & I. Samoladas (Eds.), *Emerging free and open source software practices* (pp. 215–236). Hershey, PA: IGI Global. doi:10.4018/978-1-59904-210-7.ch010

Díaz de León, A., & Greenham, L. (2001). Monetary policy and interest rates: recent experience for the case of Mexico. *Mexican Economy. New Age*, 213-258.

Diaz-Alejandro, C. F. (1984). *Good-bye Financial Repression, Hello Financial Crash.* Kellog Institute Working Papers Series No. 24.

Diesner, J., & Carley, K. M. (2005). Revealing social structure from texts: Meta-matrix text analysis as a novel method for network text analysis. In V. Narayanan & D. Armstrong (Eds.), *Causal mapping for research in information technology* (pp. 81–108). Hershey, PA: IGI Global. doi:10.4018/978-1-59140-396-8.ch004

Dologite, D. G., Mockler, R. J., Bai, Q., & Viszhanyo, P. F. (2006). IS change agents in practice in a US-Chinese joint venture. In M. Hunter & F. Tan (Eds.), *Advanced topics in global information management* (Vol. 5, pp. 331–352). Hershey, PA: IGI Global. doi:10.4018/978-1-59140-923-6.ch015

Drnevich, P., Brush, T. H., & Luckock, G. T. (2011). Process and structural implications for IT-enabled outsourcing. *International Journal of Strategic Information Technology and Applications*, *2*(4), 30–43. doi:10.4018/jsita.2011100103

Dwivedi, A. N. (2009). Handbook of research on information technology management and clinical data administration in healthcare (Vols. 1–2). Hershey, PA: IGI Global. doi:10.4018/978-1-60566-356-2

ECLAC. (2015). *Panorama Fiscal de América Latina y el Caribe 2015: Dilemas y espacios de políticas*. United Natinos.

Elbeltagi, I., McBride, N., & Hardaker, G. (2006). Evaluating the factors affecting DSS usage by senior managers in local authorities in Egypt. In M. Hunter & F. Tan (Eds.), *Advanced topics in global information management* (Vol. 5, pp. 283–307). Hershey, PA: IGI Global. doi:10.4018/978-1-59140-923-6.ch013

Eom, S., & Fountain, J. E. (2013). Enhancing information services through public-private partnerships: Information technology knowledge transfer underlying structures to develop shared services in the U.S. and Korea. In J. Gil-Garcia (Ed.), *E-government success around the world: Cases, empirical studies, and practical recommendations* (pp. 15–40). Hershey, PA: IGI Global. doi:10.4018/978-1-4666-4173-0.ch002

Esteves, T., Leuenberger, D., & Van Leuven, N. (2012). Reaching citizen 2.0: How government uses social media to send public messages during times of calm and times of crisis. In K. Kloby & M. D'Agostino (Eds.), *Citizen 2.0: Public and governmental interaction through web 2.0 technologies* (pp. 250–268). Hershey, PA: IGI Global. doi:10.4018/978-1-4666-0318-9.ch013

Estevez, E., Fillottrani, P., Janowski, T., & Ojo, A. (2012). Government information sharing: A framework for policy formulation. In Y. Chen & P. Chu (Eds.), *Electronic governance and cross-boundary collaboration: Innovations and advancing tools* (pp. 23–55). Hershey, PA: IGI Global. doi:10.4018/978-1-60960-753-1.ch002

Ezz, I. E. (2008). E-governement emerging trends: Organizational challenges. In A. Anttiroiko (Ed.), *Electronic government: Concepts, methodologies, tools, and applications* (pp. 3721–3737). Hershey, PA: IGI Global. doi:10.4018/978-1-59904-947-2.ch269

F. R., & F. S. (2015). Costa Rica: favorecer a los exportadores, sacrificando la inversión social y el desarollo democrático. In I. C. Fiscales (Ed.), *Política fsical: expresión del poder de las élites centroamericanas* (pp. 313-390). FyG.

Fabri, M. (2009). The Italian style of e-justice in a comparative perspective. In A. Martínez & P. Abat (Eds.), *E-justice: Using information communication technologies in the court system* (pp. 1–19). Hershey, PA: IGI Global. doi:10.4018/978-1-59904-998-4.ch001

Fagbe, T., & Adekola, O. D. (2010). Workplace safety and personnel well-being: The impact of information technology. *International Journal of Green Computing*, *1*(1), 28–33. doi:10.4018/jgc.2010010103

Fagbe, T., & Adekola, O. D. (2011). Workplace safety and personnel well-being: The impact of information technology. In *Global business: Concepts, methodologies, tools and applications* (pp. 1438–1444). Hershey, PA: IGI Global. doi:10.4018/978-1-60960-587-2.ch509

Farmer, L. (2008). Affective collaborative instruction with librarians. In S. Kelsey & K. St.Amant (Eds.), *Handbook of research on computer mediated communication* (pp. 15–24). Hershey, PA: IGI Global. doi:10.4018/978-1-59904-863-5.ch002

Favier, L., & Mekhantar, J. (2007). Use of OSS by local e-administration: The French situation. In K. St.Amant & B. Still (Eds.), *Handbook of research on open source software: Technological, economic, and social perspectives* (pp. 428–444). Hershey, PA: IGI Global. doi:10.4018/978-1-59140-999-1.ch033

Fernando, S. (2009). Issues of e-learning in third world countries. In M. Khosrow-Pour (Ed.), *Encyclopedia of information science and technology* (2nd ed.; pp. 2273–2277). Hershey, PA: IGI Global. doi:10.4018/978-1-60566-026-4.ch360

Filho, J. R., & dos Santos Junior, J. R. (2009). Local e-government in Brazil: Poor interaction and local politics as usual. In C. Reddick (Ed.), *Handbook of research on strategies for local e-government adoption and implementation: Comparative studies* (pp. 863–878). Hershey, PA: IGI Global. doi:10.4018/978-1-60566-282-4.ch045

Fisher, S. (1986). *The inflationary process: Shocks and Accommodation in the Israeli Economy: Maturing through crisis*. Harvard University Press.

Fletcher, P. D. (2004). Portals and policy: Implications of electronic access to U.S. federal government information services. In A. Pavlichev & G. Garson (Eds.), *Digital government: Principles and best practices* (pp. 52–62). Hershey, PA: IGI Global. doi:10.4018/978-1-59140-122-3.ch004

Fletcher, P. D. (2008). Portals and policy: Implications of electronic access to U.S. federal government information services. In A. Anttiroiko (Ed.), *Electronic government: Concepts, methodologies, tools, and applications* (pp. 3970–3979). Hershey, PA: IGI Global. doi:10.4018/978-1-59904-947-2.ch289

Fondo Monetario Internacional. (2011). *Data mapper*. Obtenido de la siguiente dirección: http://www.imf.org/external/datamapper/index.php

Forlano, L. (2004). The emergence of digital government: International perspectives. In A. Pavlichev & G. Garson (Eds.), *Digital government: Principles and best practices* (pp. 34–51). Hershey, PA: IGI Global. doi:10.4018/978-1-59140-122-3.ch003

Franzel, J. M., & Coursey, D. H. (2004). Government web portals: Management issues and the approaches of five states. In A. Pavlichev & G. Garson (Eds.), *Digital government: Principles and best practices* (pp. 63–77). Hershey, PA: IGI Global. doi:10.4018/978-1-59140-122-3.ch005

Fuentes, N., & Rojas, M. (2001). Economic Theory and Subjective Well-Being: Mexico. In *Social Indicator Research*. Dialogos Bienestera.

Fundación Enrique Bolaños. (2001). *Fundación Enrique Bolaños*. Retrieved from Vicente Filísola: http://www.enriquebolanos.org/data/docs/Biografia%20de%20 Vicente%20Filisola%20v1.pdf

Gaivéo, J. M. (2013). Security of ICTs supporting healthcare activities. In M. Cruz-Cunha, I. Miranda, & P. Gonçalves (Eds.), *Handbook of research on ICTs for human-centered healthcare and social care services* (pp. 208–228). Hershey, PA: IGI Global. doi:10.4018/978-1-4666-3986-7.ch011

Garson, G. D. (1999). *Information technology and computer applications in public administration: Issues and trends*. Hershey, PA: IGI Global. doi:10.4018/978-1-87828-952-0

Garson, G. D. (2003). Toward an information technology research agenda for public administration. In G. Garson (Ed.), *Public information technology: Policy and management issues* (pp. 331–357). Hershey, PA: IGI Global. doi:10.4018/978-1-59140-060-8.ch014

Garson, G. D. (2004). The promise of digital government. In A. Pavlichev & G. Garson (Eds.), *Digital government: Principles and best practices* (pp. 2–15). Hershey, PA: IGI Global. doi:10.4018/978-1-59140-122-3.ch001

Garson, G. D. (2007). An information technology research agenda for public administration. In G. Garson (Ed.), *Modern public information technology systems: Issues and challenges* (pp. 365–392). Hershey, PA: IGI Global. doi:10.4018/978-1-59904-051-6.ch018

Gasco, M. (2007). Civil servants' resistance towards e-government development. In A. Anttiroiko & M. Malkia (Eds.), *Encyclopedia of digital government* (pp. 190–195). Hershey, PA: IGI Global. doi:10.4018/978-1-59140-789-8.ch028

Gasco, M. (2008). Civil servants' resistance towards e-government development. In A. Anttiroiko (Ed.), *Electronic government: Concepts, methodologies, tools, and applications* (pp. 2580–2588). Hershey, PA: IGI Global. doi:10.4018/978-1-59904-947-2.ch190

General Management of Educational Quality Management. (n.d.). *National Curriculum Base.* Ministry of Education, Guatemala.

Gensollen, M. & Laubie, A. (1995). *The role of telecommunications in economic development.* Academic Press.

Gerardo Guajardo Cantú, N. E. (2008). *Contabilidad financiera* (M. Hill, Ed.). México.

Ghere, R. K. (2010). Accountability and information technology enactment: Implications for social empowerment. In E. Ferro, Y. Dwivedi, J. Gil-Garcia, & M. Williams (Eds.), *Handbook of research on overcoming digital divides: Constructing an equitable and competitive information society* (pp. 515–532). Hershey, PA: IGI Global. doi:10.4018/978-1-60566-699-0.ch028

Gibson, I. W. (2012). Simulation modeling of healthcare delivery. In A. Kolker & P. Story (Eds.), *Management engineering for effective healthcare delivery: Principles and applications* (pp. 69–89). Hershey, PA: IGI Global. doi:10.4018/978-1-60960-872-9.ch003

Gil-Garcia, J. R. (2007). Exploring e-government benefits and success factors. In A. Anttiroiko & M. Malkia (Eds.), *Encyclopedia of digital government* (pp. 803–811). Hershey, PA: IGI Global. doi:10.4018/978-1-59140-789-8.ch122

Gil-Garcia, J. R., & González Miranda, F. (2010). E-government and opportunities for participation: The case of the Mexican state web portals. In C. Reddick (Ed.), *Politics, democracy and e-government: Participation and service delivery* (pp. 56–74). Hershey, PA: IGI Global. doi:10.4018/978-1-61520-933-0.ch004

Gobierno de Chile. (2011). *Guía práctica sobre la quiebra de una empresa. Dirección de trabajo.* Santiago de Chile.

Gobierno de la República de Guatemala. (1962). *Decreto 1559.* Retrieved from http://old.congreso.gob.gt/archivos/decretos/1962/gtdcx15591962.pdf

Gobierno de la República de Guatemala. (1966). *Congreso de Guatemala.* Retrieved from http://old.congreso.gob.gt/archivos/decretos/1966/gtdcx16271966.pdf

Gobierno de la República de Guatemala. (1974). *Decreto 50-74.* Retrieved from Congress of Guatemala: http://old.congreso.gob.gt/archivos/decretos/1974/gtdcx00501974.pdf

Gobierno de la República de Guatemala. (1980). *Decreto 51-80.* Retrieved from Congreso de Guatemala: http://old.congreso.gob.gt/archivos/decretos/1980/gtdcx00511980.pdf

Gobierno de la República de Guatemala. (1985). *Constitución Política de la República de Guatemala.* Author.

Gobierno de la República de Guatemala. (1998). *Congeso de la República.* Retrieved from Decreto 15-98: https://www.rgp.org.gt/docs/legislacion_registral/Ley%20del%20Impuesto%20Unico%20sobre%20Inmuebles.pdf

Goldfinch, S. (2012). Public trust in government, trust in e-government, and use of e-government. In Z. Yan (Ed.), *Encyclopedia of cyber behavior* (pp. 987–995). Hershey, PA: IGI Global. doi:10.4018/978-1-4666-0315-8.ch081

González Orellana, C. (2007). *History of education in Guatemala*. Editorial USAC.

Goodyear, M. (2012). Organizational change contributions to e-government project transitions. In S. Aikins (Ed.), *Managing e-government projects: Concepts, issues, and best practices* (pp. 1–21). Hershey, PA: IGI Global. doi:10.4018/978-1-4666-0086-7.ch001

Gordon, S., & Mulligan, P. (2003). Strategic models for the delivery of personal financial services: The role of infocracy. In S. Gordon (Ed.), *Computing information technology: The human side* (pp. 220–232). Hershey, PA: IGI Global. doi:10.4018/978-1-93177-752-0.ch014

Gordon, T. F. (2007). Legal knowledge systems. In A. Anttiroiko & M. Malkia (Eds.), *Encyclopedia of digital government* (pp. 1161–1166). Hershey, PA: IGI Global. doi:10.4018/978-1-59140-789-8.ch175

Graham, J. E., & Semich, G. W. (2008). Integrating technology to transform pedagogy: Revisiting the progress of the three phase TUI model for faculty development. In L. Tomei (Ed.), *Adapting information and communication technologies for effective education* (pp. 1–12). Hershey, PA: IGI Global. doi:10.4018/978-1-59904-922-9.ch001

Gramajo, J., & Ramirez, G. (2016). *Ley de Empleo favorece a maquilas y Call Centers*. Academic Press.

Grandinetti, L., & Pisacane, O. (2012). Web services for healthcare management. In D. Prakash Vidyarthi (Ed.), *Technologies and protocols for the future of internet design: Reinventing the web* (pp. 60–94). Hershey, PA: IGI Global. doi:10.4018/978-1-4666-0203-8.ch004

Groenewegen, P., & Wagenaar, F. P. (2008). VO as an alternative to hierarchy in the Dutch police sector. In G. Putnik & M. Cruz-Cunha (Eds.), *Encyclopedia of networked and virtual organizations* (pp. 1851–1857). Hershey, PA: IGI Global. doi:10.4018/978-1-59904-885-7.ch245

Gronlund, A. (2001). Building an infrastructure to manage electronic services. In S. Dasgupta (Ed.), *Managing internet and intranet technologies in organizations: Challenges and opportunities* (pp. 71–103). Hershey, PA: IGI Global. doi:10.4018/978-1-878289-95-7.ch006

Gronlund, A. (2002). Introduction to electronic government: Design, applications and management. In Å. Grönlund (Ed.), *Electronic government: Design, applications and management* (pp. 1–21). Hershey, PA: IGI Global. doi:10.4018/978-1-930708-19-8.ch001

Grub, U. (2004). *Asociación para el Fomento de los Estudios Históricos en Centroamérica*. Bustamante y Guerra.

GSMA. (2012). *Mobile telephony and taxation impact in Latin America*. GSMA.

Guatemala Imprenta Nueva. (1830). Exposición que al comenzar la actual legislatura ordinaria, hizo al Congreso Federal de esta República. Author.

Guatemala, G. d. (1987). *Decreto 97-24*. Retrieved from Congreso de Guatemala: http://old.congreso.gob.gt/archivos/decretos/1984/gtdly97-84.pdf

Gujarati, D., & Porter, D. (n.d.). Econometrics (5th ed.). McGraw Hill.

Gupta, A., Woosley, R., Crk, I., & Sarnikar, S. (2009). An information technology architecture for drug effectiveness reporting and post-marketing surveillance. In J. Tan (Ed.), *Medical informatics: Concepts, methodologies, tools, and applications* (pp. 631–646). Hershey, PA: IGI Global. doi:10.4018/978-1-60566-050-9.ch047

Gutiérrez, L. (2002). *Regulatory Governance in the Latin American Telecommunications Sector*. Universidad del Rosario.

Gutiérrez, L. (2003). The Effect of Endogenous Regulation on Telecommunications Expansion and Efficiency in Latin America. *Journal of Regulatory Economics*, *23*(3), 257–286. doi:10.1023/A:1023412226826

Gutiérrez, L., & Berg, S. (2000). *Telecommunications Liberalization and Regulatory Governance: Lessons from Latin America*. University of Florida.

H. S. (2014). State Building and Taxation in Latin America. *Latin American Research Review*, 258–262.

Hallin, A., & Lundevall, K. (2007). mCity: User focused development of mobile services within the city of Stockholm. In I. Kushchu (Ed.), Mobile government: An emerging direction in e-government (pp. 12-29). Hershey, PA: IGI Global. doi:10.4018/978-1-59140-884-0.ch002

Hallin, A., & Lundevall, K. (2009). mCity: User focused development of mobile services within the city of Stockholm. In D. Taniar (Ed.), Mobile computing: Concepts, methodologies, tools, and applications (pp. 3455-3467). Hershey, PA: IGI Global. doi:10.4018/978-1-60566-054-7.ch253

Hallin, A., & Lundevall, K. (2009). mCity: User focused development of mobile services within the city of Stockholm. In S. Clarke (Ed.), Evolutionary concepts in end user productivity and performance: Applications for organizational progress (pp. 268-280). Hershey, PA: IGI Global. doi:10.4018/978-1-60566-136-0.ch017

Hanson, A. (2005). Overcoming barriers in the planning of a virtual library. In M. Khosrow-Pour (Ed.), *Encyclopedia of information science and technology* (pp. 2255–2259). Hershey, PA: IGI Global. doi:10.4018/978-1-59140-553-5.ch397

Haque, A. (2008). Information technology and surveillance: Implications for public administration in a new word order. In T. Loendorf & G. Garson (Eds.), *Patriotic information systems* (pp. 177–185). Hershey, PA: IGI Global. doi:10.4018/978-1-59904-594-8.ch008

Hauck, R. V., Thatcher, S. M., & Weisband, S. P. (2012). Temporal aspects of information technology use: Increasing shift work effectiveness. In J. Wang (Ed.), *Advancing the service sector with evolving technologies: Techniques and principles* (pp. 87–104). Hershey, PA: IGI Global. doi:10.4018/978-1-4666-0044-7.ch006

Hawk, S., & Witt, T. (2006). Telecommunications courses in information systems programs. *International Journal of Information and Communication Technology Education, 2*(1), 79–92. doi:10.4018/jicte.2006010107

Heinz, W., & Zelner, B. A. (2001). The Institutional Environment for Telecommunications Investment. *Journal of Economics & Management Strategy, 10*(1), 123–147. doi:10.1162/105864001300122575

Helms, M. M., Moore, R., & Ahmadi, M. (2009). Information technology (IT) and the healthcare industry: A SWOT analysis. In J. Tan (Ed.), *Medical informatics: Concepts, methodologies, tools, and applications* (pp. 134–152). Hershey, PA: IGI Global. doi:10.4018/978-1-60566-050-9.ch012

Helps, A. (1868). *The Spanish conquest in America.* Harper & Brothers.

Hendrickson, S. M., & Young, M. E. (2014). Electronic records management at a federally funded research and development center. In J. Krueger (Ed.), *Cases on electronic records and resource management implementation in diverse environments* (pp. 334–350). Hershey, PA: IGI Global. doi:10.4018/978-1-4666-4466-3.ch020

Henman, P. (2010). Social policy and information communication technologies. In J. Martin & L. Hawkins (Eds.), *Information communication technologies for human services education and delivery: Concepts and cases* (pp. 215–229). Hershey, PA: IGI Global. doi:10.4018/978-1-60566-735-5.ch014

Hernández, M. S. (2014). *Centroamérica 1850-1950: los debates fundamentales sobre la unión política regional.* Universidad Nacional de Costa Rica.

Highley, J. (2001). *Elite Theory in Political Sociology.* Estados Unidos.

Hirshman, A. (1991). *Retórica de la instransigencia.* Academic Press.

Hismanoglu, M. (2011). Important issues in online education: E-pedagogy and marketing. In U. Demiray & S. Sever (Eds.), *Marketing online education programs: Frameworks for promotion and communication* (pp. 184–209). Hershey, PA: IGI Global. doi:10.4018/978-1-60960-074-7.ch012

Ho, K. K. (2008). The e-government development, IT strategies, and portals of the Hong Kong SAR government. In A. Anttiroiko (Ed.), *Electronic government: Concepts, methodologies, tools, and applications* (pp. 715–733). Hershey, PA: IGI Global. doi:10.4018/978-1-59904-947-2.ch060

Holden, S. H. (2003). The evolution of information technology management at the federal level: Implications for public administration. In G. Garson (Ed.), *Public information technology: Policy and management issues* (pp. 53–73). Hershey, PA: IGI Global. doi:10.4018/978-1-59140-060-8.ch003

Holden, S. H. (2007). The evolution of federal information technology management literature: Does IT finally matter? In G. Garson (Ed.), *Modern public information technology systems: Issues and challenges* (pp. 17–34). Hershey, PA: IGI Global. doi:10.4018/978-1-59904-051-6.ch002

Holland, J. W. (2009). Automation of American criminal justice. In M. Khosrow-Pour (Ed.), *Encyclopedia of information science and technology* (2nd ed.; pp. 300–302). Hershey, PA: IGI Global. doi:10.4018/978-1-60566-026-4.ch051

Holloway, K. (2013). Fair use, copyright, and academic integrity in an online academic environment. In *Digital rights management: Concepts, methodologies, tools, and applications* (pp. 917–928). Hershey, PA: IGI Global. doi:10.4018/978-1-4666-2136-7.ch044

Horiuchi, C. (2005). E-government databases. In L. Rivero, J. Doorn, & V. Ferraggine (Eds.), *Encyclopedia of database technologies and applications* (pp. 206–210). Hershey, PA: IGI Global. doi:10.4018/978-1-59140-560-3.ch035

Horiuchi, C. (2006). Creating IS quality in government settings. In E. Duggan & J. Reichgelt (Eds.), *Measuring information systems delivery quality* (pp. 311–327). Hershey, PA: IGI Global. doi:10.4018/978-1-59140-857-4.ch014

Hsiao, N., Chu, P., & Lee, C. (2012). Impact of e-governance on businesses: Model development and case study. In *Digital democracy: Concepts, methodologies, tools, and applications* (pp. 1407–1425). Hershey, PA: IGI Global. doi:10.4018/978-1-4666-1740-7.ch070

Huang, T., & Lee, C. (2010). Evaluating the impact of e-government on citizens: Cost-benefit analysis. In C. Reddick (Ed.), *Citizens and e-government: Evaluating policy and management* (pp. 37–52). Hershey, PA: IGI Global. doi:10.4018/978-1-61520-931-6.ch003

Hunter, M. G., Diochon, M., Pugsley, D., & Wright, B. (2002). Unique challenges for small business adoption of information technology: The case of the Nova Scotia ten. In S. Burgess (Ed.), *Managing information technology in small business: Challenges and solutions* (pp. 98–117). Hershey, PA: IGI Global. doi:10.4018/978-1-930708-35-8.ch006

Hurskainen, J. (2003). Integration of business systems and applications in merger and alliance: Case metso automation. In T. Reponen (Ed.), *Information technology enabled global customer service* (pp. 207–225). Hershey, PA: IGI Global. doi:10.4018/978-1-59140-048-6.ch012

Huurdeman, A. (2003). *The worldwide history of Telecommunications*. John Wiley & Sons, Inc. doi:10.1002/0471722243

Iazzolino, G., & Pietrantonio, R. (2011). The soveria.it project: A best practice of e-government in southern Italy. In D. Piaggesi, K. Sund, & W. Castelnovo (Eds.), *Global strategy and practice of e-governance: Examples from around the world* (pp. 34–56). Hershey, PA: IGI Global. doi:10.4018/978-1-60960-489-9.ch003

ICEFI. (2017). *Perfiles macrofiscales 8*. ICEFI.

ICONTEC. (2010). *Compendio sistema de gestión de seguridad de la información (SGSI)*. Bogota, Colombia: Editorial Kimpress.

Ihori, T. (2015). *Fiscal Privileges, Consolidation Attempts and Pigouvian Taxes*. Tokyo: Public Choice Meetings.

i. Martinez, A. C. (2008). Accessing administration's information via internet in Spain. In F. Tan (Ed.), *Global information technologies: Concepts, methodologies, tools, and applications* (pp. 2558–2573). Hershey, PA: IGI Global. doi:10.4018/978-1-59904-939-7.ch186

Imran, A., & Gregor, S. (2012). A process model for successful e-government adoption in the least developed countries: A case of Bangladesh. In F. Tan (Ed.), *International comparisons of information communication technologies: Advancing applications* (pp. 321–350). Hershey, PA: IGI Global. doi:10.4018/978-1-61350-480-2.ch014

INCIBE. (2016). *Gestión de riesgos, una guía de aproximación para el empresario*. Obtenido de Instituto Nacional de Ciberseguridad: https://www.incibe.es/extfrontinteco/img/File/empresas/guias/Guia_gestion_riesgos/guiagestionriesgos.pdf

Inoue, Y., & Bell, S. T. (2005). Electronic/digital government innovation, and publishing trends with IT. In M. Khosrow-Pour (Ed.), *Encyclopedia of information science and technology* (pp. 1018–1023). Hershey, PA: IGI Global. doi:10.4018/978-1-59140-553-5.ch180

Institute of Taxation and Economic Policy. (2013). *Tax Incentives: Costly for States, Drag on the Nation*. Retrieved from ITEP: http://itep.org/itep_reports/2013/08/tax-incentives-costly-for-states-drag-on-the-nation.php#.WOOpezs1-M8

Instituto Centroamericano de Estudios Fiscales. (2006). Guatemala ingresos de gobierno Central. Guatemala: Author.

Instituto Centroamericano de Estudios Fiscales. (2007). *Historia de la tributación en Guatemala*. Author.

Instituto Centroamericano de Estudios Fiscales. (2009). *Historia de la tributación de Guatemala*. Superintendencia de Administración Tributaria.

Instituto Centroamericano de Estudios Fiscales. (2014). *Contamos! Protegiendo la nueva cosecha*. ICEFI.

Instituto Centroamericano de Estudios Fiscales. (2015). *Política fiscal: expresión del poder de las élites centroamericanas*. FyG editores.

Instituto Centroamericano de Estudios Fiscales. (2016). *Contamos¡ ¿Dond están los ausentes?*. ICEFI.

International Monetary Fund. (2009). *What is fiscal policy?*. International Monetary Fund.

International Telecommunications Union. (1993). *The Changing Role of Government in an Era of Deregulation. ITU Regulatory Colloquium No. 1*. ITU.

Iraheta, B. J. M. (2010). Vulnerabilidad Macroeconómica en Centroamérica y República Dominicana ante la Crisis Financiera: Un Análisis Comparado con LAC7 (Documento de Trabajo No. 01–2010). San José, Costa Rica: Academic Press.

Iranzo, S. (2008). *Introducción al riesgo país. Banco de España, documentos ocasionales No. 0802*. España.

ISACA. (2013). *Manual de preparación al Examen CISM 2013*. Estados Unidos de América: ISACA. Recuperado el 20 de Septiembre de 2016, de http://www.isaca.org

Islam, M. M., & Ehsan, M. (2013). Understanding e-governance: A theoretical approach. In M. Islam & M. Ehsan (Eds.), *From government to e-governance: Public administration in the digital age* (pp. 38–49). Hershey, PA: IGI Global. doi:10.4018/978-1-4666-1909-8.ch003

ISO. IEC 27001:2013. (2013). Information technology - Security techniques - Information security management systems - Requeriments (2nd ed.). ISO.

ISO/IEC TR 13335-3:1998. (1998). *Information Technology. Guidelines for the Management of IT Security. Part 3: Techniques for the Management of IT Security*. ISO.

Izquierdo, A., Romero, R., & Talvi, E. (2008). *Booms and Busts in Latin America: The Role of External Factors*. Inter-American Development Bank: Centro de Estudio de Realidad Económica y Social.

J. H. & T. K. (2012). The impact of tax incentives on the economic activity of entrepreneurs. *NBER Working Papers*, 1-48.

J. L., & R. H. (1965). *The Origins of the Latin American Revolutions, 1808-1826*. Academic Press.

Jaca, B. B. (1988). *Causas del pronunciamiento de 1820 y de su éxito*. Madrid: Universidad Nacional de Educación a Distancia.

Jaeger, B. (2009). E-government and e-democracy in the making. In M. Khosrow-Pour (Ed.), *Encyclopedia of information science and technology* (2nd ed.; pp. 1318–1322). Hershey, PA: IGI Global. doi:10.4018/978-1-60566-026-4.ch208

Jain, R. B. (2007). Revamping the administrative structure and processes in India for online diplomacy. In A. Anttiroiko & M. Malkia (Eds.), *Encyclopedia of digital government* (pp. 1418–1423). Hershey, PA: IGI Global. doi:10.4018/978-1-59140-789-8.ch217

Jain, R. B. (2008). Revamping the administrative structure and processes in India for online diplomacy. In A. Anttiroiko (Ed.), *Electronic government: Concepts, methodologies, tools, and applications* (pp. 3142–3149). Hershey, PA: IGI Global. doi:10.4018/978-1-59904-947-2.ch233

Jamison, M., & Berg, S. (2000). *Issues and Strategies in Latin American Telecommunications: The Global E-economy*. University of Florida.

Jauhiainen, J. S., & Inkinen, T. (2009). E-governance and the information society in periphery. In C. Reddick (Ed.), *Handbook of research on strategies for local e-government adoption and implementation: Comparative studies* (pp. 497–514). Hershey, PA: IGI Global. doi:10.4018/978-1-60566-282-4.ch026

Jensen, M. J. (2009). Electronic democracy and citizen influence in government. In C. Reddick (Ed.), *Handbook of research on strategies for local e-government adoption and implementation: Comparative studies* (pp. 288–305). Hershey, PA: IGI Global. doi:10.4018/978-1-60566-282-4.ch015

Jestes, R. (2013, June 15). *Native Heritage Project.* Retrieved from Las Castas – Spanish Racial Classifications: https://nativeheritageproject.com/2013/06/15/las-castas- spanish-racial-classifications/

Jiao, Y., Hurson, A. R., Potok, T. E., & Beckerman, B. G. (2009). Integrating mobile-based systems with healthcare databases. In J. Erickson (Ed.), *Database technologies: Concepts, methodologies, tools, and applications* (pp. 484–504). Hershey, PA: IGI Global. doi:10.4018/978-1-60566-058-5.ch031

Joia, L. A. (2002). A systematic model to integrate information technology into metabusinesses: A case study in the engineering realms. In F. Tan (Ed.), *Advanced topics in global information management* (Vol. 1, pp. 250–267). Hershey, PA: IGI Global. doi:10.4018/978-1-930708-43-3.ch016

Jones, T. H., & Song, I. (2000). Binary equivalents of ternary relationships in entity-relationship modeling: A logical decomposition approach. *Journal of Database Management, 11*(2), 12–19. doi:10.4018/jdm.2000040102

Juana-Espinosa, S. D. (2007). Empirical study of the municipalitites' motivations for adopting online presence. In L. Al-Hakim (Ed.), *Global e-government: Theory, applications and benchmarking* (pp. 261–279). Hershey, PA: IGI Global. doi:10.4018/978-1-59904-027-1.ch015

Judicial Body. (n.d.). *Official statistics - Judicial Body.* Obtained from Http://www.oj.gob.gt/estadisticaj/files/population--total--by--municipal1.pdf

Jun, K., & Weare, C. (2012). Bridging from e-government practice to e-government research: Past trends and future directions. In K. Bwalya & S. Zulu (Eds.), *Handbook of research on e-government in emerging economies: Adoption, e-participation, and legal frameworks* (pp. 263–289). Hershey, PA: IGI Global. doi:10.4018/978-1-4666-0324-0.ch013

Junqueira, A., Diniz, E. H., & Fernandez, M. (2010). Electronic government implementation projects with multiple agencies: Analysis of the electronic invoice project under PMBOK framework. In J. Cordoba-Pachon & A. Ochoa-Arias (Eds.), *Systems thinking and e-participation: ICT in the governance of society* (pp. 135–153). Hershey, PA: IGI Global. doi:10.4018/978-1-60566-860-4.ch009

Junta Monetaria. (2011). Resolución JM-102-2011. Reglamento para la administración de riesgo tecnológico. Author.

Juntunen, A. (2009). Joint service development with the local authorities. In C. Reddick (Ed.), *Handbook of research on strategies for local e-government adoption and implementation: Comparative studies* (pp. 902–920). Hershey, PA: IGI Global. doi:10.4018/978-1-60566-282-4.ch047

Kamel, S. (2001). *Using DSS for crisis management*. Hershey, PA: IGI Global. doi:10.4018/978-1-87828-961-2.ch020

Kamel, S. (2006). DSS for strategic decision making. In M. Khosrow-Pour (Ed.), *Cases on information technology and organizational politics & culture* (pp. 230–246). Hershey, PA: IGI Global. doi:10.4018/978-1-59904-411-8.ch015

Kamel, S. (2009). The software industry in Egypt as a potential contributor to economic growth. In M. Khosrow-Pour (Ed.), *Encyclopedia of information science and technology* (2nd ed.; pp. 3531–3537). Hershey, PA: IGI Global. doi:10.4018/978-1-60566-026-4.ch562

Kamel, S., & Hussein, M. (2008). Xceed: Pioneering the contact center industry in Egypt. *Journal of Cases on Information Technology*, *10*(1), 67–91. doi:10.4018/jcit.2008010105

Kamel, S., & Wahba, K. (2003). The use of a hybrid model in web-based education: "The Global campus project. In A. Aggarwal (Ed.), *Web-based education: Learning from experience* (pp. 331–346). Hershey, PA: IGI Global. doi:10.4018/978-1-59140-102-5.ch020

Kapuscinski, R. (2010). *Cristo con un fusil al hombro*. Anagrama.

Kardaras, D. K., & Papathanassiou, E. A. (2008). An exploratory study of the e-government services in Greece. In G. Garson & M. Khosrow-Pour (Eds.), *Handbook of research on public information technology* (pp. 162–174). Hershey, PA: IGI Global. doi:10.4018/978-1-59904-857-4.ch016

Kassahun, A. E., Molla, A., & Sarkar, P. (2012). Government process reengineering: What we know and what we need to know. In *Digital democracy: Concepts, methodologies, tools, and applications* (pp. 1730–1752). Hershey, PA: IGI Global. doi:10.4018/978-1-4666-1740-7.ch086

Katz, R. (2009). The Economic and Social Impact of Telecommunications Output: A Theoretical Framework and Empirical Evidence for Spain. *Inter Economics*, *44*(1), 41–48. doi:10.1007/s10272-009-0276-0

Keyes, C. (1998). The Social Wellbeing. *Social Psychology Quarterly*, *61*(2).

Keynes, J. (2010). The General Theory of Employment and Interest and Money. Harcourt, Brace.

Khan, B. (2005). Technological issues. In B. Khan (Ed.), *Managing e-learning strategies: Design, delivery, implementation and evaluation* (pp. 154–180). Hershey, PA: IGI Global. doi:10.4018/978-1-59140-634-1.ch004

Khasawneh, A., Bsoul, M., Obeidat, I., & Al Azzam, I. (2012). Technology fears: A study of e-commerce loyalty perception by Jordanian customers. In J. Wang (Ed.), *Advancing the service sector with evolving technologies: Techniques and principles* (pp. 158–165). Hershey, PA: IGI Global. doi:10.4018/978-1-4666-0044-7.ch010

Khatibi, V., & Montazer, G. A. (2012). E-research methodology. In A. Juan, T. Daradoumis, M. Roca, S. Grasman, & J. Faulin (Eds.), *Collaborative and distributed e-research: Innovations in technologies, strategies and applications* (pp. 62–81). Hershey, PA: IGI Global. doi:10.4018/978-1-4666-0125-3.ch003

Kidd, T. (2011). The dragon in the school's backyard: A review of literature on the uses of technology in urban schools. In L. Tomei (Ed.), *Online courses and ICT in education: Emerging practices and applications* (pp. 242–257). Hershey, PA: IGI Global. doi:10.4018/978-1-60960-150-8.ch019

Kidd, T. T. (2010). My experience tells the story: Exploring technology adoption from a qualitative perspective - A pilot study. In H. Song & T. Kidd (Eds.), *Handbook of research on human performance and instructional technology* (pp. 247–262). Hershey, PA: IGI Global. doi:10.4018/978-1-60566-782-9.ch015

Kieley, B., Lane, G., Paquet, G., & Roy, J. (2002). e-Government in Canada: Services online or public service renewal? In Å. Grönlund (Ed.), Electronic government: Design, applications and management (pp. 340-355). Hershey, PA: IGI Global. doi:10.4018/978-1-930708-19-8.ch016

Kim, P. (2012). "Stay out of the way! My kid is video blogging through a phone!": A lesson learned from math tutoring social media for children in underserved communities. In *Wireless technologies: Concepts, methodologies, tools and applications* (pp. 1415–1428). Hershey, PA: IGI Global. doi:10.4018/978-1-61350-101-6.ch517

Kirlidog, M. (2010). Financial aspects of national ICT strategies. In S. Kamel (Ed.), *E-strategies for technological diffusion and adoption: National ICT approaches for socioeconomic development* (pp. 277–292). Hershey, PA: IGI Global. doi:10.4018/978-1-60566-388-3.ch016

Kisielnicki, J. (2006). Transfer of information and knowledge in the project management. In E. Coakes & S. Clarke (Eds.), *Encyclopedia of communities of practice in information and knowledge management* (pp. 544–551). Hershey, PA: IGI Global. doi:10.4018/978-1-59140-556-6.ch091

Kittner, M., & Van Slyke, C. (2006). Reorganizing information technology services in an academic environment. In M. Khosrow-Pour (Ed.), *Cases on the human side of information technology* (pp. 49–66). Hershey, PA: IGI Global. doi:10.4018/978-1-59904-405-7.ch004

Klem, A. (2009). Causes, Benefits, and Risks of Business Tax Incentives. *IMF Working Papers*, 1-28.

Knoell, H. D. (2008). Semi virtual workplaces in German financial service enterprises. In P. Zemliansky & K. St.Amant (Eds.), *Handbook of research on virtual workplaces and the new nature of business practices* (pp. 570–581). Hershey, PA: IGI Global. doi:10.4018/978-1-59904-893-2.ch041

Koh, S. L., & Maguire, S. (2009). Competing in the age of information technology in a developing economy: Experiences of an Indian bank. In S. Koh & S. Maguire (Eds.), *Information and communication technologies management in turbulent business environments* (pp. 326–350). Hershey, PA: IGI Global. doi:10.4018/978-1-60566-424-8.ch018

Kollmann, T., & Häsel, M. (2009). Competence of information technology professionals in internet-based ventures. In A. Cater-Steel (Ed.), *Information technology governance and service management: Frameworks and adaptations* (pp. 239–253). Hershey, PA: IGI Global. doi:10.4018/978-1-60566-008-0.ch013

Kollmann, T., & Häsel, M. (2009). Competence of information technology professionals in internet-based ventures. In I. Lee (Ed.), *Electronic business: Concepts, methodologies, tools, and applications* (pp. 1905–1919). Hershey, PA: IGI Global. doi:10.4018/978-1-60566-056-1.ch118

Kollmann, T., & Häsel, M. (2010). Competence of information technology professionals in internet-based ventures. In *Electronic services: Concepts, methodologies, tools and applications* (pp. 1551–1565). Hershey, PA: IGI Global. doi:10.4018/978-1-61520-967-5.ch094

KPMG. (2015). Retrieved from 2015 Global Tax Rate Survey: https://assets.kpmg.com/content/dam/kpmg/pdf/2015/11/global-tax-rate-survey-2015-v2- web.pdf

Kraemer, K., & King, J. L. (2006). Information technology and administrative reform: Will e-government be different? *International Journal of Electronic Government Research*, *2*(1), 1–20. doi:10.4018/jegr.2006010101

Kraemer, K., & King, J. L. (2008). Information technology and administrative reform: Will e-government be different? In D. Norris (Ed.), *E-government research: Policy and management* (pp. 1–20). Hershey, PA: IGI Global. doi:10.4018/978-1-59904-913-7.ch001

Kridel, D., & Sappington, D. (n.d.). The Effects of Incentive Regulation in the Telecommunications Industry: A Survey. Journal of Regulatory Economics, 9, 269–306.

La Ilustración Guatemalteca. (1897). Retrieved from La Ilustración Guatemalteca: https://archive.org/stream/ilustracionguate00guat#page/376/mode/2up

La República. (1897). Retrieved from https://archive.org/stream/ilustracionguate00guat#page/390/mode/2up

Lampathaki, F., Tsiakaliaris, C., Stasis, A., & Charalabidis, Y. (2011). National interoperability frameworks: The way forward. In Y. Charalabidis (Ed.), *Interoperability in digital public services and administration: Bridging e-government and e-business* (pp. 1–24). Hershey, PA: IGI Global. doi:10.4018/978-1-61520-887-6.ch001

Lane, P. R., & Milesi-Ferretti, G. M. (2010). *The Cross-Country Incidence of the Global Crisis*. IMF Working Paper No.10/171. Washington, DC: International Monetary Fund.

Lan, Z., & Scott, C. R. (1996). The relative importance of computer-mediated information versus conventional non-computer-mediated information in public managerial decision making. *Information Resources Management Journal*, *9*(1), 27–0. doi:10.4018/irmj.1996010103

Law, W. (2004). *Public sector data management in a developing economy*. Hershey, PA: IGI Global. doi:10.4018/978-1-59140-259-6.ch034

Law, W. K. (2005). Information resources development challenges in a cross-cultural environment. In M. Khosrow-Pour (Ed.), *Encyclopedia of information science and technology* (pp. 1476–1481). Hershey, PA: IGI Global. doi:10.4018/978-1-59140-553-5.ch259

Law, W. K. (2009). Cross-cultural challenges for information resources management. In M. Khosrow-Pour (Ed.), *Encyclopedia of information science and technology* (2nd ed.; pp. 840–846). Hershey, PA: IGI Global. doi:10.4018/978-1-60566-026-4.ch136

Law, W. K. (2011). Cross-cultural challenges for information resources management. In *Global business: Concepts, methodologies, tools and applications* (pp. 1924–1932). Hershey, PA: IGI Global. doi:10.4018/978-1-60960-587-2.ch704

Leonard, T. (1991). *Central America and the United States: The Search for Stability*. Academic Press.

Lipsky, J. (2011). *Latin America in an Uneven Global Recovery: Managing Abundance*. Speech of the First Deputy Managing Director, III Forum économique International Amérique Latine et Caraïbes, International Monetary Fund, Paris, France.

List of IPOs During 2003-2013 Through NSE. (n.d.). Retrieved from http://www.nseindia.com/products/content/equities/ipos/ipos.htm

Llaudes, R., Salman, F., Chivakul, M., & Dadayan, L. (2010). *The impact of the great recession on emerging markets* (IMF Working Paper No. 237). IMF Working Papers. Retrieved from http://www.rockinst.org/pdf/government_finance/2012-07-16-Recession_Local_ Property_Tax.pdf

Lopez, M. (2013). Elite theory. *Sociopedia*, 1-12.

López, J. E. (1979). *Privilegios fiscales y la repoblación del Reino de Granada (1495-1520)*. Universidad de Málaga.

Luengo Navas, J. (2004). Education as an object of knowledge. He Concept of education. In M. d. Pozo Andrés, J. L. Álvarez Castillo, J. Luengo Navas, & E. Otero Urtza (Eds.), Theories and contemporary educational institutions. Madrid: Academic Press.

MacLeod, M. (2007). *Spanish Central America: A Socioeconomic History, 1520–1720*. LLILAS Special Publications.

Malkia, M., & Savolainen, R. (2004). eTransformation in government, politics and society: Conceptual framework and introduction. In M. Malkia, A. Anttiroiko, & R. Savolainen (Eds.), eTransformation in governance: New directions in government and politics (pp. 1-21). Hershey, PA: IGI Global. doi:10.4018/978-1-59140-130-8.ch001

Mandujano, S. (2011). Network manageability security. In D. Kar & M. Syed (Eds.), *Network security, administration and management: Advancing technology and practice* (pp. 158–181). Hershey, PA: IGI Global. doi:10.4018/978-1-60960-777-7.ch009

Marich, M. J., Schooley, B. L., & Horan, T. A. (2012). A normative enterprise architecture for guiding end-to-end emergency response decision support. In M. Jennex (Ed.), *Managing crises and disasters with emerging technologies: Advancements* (pp. 71–87). Hershey, PA: IGI Global. doi:10.4018/978-1-4666-0167-3.ch006

Markov, R., & Okujava, S. (2008). Costs, benefits, and risks of e-government portals. In G. Putnik & M. Cruz-Cunha (Eds.), *Encyclopedia of networked and virtual organizations* (pp. 354–363). Hershey, PA: IGI Global. doi:10.4018/978-1-59904-885-7.ch047

Martínez Rizo, F. (2004). Pass or fail? The meaning of the evaluation in basic education. *Mexican Journal of Educational Research*, *9*(23), 817–839.

Martin, N., & Rice, J. (2013). Evaluating and designing electronic government for the future: Observations and insights from Australia. In V. Weerakkody (Ed.), *E-government services design, adoption, and evaluation* (pp. 238–258). Hershey, PA: IGI Global. doi:10.4018/978-1-4666-2458-0.ch014

Maslow, A. (1943). *A Theory of Human Motivation.* Kindle Edition.

Mbarika, V. W., Meso, P. N., & Musa, P. F. (2006). A disconnect in stakeholders' perceptions from emerging realities of teledensity growth in Africa's least developed countries. In M. Hunter & F. Tan (Eds.), *Advanced topics in global information management* (Vol. 5, pp. 263–282). Hershey, PA: IGI Global. doi:10.4018/978-1-59140-923-6.ch012

Mbarika, V. W., Meso, P. N., & Musa, P. F. (2008). A disconnect in stakeholders' perceptions from emerging realities of teledensity growth in Africa's least developed countries. In F. Tan (Ed.), *Global information technologies: Concepts, methodologies, tools, and applications* (pp. 2948–2962). Hershey, PA: IGI Global. doi:10.4018/978-1-59904-939-7.ch209

MCK. IM Bloomberg. (2016). Obtenido de Bloomberg: http://www.bloomberg.com/quote/MCK:IM

Means, T., Olson, E., & Spooner, J. (2013). Discovering ways that don't work on the road to success: Strengths and weaknesses revealed by an active learning studio classroom project. In A. Benson, J. Moore, & S. Williams van Rooij (Eds.), *Cases on educational technology planning, design, and implementation: A project management perspective* (pp. 94–113). Hershey, PA: IGI Global. doi:10.4018/978-1-4666-4237-9.ch006

Medal, J. L. (2015). Nicaragua: Política Fiscal para cargar a los contribuyentes las pérdidas privadas y los privilegios de las élites. In I. C. Fiscales (Ed.), *Política Fiscal: Expresión del poder de las élites centroamericanas* (pp. 273–319). FyG Editores.

Megginson, W., & Netter, J. (2000). *From State to Market: A Survey of Empirical Studies on Privatization.* Academic Press.

Melitski, J., Holzer, M., Kim, S., Kim, C., & Rho, S. (2008). Digital government worldwide: An e-government assessment of municipal web sites. In G. Garson & M. Khosrow-Pour (Eds.), *Handbook of research on public information technology* (pp. 790–804). Hershey, PA: IGI Global. doi:10.4018/978-1-59904-857-4.ch069

Memmola, M., Palumbo, G., & Rossini, M. (2009). Web & RFID technology: New frontiers in costing and process management for rehabilitation medicine. In L. Al-Hakim & M. Memmola (Eds.), *Business web strategy: Design, alignment, and application* (pp. 145–169). Hershey, PA: IGI Global. doi:10.4018/978-1-60566-024-0.ch008

Menger, C. (1997). Principios de economía política (2nd ed.). Madrid: Unión Editorial, S.A.

Menger, C. (2003). *Economía y Bienestar Económico*. Barcelona: Ediciones Orbis.

Meng, Z., Fahong, Z., & Lei, L. (2008). Information technology and environment. In Y. Kurihara, S. Takaya, H. Harui, & H. Kamae (Eds.), *Information technology and economic development* (pp. 201–212). Hershey, PA: IGI Global. doi:10.4018/978-1-59904-579-5.ch014

Mentzingen de Moraes, A. J., Ferneda, E., Costa, I., & Spinola, M. D. (2011). Practical approach for implementation of governance process in IT: Information technology areas. In N. Shi & G. Silvius (Eds.), *Enterprise IT governance, business value and performance measurement* (pp. 19–40). Hershey, PA: IGI Global. doi:10.4018/978-1-60566-346-3.ch002

Merwin, G. A. Jr, McDonald, J. S., & Odera, L. C. (2008). Economic development: Government's cutting edge in IT. In M. Raisinghani (Ed.), *Handbook of research on global information technology management in the digital economy* (pp. 1–37). Hershey, PA: IGI Global. doi:10.4018/978-1-59904-875-8.ch001

Meso, P. N., & Duncan, N. B. (2002). Can national information infrastructures enhance social development in the least developed countries? In F. Tan (Ed.), *Advanced topics in global information management* (Vol. 1, pp. 207–226). Hershey, PA: IGI Global. doi:10.4018/978-1-930708-43-3.ch014

Meso, P., & Duncan, N. (2002). Can national information infrastructures enhance social development in the least developed countries? An empirical investigation. In M. Dadashzadeh (Ed.), *Information technology management in developing countries* (pp. 23–51). Hershey, PA: IGI Global. doi:10.4018/978-1-931777-03-2.ch002

Middleton, M. (2008). Evaluation of e-government web sites. In G. Garson & M. Khosrow-Pour (Eds.), *Handbook of research on public information technology* (pp. 699–710). Hershey, PA: IGI Global. doi:10.4018/978-1-59904-857-4.ch063

MINEDUC. (January 6, 2016). *Population exceeds 17.1 million*. Press Free.

MINFIN. (2016). Obtenido de Ministerio de Finanzas Públicas: http://www.minfin.gob.gt/index.php/comunicados-2014a/1839-22-fitch-ratings-asigna-calificacion-de-riesgo-crediticio

Mingers, J. (2010). Pluralism, realism, and truth: The keys to knowledge in information systems research. In D. Paradice (Ed.), *Emerging systems approaches in information technologies: Concepts, theories, and applications* (pp. 86–98). Hershey, PA: IGI Global. doi:10.4018/978-1-60566-976-2.ch006

Mishra, P. K. (2012). Global Financial Crisis and Indian Capital Market- An Econometric Analysis. *International Journal of Applied Business and Economics Research.*, *10*(1), 11–29.

Mital, K. M. (2012). ICT, unique identity and inclusive growth: An Indian perspective. In A. Manoharan & M. Holzer (Eds.), *E-governance and civic engagement: Factors and determinants of e-democracy* (pp. 584–612). Hershey, PA: IGI Global. doi:10.4018/978-1-61350-083-5.ch029

Mizell, A. P. (2008). Helping close the digital divide for financially disadvantaged seniors. In F. Tan (Ed.), *Global information technologies: Concepts, methodologies, tools, and applications* (pp. 2396–2402). Hershey, PA: IGI Global. doi:10.4018/978-1-59904-939-7.ch173

Molinari, F., Wills, C., Koumpis, A., & Moumtzi, V. (2011). A citizen-centric platform to support networking in the area of e-democracy. In H. Rahman (Ed.), *Cases on adoption, diffusion and evaluation of global e-governance systems: Impact at the grass roots* (pp. 282–302). Hershey, PA: IGI Global. doi:10.4018/978-1-61692-814-8.ch014

Molinari, F., Wills, C., Koumpis, A., & Moumtzi, V. (2013). A citizen-centric platform to support networking in the area of e-democracy. In H. Rahman (Ed.), *Cases on progressions and challenges in ICT utilization for citizen-centric governance* (pp. 265–297). Hershey, PA: IGI Global. doi:10.4018/978-1-4666-2071-1.ch013

Monteverde, F. (2010). The process of e-government public policy inclusion in the governmental agenda: A framework for assessment and case study. In J. Cordoba-Pachon & A. Ochoa-Arias (Eds.), *Systems thinking and e-participation: ICT in the governance of society* (pp. 233–245). Hershey, PA: IGI Global. doi:10.4018/978-1-60566-860-4.ch015

Moodley, S. (2008). Deconstructing the South African government's ICT for development discourse. In A. Anttiroiko (Ed.), *Electronic government: Concepts, methodologies, tools, and applications* (pp. 622–631). Hershey, PA: IGI Global. doi:10.4018/978-1-59904-947-2.ch053

Moodley, S. (2008). Deconstructing the South African government's ICT for development discourse. In C. Van Slyke (Ed.), *Information communication technologies: Concepts, methodologies, tools, and applications* (pp. 816–825). Hershey, PA: IGI Global. doi:10.4018/978-1-59904-949-6.ch052

Mora, M., Cervantes-Perez, F., Gelman-Muravchik, O., Forgionne, G. A., & Mejia-Olvera, M. (2003). DMSS implementation research: A conceptual analysis of the contributions and limitations of the factor-based and stage-based streams. In G. Forgionne, J. Gupta, & M. Mora (Eds.), *Decision-making support systems: Achievements and challenges for the new decade* (pp. 331–356). Hershey, PA: IGI Global. doi:10.4018/978-1-59140-045-5.ch020

Morgan, G., & Saunders, R. (1994). *Telecommunications and Economic Development*. Baltimore, MD: The John Hopkins University Press.

Mörtberg, C., & Elovaara, P. (2010). Attaching people and technology: Between e and government. In S. Booth, S. Goodman, & G. Kirkup (Eds.), *Gender issues in learning and working with information technology: Social constructs and cultural contexts* (pp. 83–98). Hershey, PA: IGI Global. doi:10.4018/978-1-61520-813-5.ch005

Muñoz, R. (2009). *Política anticíclica*. Retrieved from http://ocw.usal.es/eduCommons/ciencias-sociales-1/hacienda-publica-i/contenidos/Comentarios/Comentario%201.pdf

Murphy, J., Harper, E., Devine, E. C., Burke, L. J., & Hook, M. L. (2011). Case study: Lessons learned when embedding evidence-based knowledge in a nurse care planning and documentation system. In A. Cashin & R. Cook (Eds.), *Evidence-based practice in nursing informatics: Concepts and applications* (pp. 174–190). Hershey, PA: IGI Global. doi:10.4018/978-1-60960-034-1.ch014

Mutula, S. M. (2013). E-government's role in poverty alleviation: Case study of South Africa. In H. Rahman (Ed.), *Cases on progressions and challenges in ICT utilization for citizen-centric governance* (pp. 44–68). Hershey, PA: IGI Global. doi:10.4018/978-1-4666-2071-1.ch003

NASDAQ. (2016). *National Association of Securities Dealers Automated Quotation*. Obtenido de Mercado de Valores: http://www.nasdaq.com/

Nath, R., & Angeles, R. (2005). Relationships between supply characteristics and buyer-supplier coupling in e-procurement: An empirical analysis. *International Journal of E-Business Research, 1*(2), 40–55. doi:10.4018/jebr.2005040103

Nissen, M. E. (2006). Application cases in government. In M. Nissen (Ed.), *Harnessing knowledge dynamics: Principled organizational knowing & learning* (pp. 152–181). Hershey, PA: IGI Global. doi:10.4018/978-1-59140-773-7.ch008

Nordhaus, D., & Tobin, J. (1972). Is growth obsolete?. *Economic Research Journal, 38*.

Norris, D. F. (2003). Leading-edge information technologies and American local governments. In G. Garson (Ed.), *Public information technology: Policy and management issues* (pp. 139–169). Hershey, PA: IGI Global. doi:10.4018/978-1-59140-060-8.ch007

Norris, D. F. (2008). Information technology among U.S. local governments. In G. Garson & M. Khosrow-Pour (Eds.), *Handbook of research on public information technology* (pp. 132–144). Hershey, PA: IGI Global. doi:10.4018/978-1-59904-857-4.ch013

Northrop, A. (1999). The challenge of teaching information technology in public administration graduate programs. In G. Garson (Ed.), *Information technology and computer applications in public administration: Issues and trends* (pp. 1–22). Hershey, PA: IGI Global. doi:10.4018/978-1-87828-952-0.ch001

Northrop, A. (2003). Information technology and public administration: The view from the profession. In G. Garson (Ed.), *Public information technology: Policy and management issues* (pp. 1–19). Hershey, PA: IGI Global. doi:10.4018/978-1-59140-060-8.ch001

Northrop, A. (2007). Lip service? How PA journals and textbooks view information technology. In G. Garson (Ed.), *Modern public information technology systems: Issues and challenges* (pp. 1–16). Hershey, PA: IGI Global. doi:10.4018/978-1-59904-051-6.ch001

NTC5254. (2004). *Norma tecnica Colombiana, Gestión de Riesgos*. Bogotá, Colombia: ICONTEC.

Null, E. (2013). Legal and political barriers to municipal networks in the United States. In A. Abdelaal (Ed.), *Social and economic effects of community wireless networks and infrastructures* (pp. 27–56). Hershey, PA: IGI Global. doi:10.4018/978-1-4666-2997-4.ch003

OEC. (2014). *The observatory of economic complexity.* Retrieved from http://atlas.media.mit.edu/en/

Okunoye, A., Frolick, M., & Crable, E. (2006). ERP implementation in higher education: An account of pre-implementation and implementation phases. *Journal of Cases on Information Technology, 8*(2), 110–132. doi:10.4018/jcit.2006040106

Olasina, G. (2012). A review of egovernment services in Nigeria. In A. Tella & A. Issa (Eds.), *Library and information science in developing countries: Contemporary issues* (pp. 205–221). Hershey, PA: IGI Global. doi:10.4018/978-1-61350-335-5.ch015

Organisation for Economic Co-operation and Development. (2013). *Organisation for Economic Co-operation and Development.* Retrieved from What drives tax morale?: http://www.oecd.org/ctp/tax-global/TaxMorale_march13.pdf

Orgeron, C. P. (2008). A model for reengineering IT job classes in state government. In G. Garson & M. Khosrow-Pour (Eds.), *Handbook of research on public information technology* (pp. 735–746). Hershey, PA: IGI Global. doi:10.4018/978-1-59904-857-4.ch066

Oslin, G. P. (1992). *The Story of Telecommunications.* Mercer University Press.

Owsinski, J. W., & Pielak, A. M. (2011). Local authority websites in rural areas: Measuring quality and functionality, and assessing the role. In Z. Andreopoulou, B. Manos, N. Polman, & D. Viaggi (Eds.), *Agricultural and environmental informatics, governance and management: Emerging research applications* (pp. 39–60). Hershey, PA: IGI Global. doi:10.4018/978-1-60960-621-3.ch003

Owsiński, J. W., Pielak, A. M., Sęp, K., & Stańczak, J. (2014). Local web-based networks in rural municipalities: Extension, density, and meaning. In Z. Andreopoulou, V. Samathrakis, S. Louca, & M. Vlachopoulou (Eds.), *E-innovation for sustainable development of rural resources during global economic crisis* (pp. 126–151). Hershey, PA: IGI Global. doi:10.4018/978-1-4666-4550-9.ch011

Pagani, M., & Pasinetti, C. (2008). Technical and functional quality in the development of t-government services. In A. Anttiroiko (Ed.), *Electronic government: Concepts, methodologies, tools, and applications* (pp. 2943–2965). Hershey, PA: IGI Global. doi:10.4018/978-1-59904-947-2.ch220

Pani, A. K., & Agrahari, A. (2005). On e-markets in emerging economy: An Indian experience. In M. Khosrow-Pour (Ed.), *Advanced topics in electronic commerce* (Vol. 1, pp. 287–299). Hershey, PA: IGI Global. doi:10.4018/978-1-59140-819-2.ch015

Papadopoulos, T., Angelopoulos, S., & Kitsios, F. (2011). A strategic approach to e-health interoperability using e-government frameworks. In A. Lazakidou, K. Siassiakos, & K. Ioannou (Eds.), *Wireless technologies for ambient assisted living and healthcare: Systems and applications* (pp. 213–229). Hershey, PA: IGI Global. doi:10.4018/978-1-61520-805-0.ch012

Papadopoulos, T., Angelopoulos, S., & Kitsios, F. (2013). A strategic approach to e-health interoperability using e-government frameworks. In *User-driven healthcare: Concepts, methodologies, tools, and applications* (pp. 791–807). Hershey, PA: IGI Global. doi:10.4018/978-1-4666-2770-3.ch039

Papaleo, G., Chiarella, D., Aiello, M., & Caviglione, L. (2012). Analysis, development and deployment of statistical anomaly detection techniques for real e-mail traffic. In T. Chou (Ed.), *Information assurance and security technologies for risk assessment and threat management: Advances* (pp. 47–71). Hershey, PA: IGI Global. doi:10.4018/978-1-61350-507-6.ch003

Papp, R. (2003). Information technology & FDA compliance in the pharmaceutical industry. In M. Khosrow-Pour (Ed.), *Annals of cases on information technology* (Vol. 5, pp. 262–273). Hershey, PA: IGI Global. doi:10.4018/978-1-59140-061-5.ch017

Pareto, V. (1935). *The mind and society. A treaty on general sociology*. Dover: Nueva York.

Parsons, T. W. (2007). Developing a knowledge management portal. In A. Tatnall (Ed.), *Encyclopedia of portal technologies and applications* (pp. 223–227). Hershey, PA: IGI Global. doi:10.4018/978-1-59140-989-2.ch039

Passaris, C. E. (2007). Immigration and digital government. In A. Anttiroiko & M. Malkia (Eds.), *Encyclopedia of digital government* (pp. 988–994). Hershey, PA: IGI Global. doi:10.4018/978-1-59140-789-8.ch148

Paulson, H. (2011). *On the Brink: Inside the Race to Stop the Collapse of the Global Financial System*. New York: Grand Central Publishing.

Pavlichev, A. (2004). The e-government challenge for public administration. In A. Pavlichev & G. Garson (Eds.), *Digital government: Principles and best practices* (pp. 276–290). Hershey, PA: IGI Global. doi:10.4018/978-1-59140-122-3.ch018

Penrod, J. I., & Harbor, A. F. (2000). Designing and implementing a learning organization-oriented information technology planning and management process. In L. Petrides (Ed.), *Case studies on information technology in higher education: Implications for policy and practice* (pp. 7–19). Hershey, PA: IGI Global. doi:10.4018/978-1-878289-74-2.ch001

Pino, H. N. (2015). Honduras: El abuso de las exoneraciones tributarias como dogma fiscal. In I. C. Fiscales (Ed.), *Política fiscal: expresión del poder de las élites centroamericanas* (pp. 211–273). FyG Editores.

Planas-Silva, M. D., & Joseph, R. C. (2011). Perspectives on the adoption of electronic resources for use in clinical trials. In M. Guah (Ed.), *Healthcare delivery reform and new technologies: Organizational initiatives* (pp. 19–28). Hershey, PA: IGI Global. doi:10.4018/978-1-60960-183-6.ch002

Polimeni, R. S., Fabozzi, F. J., & Adelberg, A. H. (2008). Contabilidad de Costos (Conceptos y Aplicaciones para la Toma de Decisioens Gerenciales). McGraw-Hill.

Pomazalová, N., & Rejman, S. (2013). The rationale behind implementation of new electronic tools for electronic public procurement. In N. Pomazalová (Ed.), *Public sector transformation processes and internet public procurement: Decision support systems* (pp. 85–117). Hershey, PA: IGI Global. doi:10.4018/978-1-4666-2665-2.ch006

Pompejano, D. (1997). *La crisis del antiguo régimen en Guatemala, 1839-1871*. Editorial Universitaria.

Postorino, M. N. (2012). City competitiveness and airport: Information science perspective. In M. Bulu (Ed.), *City competitiveness and improving urban subsystems: Technologies and applications* (pp. 61–83). Hershey, PA: IGI Global. doi:10.4018/978-1-61350-174-0.ch004

Poupa, C. (2002). Electronic government in Switzerland: Priorities for 2001-2005 - Electronic voting and federal portal. In Å. Grönlund (Ed.), *Electronic government: Design, applications and management* (pp. 356–369). Hershey, PA: IGI Global. doi:10.4018/978-1-930708-19-8.ch017

Powell, S. R. (2010). Interdisciplinarity in telecommunications and networking. In *Networking and telecommunications: Concepts, methodologies, tools and applications* (pp. 33–40). Hershey, PA: IGI Global. doi:10.4018/978-1-60566-986-1.ch004

Prensa Libre. (2015). *Pobreza sube a 59.3%: son 9.6 millones de guatemaltecos los afectados*. Author.

Priya, P. S., & Mathiyalagan, N. (2011). A study of the implementation status of two e-governance projects in land revenue administration in India. In M. Shareef, V. Kumar, U. Kumar, & Y. Dwivedi (Eds.), *Stakeholder adoption of e-government services: Driving and resisting factors* (pp. 214–230). Hershey, PA: IGI Global. doi:10.4018/978-1-60960-601-5.ch011

Programa de las Naciones Unidas para el Desarrollo Humano. (2004). *Curso de Desarrollo Humano*. PNUD, República Dominicana.

Prysby, C. L., & Prysby, N. D. (2003). Electronic mail in the public workplace: Issues of privacy and public disclosure. In G. Garson (Ed.), *Public information technology: Policy and management issues* (pp. 271–298). Hershey, PA: IGI Global. doi:10.4018/978-1-59140-060-8.ch012

Prysby, C. L., & Prysby, N. D. (2007). You have mail, but who is reading it? Issues of e-mail in the public workplace. In G. Garson (Ed.), *Modern public information technology systems: Issues and challenges* (pp. 312–336). Hershey, PA: IGI Global. doi:10.4018/978-1-59904-051-6.ch016

Prysby, C., & Prysby, N. (2000). Electronic mail, employee privacy and the workplace. In L. Janczewski (Ed.), *Internet and intranet security management: Risks and solutions* (pp. 251–270). Hershey, PA: IGI Global. doi:10.4018/978-1-878289-71-1.ch009

R. B., & W. F. (2015). Guatemala: Poder de veto a la legislación tributaria y captura fallida del negocio de la inversión pública. In I. C. Fiscales (Ed.), *Política Fiscal: epresión del poder de las élites centroamericanas* (pp. 25-128). FyG.

R. B., R. C., M. G., L. M., J. U., C. A., . . . Trejo, C. P. (2015). El Salvador: una política fiscal diseñada como base y garant{ia para un sistema económico rentista y expoliador. In I. C. Fiscales (Ed.), Política fiscal: expresión del poder de las élites centroamericans (pp. 129-208). FyG Editores.

Radl, A., & Chen, Y. (2005). Computer security in electronic government: A state-local education information system. *International Journal of Electronic Government Research, 1*(1), 79–99. doi:10.4018/jegr.2005010105

Rahman, H. (2008). Information dynamics in developing countries. In C. Van Slyke (Ed.), *Information communication technologies: Concepts, methodologies, tools, and applications* (pp. 104–114). Hershey, PA: IGI Global. doi:10.4018/978-1-59904-949-6.ch008

Ramanathan, J. (2009). Adaptive IT architecture as a catalyst for network capability in government. In P. Saha (Ed.), *Advances in government enterprise architecture* (pp. 149–172). Hershey, PA: IGI Global. doi:10.4018/978-1-60566-068-4.ch007

Ramos, I., & Berry, D. M. (2006). Social construction of information technology supporting work. In M. Khosrow-Pour (Ed.), *Cases on information technology: Lessons learned* (Vol. 7, pp. 36–52). Hershey, PA: IGI Global. doi:10.4018/978-1-59140-673-0.ch003

Ray, D., Gulla, U., Gupta, M. P., & Dash, S. S. (2009). Interoperability and constituents of interoperable systems in public sector. In V. Weerakkody, M. Janssen, & Y. Dwivedi (Eds.), *Handbook of research on ICT-enabled transformational government: A global perspective* (pp. 175–195). Hershey, PA: IGI Global. doi:10.4018/978-1-60566-390-6.ch010

Real Academia Española. (2016). *Diccionario de la lengua española* (E. D. Tricentenario, Ed.). Obtenido de RAE: www.rae.es

Real Instituto Elcano. (2008). *Tratado de la Unión Europea*. España.

Reddick, C. G. (2007). E-government and creating a citizen-centric government: A study of federal government CIOs. In G. Garson (Ed.), *Modern public information technology systems: Issues and challenges* (pp. 143–165). Hershey, PA: IGI Global. doi:10.4018/978-1-59904-051-6.ch008

Reddick, C. G. (2010). Citizen-centric e-government. In C. Reddick (Ed.), *Homeland security preparedness and information systems: Strategies for managing public policy* (pp. 45–75). Hershey, PA: IGI Global. doi:10.4018/978-1-60566-834-5.ch002

Reddick, C. G. (2010). E-government and creating a citizen-centric government: A study of federal government CIOs. In C. Reddick (Ed.), *Homeland security preparedness and information systems: Strategies for managing public policy* (pp. 230–250). Hershey, PA: IGI Global. doi:10.4018/978-1-60566-834-5.ch012

Reddick, C. G. (2010). Perceived effectiveness of e-government and its usage in city governments: Survey evidence from information technology directors. In C. Reddick (Ed.), *Homeland security preparedness and information systems: Strategies for managing public policy* (pp. 213–229). Hershey, PA: IGI Global. doi:10.4018/978-1-60566-834-5.ch011

Reddick, C. G. (2012). Customer relationship management adoption in local governments in the United States. In S. Chhabra & M. Kumar (Eds.), *Strategic enterprise resource planning models for e-government: Applications and methodologies* (pp. 111–124). Hershey, PA: IGI Global. doi:10.4018/978-1-60960-863-7.ch008

Reeder, F. S., & Pandy, S. M. (2008). Identifying effective funding models for e-government. In A. Anttiroiko (Ed.), *Electronic government: Concepts, methodologies, tools, and applications* (pp. 1108–1138). Hershey, PA: IGI Global. doi:10.4018/978-1-59904-947-2.ch083

Reinhart, C. M., & Rogoff, K. (2009). *This time is different. In Eight Centuries of Financial Folly*. Princeton, NJ: Princeton University.

Revolution of 1871. (n.d.). Retrieved from Revolution of 1871 - History - Guatemala - Central America: guatemala history, crop guatemala, guatemala people, guatemala money, coffee elite: http://www.countriesquest.com/central_ america/guatemala/history/revolution_of_1871.htm

Reyes, J. (2017). *La Hora*. Retrieved from La historia no miente… 1975-1986: http://lahora.gt/hemeroteca-lh/la-historia-no-miente-19751986/

Riascos, A. (1997). Sobre el costo en bienestar de la inflación en Colombia. *Borradores de Economía*, *82*, 1-25.

Riesco, D., Acosta, E., & Montejano, G. (2003). An extension to a UML activity graph from workflow. In L. Favre (Ed.), *UML and the unified process* (pp. 294–314). Hershey, PA: IGI Global. doi:10.4018/978-1-93177-744-5.ch015

Ritzhaupt, A. D., & Gill, T. G. (2008). A hybrid and novel approach to teaching computer programming in MIS curriculum. In S. Negash, M. Whitman, A. Woszczynski, K. Hoganson, & H. Mattord (Eds.), *Handbook of distance learning for real-time and asynchronous information technology education* (pp. 259–281). Hershey, PA: IGI Global. doi:10.4018/978-1-59904-964-9.ch014

Roche, E. M. (1993). International computing and the international regime. *Journal of Global Information Management*, *1*(2), 33–44. doi:10.4018/jgim.1993040103

Rocheleau, B. (2007). Politics, accountability, and information management. In G. Garson (Ed.), *Modern public information technology systems: Issues and challenges* (pp. 35–71). Hershey, PA: IGI Global. doi:10.4018/978-1-59904-051-6.ch003

Rock, D. (1992). *1516-1982: From Spanish Colonization to the Falklands War*. University of California Press.

Rodrigues Filho, J. (2010). E-government in Brazil: Reinforcing dominant institutions or reducing citizenship? In C. Reddick (Ed.), *Politics, democracy and e-government: Participation and service delivery* (pp. 347–362). Hershey, PA: IGI Global. doi:10.4018/978-1-61520-933-0.ch021

Rodriguez, S. R., & Thorp, D. A. (2013). eLearning for industry: A case study of the project management process. In A. Benson, J. Moore, & S. Williams van Rooij (Eds.), Cases on educational technology planning, design, and implementation: A project management perspective (pp. 319-342). Hershey, PA: IGI Global. doi:10.4018/978-1-4666-4237-9.ch017

Rogoff, K., & Reinhart, C. (2008). Is the 2007 US sub-prime financial crisis so different? An international historical comparison. *The American Economic Review*, *98*(2), 339–344. doi:10.1257/aer.98.2.339

Roman, A. V. (2013). Delineating three dimensions of e-government success: Security, functionality, and transformation. In J. Gil-Garcia (Ed.), *E-government success factors and measures: Theories, concepts, and methodologies* (pp. 171–192). Hershey, PA: IGI Global. doi:10.4018/978-1-4666-4058-0.ch010

Ros, A. (2003). *The Impact of Regulatory Process and Price Cap Regulation in Latin American Telecommunications Market.* Academic Press.

Rosenthal, G. (2009). *The international economic crisis and its possible Consequences in Guatemala.* Academic Press.

Ross, S. C., Tyran, C. K., & Auer, D. J. (2008). Up in smoke: Rebuilding after an IT disaster. In H. Nemati (Ed.), *Information security and ethics: Concepts, methodologies, tools, and applications* (pp. 3659–3675). Hershey, PA: IGI Global. doi:10.4018/978-1-59904-937-3.ch248

Ross, S. C., Tyran, C. K., Auer, D. J., Junell, J. M., & Williams, T. G. (2005). Up in smoke: Rebuilding after an IT disaster. *Journal of Cases on Information Technology*, *7*(2), 31–49. doi:10.4018/jcit.2005040103

Roy, J. (2008). Security, sovereignty, and continental interoperability: Canada's elusive balance. In T. Loendorf & G. Garson (Eds.), *Patriotic information systems* (pp. 153–176). Hershey, PA: IGI Global. doi:10.4018/978-1-59904-594-8.ch007

Rubeck, R. F., & Miller, G. A. (2009). vGOV: Remote video access to government services. In A. Scupola (Ed.), Cases on managing e-services (pp. 253-268). Hershey, PA: IGI Global. doi:10.4018/978-1-60566-064-6.ch017

Saekow, A., & Boonmee, C. (2011). The challenges of implementing e-government interoperability in Thailand: Case of official electronic correspondence letters exchange across government departments. In Y. Charalabidis (Ed.), *Interoperability in digital public services and administration: Bridging e-government and e-business* (pp. 40–61). Hershey, PA: IGI Global. doi:10.4018/978-1-61520-887-6.ch003

Saekow, A., & Boonmee, C. (2012). The challenges of implementing e-government interoperability in Thailand: Case of official electronic correspondence letters exchange across government departments. In *Digital democracy: Concepts, methodologies, tools, and applications* (pp. 1883–1905). Hershey, PA: IGI Global. doi:10.4018/978-1-4666-1740-7.ch094

Sagsan, M., & Medeni, T. (2012). Understanding "knowledge management (KM) paradigms" from social media perspective: An empirical study on discussion group for KM at professional networking site. In M. Cruz-Cunha, P. Gonçalves, N. Lopes, E. Miranda, & G. Putnik (Eds.), *Handbook of research on business social networking: Organizational, managerial, and technological dimensions* (pp. 738–755). Hershey, PA: IGI Global. doi:10.4018/978-1-61350-168-9.ch039

Sahi, G., & Madan, S. (2013). Information security threats in ERP enabled e-governance: Challenges and solutions. In *Enterprise resource planning: Concepts, methodologies, tools, and applications* (pp. 825–837). Hershey, PA: IGI Global. doi:10.4018/978-1-4666-4153-2.ch048

Salman, M. F., Chivakul, M., & Llaudes, M. R. (2010). The Impact of the Great Recession on Emerging Markets (No. 10-237). International Monetary Fund.

Samson, R., Mehta, M., & Chandani, A. (2014). Impact of Online Digital Communication on Customer Buying Decision. *Procedia Economics and Finance.*, *11*, 872–880. doi:10.1016/S2212-5671(14)00251-2

Sánchez, M., & María, O. J. (1997). Education in multicultural society. *Papers*, *53*, 139–148.

Sanford, C., & Bhattacherjee, A. (2008). IT implementation in a developing country municipality: A sociocognitive analysis. *International Journal of Technology and Human Interaction*, *4*(3), 68–93. doi:10.4018/jthi.2008070104

Santana, A. (2012). *Vida, obra y pensamientos de Francisco Morazán*. Fundación Biblioteca Ayaucho.

Santillán-Salgado, R. J., Fonseca-Ramírez, A., & Ortiz-Arango, F. (2015). La Crisis de la Deuda Soberana en la Eurozona (2009-2012). In La Gran Recesión (2007-2012): Lecciones y Oportunidades para México. EGADE-IMEF.

SAT. (2015). *Estimación del gasto tributario del gobierno central*. SAT.

SAT. (2016). *Gasto Tributario*. SAT.

Schelin, S. H. (2003). E-government: An overview. In G. Garson (Ed.), *Public information technology: Policy and management issues* (pp. 120–138). Hershey, PA: IGI Global. doi:10.4018/978-1-59140-060-8.ch006

Schelin, S. H. (2004). Training for digital government. In A. Pavlichev & G. Garson (Eds.), *Digital government: Principles and best practices* (pp. 263–275). Hershey, PA: IGI Global. doi:10.4018/978-1-59140-122-3.ch017

Schelin, S. H. (2007). E-government: An overview. In G. Garson (Ed.), *Modern public information technology systems: Issues and challenges* (pp. 110–126). Hershey, PA: IGI Global. doi:10.4018/978-1-59904-051-6.ch006

Schelin, S. H., & Garson, G. (2004). Theoretical justification of critical success factors. In G. Garson & S. Schelin (Eds.), *IT solutions series: Humanizing information technology: Advice from experts* (pp. 4–15). Hershey, PA: IGI Global. doi:10.4018/978-1-59140-245-9.ch002

Schneider, A. (2012). *State-Building and Tax Regimes in Central America*. Cambridge Press. doi:10.1017/CBO9781139094061

Schoonover, T. (1991). *The United States in Central America, 1860–1911: Episodes of Social Imperialism and Imperial Rivalry in the World System*. Duke University Press Books.

Schoonover, T. (1998). *Germany in Central America*. University of Alabama Press.

Scime, A. (2002). Information systems and computer science model curricula: A comparative look. In M. Dadashzadeh, A. Saber, & S. Saber (Eds.), *Information technology education in the new millennium* (pp. 146–158). Hershey, PA: IGI Global. doi:10.4018/978-1-931777-05-6.ch018

Scime, A. (2009). Computing curriculum analysis and development. In M. Khosrow-Pour (Ed.), *Encyclopedia of information science and technology* (2nd ed.; pp. 667–671). Hershey, PA: IGI Global. doi:10.4018/978-1-60566-026-4.ch108

Scime, A., & Wania, C. (2008). Computing curricula: A comparison of models. In C. Van Slyke (Ed.), *Information communication technologies: Concepts, methodologies, tools, and applications* (pp. 1270–1283). Hershey, PA: IGI Global. doi:10.4018/978-1-59904-949-6.ch088

Scott Besley, E. F. (2009). Fundamentos de administración financiera. CENGAGE Learning.

Seidman, S. B. (2009). An international perspective on professional software engineering credentials. In H. Ellis, S. Demurjian, & J. Naveda (Eds.), *Software engineering: Effective teaching and learning approaches and practices* (pp. 351–361). Hershey, PA: IGI Global. doi:10.4018/978-1-60566-102-5.ch018

Seifert, J. W. (2007). E-government act of 2002 in the United States. In A. Anttiroiko & M. Malkia (Eds.), *Encyclopedia of digital government* (pp. 476–481). Hershey, PA: IGI Global. doi:10.4018/978-1-59140-789-8.ch072

Seifert, J. W., & Relyea, H. C. (2008). E-government act of 2002 in the United States. In A. Anttiroiko (Ed.), *Electronic government: Concepts, methodologies, tools, and applications* (pp. 154–161). Hershey, PA: IGI Global. doi:10.4018/978-1-59904-947-2.ch013

Sejal, D. (2014). Underpricing of Initial Public Offerings: A study based on mega issues listed on National Stock Exchange. *International Journal of Business and Management, 1*(2), 75–85.

Sena. (2007). *La sociedad Colonial, Siglos XVI y XVII.* Banco de la República de Colombia.

Seufert, S. (2002). E-learning business models: Framework and best practice examples. In M. Raisinghani (Ed.), *Cases on worldwide e-commerce: Theory in action* (pp. 70–94). Hershey, PA: IGI Global. doi:10.4018/978-1-930708-27-3.ch004

Shareef, M. A., & Archer, N. (2012). E-government initiatives: Review studies on different countries. In M. Shareef, N. Archer, & S. Dutta (Eds.), *E-government service maturity and development: Cultural, organizational and technological perspectives* (pp. 40–76). Hershey, PA: IGI Global. doi:10.4018/978-1-60960-848-4.ch003

Shareef, M. A., & Archer, N. (2012). E-government service development. In M. Shareef, N. Archer, & S. Dutta (Eds.), *E-government service maturity and development: Cultural, organizational and technological perspectives* (pp. 1–14). Hershey, PA: IGI Global. doi:10.4018/978-1-60960-848-4.ch001

Shareef, M. A., Kumar, U., & Kumar, V. (2011). E-government development: Performance evaluation parameters. In M. Shareef, V. Kumar, U. Kumar, & Y. Dwivedi (Eds.), *Stakeholder adoption of e-government services: Driving and resisting factors* (pp. 197–213). Hershey, PA: IGI Global. doi:10.4018/978-1-60960-601-5.ch010

Shareef, M. A., Kumar, U., Kumar, V., & Niktash, M. (2012). Electronic-government vision: Case studies for objectives, strategies, and initiatives. In M. Shareef, N. Archer, & S. Dutta (Eds.), *E-government service maturity and development: Cultural, organizational and technological perspectives* (pp. 15–39). Hershey, PA: IGI Global. doi:10.4018/978-1-60960-848-4.ch002

Shukla, P., Kumar, A., & Anu Kumar, P. B. (2013). Impact of national culture on business continuity management system implementation. *International Journal of Risk and Contingency Management*, *2*(3), 23–36. doi:10.4018/ijrcm.2013070102

Shulman, S. W. (2007). The federal docket management system and the prospect for digital democracy in U S rulemaking. In G. Garson (Ed.), *Modern public information technology systems: Issues and challenges* (pp. 166–184). Hershey, PA: IGI Global. doi:10.4018/978-1-59904-051-6.ch009

SIECA. (n.d.). *Anexo A*. Retrieved from Anexo A: http://www.sieca.int/PortalData/Documentos/8F59A1A1-DC31-441F-AD66- 1B1739F37CB0.pdf

Simonovic, S. (2007). Problems of offline government in e-Serbia. In A. Anttiroiko & M. Malkia (Eds.), *Encyclopedia of digital government* (pp. 1342–1351). Hershey, PA: IGI Global. doi:10.4018/978-1-59140-789-8.ch205

Simonovic, S. (2008). Problems of offline government in e-Serbia. In A. Anttiroiko (Ed.), *Electronic government: Concepts, methodologies, tools, and applications* (pp. 2929–2942). Hershey, PA: IGI Global. doi:10.4018/978-1-59904-947-2.ch219

Singh, A. K., & Murthy, K. V. B. (2014). Short run performance of IPO Market in India. *International Journal of Financial Management.*, *4*(1), 11–22.

Singh, A. M. (2005). Information systems and technology in South Africa. In M. Khosrow-Pour (Ed.), *Encyclopedia of information science and technology* (pp. 1497–1502). Hershey, PA: IGI Global. doi:10.4018/978-1-59140-553-5.ch263

Singh, S., & Naidoo, G. (2005). Towards an e-government solution: A South African perspective. In W. Huang, K. Siau, & K. Wei (Eds.), *Electronic government strategies and implementation* (pp. 325–353). Hershey, PA: IGI Global. doi:10.4018/978-1-59140-348-7.ch014

Smith, R. S. (1948). Sales taxes in New Spain, 15751770. *The Hispanic American Historical Review*, *28*(1), 2–37. doi:10.2307/2508188

Snoke, R., & Underwood, A. (2002). Generic attributes of IS graduates: An analysis of Australian views. In F. Tan (Ed.), *Advanced topics in global information management* (Vol. 1, pp. 370–384). Hershey, PA: IGI Global. doi:10.4018/978-1-930708-43-3.ch023

Sommer, L. (2006). Revealing unseen organizations in higher education: A study framework and application example. In A. Metcalfe (Ed.), *Knowledge management and higher education: A critical analysis* (pp. 115–146). Hershey, PA: IGI Global. doi:10.4018/978-1-59140-509-2.ch007

Song, H., Kidd, T., & Owens, E. (2011). Examining technological disparities and instructional practices in English language arts classroom: Implications for school leadership and teacher training. In L. Tomei (Ed.), *Online courses and ICT in education: Emerging practices and applications* (pp. 258–274). Hershey, PA: IGI Global. doi:10.4018/978-1-60960-150-8.ch020

Spanish, R. A. (2001). *Dictionary of the Spanish Language* (22nd ed.). Retrieved from http://dle.rae.es/?id=UFbxsxz

Speaker, P. J., & Kleist, V. F. (2003). Using information technology to meet electronic commerce and MIS education demands. In A. Aggarwal (Ed.), *Web-based education: Learning from experience* (pp. 280–291). Hershey, PA: IGI Global. doi:10.4018/978-1-59140-102-5.ch017

Spitler, V. K. (2007). Learning to use IT in the workplace: Mechanisms and masters. In M. Mahmood (Ed.), *Contemporary issues in end user computing* (pp. 292–323). Hershey, PA: IGI Global. doi:10.4018/978-1-59140-926-7.ch013

Steenbergen, V. (2012). *Tax reform in Guatemala: analyzing the mechanisms of interest group influence*. Retrieved from London School of Economics: http://www.lse.ac.uk/IPA/images/Documents/PublicSphere/2013/6-tax-reform-guatemala- 2012.pdf

Stellefson, M. (2011). Considerations for marketing distance education courses in health education: Five important questions to examine before development. In U. Demiray & S. Sever (Eds.), *Marketing online education programs: Frameworks for promotion and communication* (pp. 222–234). Hershey, PA: IGI Global. doi:10.4018/978-1-60960-074-7.ch014

Straub, D. W., & Loch, K. D. (2006). Creating and developing a program of global research. *Journal of Global Information Management, 14*(2), 1–28. doi:10.4018/jgim.2006040101

Straub, D. W., Loch, K. D., & Hill, C. E. (2002). Transfer of information technology to the Arab world: A test of cultural influence modeling. In M. Dadashzadeh (Ed.), *Information technology management in developing countries* (pp. 92–134). Hershey, PA: IGI Global. doi:10.4018/978-1-931777-03-2.ch005

Straub, D. W., Loch, K. D., & Hill, C. E. (2003). Transfer of information technology to the Arab world: A test of cultural influence modeling. In F. Tan (Ed.), *Advanced topics in global information management* (Vol. 2, pp. 141–172). Hershey, PA: IGI Global. doi:10.4018/978-1-59140-064-6.ch009

Suki, N. M., Ramayah, T., Ming, M. K., & Suki, N. M. (2013). Factors enhancing employed job seekers intentions to use social networking sites as a job search tool. In A. Mesquita (Ed.), *User perception and influencing factors of technology in everyday life* (pp. 265–281). Hershey, PA: IGI Global. doi:10.4018/978-1-4666-1954-8.ch018

Suomi, R. (2006). Introducing electronic patient records to hospitals: Innovation adoption paths. In T. Spil & R. Schuring (Eds.), *E-health systems diffusion and use: The innovation, the user and the use IT model* (pp. 128–146). Hershey, PA: IGI Global. doi:10.4018/978-1-59140-423-1.ch008

Swim, J., & Barker, L. (2012). Pathways into a gendered occupation: Brazilian women in IT. *International Journal of Social and Organizational Dynamics in IT, 2*(4), 34–51. doi:10.4018/ijsodit.2012100103

Swiss Information. (2016). *Swiss Info*. Retrieved from http://www.swissinfo.ch/spa/economia/respiro-a-multinacionales_aprueban-nuevos-privilegios-fiscales-para-corporativos/42226892

Tarafdar, M., & Vaidya, S. D. (2006). Adoption and implementation of IT in developing nations: Experiences from two public sector enterprises in India. In M. Khosrow-Pour (Ed.), *Cases on information technology planning, design and implementation* (pp. 208–233). Hershey, PA: IGI Global. doi:10.4018/978-1-59904-408-8.ch013

Tarafdar, M., & Vaidya, S. D. (2008). Adoption and implementation of IT in developing nations: Experiences from two public sector enterprises in India. In G. Garson & M. Khosrow-Pour (Eds.), *Handbook of research on public information technology* (pp. 905–924). Hershey, PA: IGI Global. doi:10.4018/978-1-59904-857-4.ch076

Thesing, Z. (2007). Zarina thesing, pumpkin patch. In M. Hunter (Ed.), *Contemporary chief information officers: Management experiences* (pp. 83–94). Hershey, PA: IGI Global. doi:10.4018/978-1-59904-078-3.ch007

Thomas, J. C. (2004). Public involvement in public administration in the information age: Speculations on the effects of technology. In M. Malkia, A. Anttiroiko, & R. Savolainen (Eds.), *eTransformation in governance: New directions in government and politics* (pp. 67–84). Hershey, PA: IGI Global. doi:10.4018/978-1-59140-130-8.ch004

Tovar, G. S. (2008). *Centro de Estudios Politicos y Constitucionales*. Retrieved from La Federación Centroamericana: http://www.cepc.gob.es/Controls/Mav/getData.ashx?MAVqs=~aWQ9MzI1MjImaWRlPTEwMzcmdXJsPTEzJm5hbWU9UlBJXzAwNV8xMTgucGRmJmZpbGU9UlBJXzAwNV8xMTgucG RmJnRhYmxhPUFydGljdWxvJmNvbnRlbnQ9YXBwbGljYXRpb24vcGRm

Treiblmaier, H., & Chong, S. (2013). Trust and perceived risk of personal information as antecedents of online information disclosure: Results from three countries. In F. Tan (Ed.), *Global diffusion and adoption of technologies for knowledge and information sharing* (pp. 341–361). Hershey, PA: IGI Global. doi:10.4018/978-1-4666-2142-8.ch015

UCTAD. (1996). *Incentives and Foreign Direct Investment*. New York: United Nations.

UNISDR. (2009). *International Strategy for Disaster Reduction (UNISDR)*. Obtenido de UNISDR: http://www.unisdr.org/files/7817_UNISDRTerminologySpanish.pdf

van Grembergen, W., & de Haes, S. (2008). IT governance in practice: Six case studies. In W. van Grembergen & S. De Haes (Eds.), *Implementing information technology governance: Models, practices and cases* (pp. 125–237). Hershey, PA: IGI Global. doi:10.4018/978-1-59904-924-3.ch004

van Os, G., Homburg, V., & Bekkers, V. (2013). Contingencies and convergence in European social security: ICT coordination in the back office of the welfare state. In M. Cruz-Cunha, I. Miranda, & P. Gonçalves (Eds.), *Handbook of research on ICTs and management systems for improving efficiency in healthcare and social care* (pp. 268–287). Hershey, PA: IGI Global. doi:10.4018/978-1-4666-3990-4.ch013

Velloso, A. B., Gassenferth, W., & Machado, M. A. (2012). Evaluating IBMEC-RJ's intranet usability using fuzzy logic. In M. Cruz-Cunha, P. Gonçalves, N. Lopes, E. Miranda, & G. Putnik (Eds.), *Handbook of research on business social networking: Organizational, managerial, and technological dimensions* (pp. 185–205). Hershey, PA: IGI Global. doi:10.4018/978-1-61350-168-9.ch010

Villablanca, A. C., Baxi, H., & Anderson, K. (2009). Novel data interface for evaluating cardiovascular outcomes in women. In A. Dwivedi (Ed.), *Handbook of research on information technology management and clinical data administration in healthcare* (pp. 34–53). Hershey, PA: IGI Global. doi:10.4018/978-1-60566-356-2.ch003

Villablanca, A. C., Baxi, H., & Anderson, K. (2011). Novel data interface for evaluating cardiovascular outcomes in women. In *Clinical technologies: Concepts, methodologies, tools and applications* (pp. 2094–2113). Hershey, PA: IGI Global. doi:10.4018/978-1-60960-561-2.ch806

Villalobos, R. (2013). *Prensa Libre*. Retrieved from Criolla independencia: http://www.prensalibre.com/revista_d/Independencia_de_Guatemala-fiestas_patrias- verdadera_independencia-historia_de_la_independencia_0_991701023.html

Villatoro, D. (2015). *Plaza Pública*. Retrieved from https://www.plazapublica.com.gt/content/guatemala-es-el-pais-con-la-carga-tributaria-mas- baja-de-america-latina: https://www.plazapublica.com.gt/content/guatemala-es-el-pais-con-la- carga-tributaria-mas-baja-de-america-latina

Virkar, S. (2011). Information and communication technologies in administrative reform for development: Exploring the case of property tax systems in Karnataka, India. In J. Steyn, J. Van Belle, & E. Mansilla (Eds.), *ICTs for global development and sustainability: Practice and applications* (pp. 127–149). Hershey, PA: IGI Global. doi:10.4018/978-1-61520-997-2.ch006

Virkar, S. (2013). Designing and implementing e-government projects: Actors, influences, and fields of play. In S. Saeed & C. Reddick (Eds.), *Human-centered system design for electronic governance* (pp. 88–110). Hershey, PA: IGI Global. doi:10.4018/978-1-4666-3640-8.ch007

Vodafone Group Plc. (2014). *Annual Report 2014*. Retrieved from https://www.vodafone.com/content/annualreport/annual_report14/downloads/market_overview.pdf

Wallace, A. (2009). E-justice: An Australian perspective. In A. Martínez & P. Abat (Eds.), *E-justice: Using information communication technologies in the court system* (pp. 204–228). Hershey, PA: IGI Global. doi:10.4018/978-1-59904-998-4.ch014

Wang, G. (2012). E-democratic administration and bureaucratic responsiveness: A primary study of bureaucrats' perceptions of the civil service e-mail box in Taiwan. In K. Kloby & M. D'Agostino (Eds.), *Citizen 2.0: Public and governmental interaction through web 2.0 technologies* (pp. 146–173). Hershey, PA: IGI Global. doi:10.4018/978-1-4666-0318-9.ch009

Wangpipatwong, S., Chutimaskul, W., & Papasratorn, B. (2011). Quality enhancing the continued use of e-government web sites: Evidence from e-citizens of Thailand. In V. Weerakkody (Ed.), *Applied technology integration in governmental organizations: New e-government research* (pp. 20–36). Hershey, PA: IGI Global. doi:10.4018/978-1-60960-162-1.ch002

Warrington, P. (1993). *The distortionary impact of taxation on irish saving media: The principle of fiscal priviledges*. Student Economic Review.

Weber, M. (2012). *Sociologia del poder: Los Tipos De Dominacion*. Madrid: Alianza Editoria.

Wedemeijer, L. (2006). Long-term evolution of a conceptual schema at a life insurance company. In M. Khosrow-Pour (Ed.), *Cases on database technologies and applications* (pp. 202–226). Hershey, PA: IGI Global. doi:10.4018/978-1-59904-399-9.ch012

Whybrow, E. (2008). Digital access, ICT fluency, and the economically disadvantages: Approaches to minimize the digital divide. In F. Tan (Ed.), *Global information technologies: Concepts, methodologies, tools, and applications* (pp. 1409–1422). Hershey, PA: IGI Global. doi:10.4018/978-1-59904-939-7.ch102

Whybrow, E. (2008). Digital access, ICT fluency, and the economically disadvantages: Approaches to minimize the digital divide. In C. Van Slyke (Ed.), *Information communication technologies: Concepts, methodologies, tools, and applications* (pp. 764–777). Hershey, PA: IGI Global. doi:10.4018/978-1-59904-949-6.ch049

Wickramasinghe, N., & Geisler, E. (2010). Key considerations for the adoption and implementation of knowledge management in healthcare operations. In M. Saito, N. Wickramasinghe, M. Fuji, & E. Geisler (Eds.), *Redesigning innovative healthcare operation and the role of knowledge management* (pp. 125–142). Hershey, PA: IGI Global. doi:10.4018/978-1-60566-284-8.ch009

Wickramasinghe, N., & Geisler, E. (2012). Key considerations for the adoption and implementation of knowledge management in healthcare operations. In *Organizational learning and knowledge: Concepts, methodologies, tools and applications* (pp. 1316–1328). Hershey, PA: IGI Global. doi:10.4018/978-1-60960-783-8.ch405

Wickramasinghe, N., & Goldberg, S. (2007). A framework for delivering m-health excellence. In L. Al-Hakim (Ed.), *Web mobile-based applications for healthcare management* (pp. 36–61). Hershey, PA: IGI Global. doi:10.4018/978-1-59140-658-7.ch002

Wickramasinghe, N., & Goldberg, S. (2008). Critical success factors for delivering m-health excellence. In N. Wickramasinghe & E. Geisler (Eds.), *Encyclopedia of healthcare information systems* (pp. 339–351). Hershey, PA: IGI Global. doi:10.4018/978-1-59904-889-5.ch045

William, G., & Sullivan, E. M. (2004). *Ingenieria Económica DeDegarmo* (D. Ediciôn, Ed.). Pearson Prentice Hall.

Woodward, R. L. (1999). *Central America: A Nation Divided.* Oxford Press.

World Bank. (2014). *Guatemala Data.* Retrieved from World Bank: http://www.worldbank.org/en/country/guatemala

World Bank. (2017). *Latin America and Guatemala Data.* Retrieved from World Bank: http://data.worldbank.org/

Wortman, M. (1975). Bourbon Reforms in Central America: 1750-1786. The Americas, 222-238.

Wyld, D. (2009). Radio frequency identification (RFID) technology. In J. Symonds, J. Ayoade, & D. Parry (Eds.), *Auto-identification and ubiquitous computing applications* (pp. 279–293). Hershey, PA: IGI Global. doi:10.4018/978-1-60566-298-5.ch017

Yaghmaei, F. (2010). Understanding computerised information systems usage in community health. In J. Rodrigues (Ed.), *Health information systems: Concepts, methodologies, tools, and applications* (pp. 1388–1399). Hershey, PA: IGI Global. doi:10.4018/978-1-60566-988-5.ch088

Yeager, T. (1995). Encomienda or Slavery? The Spanish Crowns choice of labour organization in Sixteen-Century Spanish America. *The Journal of Economic History*, *55*(04), 842–859. doi:10.1017/S0022050700042182

Yee, G., El-Khatib, K., Korba, L., Patrick, A. S., Song, R., & Xu, Y. (2005). Privacy and trust in e-government. In W. Huang, K. Siau, & K. Wei (Eds.), *Electronic government strategies and implementation* (pp. 145–190). Hershey, PA: IGI Global. doi:10.4018/978-1-59140-348-7.ch007

Yeh, S., & Chu, P. (2010). Evaluation of e-government services: A citizen-centric approach to citizen e-complaint services. In C. Reddick (Ed.), *Citizens and e-government: Evaluating policy and management* (pp. 400–417). Hershey, PA: IGI Global. doi:10.4018/978-1-61520-931-6.ch022

Young-Jin, S., & Seang-tae, K. (2008). E-government concepts, measures, and best practices. In A. Anttiroiko (Ed.), *Electronic government: Concepts, methodologies, tools, and applications* (pp. 32–57). Hershey, PA: IGI Global. doi:10.4018/978-1-59904-947-2.ch004

Yun, H. J., & Opheim, C. (2012). New technology communication in American state governments: The impact on citizen participation. In K. Bwalya & S. Zulu (Eds.), *Handbook of research on e-government in emerging economies: Adoption, e-participation, and legal frameworks* (pp. 573–590). Hershey, PA: IGI Global. doi:10.4018/978-1-4666-0324-0.ch029

Z. E., & E. A. (2012). *Tax incentives.* Washington, DC: World Bank Institute.

Zeyfer. (2006). *Historia de Honduras*. Retrieved from Reformas Borbónicas: http://www.historiadehonduras.hn/Historia/Colonial/reformasborbonicas.htm

Zhang, N., Guo, X., Chen, G., & Chau, P. Y. (2011). User evaluation of e-government systems: A Chinese cultural perspective. In F. Tan (Ed.), *International enterprises and global information technologies: Advancing management practices* (pp. 63–84). Hershey, PA: IGI Global. doi:10.4018/978-1-60960-605-3.ch004

Zuo, Y., & Hu, W. (2011). Trust-based information risk management in a supply chain network. In J. Wang (Ed.), *Supply chain optimization, management and integration: Emerging applications* (pp. 181–196). Hershey, PA: IGI Global. doi:10.4018/978-1-60960-135-5.ch013

About the Contributors

Arti Chandani's specialization is finance and her interest area includes financial accounting, cost and management accounting and financial management. She has more than 14 years of Post graduate teaching experience. She has attended many conferences, national and international and presented papers in those conferences. She has written a chapter in book titled, "Emerging Trends in Service Sector". She has also taught in Brunei Darussalam for 4 years. Presently, she has Ph.D from University of Madras, Chennai. She has been certified by AIMA as AMT (Accredited Management Teacher).

Rakshita Dubey, an MBA Finance Graduate from SIMS, is passionate researcher and currently works as a Financial Risk Analyst in Credit Suisse India Services Ltd. She was the Senior Coordinator for the Research Cell at SIMS and has written many articles for various college events and magazines, broadly in the field of finance, few of them being "SEZ: Boon or Bane to the Society", "Plastic Money and Its Long-Term Effects". She is an avid nature and animal lover and pursues basketball as a hobby.

Edgardo Arturo Ayala Gaytán holds a PhD from Tulane University. His research areas are sectorial and regional analysis, and economic growth. In this regard, he has published articles in indexed journals on binational integration, regional general equilibrium models and economic growth, and he is co-author of three books in the areas of finance and regional development. Professor Ayala has been recognized as a member of the National System of Researchers, Level II at CONACYT. He obtained the second place of the 2016 Public Finance Award of Mexico granted by the Center for Public Finance of the House of Representatives in Mexico, the Raúl Conde Hernández Prize 2014 awarded by the Academy of Administrative Sciences and the Social Science Research Award from the Autonomous University of Nuevo León (UANL) 2009, as well as honorific mentions in the Victor L. Urquidí Prize 2011 and the Rómulo Garza Award. He was director the UANL Economic Research Center and the Mexico-United States-Canada Studies program of the Center for

Strategic Studies of ITESM, he held directive positions in financial institutions and has been consultant for companies and state governments. He is currently associate professor at the National School of Social Sciences and Government of the Tecnológico de Monterrey.

Mita Mehta is Ph.D., M.com, and UGC-SET qualified. She has more than 13 years of experience in teaching. Dr. Mita Mehta's current areas of interest are Human resource management, Communication skills, Organizational Behavior and Business ethics. She has done her doctorate in Corporate governance in Indian Corporate Sectors area. She has cleared UGC-SET form M.S.U. Baroda, Gujarat in Commerce Subject. She has various international and national publications in reputed magazines, journals and refereed books related to the area of Business Ethics and HR. She has been awarded as best professor–Human Resource Management by Dewang Mehta Business School Award-2012, She has authored a book on Corporate Governance in India.

Luis Rodrigo Asturias is an Economist with masters in public administration. Currently serving a position in research at the Universidad Rafael Landivar de Guatemala and has been advisor to the Minister of Development at Guatemala.

Celso Cereso has more than 20 years of experience in the telecommunications industry. More than 14 years as an academic. Social entrepreneur. (as for 2017)

Mayra Irasema Gaitan is a public accountant with a master of finance for the Universidad Galileo in Guatemala and a Master in Advanced Finance from the Universidad del Valle de Guatemala.

Mauricio Garita is a researcher at the Universidad del Valle de Guatemala. He has a PhD from the Universidad Pontificia de Salamanca in sociology and politics and an MS from Manchester Business School in International Business and Management. His research centers on economic policy and its impact on the business environment. As a consequence he has developed research concerning economic growth and equality, business and politics and the impact of economic and political issues on the financial aspects of companies. He has worked with the private sector of Guatemala, the Secretariat for Economic Integration, the World Bank and the Central American Institute of Fiscal Studies.

Sofía Jimena Roca is an Industrial Engineer, Master's student in Advanced Finance, both at the Universidad Del Valle de Guatemala.

Israel Ebenezer Mendoza Bautista, Electronic Engineer, MSC. Electronic Business, Master in Advanced Finance Universidad del Valle de Guatemala, C.A.

Roberto Joaquín Santillán Salgado is currently Full Professor of Finance at EGADE Business School, Tecnológico de Monterrey, Campus Monterrey (www.egade.mx), and has worked at the Mexico City and Veracruz campus of the same institution. During the 1990s he was Visiting Professor at the University of Texas at Austin and the Universidad Católica de Chile. Professor Santillán Salgado is currently a Level III member of the National Researchers System (Sistema Nacional de Investigadores) in Mexico, and frequently lectures in universities in Europe, the United States and South America. He is also the President of the American Academy of Financial Management for Latin America. His research areas include Corporate Finance, International Finance, Valuation and Risk Management. He has published extensively on economic and financial topics in regional and international journals, and has published a book on the 2007-2009 Financial Crisis. Dr. Santillán serves as an Editorial Member in: Panoeconomicus, Contaduría y Administración, Estudios Gerenciales, Estocástica, and the Journal of Global Business. He earned a bachelor's degree in economics from the National Autonomous University of Mexico (distinguished with Honors), a Master's degree in Public Administration from the Universidad Autónoma Metropolitana, a second Master's degree in Business Administration from the Tecnológico de Monterrey, a Doctorate in Business Administration with a major in Finance, from Tecnológico de Monterrey/University of Texas at Austin, conducted a first postdoctoral fellow of Corporate Finance at the University of Texas at Austin and is currently undertaking a second postdoctoral fellowship in Financial Economics at the Instituto Politécnico Nacional. Dr. Santillán-Salgado has a professional certification as a Registered Financial Specialist and Financial Executive Certificate, from the American Academy of Financial Management (AAFM).

Index

J

L

M

N

P

R

S

T

U

V

W

Y

Encyclopedia of
Information Science and Technology
Fourth Edition

www.ingramcontent.com/pod-product-compliance
Lightning Source LLC
LaVergne TN
LVHW080853300926
849162LV00003B/417